# Sex Crimes and Sex Offenders

*Sex Crimes and Sex Offenders: Research and Realities* provides an overview of social scientific theory and research on sex crimes and sex offenders. Most other books on the market are focused on a single issue—such as treatment, rape, pedophilia, theory, etc. This book is unique in that it covers the most current theory and research along with individual cases of sex crimes (e.g., Kobe Bryant, Jerry Sandusky, and other case studies), effectively linking theory and research with the realities of sex crimes and sex offenders as well as their victims. Vandiver, Braithwaite, and Stafford are careful to dispel myths and focus on the heterogeneity of sex crimes and sex offenders, and not on any one type of population or theory. Instead, they weave a framework using a full range of theoretical concepts and research data to integrate their discussions of crimes, offenders, victims, treatments, and policy implications. The result is a valuable resource for students and early-stage researchers investigating sex crimes or offenders.

**Donna Vandiver,** PhD, is a Professor in the School of Criminal Justice at Texas State University in San Marcos, Texas. She co-authored *Juvenile sex offenders: What the public needs to know.* She has published on a broad range of topics related to sex crimes and sex offenders with a focus on female and juvenile sex offenders. She has authored/co-authored refereed articles and book chapters.

**Jeremy Braithwaite** is an Evaluation Manager at Social Solutions International, Inc., in Rockville, Maryland. He has published 12 refereed articles and over 50 technical reports for agencies, including Health and Human Services and the U.S. Air Force. He is working on a book on rape and domestic violence in rural Alaskan communities.

**Mark Stafford,** PhD, is a Professor in the School of Criminal Justice at Texas State University in San Marcos. He is the co-author of *American delinquency: Its meaning and construction* (6th ed.) and has published more than 30 refereed articles and book chapters.

[*Sex Crimes and Sex Offenders*] will appeal to a broad audience of students who desire employment as social workers, law enforcement officers, probation and/or parole officers, case managers, etc. The inclusion of a discussion of crime investigation will make this book very attractive to budding criminal justice professionals.

—**Lisa Sample,** *University of Nebraska Omaha*

# Sex Crimes and Sex Offenders

## Research and Realities

*Donna Vandiver*

*Jeremy Braithwaite*

*Mark Stafford*

Routledge
Taylor & Francis Group

NEW YORK AND LONDON

**Please visit the companion website at**
**www.routledge.com/cw/vandiver**

First published 2017
by Routledge
711 Third Avenue, New York, NY 10017

and by Routledge
2 Park Square, Milton Park, Abingdon, Oxon, OX14 4RN

*Routledge is an imprint of the Taylor & Francis Group, an informa business*

*Library of Congress Cataloging in Publication Data*
Names: Vandiver, Donna M., 1972– author. | Braithwaite, Jeremy,
    author. | Stafford, Mark C., author.
Title: Sex crimes and sex offenders : theory, research, and realities /
    Donna Vandiver, Jeremy Braithwaite, Mark Stafford.
Description: New York, NY : Routledge, 2016.
Identifiers: LCCN 2016025162 | ISBN 9781138937093 (hardback) |
    ISBN 1138937096 (hardback) | ISBN 9781138937109 (pbk.) |
    ISBN 113893710X (pbk.)
Subjects: LCSH: Sex crimes. | Sex offenders.
Classification: LCC HV6556 .V36 2016 | DDC 364.15/3—dc23
LC record available at https://lccn.loc.gov/2016025162

ISBN: 978-1-138-93709-3 (hbk)
ISBN: 978-1-138-93710-9 (pbk)
ISBN: 978-1-31567-646-3 (ebk)

Typeset in Stone Serif
by Apex CoVantage, LLC

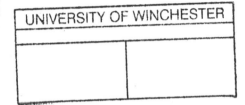

MIX
Paper from
responsible sources
FSC    FSC® C013056
www.fsc.org

Printed and bound in Great Britain by
TJ International Ltd, Padstow, Cornwall

# TABLE OF CONTENTS

# PREFACE

Teaching a course on sex crimes and sex offenders has often required that instructors cobble together resources, from journal articles to newspaper articles, and sections of books written on narrow topics. After repeating this exercise too many times, we opted to write a textbook. We first had to consider the common stereotypes, misconceptions, and other biases about sex crimes and sex offenders. Our students brought them to our attention, as they often asked questions that reflected them (e.g., all sex offenders recidivate, right?), which they had discerned from the media and their own "commonsense" perspectives. This became the foundation of the textbook: identifying common myths and subsequently addressing them with the most recent and best research available.

After several semesters of teaching the course, we realized that the core themes must involve discussion of theories about sex crimes and sex offenders and different types of sex crimes (e.g., rape, child molestation, and child pornography), identification of salient groups of offenders and the contexts in which they commonly commit their crimes (e.g., juveniles, females, and those who offend in the context of an institution), and providing information about the identification, control, and treatment of sex offenders in the criminal justice system. This subsequently became an outline of chapter topics that we believed would provide a comprehensive perspective.

This textbook was written with students in mind, as it considers what is often thought about sex crimes and sex offenders by people who have not studied the topic closely. It is appropriate for use in any undergraduate or graduate-level course that is geared specifically towards sex crimes and sex offenders. Also, it can be used in a course that is more broadly oriented toward criminal behavior and/or deviant sexual behavior. It should be useful for instructors not just in criminal justice, but also public policy, social work, and sociology.

This textbook differs from competing textbooks in several ways. First, it focuses on sex crimes and sex offenders in a comprehensive way. There are many trade books on narrow aspects of the topic, such as juvenile sex offenders, investigation of sex crimes, and treatment of sex offenders. There are also many textbooks about crime and criminals in general, but this textbook provides an in-depth discussion of sex crimes and sex offenders in particular. Second, this book incorporates several broad themes related to criminology (why people commit crimes), policy-related issues (e.g., sex-crime and sex-offender-based laws), and the assessment and treatment of sex offenders—yet this is done with sex crimes and sex offenders in mind. Thus, this textbook integrates many core themes from psychology, sociology, criminology, and law.

On the Alice in Wonderland art on the cover:

Rev. Charles Lutwidge Dodgson, better known as Lewis Carroll, was a nineteenth-century, English mathematician, logician, and cleric, who wrote *Alice's Adventures in Wonderland* and its sequels. Many people around the world know of Alice's fantastical experiences with Mad Hatter, Queen of Hearts, Cheshire Cat, White Rabbit, March Hare, and Jabberwock, but few know of the controversy surrounding Carroll's interest in little girls. Carroll was besotted with little girls and often photographed them in various states of undress. His most famous model was Alice Riddell who was the inspiration for his famous book and to whom Carroll first told the story of wonderland. He once photographed Alice as a young beggar, barely covered by a tattered dress with the hint of a nipple peeping from under it. Alfred Tennyson described it as the most beautiful photograph he had ever seen. However, Vladimir Nabokov, himself controversial because of his book *Lolita* about a middle-aged man, Humbert Humbert, who was obsessed with a 12-year-old girl with whom he eventually had sex, said this about Carroll and his photographs:

He has a pathetic affinity with H.H. [Humbert Humbert], but some odd scruple prevented me from alluding in *Lolita* to his perversion and to those ambiguous photographs he took in dim rooms. He got away with it, as so many other Victorians got away with pederasty and nympholepsy. His were sad scrawny little nymphets, bedraggled and half-undressed, or rather semi-undraped, as if participating in some dusty and dreadful charade (Appel & Nabokov, 1967, pp. 142–143).

Carroll's photographs were taken with the consent of his models and their parents. While many of the photographs would be considered child pornography today, they would not have disturbed 19th-century Victorians who viewed naked children as cherubs void of sexuality. Moreover, even if Carroll's interest in little girls was at least partly pedophilic rather than entirely artistic, there was no evidence he had sex with any of them, though he was known to have bounced them on his knee and kissed them. Carroll's interest in little girls and his photographs can be viewed through two looking glasses—one innocent and the other dark. The view in this textbook is not so equivocal; it is the darkness of sex offenders and the sex crimes they commit.

Appel, A. Jr., & Nabokov, V. (1967). An Interview with Vladimir Nabokov. *Wisconsin Studies in Contemporary Literature*, 8(2): 127–152.

## CHAPTER 1

# *Introduction*

## CHAPTER OBJECTIVES

- Discuss the moral panic towards sex crimes and sex offenders.
- Define a sex crime.
- Identify sources and current numbers of sex crimes/sex offenders.
- Identify the historical roots of conducting sex research.
- Identify paraphilias identified in the Diagnostic and Statistical Manual of Mental Disorders (fifth edition) (DSM-5).
- Assess sexual recidivism rates of known sex offenders.
- Provide an overview of myths about sex crimes and sex offenders.

What we know about sex crimes and sex offenders has changed substantially over the past several decades. For example, Robert Longo, now the director of a psychiatric hospital in Winston-Salem, North Carolina, "remembers appearing on 'Donahue' and 'Oprah' in the 1980s, making pronouncements like 'sex offenders can't be cured,' and 'victims are damaged for life.' Neither statement was based on good research, he now says. 'We were desperately trying to bring attention to the issue,' Longo says of himself and other sex-abuse experts, 'and we went way overboard'" (Jones, 2007, n.p.).

Bring up sex offenders to any group of people, and most, if not all, will agree they are morally reprehensible—monsters. They inflict harm on victims and engage in disgusting behaviors. Differences of opinion among community members and experts in the field, however, begin to emerge when you ask questions such as: should sex offenders be treated or locked up in prison for life? Are sex offenders treatable? Do they all recidivate? The goal of this textbook is to identify many of the myths that exist regarding sex offenders and to identify what the research reveals. In some instances, the research may be definitive. Yet, in other instances, the research is murky. We will highlight not only what the research says, but also where gaps exist.

In order to identify the myths and, subsequently, the research and realities of sex crimes and sex offenders, several overarching themes are examined. For example, a great deal of ***moral panic*** has been generated towards sex crimes and sex offenders. With regard to the research on this topic, official statistics over the past decade are examined. What is considered sexually deviant is also examined by providing an overview of **paraphilias**. A brief examination of the historical roots of conducting sex-crime and sex-offender research is provided, as it is still relatively new, especially when compared with research on other types of crime. Last, an outline of many of the existing myths regarding sex crimes and sex offenders is presented. Each chapter examines some aspect of the overarching myth that all sex offenders are the same. This is presented alongside research that refutes the myth. An in-depth discussion of the first myth—once a sex offender, always a sex offender—is presented as an introduction to understanding a critical characteristic of this group of offenders.

## MORAL PANIC AND REALITY

It has been well documented that many of the current perceptions regarding sex offenders are inaccurate (Stafford & Vandiver, 2016). In 1972, Cohen introduced the term moral panic, which can be applied to the current reaction towards sex offenders in today's media:

> Societies appear to be subject, every now and then, to periods of moral panic. A condition, episode, person or group of persons emerges to become defined as a threat to societal values and interests; its nature is presented in a stylized and stereotypical fashion by the mass media; the moral barricades are manned by editors, bishops, politicians and other right-thinking people; socially accredited experts pronounce their diagnoses and solutions; ways of coping are evolved or (more often) resorted to; the condition then disappears, submerges or deteriorates and becomes more visible. Sometimes the object of the panic is quite novel and at other times it is something which has been in existence long enough, but suddenly appears in the limelight. Sometimes the panic passes over and is forgotten, except in folklore and collective memory; at other times it has more serious and long-lasting repercussions and might produce such changes … in legal and social policy or even in the way the society conceives itself.
>
> (Cohen, 1972, p. 1)

In his book, *Moral Panic: Changing Concepts of the Child Molester in Modern America*, Phillip Jenkins examines the current perceptions of sex offenders as a product of moral panic (Jenkins, 1998). He details the changing laws, media portrayals, and the public's general views about sex offenders in American history. He provides examples of the pendulum swing, by noting that in the 1960s children were viewed as seducers, whereas in the 1940s and 1950s, children were viewed as potential victims of sex offenders. He describes the view of sex offenders as cyclical, describing the current panic that exists as a swing in the pendulum that causes fear among the public.

A noteworthy point made throughout this textbook, is that the current reaction to sex offenders is largely found in the Americas, with a central focus in the U.S. For example, you will learn in Chapter 11 that the U.S. leads the way in developing sex-offender laws. Many of the assessment tools and treatment paradigms were developed in Canada and the U.S. Much of the research also originates in these countries.

## WHAT IS A SEX CRIME?

Current U.S. federal law defines a sex crime as "a criminal offense that has an element involving a sexual act or sexual contact with another" (42 U.S. Code § 16911 (5)(a)(1)). This extremely broad and somewhat non-specific definition is reflective of the extensive range of sexual behaviors and activities that have been identified as crimes.

Some sex crimes are violent crimes that involve sexual activity. These include rape, sexual assault, and sexual abuse of adults and children. Other sex crimes involve the exploitation of children, including child sexual abuse, child pornography production, and engaging children in prostitution and sex trafficking. Other sex crimes involve social taboos (also known as nuisance offenses), including exhibitionism (i.e., indecent exposure), voyeurism (i.e., peeping), bestiality (i.e., sexual activity with animals), necrophilia (i.e., sexual activity with bodies of dead persons), and many others.

As you will learn throughout this textbook, the definition of a sex crime (as well as the social and legal response to these crimes) is largely time-variant, meaning that definitions are not fixed, but change over time as a result of social, legal, moral, and even technological changes. In Chapter 3, we will discuss how the legal definition of rape, until recently, was exclusively limited to acts involving forceful penetration of a female victim. Likewise, in Chapter 5, we examine how the legal definition of child pornography has evolved over the past 40 years, particularly emphasizing how the advent of the Internet influenced its definition.

Sex-crime definitions are also largely contingent on place and culture. For example, only rapes involving White female victims were prosecuted under the apartheid system in South Africa. Rape of Black women was socially accepted (Armstrong, 1994). Child marriages in particular parts of rural India involve marriage and sexual relationships between adult men and girls who are not adults, and this is legally sanctioned (Ouattara, Sen, & Thomson, 1998). Even within the U.S., what constitutes a sex crime varies among states. For example, most, but not all states, classify indecent exposure as a sex crime and mandate sex-offender registration for convicted offenders (Levenson, Letourneau, Armstrong, & Zgoba, 2010). Throughout this textbook, these state and jurisdictional differences occasionally are discussed.

Though it is beyond the scope of this textbook to discuss all of the differences in sex-crime definitions across all states and jurisdictions, as well as across every time point in American history, the point to be made here is that there is a great deal of heterogeneity regarding the definition of a sex crime.

## SOURCES AND NUMBERS OF SEX CRIMES AND OFFENDERS

How many sex crimes and sex offenders are there? To address the question, one must first examine the sources of reliable estimates. Here, the strengths and weaknesses of each source, with regard to measuring sex crimes, are assessed. We begin, first, by examining an international source of sexual-violence data, and subsequently, several sources of U.S. data—as the majority of sex-crime and sex-offender estimates come from such data.

### United Nations Office on Drugs and Crime (UNODC)

This is one source of data for sexual-violence estimates. The **United Nations Office on Drugs and Crime** (UNODC) data rely on multiple sources, including an annual report questionnaire, an annual self-report survey on crime trends and operations of criminal justice systems, and other national surveys administered in countries that are members of the United Nations (UNODC, 2015). The data, however, are constrained by the fact that countries define sexual violence differently, making comparisons between them difficult. Also, some of the countries change their definition of sexual violence over time, making temporal comparisons difficult. These data, however, are beneficial in that they provide estimates by relying on several sources. Data from selected regions and countries are presented in Table 1.1.[1] These data reveal high rates in both years (2009 and 2013) in Costa Rica, United Kingdom (U.K.), and Canada. The data may reveal real differences, or those differences may simply be due to different methods of measuring sexual violence in these countries.

### Uniform Crime Reports (UCR)

In the U.S., the Federal Bureau of Investigation (FBI) began reporting crime data in 1930. Currently, over 18,000 law enforcement agencies at various levels voluntarily report crime data. These law enforcement agencies include city, university/college, county, state, tribal, and federal agencies. The FBI publishes an annual report on crimes, *Crime in the United States*. Data for two types of sex crimes are reported: rape and other sex crimes. More commonly known as the Uniform Crime Reports (UCR), this publication also provides counts of offenses known to law enforcement officials and arrest data.

In 2013, the UCR began using a revised definition of rape: "penetration, no matter how slight, of the vagina or anus with any body part or object, or oral penetration by a sex organ of another person, without the consent of the victim." The difference between this definition and the older definition is that the new definition is gender-neutral (i.e., the victim and the offender can be either male or female). Also, the new definition does not require "force," but rather lack of consent. This includes statutory rape and incest. It also includes attempted offenses. In 2014,

**TABLE 1.1**  *Sexual Violence Rates in 2009 and 2013 Among Various Countries*

| REGION | COUNTRY | RATE PER 100,000 | |
|---|---|---|---|
| | | 2009 | 2013 |
| Africa | Kenya | 10.2 | 10.8 |
| | Rwanda | n/a | 14.7 |
| | Morocco | 10.4 | 13.1 |
| Americas | Costa Rica | 141.3 | 149.4 |
| | Mexico | 29.0 | 32.0 |
| | Colombia | 16.8 | 24.0 |
| | Canada | 73.5 | 75.6 |
| Asia | Kazakhstan | 2.2 | 3.1 |
| | Japan | 6.4 | 7.1 |
| | China | 8.8 | 9.4 |
| | Philippines | 1.7 | n/a |
| | India | 6.0 | 9.3 |
| | Kuwait | 17.9 | n/a |
| Europe | Hungary | 14.4 | 59.6 |
| | Russian Federation | 12.5 | 9.2 |
| | Ireland | 33.6 | 43.7 |
| | U.K. (England & Wales) | 79.1 | 99.3 |
| | Greece | 8.3 | 7.7 |
| | Germany | 59.0 | 56.6 |
| Oceania | Australia | 28.8 | 85.3 |
| | New Zealand | 65.4 | n/a |

Source: (UNODC, 2015)

utilizing the new definition of rape, 116,645 rapes were reported to law enforcement agencies. The rape rate per 100,000 individuals was 36.6. This is a slight increase from 2013, when 113,695 rapes were reported to law enforcement agencies, and the rate was 35.9 per 100,000 individuals (Federal Bureau of Investigation, 2016).

Figure 1.1 shows the number of reported rapes, by year, from 2004–2014. Figure 1.2 shows the corresponding rates. Even taking into account that the FBI revised its definition of rape, both the number of rapes and rape rates have been decreasing during this time period.

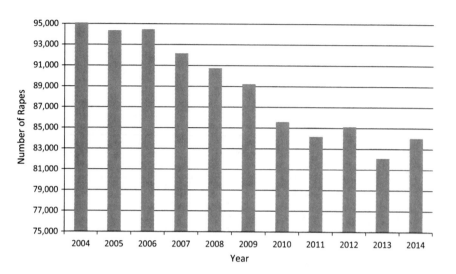

**FIGURE 1.1** *Number of Rapes Reported to Law Enforcement Agencies, 2004–2014*
*Source: Adapted from: Federal Bureau of Investigation (2016). Crimes in the United States: 2014. Washington DC: Government Printing Office.*

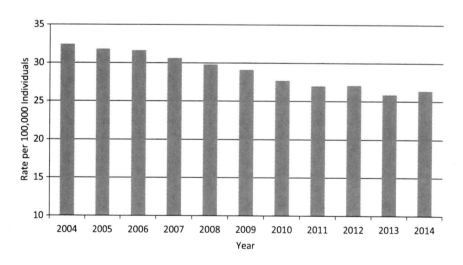

**FIGURE 1.2** *Rape Rates, 2004–2014*
*Source: Adapted from: Federal Bureau of Investigation (2016). Crimes in the United States: 2014. Washington DC: Government Printing Office.*

In addition to rapes, the UCR reports arrest data for other sex crimes (excluding prostitution). These data, however, include only arrests and not the number of offenses known to law enforcement. Other sex crimes include "offenses against chastity, common decency, morals, and the like." It does not include indecent exposure or statutory rape. It does, however, include attempted sex crimes. In 2005, there were 46,036 arrests for other sex crimes compared to 29,784 in 2014. Thus, there was a 35% reduction in the number of arrests.

One of the disadvantages of relying on the UCR for sex crimes is that it only includes crimes known to law enforcement agencies and arrests. Thus, crimes not reported to law enforcement or crimes that did not result in arrests are not included. One should also be aware that sex crimes are one of the offenses least likely to be reported to law enforcement officials. The reasons vary: embarrassment, fear of not being believed, fear of retribution, and/or fear of the criminal justice system. The victim can hold to myths as well and, therefore, may believe he or she did something wrong (e.g., drank alcohol or did not fight back hard enough) or believe that it was not rape because the victim knew the offender.

The UCR, however, is advantageous in that it provides a consistent estimate of how many sex crimes and arrests for sex crimes occur. The data are presented in an easy-to-read format. It allows anyone to compare rates across multiple years, even decades, since its inception. The UCR also includes a breakdown by states and regions of the U.S.

## National Incident-Based Reporting System (NIBRS)

The FBI, in an attempt to improve crime-data collection, developed the *National Incident-Based Reporting System* (NIBRS). Planning began in the 1980s, with formal implementation taking place in 1989 (Federal Bureau of Investigation, n.d.-b). It was recognized that there is a need for more details about crimes. For example, instead of simply reporting the number of rapes known to law enforcement officials, there is a need to know offender information, victim information, and other circumstances associated with the incident. NIBRS collects information about multiple offenders, multiple victims, and multiple offenses committed per incident.

By 2012, 32 states contributed to NIBRS. Though in each state, not all jurisdictions were reporting. The 2012 NIBRS data assessed 30% of the U.S. population and accounted for 28% of all U.S. crime. With regard to sex crimes, NIBRS collects information on incidents for the following offenses: (1) kidnapping/abduction, (2) pornography/obscene material, (3) prostitution offenses: prostituting, assisting or promoting prostitution, (4) sex offenses, forcible: forcible rape, forcible sodomy, sexual assault with an object, and forcible fondling, (5) sex offenses, non-forcible: incest and statutory rape, and (6) peeping tom (Federal Bureau of Investigation, n.d.-a). Although all of these data are available for anyone to access, only a few categories have been summarized in FBI publications.

Table 1.2 summarizes 2012 data for selected sex crimes. What should be noted is that some incidents involve more than one offender, one victim, and one criminal

**TABLE 1.2**   *Summary of NIBRS 2012 Sex Crimes*

| SEX CRIME | NUMBER OF: | | | |
| --- | --- | --- | --- | --- |
| | INCIDENTS | OFFENDERS | VICTIMS | CRIMES |
| Sex Offenses, Forcible | 67,861 | 70,441 | 73,132 | 73,132 |
| Sex Offenses, Non-forcible | 6,137 | 6,486 | 6,493 | 6,493 |
| Pornography/Obscene Offenses | 6,026 | 5,962 | 6,031 | 6,026 |

Source: Adapted from: Federal Bureau of Investigation (2014). National Incident-Based Reporting System: 2012. Washington DC: Government Printing Office.

offense. For example, if two offenders rape and assault one victim, that is considered a single incident, with two offenders, two victims, and two crimes (rape and assault).

Also notable from NIBRS data, a majority of forcible sex offenders were male, White, and young. In 2012, 95% of the offenders of forcible rape offenses were male. Also, 60% of offenders were White. Slightly more than half of offenders (55%) were between the ages of 16 and 35. With regard to victims, most were female, White, and young. According to the 2012 data, 98% of victims of forcible rape were female. Approximately three-quarters (76%) of the victims were White. The victims ranged in age from infancy to elderly with the largest percentage (37%) being between ages 11 and 20 (Federal Bureau of Investigation, 2014).

One of the advantages of NIBRS is the amount of detail collected about each criminal incident. For each incident, details regarding all of the offenders and victims are included. Also, details of all of the offenses related to that incident are included. This is an advantage over the UCR, which only includes the most serious offense (known as the *hierarchy rule*). NIBRS also measures a broader range of crimes than the UCR and includes more details about each offense. A disadvantage of NIBRS is that it is still relatively new and still developing. Each year, it includes more of the U.S. population, which must be taken into consideration when making comparisons from year to year.

## National Crime Victimization Survey (NCVS)

Given that many sex crimes go unreported to law enforcement officials, another way to measure them is through victimization surveys. Rather than collecting information about reported crimes, the *National Crime Victimization Survey* (NCVS) collects information about the number and type of victimizations in the U.S., regardless of whether they have been reported to law enforcement officials. A goal of the NCVS is to highlight the "dark figure of crime." Each year, the NCVS samples a large number of U.S. households and interviews each household member age 12 and older twice a year for three successive years. It assesses a wide range of crime victimizations—property and personal crimes, including sex crimes.

There were 300,170 rape victimizations according to the NCVS in 2013. This is a slight decrease from the year before: 346,830. It should be recognized, however, that these counts do not take population changes into account. To estimate these changes, it is helpful to examine victimization rate changes. This takes into account the number of victimizations per 1,000 individuals who were at least 12 years old. For 2013, the rape rate was 1.1. This is compared to a rate of 1.3 for the year before, showing a slight decline in the rate of reported rape occurrences. To assess trends over a longer period, the rate of rape in 2004 was 1.1 per 1,000 persons aged 12 and older. Thus, the rate in 2004 was identical to the 2013 rate (Truman & Langton, 2014).

Given that girls and women account for the majority of rape victimizations, the Bureau of Justice Statistics assessed victim characteristics of just this population of victims. Ninety-four percent of all completed rapes between 1992 and 2000 were committed against female victims (Rennison, 2002). The following characteristics of female victims of sexual violence were also revealed:

- The rape rate declined 58% from 1995 to 2010.
- Women who experienced the highest rape rate from 2005–2010 were younger than 35, lived in lower income households, and lived in rural areas.
- Between 2005 and 2010, 78% of rapes were committed by a family member, intimate partner, acquaintance, or friend.
- The proportion of those victims who reported sexual violence to the police ranged from a high of 56% in 2003 to a low of 35% in 2010 (Planty, Langston, Krebs, & Smiley-McDonald, 2013).

According to the NCVS, approximately half of all violent victimizations are not reported to law enforcement officials. Sixty-five percent of rapes, however, were not reported from 2006–2010. Victims gave the following reasons for not reporting: fear of reprisal or getting offender into trouble (28%), dealt with in another way/personal matter (20%), police would not or could not help (13%), not important enough to report (6%), or other reason (33%) (Langton, Berzofsky, Krebs, & Smiley-McDonald, 2012).

While there are many advantages of the NCVS (e.g., includes offenses not reported to law enforcement officials, allows comparison across several years and decades), it has its limitations. For example, it includes only crimes that involve victims who are at least 12 years old. Also, although the interviewed individual was a sex crime victim, he or she may choose not to report it to the NCVS, for a variety of reasons (e.g., embarrassment, shame, etc.).

## National Child Abuse and Neglect Data System (NCANDS)

In 1988, the Child Abuse Prevention and Treatment Act was passed. This led to the development of the *National Child Abuse and Neglect Data System* (NCANDS), which includes data from all U.S. states for all forms of child abuse and neglect.

Thus, the data are not limited to sexual-abuse victimizations. The data-collection process is based on voluntary reporting, and the data are reported annually (Administration on Children Youth and Families, 2014).

Data from NCANDS indicate that in 2013, there were 679,000 child victims of abuse or neglect in the U.S. This translates into a rate of 9.1 victims per 1,000 children. This reveals a 3.8% decrease in such victimization from 2009–2013. Nine percent of the 679,000 children were sexually abused (Administration on Children Youth and Families, 2014).

NCANDS is advantageous in that it provides information about child sexual victimizations that may not have been reported to law enforcement officials. It focuses on child victims of all types of abuse, including neglect. The data are limited in that they focus broadly on abuse and neglect and do not provide detailed information regarding victims of sex crimes.

### National Violence Against Women Survey

Recognizing gaps that exist in rape research, the National Institute of Justice (NIJ) and the Centers for Disease Control and Prevention (CDC) partnered to conduct a national telephone survey, the *National Violence Against Women Survey*. The survey conducted in 1995–1996 included a random sample of 8,000 women and 8,005 men who were asked about rape victimizations (Tjaden & Thoennes, 2006).

The survey revealed that about 18% of women and 3% of men had been a victim of rape at some point during their lives. Thus, one out of every six women and one out of every 33 men had been raped. Female rape victims experienced vaginal penetration (68%), mouth penetration (24%), anal penetration with a penis (13%), anal or vaginal penetration by objects/fingers (31%), and/or attempted vaginal, anal, or mouth penetration (49%). In an examination of female victim's race/ethnicity, American Indians/Alaskan Natives (34%) and those of mixed races (24%) were substantially more likely to have been raped as compared to those who were non-Hispanic White (18%), Hispanic White (12%), African American (19%), and Asian/Pacific Islander (6%) (Tjaden & Thoennes, 2006).

A limitation of the National Violence Against Women Survey is that it is a one-time survey and includes only individuals who are at least 18 years old. It, however, is advantageous in that it provides a wealth of information regarding women and men's likelihood of rape victimization over their lifetimes.

## HISTORICAL ROOTS OF CONDUCTING SEX RESEARCH

One of the first researchers to discuss childhood sexual abuse was Sigmund Freud. In the late 1800s, he proposed his *seduction theory of childhood sexuality* (Laws & Marshall, 2003), which stated that adult hysteria was rooted in suppressed, childhood incidents of sexual abuse. This theory was not well received by Freud's peers, as one of them noted it sounded like a fairy tale (Hunt, 1993). Freud abandoned his theory and later suggested that sexual abuse was imagined by the purported victims (Laws & Marshall, 2003). Freud, in 1905, published *Three Essays on the Theory of Sexuality*, which discussed sexual deviations, infantile sexuality, and sexuality in puberty. In Europe and North America, Freud was considered by many to be a "pervert" for his research (Hunt, 1993).

What can be learned from Freud's attempt to study sexuality and sex crimes? First, studying sexuality is risky. It is not a popular topic to study scientifically as the topic is risqué, and studying it objectively is difficult. Second, Freud was the first to discuss adult emotional problems (e.g., hysteria) as a consequence of childhood events—a causal logic that is still relied upon today.

Other researchers were also studying sex and sexual deviations at the same time. For example, Adolf Patze recognized that children ages three to six years displayed a strong sexual drive. Another researcher, Henry Maudsley, also mentioned sexual behaviors among infants. Richard von Krafft-Ebing (Krafft-Ebing 1886) also published accounts of deviant sexual behavior.

A grand-scale attempt to describe human sexuality, as well as variations of it, was made by Alfred Kinsey. He was an entomologist who studied variations in gall wasps. He was influenced by Sigmund Freud, believing that human behavior is driven by sexual desires (Laws & Marshall, 2003). Kinsey conducted interviews with Americans of all ages and from diverse backgrounds. He published the results in *Sexual Behavior in the Human Male* in 1948, and later, *Sexual Behavior in the Human Female* in 1953. Some of the results of his research are reported in Focus Box 1.1.

---

*Focus Box 1.1    Results of Alfred Kinsey's Research (1948/1953) on Human Sexuality*

### HOMOSEXUAL BEHAVIOR

Men: 46% engaged in heterosexual and homosexual behavior or were aroused by persons of both sexes. Only 12% of White males (between the ages of 20–35) received a score of 3 on a 7-point scale, indicating about equal heterosexual and homosexual experiences/responses.

Women: Between 6 and 14% had more than an incidental homosexual experience.

### AGE OF FIRST INTERCOURSE

**For men:**

By age 16: 21%
At age 17: 11%
At age 18: 12%
At age 19: 11%

## For women:

By age 16: 6%
At age 17: 5%
At age 18: 9%
At age 19: 11%

## MASTURBATION

Men: 92%
Women: 62%

## SEXUAL FANTASY

### Men:

84% were aroused by sexual fantasy with women.
**89% relied on sexual fantasy while masturbating.**
Rarely (3 or 4 out of 5,000 times) do men experience ejaculation by fantasy alone.

### Women:

31% had never been aroused by thinking about men.
**69% reported having erotic fantasies about men.**
**64% relied on sexual fantasy while masturbating.**
2% of women experience an orgasm by fantasy alone.

## EXPERIENCED PREMARITAL SEX

Men: 67–98%, depending on socioeconomic status.
Women: Approximately 50%.

Source: (Kinsey, Pomeroy, & Martin,1948; Kinsey, Pomeroy, Martin, & Gebhard, 1953)

Despite a wide interest in sexuality among scientists, there was still "a widespread resistance in society to allow scientists to straightforwardly study human sexuality, particularly in its more unusual forms" (Laws & Marshall, 2003, p. 80). Few scholars were interested in sex-crime research, and even fewer were interested in studying sex offenders (Soothill, 2010). The results of Kinsey's research "have been scorned and attacked from a variety of perspectives" (Laws & Marshall, 2003, p. 80). Still noteworthy, his data remain the largest collection of empirical information on human sexuality (Laws & Marshall, 2003).

Thus, research on sex, sexuality, and deviant sex acts, including sex crimes, occurred early on under an umbrella of taboo. The early researchers in this area were true pioneers. Today, while conducting research on sex, sexuality, and sex crimes is less of a taboo, it still remains less studied than other research areas. Over the past several decades, however, large strides have been made in studying sex offenders and sex crimes.

## SEXUAL DEVIANCES: PARAPHILIAS

Critical to assessing sex crimes and sex offenders is to distinguish what is considered "normal" sexual behavior from "abnormal" sexual behavior—as many sex offenders exhibit sexual deviances. Paraphilias are defined by the American Psychiatric Association in their *Diagnostic and Statistical Manual of Mental Disorders* (DSM)—a sort of "bible of mental disorders."

The American Psychiatric Association in the most recent edition (fifth) of the DSM provide the diagnosis criteria for paraphilias. The criteria established, however, are not without controversy, as what is considered sexually abnormal is culturally dependent (McManus, Hargreaves, Rainbow, & Alison, 2013). That is, what is considered a paraphilia varies between places and over time. For example, up until 1973, the DSM included homosexuality as a paraphilia (McManus et al., 2013).

A paraphilia is defined as "any intense and persistent sexual interest other than sexual interest in genital stimulation or preparatory fondling with phenotypically normal, physically mature, consenting human partners" (American Psychiatric Association, 2013, p. 685). A *paraphilic disorder* is defined as a "paraphilia that is currently causing distress or impairment to the individual or a paraphilia whose satisfaction has entailed personal harm, or risk of harm, to others" (American Psychiatric Association, 2013, pp. 685–686). This definition varies from an earlier version in that it requires that some sort of distress or impairment be caused from the sexual attraction. Also, the symptoms of disorder must exist for at least six months.

The following eight paraphilic disorders are identified in the DSM-5, along with a residual "other" category:

*Exhibitionist Disorder*: Deriving sexual pleasure from exposing one's private parts to an unsuspecting person or performing sexual acts that can be watched by others.

*Frotteuristic Disorder*: Deriving sexual pleasure form touching/rubbing against a non-consenting person.

*Voyeuristic Disorder*: Deriving sexual pleasure from observing an unsuspecting person who is naked, undressing or engaging in sexual activities, or in activities deemed to be of a private nature.

*Fetishistic Disorder*: Deriving sexual pleasure from specific inanimate objects.

*Pedophilic Disorder*: Sexual preference for prepubescent children.

*Sexual Masochism Disorder*: Deriving sexual pleasure from wanting to be humiliated, beaten, bound or otherwise made to suffer.

*Sexual Sadism Disorder*: Deriving sexual pleasure from inflicting pain or humiliation on another person.

*Transvestic Fetishism*: Deriving sexual pleasure from clothing associated with members of the opposite sex.

*Other Specified Paraphilic Disorder*: These include a variety of other paraphilic behaviors not already listed (Brannon, n.d.).

It should be noted that many of the paraphilic disorders are not sex crimes unless a non-consenting person is involved. For example, a fetish that involves a sexual attraction to ladies' shoes is not a crime. If an individual with a fetishistic disorder, however, breaks into a house to steal ladies' shoes, a crime has been committed.

## ONCE A SEX OFFENDER, ALWAYS A SEX OFFENDER?

One particular myth is worth examining in this chapter, as it permeates most aspects of sex crimes and sex offenders. Many believe that all sex offenders recidivate, that is, they commit sex crimes one after another. In addressing this myth, it is important to first examine a few methodological obstacles in measuring "true" recidivism rates. *Recidivism*, broadly defined, simply refers to committing a crime again. Most researchers acknowledge that this is nearly impossible to accurately measure, as many will commit another crime, but the crime will not become known to law enforcement officials. Researchers are often left to rely on other indicators that someone has committed a crime, usually arrest records, re-incarceration records, or self-report data. Each of these sources has its own limitations. The primary limitation is that they do not capture all sex crimes. Many sex offenders go unnoticed by law enforcement officials and many, if asked in a self-report survey, will underestimate the number of crimes they have committed. Thus, as researchers, we rely on imperfect measures of recidivism.

Numerous studies have been conducted on sex offender recidivism. Many, however, are limited by small, localized samples and do not follow offenders for an extended time. The best way to find the answer to the question of how many sex offenders recidivate is to rely on *meta-analyses*. A meta-analysis is a sort of study of studies, where a researcher gathers all relevant studies on a particular topic and analyzes all of the results to gain a more comprehensive answer to the research question posed. It is advantageous in that it creates a larger sample of studies. It also provides a comprehensive perspective of the research question addressed.

Two meta-analyses of sex offenders stand out as being the most comprehensive. The first was published in 1998 and included 61 studies. A total of 23,393 sex offenders were included. The majority (84%) of the studies relied on reconviction to measure recidivism. Studies also relied on arrests (54%), self-reports (25%), and parole violations (16%). Given that some of the studies relied on multiple measures, the percentages here exceed 100%. Studies were included only if they were deemed to have reliable methods as determined by the two researchers. The sex offenders were followed for an average of four to five years (Hanson & Bussière, 1998).

The results indicated that, on average, 13.4% of sex offenders sexually recidivated (i.e., committed another sex crime) (Hanson & Bussière, 1998). The rate of sexual recidivism, however, varied for sub-groups of sex offenders. Rapists recidivated at a slightly higher rate (18.9%) than child molesters (12.7%). Again, it is important to note that although these rates are low, many sex crimes go undetected. The evidence, however, suggests that not all sex offenders recidivate, and their sexual recidivism rates are lower than expected. This study also found that criminal lifestyle, sexual deviance, and psychological maladjustment were predictors of sexual recidivism. More factors associated with predicting recidivism are reported in Chapter 10, Assessment Tools and Treatment of Sex Offenders.

Another meta-analysis was conducted in 2005. It was based on 82 studies and 29,450 known sex offenders. Although the majority of the sex offenders were from the U.S., these studies also included sex offenders from Canada, U.K., Austria, Sweden, Australia, France, Netherlands, and Denmark. Most of the studies incorporated multiple measures of recidivism (i.e., arrest, parole violations, and other reports), but some relied solely on arrest or reconviction data. The offenders were followed for an average of five to six years (Hanson & Morton-Bourgon, 2005).

The results of this meta-analysis, similar to the previous meta-analysis, revealed a 13.7% sexual recidivism rate. The researchers noted that these "should be considered underestimates because not all offenses are detected" (Hanson & Morton-Bourgon, 2005, p. 1157). The strongest predictors of sexual recidivism included sexual deviancy and antisocial orientation.

While these studies use imperfect measures of recidivism—less than "true" recidivism measures—other studies may yield further insights. Albeit controversial, much has been learned from utilizing polygraph testing to estimate recidivism. In one study of 147 sex offenders who were polygraphed, one was re-arrested for sexual recidivism, while an additional 20 self-reported sexually abusing victims after their initial sex-offense conviction (English, Jones, Pasini-Hill, Patrick, & Cooley-Towell, 2000). Thus, 14% would have avoided detection if using re-arrest as the measure of recidivism. What this tells us is that while the estimates of approximately 13–14% suggest low rates of sexual recidivism, utilizing polygraphs (a potentially more accurate measure) reveals an additional (approximately) 14% may go undetected. While these point to possible higher rates of recidivism than are reported in the literature, they still indicate that a majority of those detected and identified as sex offenders do not go on to commit another sex crime.

## ADDRESSING SEX-OFFENDER AND SEX-CRIME MYTHS

Although there are many myths regarding sex offenders and sex crimes, one myth is embedded in most of them: *all sex offenders are the same.* Throughout all of the subsequent chapters, research is presented that highlights that sex offenders are heterogeneous (i.e., vary in their characteristics and behaviors). They are a diverse group of offenders. They vary a great deal in their characteristics, from young to old, and having no job skills to having highly trained positions, such as teacher, coach, or professional sports figure. They vary in their victim choice, from choosing a child or an adult, someone they know, or someone they have never met. And they vary in how they approach their victims, from years of slowly eroding boundaries to a split-second attack. This textbook is laid out by addressing various overarching myths regarding sex crimes and sex offenders.

## Myths About the Number of, and Trends Associated with, Sex Offenders

As discussed in this chapter, much information refutes common beliefs about who is a sex offender, how many there are, and what the trends show. Sex offenders are diverse: male, female, young, old, wealthy, poor, employed, and unemployed. As revealed from a brief examination of the table of contents, sex offenders commit diverse crimes (sexual assault, child molesting, and child pornography) and affect a wide range of victims. Given the media attention that sex crimes and sex offenders receive, it is no wonder why it is believed that sex crime rates are high and continue to increase (Center for Sex Offender Management, 2000). This is refuted in this chapter by closely examining sex-crime and sex-offender estimates from various sources. Like all other violent crimes, sex crimes have been decreasing recently. Also, it has been (wrongly) proposed that all sex offenders re-offend (Center for Sex Offender Management, 2000). Research, however, shows that a small portion of convicted sex offenders commit subsequent sex crimes.

## Myths Regarding Why Sex Offenders Commit Sex Crimes

Many myths exist regarding why sex offenders commit sex crimes. For example, it has been (wrongly) proposed that one must be mentally ill to commit a sex crime (Center for Sex Offender Management, n.d.) and rape, in particular, is caused by offenders who have uncontrollable sexual urges (Michigan State University, 2015). The reasons why people commit sex crimes are varied, and no single theory explains all sex crimes. Chapter 2 presents various theories proposed to explain sex crimes and sex offenders. It should be noted, however, that many of these theories have only moderate empirical support, meaning we still do not know exactly why people commit sex crimes.

## Myths Regarding Rapists, Rape, and Rape Victims

It has been proposed that women should be careful when walking alone at night, for fear that a stranger may rape them (Koester, 2015). The research shows that most rape victims know their rapists (Planty et al., 2013). It is also proposed that rape is (always) about sex, female victims are often at fault, and there is a "right" way to respond to a rape (University of Minnesota Duluth, 2001). An entire set of "rape myths" has been identified in the literature, and affects the way many people perceive rape. All of these myths are refuted by research, and are discussed in Chapter 3.

## Myths Regarding Child Molesters, Child Molestation, and Child Victims

There are many myths about child molesters, the process of an offender eroding boundaries to molest the child, and the characteristics of child molestation victims. For example, many (wrongly) believe that child molesters are "boogeymen," who don't appear to be normal (One with Courage, n.d.). Chapter 4 discusses research regarding the characteristics of child molesters, the process involved, and victim characteristics. You will learn that child molesters are a diverse group of offenders. Some choose employment based on their access to children. Also, characteristics of the child-molestation process vary, and there is a wide range of victims.

## Myths Regarding Child Pornographers, Child Pornography, and Victims of Child Pornography

One may (wrongly) believe that the child-pornography industry is small and that the victims of child pornography are not harmed to the same degree as victims of hands-on crimes (Pulido, 2013). Neither of these myths is true. In Chapter 5, you will learn that child pornography is a multi-billion dollar industry, and the victims are harmed through sharing of pornographic images, and, again, offender characteristics vary considerably.

## Myths Regarding Juvenile Sex Offenders, Offenses, and Victims

Many of the myths associated with adult sex offenders apply to juvenile sex offenders. For example, the myth that once a sex offender, always a sex offender has been applied to juveniles. There are additional myths for juvenile sex offenders, such as they always grow into adult sex offenders, they are not treatable, they abuse because they have been sexually abused themselves, and they are all pedophiles (Fagundes, 2014). The research does not support these myths. This research is discussed in Chapter 6.

## Myths Regarding Female Sex Offenders, Offenses, and Victims

It is often assumed that all sex offenders are male (Office of the Attorney General, 2001). Although female offenders comprise a small percentage of sex offenders, their numbers are large enough to warrant concern. Although the schoolteacher who molests a male student has been covered at length in the media, Chapter 7 shows this is only one type of female sex offender. Chapter 7 reveals the diverse range of female sex offenders that have been identified in the research. Also, victims of female sex offenders can be either male or female and of any age.

### Myths Regarding Institutional Abuse

It has been (wrongly) assumed that child molestation and rape occur only under certain circumstances: by a stranger, unsupervised, and by someone who should not be trusted. The reality, however, is that many incidents of child abuse and rape are committed by someone the victim knows and who is in a trusted position (e.g., daycare provider). They can occur at church by a clergy member, at school by a teacher, at sports practice by a coach, or by a volunteer at a civic organization. Such instances are discussed in Chapter 8.

### Myths Regarding Investigating Abuse

Many of the myths already discussed permeate the investigations process. For example, it is not uncommon for someone to believe that women will claim to be raped when they regret having sex (University of Minnesota Duluth, 2001). This, along with other rape myths, can affect the investigation of sex crimes—from the 911 operator to the detective who leads an investigation. The investigation process is discussed in depth in Chapter 9.

### Myths Regarding Assessment and Treatment of Sex Offenders

A common sex-offender myth is that treatment is ineffective for sex offenders (Center for Sex Offender Management, 2000). Chapter 10 provides an overview of treatment methods, along with their effectiveness. Research reveals many convicted sex offenders are not re-arrested for another sex crime (Hanson & Bussière, 1998), and treatment, specifically, results in lower recidivism rates (Lösel & Schmucker, 2005).

### Myths Regarding Which Community Sanctions Should Exist for Sex Offenders

It is often wrongly assumed that most sex offenders are caught, convicted, and imprisoned (Center for Sex Offender Management, 2000). Sixty percent of convicted sex offenders are serving probation and live in the community (Greenfeld, 1997). They are, however, often subjected to registration laws and other restrictions, such as not living within 500 feet of a school or other area where children congregate. Many of the laws, unfortunately, are based on some of the common misperceptions regarding sex offenders. These laws, and their effectiveness, are discussed in Chapter 11.

## REVIEW POINTS

- Much of the information we knew about sex offenders in the 1980s was wrong.

- The current (over-)emphasis on the dangerousness of sex offenders is embedded in the current moral panic culture.

- A sex crime is broadly defined in the U.S. as a crime that involves a sexual act or sexual contact. Much of what is considered a sex crime changes over time and is highly dependent upon the current culture.

- There are various sources of the number of sex crimes and sex offenders: United Nations Office on Drugs and Crime (UNODC), Uniform Crime Reports (UCR), National Incident-Based Reporting System (NIBRS), National Crime Victimization Survey (NCVS), National Child Abuse and Neglect Data System (NCANDS), and the National Violence Against Women Survey.

- In the U.S., the number of sex crimes and sex offenders has been declining over the past several years.

- Some of the first researchers who studied sex (Sigmund Freud and Alfred Kinsey) were not well received by their peers due to the taboo nature of the topic.

- Sexual deviances are defined as paraphilias in the Diagnostic and Statistical Manual of Mental Disorders, fifth edition.

- Meta-analyses conducted on known sex offenders reveal a relatively low rate of sexual recidivism, contrary to popular belief that all sex offenders sexually recidivate.

- Many myths exist regarding sex crimes and sex offenders.

## REFERENCES

42 U.S. Code § 16911 (5)(a)(1).

Administration on Children Youth and Families. (2014). *Child maltreatment, 2013*. Washington DC: Government Printing Office.

American Psychiatric Association. (2013). *Diagnostic and statistical manual of mental disorders, fifth edition*. Washington DC: American Psychiatric Publishing.

Armstrong, S. (1994). Rape in South Africa: An invisible part of apartheid's legacy. *Gender and Development, 2*(2), 35–39.

Brannon, G. E. (n.d.). Paraphilic disorders. Retrieved January 10, 2016, from http://emed icine.medscape.com/article/291419-overview

Center for Sex Offender Management. (2000). *Myths and facts about sex offenders*. Washington, DC: U.S. Department of Justice, Office of Justice Programs.

Center for Sex Offender Management. (n.d.). Section 3: Characteristics of sex offfenders. Retrieved October 25, 2015, from http://www.csom.org/train/etiology/3/3_1.htm

Cohen, S. (1972). *Folk devils and moral panics: The creation of the mods and rockers*. Oxford: Martin Robertson.

English, K., Jones, L., Pasini-Hill, D., Patrick, D., & Cooley-Towell, S. (2000). *The value of polygraph testing in sex offender management*. Washington DC: U.S. Department of Justice, National Institute of Justice.

Fagundes, M. (2014). Dangerous myths about juvenile sex offenders: Meghan Fagundes at TEDxAustinWomen. Retrieved October 25, 2015, from http://tedxtalks.ted.com/video/Dangerous-myths-about-juvenile

Federal Bureau of Investigation. (2014). *National Incident-Based Reporting System: 2012*. Washington DC: Government Printing Office. Retrieved January 15, 2016 from https://www.fbi.gov/about-us/cjis/ucr/nibrs/2012/data-tables.

Federal Bureau of Investigation. (2016). *Crime in the United States: 2014.* Washington DC: Government Printing Office. Retrieved January 15, 2016 from https://www.fbi.gov/about-us/cjis/ucr/crime-in-the-u.s/2014/crime-in-the-u.s.-2014.

Federal Bureau of Investigation. (n.d.-a). National Incident-Based Reporting System: General information. Retrieved January 17, 2016, from https://www.fbi.gov/about-us/cjis/ucr/nibrs-overview

Federal Bureau of Investigation. (n.d.-b). NIBRS. Retrieved January 17, 2016, from https://www.fbi.gov/about-us/cjis/ucr/nibrs-overview

Greenfeld, L. (1997). *Sex offenses and offenders: An analysis of data on rape and sexual assault.* U.S. Department of Justice, Office of Justice Programs, Bureau of Justice Statistics.

Hanson, R. K., & Bussière, M. T. (1998). Predicting relapse: A meta-analysis of sexual offender recidivism studies. *Journal of Consulting and Clinical Psychology, 66*(2), 348–362.

Hanson, R. K., & Morton-Bourgon, K. E. (2005). The characteristics of persistent sexual offenders: A meta-analysis of recidivism studies. *Journal of Consulting and Clinical Psychology, 73*(6), 1154–1163.

Hunt, M. (1993). *The story of psychology.* New York: Doubleday.

Jenkins, P. (1998). *Moral panic: Changing concepts of the child molester in modern America.* New Haven, CT: Yale University Press.

Jones, M. (2007). How can you distinguish a budding pedophile from a kid with real boundary issues. Retrieved May 1, 2013, from http://www.nytimes.com/2007/07/22/magazine/22juvenile-t.html?pagewanted=all&_r=0

Kinsey, A. C., W. B. Pomeroy, & C. E. Martin. (1948). *Sexual behavior in the human male.* Philadelphia: Saunders.

Kinsey, A., Pomeroy, W. B., Martin, C., & Gebhard, P. (1953). *Sexual behavior in the human female.* Philadelphia: Saunders.

Koester, M. (2015). On safety, fear, and walking home alone at night as a woman. *Vice.* Retrieved October 25, 2015, from http://www.vice.com/read/i-was-assaulted-on-the-street-but-i-still-walk-home-alone-at-night-408

Krafft-Ebing, R. V. (1886). *Psychopathia sexualia.* Stuttgart, Germany: Ferdinand Enke.

Langton, L., Berzofsky, M., Krebs, C., & Smiley-McDonald, H. (2012). *Victimizations not reported to the police, 2006–2010.* (NCJ 238536). Washington DC: Government Printing Office.

Laws, D. R., & Marshall, W. L. (2003). A brief history of behavioral and cognitive behavioral approaches to sexual offenders: Part 1. Early developments. *Sexual Abuse: A Journal of Research and Treatment, 15*(2), 75–92.

Levenson, J., Letourneau, E. J., Armstrong, K., & Zgoba, K. (2010). Failure to register as a sex offender: Is it associated with recidivism? *Justice Quarterly, 27*(3), 305–331.

Lösel, F., & Schmucker, M. (2005). The effectiveness of treatment for sexual offenders: A comprehensive meta-analysis. *Journal of Experimental Criminology, 1*(1), 117–146.

McManus, M. A., Hargreaves, P., Rainbow, L., & Alison, L. J. (2013). Paraphilias: Definition, diagnosis and treatment. *F1000 Prime Reports, 5*(36), 36–41.

Michigan State University. (2015). Sexual assault prevention and awareness center: Myths and facts. Retrieved October 25, 2015, from https://sapac.umich.edu/article/52

Office of the Attorney General, S. o. C. (2001). Megan's Law - Facts about sex offenders. Retrieved January 15, 2016 from http://meganslaw.ca.gov/facts.htm

One with Courage. (n.d.). Myths about child sexual abuse. Retrieved October 25, 2015, from http://www.onewithcourage.org/wp-content/uploads/2011/09/myths-about-abuse1.pdf

Ouattara, M., Sen, P., & Thomson, M. (1998). Forced marriage, forced sex: The perils of childhood for girls. *Gender and Development, 6*(3), 27–33.

Planty, M., Langston, L., Krebs, C., & Smiley-McDonald, H. (2013). *Female victims of sexual violence, 1994–2010.* (NCJ 240655). Washington: DC: Government Printing Office.

Pulido, M. L. (2013). Child pornography: Basic facts about a horrific crime. The Huffington Post. Retrieved September 26, 2016 from "https://bobcatmail.txstate.edu/owa/redir.aspx?C=VX_GdT1DuQlb3OMT-VI5H9rOX7wxfqDGL_rEJAv-VvEa-WVmIObTCA..&URL=http%3a%2f%2fwww.huffingtonpost.

com%2fmary-l-pulido-phd%2fchild-pornography-basic-f_b_4094430.html" \t "_blank"
http://www.huffingtonpost.com/mary-l-pulido-phd/child-pornography-basic-f_b_4094430.
html.

Rennison, C. M. (2002). *Rape and sexual assault: Reporting to police and medical attention, 1992–2000.* (NCJ 194530). Washington DC: Government Printing Office.

Soothill, K. L. (2010). Sex offender recidivism. *Crime and Justice, 39*(1), 145–211.

Stafford, M. C., & Vandiver, D. M. (2016). Public perceptions of sex crimes and sex offenders. In B. Francis & T. Sanders (Eds.), *Oxford Handbook of Sex Offences and Sex Offenders.* Oxford: Oxford University Press.

Tjaden, P., & Thoennes, N. (2006). *Extent, nature, and consequences of rape victimization: Findings from the National Violence Against Women Survey.* (NCJ 210346). Washington DC: Government Printing Office.

Truman, J. L., & Langton, L. (2014). *Criminal victimization, 2013.* (NCJ 247648). Washington: DC: Government Printing Office.

United Nations Office on Drugs and Crime. (2015). Sexual violence statistics. Retrieved January 15, 2016 from: http://www.unodc.org/unodc/en/data-and-analysis/statistics.html

University of Minnesota Duluth. (2001). List of rape myths: Sociology of rape. Retrieved January 15, 2016 from http://www.d.umn.edu/cla/faculty/jhamlin/3925/myths.html

## DEFINITIONS

**Diagnostic and Statistical Manual of Mental Disorders (DSM):** A publication by the American Psychiatric Association that provides a list and diagnosis criteria of all the recognized mental disorders.

**Exhibitionist Disorder:** A paraphilic disorder that involves deriving sexual pleasure from exposing one's private parts to an unsuspecting person or performing sexual acts that can be watched by others.

**Fetishistic Disorder:** A paraphilic disorder that involves deriving sexual pleasure from specific inanimate objects.

**Frotteuristic Disorder:** A paraphilic disorder that involves deriving sexual pleasure from touching/rubbing against a non-consenting person.

**Hierarchy Rule:** A rule implemented in Uniform Crime Reports; when more than one offense is committed, only the most serious offense is reported.

**Meta-analysis:** A type of study that involves gathering all past, relevant studies on a particular topic and analyzing all of the results to gain a more comprehensive answer to the research question posed.

**Moral Panic:** A collective response to a perceived threat from an individual or group. The response often exceeds the actual threat, and is manifested through an us-versus-them, do-something-about-them sentiment.

**National Child Abuse and Neglect Data System (NCANDS):** A data source based on data from all U.S. states regarding child abuse and neglect claims each year.

**National Crime Victimization Survey (NCVS):** A data source including the number and type of victimizations that occur in the U.S. each year.

**National Incident-Based Reporting System (NIBRS):** A detailed reporting of crimes that have occurred in the U.S., published by the Federal Bureau of Investigation.

**National Violence Against Women Survey:** A survey conducted in 1995–1996 by the National Institute of Justice (NIJ) and the Centers for Disease Control and Prevention (CDC). It includes a random sample of 8,000 women and 8,005 men and identifies information regarding rape victimizations.

**Other Specified Paraphilic Disorder:** These include a variety of other paraphilic behaviors not already listed in the DSM-5.

**Paraphilia:** any intense and persistent sexual interest in anything other than genital stimulation or preparatory fondling with physically mature, phenotypically normal, consenting human partners.

**Paraphilic Disorder:** The presence of a paraphilia that causes distress or impairment to the individual or has led to personal harm or risk of harm to others.

**Pedophilic Disorder:** A paraphilic disorder that involves having a sexual preference for prepubescent children.

**Recidivism:** An individual's return or relapse into criminal behavior, often after having received sanctions or punishment for previous criminal behavior.

**Seduction Theory of Childhood Sexuality:** Sigmund Freud proposed a theory that adult hysteria was rooted in suppressed childhood incidents of sexual abuse.

**Sexual Masochism Disorder:** A paraphilic disorder that involves deriving sexual pleasure from wanting to be humiliated, beaten, bound or otherwise made to suffer.

**Sexual Sadism Disorder:** A paraphilic disorder that involves deriving sexual pleasure from inflicting pain or humiliation on another person.

**Transvestic Fetishism:** A paraphilic disorder that involves deriving sexual pleasure from clothing associated with members of the opposite sex.

**Uniform Crime Reports (UCR):** An annual report of crimes and arrests that have occurred in the U.S., published by the Federal Bureau of Investigation.

**United Nations Office on Drugs and Crime (UNODC):** An international source of crime statistics, including sexual violence. It is developed from an annual survey on crime trends and operations of criminal justice systems, and other national surveys administered in countries that are members of the United Nations.

**Voyeuristic Disorder:** A paraphilic disorder that involves deriving sexual pleasure from observing an unsuspecting person who is naked, undressing, or engaging in sexual activities, or in activities deemed to be of a private nature.

## CHAPTER 2

# Theories about Sex Crimes and Sex Offenders

## CHAPTER OBJECTIVES

- Discuss two broad categories of theories regarding sex crimes and sex offenders: (1) sex-crime/sex-offender specific and (2) crime in general.
- Discuss several single-factor sex-crime/sex-offender specific theories: biological, behavioral, cognitive, and psychological.
- Provide an overview of several multiple-factor sex-crime/sex-offender theories: precondition theory, quadripartite theory, and integrated theory.
- Provide an overview of several criminological theories that have been relied upon to explain sex crimes/sex offenders: social control (bonding) theory, self-control theory, routine activity theory, and social learning theory.
- Describe a logic model of sex-offender characteristics and behaviors.

What causes people to commit sex crimes and how do sex offenders differ from non-sex offenders? There is no single, universally accepted answer. Instead, there are different answers linked to different theories of sex crimes and sex offenders. But that begs the question: What is a theory? A theory is more than a mere hunch, and it is more than someone's personal ideas about the causes of something. Theories may involve hunches and ideas, but they are more than that. A conventional definition is that a theory is a "set of logically interrelated statements in the form of empirical assertions about properties of infinite classes of events or things" (Gibbs, 1972, p. 5). As the definition indicates, a theory is first a set of logically interrelated statements. A theory might claim that certain types of brain abnormalities cause people to commit sex crimes and then add that certain types of brain abnormalities cause people to have low impulse control and low impulse control is the proximate cause of sex crimes. There are three interrelated statements here. One statement is that certain types of brain abnormalities cause low impulse control. A second statement is that low impulse control causes sex crimes. A third statement is that certain types of brain abnormalities cause sex crimes indirectly through (or because of) low impulse control.

If these interrelated statements comprise a theory about sex crimes and sex offenders, they must be in the form of empirical assertions (the second part of Gibbs' definition). That is, at least some of the statements in the theory must be *testable*. Thus, there must be a possibility of bringing evidence to bear on the theory's statements about the extent to which they are true or false. This is what primarily distinguishes theories from mere hunches and ideas. To the extent theories involve hunches and ideas, they must lead to testable statements.

Theories are also about "properties of infinite classes of events or things" (the third part of Gibbs' definition). A theory cannot be about why a particular person has committed (or will commit) sex crimes. There might be an identifiable answer, and the answer might be different from why another person has committed sex crimes. But theories are not about particular people. Instead, they are generalizations about classes of people, and the generalizations must not be limited to a particular time and place. For example, it would not be a theory if someone proposed to explain why young males were more likely than other people to have committed sex crimes in the U.S. last March. If someone proposed a theory to explain why young males are more likely than other people to commit sex crimes, the theory should apply to all young males, preferably in all places and at all times and not just in the U.S. at a particular time.

Theories about sex crimes and sex offenders help us to make sense of what we know about them. Using the young-male example again, you read in the preceding chapter there is considerable evidence from various sources that young males are more likely than others to commit many sex crimes. A theory can help us to understand why this is the case. It might be due to hormone levels, or it might be learned behavior.

Why theorize at all about the causes of sex crimes and sex offenders? Some people see theories as academic navel-gazing, aimed only at creating knowledge for knowledge's sake. Academic navel-gazing should always be avoided, but there is something to be said in favor of knowledge for knowledge's sake—for example, the understanding that comes from gazing at the stars and knowing why they move in the sky. It helps us to understand the universe in which we live. Theories of sex crimes and sex offenders, however, are important not only because they provide understanding—they are also essential for identifying effective policies about control and treatment. For example, cognitive-behavioral theory (to be discussed subsequently) is the foundation of many (cognitive-behavioral) sex-offender treatment programs today. Without accurate theories about the causes of sex crimes and sex offenders, we would be clueless about how to effectively respond to them. Theories can be seen as policy guides. Good policies are based on good theories.

## TWO TYPES OF THEORIES ABOUT SEX CRIMES AND SEX OFFENDERS

This chapter summarizes a wide range of theories, but they can be divided into two types, theories about: (1) sex crimes and sex offenders only and (2) crimes in general—what accounts for sex crimes and sex offenders also accounts for other types of crimes and offenders. Psychological theories are an example of the first type. One version is that particular psychological traits, such as narcissism, are common among sex offenders (Baumeister, Catanese, & Wallace, 2002). Self-control theory (Gottfredson & Hirschi, 1990) is an example of the second type. According to self-control theory, young children with parents who fail to monitor their behavior and sanction it when it is deviant will grow up to have low self-control. People with low self-control are impulsive, prone to risk-taking, self-centered, and hot-tempered, and they commit crimes to pursue self-interest and obtain "immediate, easy, and certain short-term pleasure" (Gottfredson & Hirschi, 1990, p. 41). Self-control theory is about all types of crimes and offenders, not just sex crimes and sex offenders.

## PROBABILISTIC NATURE OF THEORIES

Whether the theories are about sex crimes and sex offenders only or crime in general, it is important to emphasize that both types of theory propose ***probabilistic causes*** (i.e., a cause may result in a specified outcome) rather than ***deterministic causes*** (i.e., a cause *always* results in a specified outcome). A theory might say some particular factor (e.g., some biological abnormality) always causes one to commit a sex crime, which is to say the theory would propose the factor is a deterministic cause. Neither the version of psychological theory described above nor self-control theory (or any theory we will consider) proposes deterministic causes. Self-control theory does not propose that low self-control *always* causes crime. Instead, it says that low self-control increases the likelihood of committing crimes, including sex crimes.

Probabilistic theories are not inferior to deterministic theories; they are just different. Some causes are deterministic, while others are probabilistic. Today, few deny that cigarette smoking causes lung cancer. Cigarette smoking, however, does not always cause lung cancer, and it is also the case that lung cancer is not always caused by cigarette smoking. Some cigarette smokers never get lung cancer, and some people with lung cancer never smoked cigarettes or were never around cigarette smokers. Cigarette smoking only increases the likelihood of lung cancer, and the more cigarettes people smoked (or the longer the period they smoked), the greater their likelihood of lung cancer. That cigarette smoking is a probabilistic cause of lung cancer does not make it any less of a cause. That is also true of probabilistic causes of sex crimes and sex offenders.

## SEX-CRIME AND SEX-OFFENDER SPECIFIC THEORIES

Several researchers have developed unique theories to explain sex crimes and sex offenders. These sex-crime and sex-offender specific theories are often rooted in other theories that have been developed to explain a broader range of aberrant conditions and behaviors. For example, biological theories are relied upon to account for various diseases—here, biological concepts are relied upon to account for sex crimes. Researchers have developed theories to explain deviant sexual arousal, paraphilias, child molestation, rape, and/or accessing child pornography. You will notice some of these theories explain sex crimes broadly, whereas others focus on only one type of sex crime (e.g., rape). In this section, we describe biological, behavioral, and psychological theories that have been proposed to specifically explain sex crimes and/or sex offenders.

## Biological Theories

As scientific discoveries are made about various biological processes, it is not surprising that they are being linked to particular behaviors, including sex crimes. An examination of a broad range of studies revealed that 33% to 100% of sex offenders (in various studies) had brain abnormalities. For those who were not sex offenders, such brain abnormalities were present in 0% to 17% of individuals (see Stinson, Sales, & Becker, 2008 for discussion). The following abnormalities have been identified: hormones/neurotransmitters, brain structure, sex chromosomes/genetic traits, and intelligence deficits (i.e., mental retardation) (Stinson et al., 2008).

### *Hormones and neurotransmitters*

It is widely accepted that *hormones* (chemical secretions) affect a wide range of bodily functions. Also, *neurotransmitters* (chemicals in the brain) affect brain function, mood, and autonomic reactions (heart rate, breathing, and other bodily functions that respond to anxiety-provoking situations) (Stinson et al., 2008). With regard to hormones, testosterone is most closely associated with sexual arousal of boys/men. It has been speculated that sexual violence is the result of high levels of testosterone, yet research has produced mixed results (Bain, Langevin, Dickey, & Ben-Aron, 1987). Other hormones have been examined as possible contributors to sex crimes (e.g., luteinizing hormone (LH), follicle-stimulating hormone (FSH), dehydroepiandrosterone sulfate, androstenedione, prolactin, and estradiol (Marieb, 2001), with inconclusive results. Neurotransmitters, such as serotonin, have been assessed for their link to violent behavior, including sex crimes. This research, however, is considered to be in its infancy (Stinson et al., 2008).

### *Temporal lobe abnormalities*

Left temporal abnormalities affect sexual interest/drive, emotional responses, and verbal learning (Lang, 1993). Abnormalities in this part of the brain have been found among persons who are attracted to children (Galski, Thornton, & Shumsky, 1990), but not necessarily among incest offenders. This, perhaps, may explain the development of pedophilia. Right temporal abnormalities have been identified among people who have committed violent/sadistic sex crimes (Aigner et al., 2000). It is speculated that the communication between the temporal and frontal lobes results in greater aggression (Aigner et al., 2000). It has also been speculated that frontal lobe abnormalities can result in deficits of inhibition, which can cause aggression (Raine & Buchsbaum, 1996). If such factors are combined with inappropriate sexual feelings, sex crimes can occur (Stinson et al., 2008). Also, research has revealed that low/abnormal cerebral blood flow is a risk factor for paraphililas (Hendricks et al., 1988). It is unclear, however, how it leads to paraphilias (Stinson et al., 2008). As noted in Focus Box 2.1, in rare cases, there is a causal link between a brain tumor and pedophilia, yet the *how* of the causal link is not clearly specified.

---

*Focus Box 2.1    Brain Tumor and Pedophilia*

Albeit a rare event, a report of a brain tumor causing pedophilia has been made. A 40-year-old teacher began to exhibit hypersexual behavior, including pedophilic interests. The man, who previously had not engaged in sexually deviant behavior, began viewing child pornography on the Internet and soliciting prostitutes. The man's wife reported his sexual advances towards children. He was found guilty for these sex crimes and sentenced to prison. The man recognized that the behavior was problematic and wrong, but indicated he did not have the restraint to overcome these feelings. The night before his prison sentence began, he complained of a headache and balance problems, along with the urge to rape his landlady. After going to the hospital, he was diagnosed with a brain tumor. It was removed and the symptoms disappeared. The man, seven months later, again reported headaches and began collecting child pornography. The tumor had returned. It was removed, and the symptoms disappeared again. A neurologist commented on the case, wondering if the tumor caused hormonal changes, which in turn caused the abnormal sexual behavior.

Source: (Choi, 2002)

---

## Genetics and Sex Chromosome Abnormalities

Research has found that genetics (i.e., inheriting certain characteristics) alone does not explain sex crimes (Stinson et al., 2008). Recently, a controversial theory of rape was proposed by Thornhill and Palmer (2000), claiming rape is the product of evolution, and that under certain conditions, all men have the capacity to rape. This theory, however, has been highly criticized for lack of systematic evidence (Zion, 2000).

With regard to chromosome abnormalities, males typically have an X and a Y chromosome (XY), whereas females have two X chromosomes (XX). Thus, these chromosomes determine biological sex, either male or female. Occasionally, rare combinations of chromosomes occur (e.g., XXY, XXXY, XYY), and it has been suggested these may be linked to the commission of sex crimes (Harrison, Clayton-Smith, & Bailey, 2001). Among a sample of male sex offenders, chromosomal abnormalities occurred at a slightly higher rate (4%) than among persons who had not sexually offended (0.1%) (Harrison et al., 2001). Chromosomal abnormalities may be associated with behavior problems, including impulsive behaviors, which can cause sex crimes. More research, however, is needed.

### Intelligence Deficits (Mental Retardation)

Sex crimes occur at a higher rate among persons with intelligence deficits than those within normal range of intelligence functioning (Blanchard et al., 1999). First, it is theorized that there are four characteristics of persons with mental retardation, which could cause them to act out sexually: (1) impulsive behavior, (2) aggression/acting out, (3) poor interpersonal skills, and (4) poor coping skills and self-esteem issues (Stinson et al., 2008). Second, it is also theorized that there is a link between mental retardation and sex crimes due to the mental age of the offenders. For example, it has been proposed that people with mental retardation molest children because the actual age of the victim matches the mental age of the offender (O'Callaghan, 1998). The exact causal mechanism warrants further research (Stinson et al., 2008).

In summary, biological theories identify many possible causes of sex crimes (e.g., temporal lobe abnormality, excessive testosterone, genetic defect), yet there is little information about the underlying biological mechanisms. This research is still relatively new, and more will be learned when more research is conducted.

## Behavioral Theories

Behavioral theories have been relied upon to explain diverse behaviors (Stinson et al., 2008). With regard to sex crimes, they have been relied upon to explain deviant sexual arousal of sex offenders. Behavioral theories rely exclusively on the association between giving a stimulus and eliciting a known and predictable response. That is, it takes into account a stimulus (e.g., give a dog food) and the response (e.g., salivate). It does not consider the cognitive processes that occur from the time a stimulus is given and a response occurs.

The foundations of behavioral theories are rooted in *classical conditioning* and *operant conditioning.* Classical conditioning was developed by Ivan Pavlov and involves eliciting a response (e.g., a sexual response) from a neutral stimulus (e.g., women's shoes) after successively pairing the two (perhaps through masturbation). Normally, the neutral stimulus (e.g., women's shoes) does not instantly elicit a response (e.g., a sexual response), but eventually (perhaps after masturbating many times while viewing women's shoes) the neutral stimulus by itself will elicit a (sexual) response (Pavlov, 1927).

Operant conditioning was developed by B. F. Skinner and explains acquisition and maintenance of behaviors through a process of reinforcement and punishment. Reinforcement results in an increase in the likelihood of a certain behavior, while punishment decreases the probability of the behavior. Reinforcement refers to anything that is rewarding (e.g., money, sexual arousal, etc.). Punishment refers to anything that is noxious (e.g., a negative feeling, pain) (Skinner, 1932).

## Self-Regulation Model of Sexual Offending.

Building on the key concepts of behavioral theories, Ward and Hudson (1998) proposed the *self-regulation model of sexual offending*. This model proposes that people behave in a way that is goal-directed. They act certain ways to achieve a desired state or to avoid an undesired state. That is, they seek pleasure and/or avoid pain. Ward and Hudson identify nine paths people can take, with four of them resulting in committing a sex crime. Here, we will focus on the four paths resulting in a sex crime:

1. *Avoidant-passive pathway:* An individual has a desire to commit a sex crime. They try not to offend but are underregulated or disinhibited. They either lack the ability or refuse to cease a behavioral pattern that has developed.

2. *Avoidant-active pathway:* This individual also lacks the desire or ability to cease committing sex crimes. They do have a goal of avoiding committing a sex crime. This individual will engage in ineffective actions, such as substance abuse, to not commit a sex crime. These actions often lead to committing a sex crime.

3. *Approach-automatic pathway:* This individual does have a goal of committing a sex crime. Here, cognitive and behavioral patterns are well established that lead to committing a sex crime. They are affected by situational factors and do not have sophisticated details of planning.

4. *Approach-explicit pathway:* This individual has a childhood history that led to sexual aggression cognitions. This type of individual engages in planning, including detailed **grooming** behaviors. They have an established goal of committing a sex crime (Ward & Hudson, 1998, 2000).

## Cognitive Theories

A variety of cognitive processes (interpretation of emotions, cue perception, information processing) affect behaviors and have been relied upon to explain dysfunctional behaviors, including sexual offending (Stinson et al., 2008). Cognitive theories have focused on explaining both the development of sexual offending and the maintenance of such behaviors. There are essentially three areas of development related to cognitive theories that focus on explaining the commission of a sex crime: *attachment theory*, *cognitive schemas*, and *cognitive biases*.

### Attachment Theory
Originally proposed as an explanation for dysfunctional adulthood behavior, Bowlby (1958, 1988) proposed that the relationship children have with their primary caretaker affects adulthood functioning. Children develop a perception of the world and how to process information, which will remain relatively stable throughout life (Bowlby, 1977). Research that has assessed attachments has found that sex offenders

disproportionately had poor parental attachment and high levels of parental rejection (Marshall, 1989; Marshall, Hudson, Jones, & Fernandez, 1995).

Subsequent research specifically identified two attachment styles in explaining sexually deviant behavior: (a) anxious-ambivalent attachment style and (b) avoidant attachment style (Ward, Polaschek, & Beech, 1995). With regard to those who develop an anxious-ambivalent attachment style, they have low self-esteem and poor self-confidence, are dependent on others for approval, and are easily frustrated by interpersonal relationships (Ward et al., 1995). Sexual abuse is the result of engaging in self-serving behavior based on feelings towards others (Marshall, 1993). It assumes the victim is deserving of the abuse (Marshall, 1993). This explanation, therefore, has been relied upon in explaining child molestation (Marshall & Mazzucco, 1995).

With regard to those who develop avoidant attachment style, they often devalue relationships. Also, they have low empathy, and demonstrate hostility towards others (Ward et al., 1995). This type of attachment style *may* lead to sexual offending. For example, if combined with sexual and aggressive urges, a sense of entitlement and desire for power can lead to committing a sex crime (Marshall, 1993). Such behaviors can be maintained to reduce frustration and isolate one's self from intimate relationships (Marshall, 1993). Alternatively, it is hypothesized that someone with avoidant attachment style may commit sex crimes because of an interaction of no/low empathy skills, which is caused from the lack of attachment formed in early childhood, and feelings of hostility (Ward et al., 1995). This person would not be likely to invest in the work associated with forming an intimate relationship. This can lead to rape or other sex crimes.

### Cognitive Schemas

Cognitive schemas help us organize information and make sense of the world. They involve creating organized patterns of previous experiences, which are relied upon to interpret new information (Fiske & Taylor, 1991). With regard to sex offenders and cognitive schemas, two related areas of research have emerged: (a) cognitive distortions and (b) causal and blame attributions (Stinson et al., 2008).

*Cognitive distortions* are a type of automatic thought process that develops and assists in minimizing the seriousness of the offense (Ward, 2000). For child molesters, they may believe they are "educating" children. For rapists, they may believe that women secretly desire to be raped. These cognitive distortions are discussed in more depth in Chapters 3 and 4.

Also, explanations of sexual offending have been linked to causal and blame attributions (Stinson et al., 2008). Causal attributions involve offenders' perceptions of the world and how they evaluate their own behaviors. Blame attributions refer to how much an offender blames himself and others for his own behavior. Research has found that rapists often focus on external factors (e.g., victim availability) (McKay, Chapman, & Long, 1996). It is also found that child molesters often rely on internal factors as a cause of sexual offending, such as a mental disorder.

### Cognitive Biases

Cognitive biases refer to illogical thoughts that skew one's perception of the world. For sex offenders, many biases have been identified that contribute to their sexual offending. For example, it has been theorized that sex offenders engage in self-serving and self-protective biases due to low self-esteem, and a lack of attachment to others (Marshall, Anderson, & Champagne, 1997). It has also been speculated that sex offenders possess a sense of sexual entitlement—that is, their needs are greater than their victims (Hanson, Gizzarelli, & Scott, 1994).

# Psychological Theories

Psychological theories have been relied upon as well to explain a broad range of abnormal behavior, including sexually deviant behavior. Psychological theories are deeply rooted in concepts developed by Sigmund Freud, who relied heavily upon sexual development as a key construct to explaining why people behaved the way they did. Here, we will discuss the work of Freud and more recent research that has proposed specific personality traits as factors that do not necessarily directly *cause* someone to commit a sex crime, but rather indirectly contribute to the development of sexually deviant behavior.

## *Freud*

Freud developed several psychological concepts that he would later rely upon in his explanation of the development of sexually deviant behavior. First, he proposed that there are five stages of *psychosexual development*: (1) oral (focus on mouth, sucking behavior), (2) anal (focus on the anus, controlling bodily functions), (3) phallic (focus on genitals), (4) latency (relatively calm period with no specific focus), and (5) genital (focus on genitals).

Freud proposed that individuals prone to sexually deviant behavior fixate on certain stages—they get "stuck" during development—or they successfully progress through each stage and possibly, later, regress to a particular stage. Thus, fixation and regression can result in sexually deviant behavior. Additionally, he proposed that problems can occur during the phallic stage. *Castration anxiety* can occur, where boys are fearful of losing or having damage done to their penis. For girls, they experience *penis envy*, which is a feeling of anxiety that occurs when they realize they do not have a penis. This occurs around the ages of three to five years (Freud, 1962).

Freud also proposed three parts to one's personality: (1) *id*, (2) *ego*, and (3) *superego*. The id is responsible for seeking self-pleasure. The ego acts as a mediator between the id and superego. The superego is associated with one's moral principles, acting as one's conscience. These aspects are often in a state of struggle, yet eventually determining one's sexual behaviors. For someone who engages in sexual deviance, it is the result of the id not being regulated by the ego and the superego.

With regard to child molestation, Freud speculated that the individual's childhood must have involved trauma and the sexual attraction to children results from their attempt to compensate for their own childhood (Freud, 1962).

### Personality Profile and Traits of Sex Offenders

Researchers have proposed the possibility that sex offenders have a unique personality profile, distinguishing them from non-sex offenders. Research has not consistently identified a unique personality profile among sex offenders. Although sex offenders may exhibit particular personality types, such personality inventory assessments would not distinguish sex offenders from non-sex offenders (Stinson et al., 2008).

Research, however, has identified particular personality traits that may combine with biological, cognitive, and social factors to cause sexual offending (Stinson et al., 2008). The traits that have been identified (*impulsivity*, *callousness* and *lack of empathy*, *narcissism*, *sadism*, and *personality pathology*) are discussed below.

1. *Impulsivity:* A common characteristic identified among sex offenders is impulsivity, a need for instant gratification and an inability to control impulses (Stinson et al., 2008). For example, impulsivity was found to be prevalent among a sample of male college students who committed rape, but not among those who had not committed rape (Mouilso, Calhoun, & Rosenbloom, 2013).

2. *Callousness and Lack of Empathy:* Callousness refers to a blunted emotional response to others, whereas lack of empathy refers to an inability to respond to someone else with appropriate emotions. Both of these have been speculated to affect those who commit sex crimes (Barnett & Mann, 2013; Porter, Campbell, & Birth, 2001). More specifically, it was proposed that child abuse caused one to develop callousness and lack of empathy, increasing the likelihood of engaging in a sex crime (Porter et al., 2001).

3. *Narcissism:* Narcissism refers to self-love, grandiose perceptions of one's self, and a sense of entitlement. Narcissistic traits have been found to exist among rapists, who attack women perceived to be unattainable (Baumeister et al., 2002).

4. *Sadism:* Sadism, achieving sexual arousal from inflicting pain or humiliation on another person, also has been identified as a trait that exists among sex offenders. More specifically, it is found among those who commit sexual murder and those who commit violent sex crimes (Berger, Berner, Bolterauer, Gutierrez, & Berger, 1999).

5. *Personality Pathology:* Many personality disorders have been identified by the American Psychiatric Association (2013) and have a host of common traits: impulsivity, egocentricity, mood problems, self-identity issues, harm to self

and others, and unpredictable behaviors. Personality pathologies involve a set of emotional and behavioral characteristics that cause maladaptive behaviors, including committing sex crimes. Sex offenders, in general, exhibit problems with interpersonal relationships (Stinson et al., 2008).

In summary, psychological theories have focused on personality development and how that results in sexually deviant behavior, including the commission of sex crimes. Although a "personality profile" has not been identified from research efforts, specific traits have been found to be prevalent among sex offenders. Although these traits by themselves do not predict whether one will sexually offend, they do seem to interact with other internal and external factors to potentially lead one to commit a sex crime.

# MULTIPLE-FACTOR THEORIES OF SEX CRIMES AND SEX OFFENDERS

Believing that the causes of sex crimes and sex offenders are more complex than indicated in any single-factor theory, some researchers have proposed theories that include multiple factors. In this section, three prominent multiple-factor theories are considered.

## Finkelhor's (1984) Precondition Theory

Finkelhor's (1984) theory is only about child sexual abuse, not all sex crimes, and it proposes four preconditions for it to occur:

1.  *There must be an offender with the motivation to sexually abuse children.* With the exception of reflexive behaviors, such as sneezing and blinking, human behavior is preceded by thought or premeditation. Child sexual abuse is no exception. People sexually abuse children because they desire to; they are motivated to sexually abuse children. Their motivation can be manifested in three ways:

    a.  *Sexual arousal*: Offenders are aroused by sex with children.
    b.  *Emotional congruence*: Child sexual abuse satisfies some emotional need, such as intimacy.
    c.  *Blockage*: There is no other viable source of sexual gratification, or nothing as satisfying as sexual abuse of children.

    Professionals, such as police officers and mental-health providers, who work with child sexual abusers often hear sex offenders claim that the offense occurred "out of the blue." It was "completely out of character." It is important to note, however, that the motivation to sexually abuse a child may have come from as far back as the offender's childhood. Attitudes and beliefs that support deviant sexuality, anger, hostility, and desire for power over sex partners can be rooted in early childhood experiences. Sexual behavior that is too early in a child's development, or that is too explicit or abusive, can blur sexual boundaries and lead to deviant sexual desires and fantasies. This generally does not happen all at once; offenders engage in thought and premeditation. It is unusual for child sexual abuse to "just happen."

2. *The offender must overcome internal inhibitions against child sexual abuse.* In deciding whether to sexually abuse children, people might consider its illegality, the consequences if caught (e.g., imprisonment), its immorality, and the harm to victims. To overcome such inhibitions, motivated offenders often subscribe to cognitive distortions that weaken or even eliminate such obstacles, thus granting themselves "permission" to sexually abuse children. Cognitive distortions minimize or deny the dangerousness of the behavior, justify it, and relieve the offender of responsibility. Cognitive distortions, such as "children need to be taught about sex," "children are very seductive," and "the child is too young to know what is happening" can cause child sexual abusers to believe they are doing nothing wrong. Impulse disorder, senility, psychosis, severe stress, alcoholism, and strong patriarchal beliefs that women and children are inferior also weaken internal inhibitions (Beech & Ward, 2004).

3. *The offender must overcome external obstacles to the abuse.* This involves creating opportunities to sexually abuse children so that the victim is alone (vulnerable) and the offender is unlikely to be caught. Offenders may create opportunities for child sexual abuse by **grooming** potential victims, which, as discussed in more detail in Chapter 4, involves manipulating children into situations where they can be more easily sexually abused and there is less of a chance to be detected.

4. *The offender must overcome resistance by the child.* In some instances of sexually violent offenses, physical violence, weapons, bindings, or verbal intimidation are used to overcome resistance. Sometimes, alcohol and other drugs are used. More often, resistance is overcome by manipulating the child into giving trust, loyalty, and affection. This can also be part of grooming a potential victim.

## Hall and Hirschman's Quadripartite Theory

This theory is about sexual aggression against women. "The [theory's] components … – physiological sexual arousal, cognitions that justify sexual aggression, affective dyscontrol, and personality problems – function as motivational precursors that increase the probability of sexually aggressive behavior" (Hall & Hirschman, 1991, p. 662).

1. *Physiological sexual arousal.* While child sexual abuse might result from deviant sexual arousal, sex crimes against adults can result from non-deviant

sexual arousal. "Similar psychological processes may underlie sexual arousal that results in appropriate sexual behavior as well as sexual arousal that results in sexual aggression" (Hall & Hirschman, 1991, p. 664). As such, sexual arousal alone does not cause sexual aggression against women. Other components must be considered.

2. *Cognitions that justify sexual aggression.* Physiological sexual arousal must be cognitively appraised before it is acted upon. These cognitions can include justifications and myths suggesting that sexual aggression against women is acceptable, perhaps even appropriate in some situations. For example, a person might support **rape myths** (see Chapter 3) that any sex act, regardless of coercion, is enjoyable for the victim, resulting in a belief that rape is acceptable. When physiological arousal is coupled with this kind of cognitive appraisal, there is an increased probability of sexual aggression.

3. *Affective dyscontrol.* According to Hall and Hirschman (1991), negative emotions often precede cognitive appraisals about committing a sex crime. Anger might be an important negative emotion for rape, while, for child molesting, it might be depression. Most people control their negative emotions so that their sexual behavior is expressed appropriately (e.g., among consenting adults). Sexual aggression, however, may occur "when these affective states become so compelling and powerful that they overcome inhibitions (e.g., guilt, moral conviction, anxiety, empathy for the victim)" (Hall & Hirschman, 1991, p. 664).

4. *Personality problems.* Personality problems are more enduring than physiological sexual arousal, cognitions that justify sexual aggression, and affective dyscontrol. Negative childhood and adolescent experiences (e.g., parental neglect or divorce and physical or sexual abuse) and developmental limitations (e.g., limited education and poor social skills) cause enduring personality problems. Sexual aggressors against women may be selfish, exploitative of others, remorseless, and antisocial, with a history of committing other, nonsexual crimes.

## Marshall and Barbaree's Integrated Theory

Like Hall and Hirschman (1991), Marshall and Barbaree (1990) say that early, negative childhood experiences can be a precursor to committing a sex crime. Early childhood physical or sexual abuse, neglect, and inconsistent discipline cause children to see their caregivers as emotionally absent and view themselves as unworthy of being loved. They later become adolescents and adults who are hostile, insensitive to others, and use aggression as a way to solve problems. They also have low self-esteem, and poor interpersonal and coping skills. A man who considers himself socially inadequate and unworthy of love might develop fantasies of power over and contempt for women.

An important part of the theory is a biological connection between sexual impulses and aggression. Males have a "biologically endowed propensity for self-interest associated with a tendency to fuse sex and aggression" (Marshall & Barbaree, 1990, p. 257). Both types of impulses come from the same part of the brain, which makes it difficult for young boys to distinguish between anger and sexual arousal. They must learn to use inhibitory controls to constrain their sexual and aggressive self-interested behavior in socially acceptable ways. Together with increasing hormone levels that occur during puberty, male adolescents and young men are vulnerable to commit sex crimes. Many sex crimes provide a release of sexual tension, a sense of control over others, interpersonal intimacy, self-esteem, and feelings of masculinity.

## THEORIES ABOUT CRIME IN GENERAL

Many criminological theories purport to explain a broad range of crimes (e.g., theft, robbery, murder), including sex crimes (e.g., rape, child molestation, child-pornography). To the extent that sex offenders also commit non-sex crimes, broad-based criminological theories are valuable, pointing to causes that are common to all offenders. In this section, we identify a few theories about crime in general that can be applied to sex crimes. They are social control (bonding) theory, self-control theory, routine activity theory, and social learning theory.

### Hirschi's Social Control (Bonding) Theory

Hirschi's (1969) social control theory is often referred to as "social bonding theory" because of the emphasis on the strength of people's bonds to society, including bonds to other people. There are four principal types of bonds: (1) *attachment*, (2) *commitment*, (3) *involvement*, and (4) *belief*. The stronger people's bonds, the less likely they are to commit crime. The weaker the bonds, the more likely it is they will violate the law. Hirschi (1969) saw the bonds as strongly interrelated. For example, if a person had weak attachment, then he usually would have weak commitment, involvement, and belief.

Attachment involves the extent to which people have strong affectional ties to other people. Individuals will refrain from committing crime if they admire other people and care what others think of them. Crime could jeopardize these affectional ties, and in that way strong attachment should be a barrier to crime. Commitment refers to the extent to which individuals have an investment (a "stake in conformity") in conventional goals, such as education and employment. The cost of losing these investments should help to prevent people from committing crime. Involvement pertains to the amount of time spent in conventional activities. The greater the amount of time spent in conventional activities, the less time there is to commit crime. Belief is the last type of bond, and it is an endorsement of conventional norms, including laws. A belief in the moral validity of law should act as a strong barrier to committing crime, according to Hirschi.

Tests of social control theory have examined all of the types of bonds and a wide range of offenses, including juvenile delinquency, and alcohol and other drug abuse (for a review see: Akers & Sellers, 2012; Loeber, 1990). Research on sex crimes and sex offenders, however, has mainly examined attachment. Recall that attachment is an important factor in some of the sex-crime and sex-offender specific theories that we considered earlier in this chapter, so it is hardly surprising that many researchers have focused on sex-offenders' attachment to other people. For example, Awad and colleagues (Awad, Saunders, & Levene, 1984; Saunders, Awad, & White, 1986) found that a large percentage of juvenile sex offenders came from dysfunctional families and they were loners with superficial friendships.

Tingle, Barnard, Robbins, Newman, and Hutchinson (1986) revealed that child molesters had weak relationships with their fathers. They were frequently abandoned by their parents, and they had problems relating to other students in school. Aside from early childhood experiences, Marshall (2010) reported in a recent literature review that adult sex offenders have been found to be lonely and to suffer from severe intimacy problems. There is contrary evidence, however. In a recent meta-analysis involving 59 studies of 3,855 male adolescent sex offenders and 13,393 male adolescent non-sex offenders, Seto and Lalumière (2010, p. 549) found the two groups did not differ with regard to "problematic family relationships, communication, and satisfaction [with family]."

## Gottfredson and Hirschi's Self-Control Theory

Hirschi later seemed to move away from his social control (bonding) theory and collaborated with Gottfredson on a self-control theory (Gottfredson & Hirschi, 1990). Self-control theory is a general theory in that it purports to explain all crimes and deviance committed by people of all ages. The cause of sex crimes, therefore, is the same as the cause of all other crimes.

According to Gottfredson and Hirschi (1990), people with low self-control are impulsive, self-centered, and hot-tempered, and they are risk-takers who prefer easy gratification, simple tasks, and physical rather than mental activities. They commit crimes when opportunities are available. Speaking specifically about rape, they say several conditions must be met:

> First, there must be a victim who is attractive to an offender, available to the offender, unwilling to engage in sexual activity, and unable to resist the offender's advances. Second, there must be an offender who is insufficiently restrained.
>
> (Gottfredson & Hirschi, 1990, p. 39)

Reduction of opportunities to commit rape can help to prevent it. Rape of women in public places by strangers can be prevented by increasing women's ability to resist—for example, by traveling with companions or carrying pepper spray. Women who live alone can reduce their risk of rape by locking their doors and windows.

Low self-control originates in early childhood from ineffective child rearing. Children with low self-control have parents who do not closely monitor their behavior and sanction deviance when it occurs (e.g., a young boy shoving his sister to get to toys). It is primarily the family, then, that shapes a child's self-control. According to the theory, self-control is stable. This means that children with lower self-control than other children will continue to have lower self-control throughout their lives. And they will have a greater likelihood of committing crime and deviance.

Gottfredson and Hirschi (1990) believe there is considerable versatility in the types of crime committed by people with low self-control. Criminal offenders are generalists, not specialists. That is, they commit different types of crime rather than specializing in one. Moreover, they are likely to engage in diverse deviant behaviors that are "analogous" to crime, such as smoking, drinking, gambling, and illicit sex. There is considerable evidence that most criminal offenders do not limit themselves to one type of crime; that is, they are generalists rather than specialists. Researchers however, have shown that many criminal offenders are both generalists and specialists (Sullivan, Mcgloin, Pratt, & Piquero, 2006). There is considerable specialization by offenders in the short term (say, over a period of a few months), but they tend to be crime generalists over the long term.

What about sex offenders? An assumption underlying much current public policy and sex-crime control efforts is that sex offenders are specialists—they commit only sex crimes, not other crimes, and they are specialists even with regard to the type of sex crimes they commit. It is assumed that rapists do not molest children, and exhibitionists do not commit either type of crime.

Consistent with self-control theory, there is considerable evidence that sex offenders do not limit themselves to sex crimes (e.g., Lussier, 2005; Miethe, Olson, & Mitchell, 2006; Sample & Bray, 2003; Simon, 1997; Smallbone, Wheaton, & Hourigan, 2003). Their offending is often characterized by versatility. While they might be generalists, however, as far as crime in general is concerned, they still might be specialists with regard to sex crimes (Soothill, Francis, Sanderson, & Ackerly, 2000). They might limit their sex offending to a particular type of sex crime (e.g., child molesting), and they might specialize in their choice of victim (e.g., young rather than old, female rather than male, and a family member rather than a stranger). The evidence is mixed.

Researchers have assessed convicted sex offenders by using information gained from polygraph examinations (English, Jones, Patrick, & Pasini-Hill, 2003). While most of the sex offenders had been convicted of offenses against children, the polygraph results revealed that 39% had previously sexually assaulted adults. Approximately one-third (31%) had sexually assaulted both male and female victims. Two-thirds of the offenders who had committed incest also had sexually assaulted victims outside the family. Hence, there was considerable evidence of *"crossover"* (versatility) in their offending (see also: Abel & Rouleau, 1990). Other researchers, however, say crossover is more characteristic of some sex offenders (Lussier, Leclerc, Healey, & Proulx, 2008). Persistent sex offenders are not as likely to switch from male to female victims (and the opposite) or change the level of violence in their sex crimes. Moreover, only about 25% of a sample of incarcerated sex offenders was versatile with regard to victim age and gender, as well as victim-offender relationship (Cann, Friendship, & Gonzna, 2007).

One of the themes in this textbook is that sex offenders are heterogeneous. There are important differences among them, and one difference is the rate at which they recidivate by committing another sex crime. In a review of follow-up studies of sex offenders, researchers concluded that male rapists have a higher sexual recidivism rate than male child molesters (Quinsey, Lalumière, Rice, & Harris, 1995). Among child molesters, those with male victims have the highest recidivism rate, followed by men who have molested unrelated females and then incest offenders. Moreover, while sex crimes account for only about 4%–14% of the criminal behavior of rapists, it is about 40% for child molesters (Lussier, LeBlanc, & Proulx, 2005). Hanson and Bussière (1998), however, found that when sex offenders recidivate, they are most likely to commit non-sex crimes—a recidivism rate of 36% for general crimes, 12% for violent crimes, and 13% for sex crimes. Moreover, Zimring, Piquero, and Jennings (2007, p. 507) found that "the best predictor … for adult sex offending was the frequency of offending [for any crime] as a juvenile rather than whether a boy committed a sexual offense" (see also Harris, Mazzerolle, & Knight, 2009).

There are surprisingly few studies of the relationship between self-control and sex crimes. However, one study found that male undergraduate students who self-reported sexual assault had lower self-control than those who did not report sexual assault (Franklin, Bouffard, & Pratt, 2012). Low self-control increased acceptance of a non-egalitarian gender-role ideology and alcohol consumption, which are two "abuse-facilitating variables" that increase the likelihood of sexual assault (Franklin et al., 2012, p. 1470). Other researchers have revealed that low self-control increases the likelihood of sexual assault victimization (Franklin, Franklin, Nobles, & Kercher, 2012). This is consistent with other research that has found low self-control is related to stalking victimization among women (Fox, Gover, & Kaukinen, 2009).

## Cohen and Felson's Routine Activity Theory

Routine activity theory directs attention away from offenders to other parts of a crime, including victims (Cohen & Felson, 1979). According to routine activity theory, three elements must come together for a crime to occur: (1) a motivated offender, (2) a suitable target, and (3) the absence of a capable guardian (anything or anyone whose presence could prevent commission of a crime). People's routine (everyday) activities affect where, when, and how these elements come together, creating situational opportunities for crime. For example, in discussing sex crimes, Felson and Eckert (2015, p. 53) note "how easy it is for stepparents to gain [sexual] access to stepchildren, priests to choirboys, and child care workers to young children. Offenses usually occur in settings with guardians absent and unable to intervene." Children can also be vulnerable to parents or other family members when there is no one to protect them.

Sometimes, commission of a non-sex crime produces an opportunity for a sex crime as when a burglar breaks into a home and finds a woman there alone. He might rape her even though that was not his original intent (Warr, 1988). More will be said about this later.

Routine activity theory emphasizes situational crime prevention to reduce opportunities to commit crimes (Felson & Clarke, 1988). This may involve increasing the effort required to commit a crime (e.g., electronic access to garages), increasing the risk of detection (e.g., surveillance cameras), decreasing the anticipated rewards for crime (e.g., access to women's shelters), and removing excuses for crime (e.g., debunking rape myths).

Two related studies offer evidence for the importance of situational opportunities for sex crimes. In one study, Wortley and Smallbone (2006) examined child sexual abuse by priests in Queensland. Most (70%) of the abuse occurred in the priest's residence. About 20% occurred in the victim's home. Twenty percent of the priests also took children on overnight trips to be alone with them. A related study of child sexual abuse by priests in the U.S., modeled after the Queensland study, found that a relatively high proportion (41%) of it occurred in a parish residence or cleric's home (Terry & Ackerman, 2008). "Living alone in the parish residence or with only one pastor or associate pastor ... allows for the priest to have the opportunity to abuse" (Terry & Ackerman, 2008, p. 651). Approximately 16% of abuse occurred in a church, 12% in the victim's home, 10% in a vacation home, and 10% in school. About 18% of the abusers said it occurred on planned overnight trips with children so the children would be more vulnerable (fewer capable guardians to prevent the abuse).

Planning overnight trips to be alone with children is an example of how sex offenders create opportunities for sex crimes. Sullivan and Beech (2004) studied men who admitted sexually abusing children in the course of their work and found that 15% had chosen the work to provide them with access to children. Another 42% said that access to children was not the only reason for their work, but it was part of the reason. Similarly, other researchers found in a study of a small sample of child sexual abusers in the U.K. that they were drawn to particular educational and voluntary organizations that provided them with easy access to potential victims (Colton, Roberts, & Vanston, 2010).

Earlier it was said that sometimes the commission of a non-sex crime produces an opportunity for a sex crime. A rape might be an "added bonus" for a burglar who breaks into a home for material gain and finds a woman there alone. This is indicative of an opportunistic rapist identified in some typologies (e.g., Knight & Prentky, 1990). A recent study by Pedneault, Beauregard, Harris, and Knight (2015), though not rejecting such a scenario, suggests that this is usually not the case—sexual and "regular" burglars respond to different situational opportunities. Comparing cases of burglaries of residences by sex offenders with regular residential burglaries, they found differences that seemed to disconfirm the "opportunistic sexual burglary" (Pedneault et al., 2015, p. 391). Sexual burglars were more likely to break into occupied residences, which regular burglars tended to avoid. Moreover, sexual burglaries more often occurred at times when people were more likely to be at home—midnight to 3 a.m. Sexual burglars also were more likely than regular burglars to carry weapons, as if prepared to find someone at home. These findings suggest that there may be more to understanding sex crimes and sex offenders than situational opportunities alone. Sexual and regular burglars may have different motivations, even different expertise.

## Akers' Social Learning Theory

Social learning theory (Akers, 1985) has been relied upon in a variety of studies to account for sex crimes and sex offenders. Like the other theories discussed in this section of the chapter, social learning theory is about crime in general. In comparison to other general-crime theories, however, social learning theory allows for more offender specialization. The reason is that one of the principal themes in social learning theory is imitation. According to social learning theory, people learn behavior, in part, by observing the behavior of other people, and subsequently imitating (or modeling) it (Bandura, 1978).

Through *vicarious learning*, people can learn from what they observe has happened to others. Also they can learn through *experiential learning*, which involves learning through personal direct experience. In this way, a victim of child sexual abuse can become a child abuser. As Felson and Lane (2009) indicate, imitation need not be behavior-specific. "There may be stimulus generalization whereby the model's response to one type of stimulus leads the observer to imitate that response to similar stimuli" (Felson & Lane, 2009, p. 489). It is possible, then, that people can observe a particular type of violence (e.g., sexual violence) and generalize it to other (non-sexual) violence. "Still, a social learning perspective implies that modeling [imitation] of specific behaviors should be strongest as it is the most direct lesson learned from the model" (Felson & Lane, 2009, p. 490).

Chapter 4 on child sexual abuse examines the literature on the "abused-abuser" hypothesis that sexual abuse during childhood can cause people to later commit child sexual abuse themselves. It is clear that childhood sexual victimization is not a deterministic cause of adult child sexual abuse. It is a myth that it always causes people to commit child sexual abuse as adults. Most sexually abused children do not grow up to become adults who sexually abuse children. Moreover, most adults convicted of child sexual abuse do not repeat their offense. Social learning theory, however, suggests that childhood sexual victimization may increase the likelihood that a child victim will later become an adult sex offender. The adult offender may be imitating a childhood experience. The evidence is mixed. In a large study of state and federal prisons, Felson and Lane (2009) tested two hypotheses:

(1) Sexual abuse during childhood is associated with adult sexual offending, and particularly sex offenses against children.

(2) Physical abuse during childhood is associated with adult violent offending.

Suggestive of imitation, they found that offenders who had experienced sexual abuse as a child were much more likely to commit sex offenses, particularly against children, than other offenses. Moreover, offenders who had experienced childhood physical abuse were more likely to commit violent than non-violent offenses as adults. Other studies, however, have not found an association between childhood sexual victimization and adult sex offending. For example, Widom (1995) found that childhood physical abuse, not sexual abuse, was related to later arrest for sodomy or rape.

## LOGIC MODEL OF SEX-OFFENDER CHARACTERISTICS AND BEHAVIORS

Although many different theories have been proposed about sex crimes and sex offenders, several common characteristics exist (see Figure 2.1). While not all sex offenders exhibit all of the characteristics, typically a cluster of several factors is present for any given sex offender. When these factors exist, they do not always lead to commission of a sex crime—they simply increase the probability that an individual commits a sex crime. Also, many of the proposed theories vary in their explanation of how these characteristics develop. Most indicate the foundation is laid during childhood, culminating in poor adaptation, interpersonal difficulties, and subsequent behaviors that involve sex crimes: rape, child molestation, and/ or viewing child pornography. The next chapters discuss each of these sex crimes.

## CONCLUSION

Many theories have been proposed to explain criminal behavior, and more specifically, sex crimes. These theories help us develop sound treatment approaches and guide policy, including legal responses to sex crimes and sex offenders. Throughout this chapter, you should have noticed that many factors that lead to committing crime, also pertain to committing sex crimes. We have also noted that sex offenders often commit non-sex crimes as well, leading to murky conclusions about sex offenders as "unique" offenders.

Theories that specifically focus on sex offenders often are narrowly focused on explaining a particular type of sex crime (e.g., child sexual abuse or rape) and the research is relatively mixed with regard to identifying specific characteristics or traits that distinguish sex offenders from non-sex offenders. Instead, research has largely identified factors that are common to sex offenders, but which in and of themselves do not necessarily equate to the commission of subsequent sex crimes. Thus, we cannot at the current time distinguish sex offenders from non-sex offenders based on a given set of existing characteristics. Nevertheless, theories assist in providing explanations about sex crimes and sex offenders for the purpose of control and treatment.

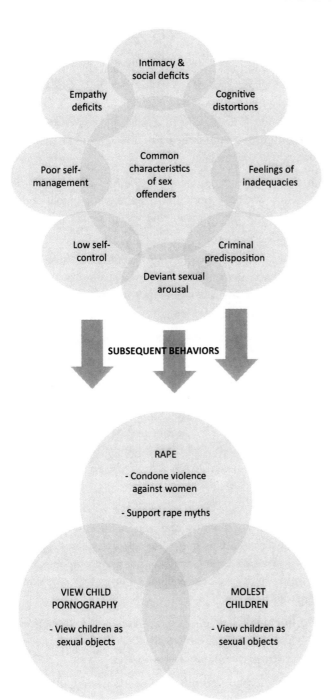

**FIGURE 2.1** *Logic Model of Sex-Offender Characteristics and Behavior*

## REVIEW POINTS

- Theories provide a logical set of statements that explain some sort of phenomenon. Theories help to provide a framework for understanding sex crimes.

- Theories have been developed to explain (1) sex crimes and sex offenders specifically, and (2) crimes in general. Both groups of theories are helpful to understanding sex crimes.

- Theories are probabilistic in nature, meaning when factors have been identified as a cause of crime, they simply increase the likelihood of crime occurring. By no means does it mean that when the cause is present, crime will result every time.

- Biological theories propose that sex crimes are caused by abnormalities among hormones, neurotransmitters, various brain structures, or sex chromosomes/genetic traits. They also link mental retardation to the commission of sex crimes.

- Cognitive theories encompass attachment theory, inappropriate cognitive schemas, and cognitive biases, and propose that the cognitive processes one develops (usually during childhood) affect subsequent behavior, which can include committing sex crimes.

- Psychological theories are deeply rooted in key concepts developed by Sigmund Freud, including the stages of psychosexual development (oral, anal, phallic, latency, genital) and three personality components (id, ego, and superego). Deviant sexual behavior may be the result of fixations and/or regression or underdevelopment of the ego/superego occurring in conjunction with an overactive id.

- Research has not successfully identified a specific personality profile that distinguishes sex offenders from non-sex offenders. Research has, however, found that certain traits appear to be common among sex offenders. These include: impulsivity, callousness/lack of empathy, narcissism, sadism, and personality pathology.

- Realizing the complex nature of sex crimes and sex offenders, several multiple-factor theories of sex crimes have also been proposed: precondition theory, quadripartite theory, and integrated theory.

- Several (broad-based) criminological theories, such as social control (bonding) theory, self-control theory, routine activity theory, and social learning theory have been applied to explain sex crimes and sex offenders.

- Social control theory posits that due to weak attachment, commitment, involvement, and belief, individuals are predisposed to commit crimes.

- Self-control theory suggests that due to poor parenting, individuals develop low self-control, predisposing them to commit crimes.

- Routine activity theory posits that crimes occur when three factors converge in space and time: a motivated offender, a suitable target, and a lack of capable guardian.

- Several common characteristics occur among sex offenders that can result in the commission of rape, child molestation, and/or viewing pornography.

# REFERENCES

Abel, G. G., & Rouleau, J. L. (1990). The nature and extent of sexual assault. In W. L. Marshall, Laws, D. R. and H. E. Barbaree (Eds.), *Handbook of sexual assault* (pp. 9–21). New York: Springer US.

Aigner, M., Eher, R., Fruehwald, S., Forttier, P., Gutierrez-Lobos, K., & Dwyer, S. M. (2000). Brain abnormalities and violent behavior. *Journal of Psychology and Human Sexuality, 11*(3), 57–64.

Akers, R., & Sellers, C. S. (2012). *Criminological theories: Introduction, evaluation, and application (6th ed.).* New York: Oxford University Press.

Akers, R. L. (1985). *Deviant behavior: A social learning approach.* Belmont, CA: Wadsworth.

American Psychiatric Association. (2013). *Diagnostic and statistical manual of mental disorders, fifth edition.* Washington DC: American Psychiatric Publishing.

Awad, G., Saunders, E., & Levene, J. (1984). A clinical study of male sex offenders. *International Journal of Offender Therapy and Comparative Criminology, 28*(2), 105–115.

Bain, J., Langevin, R., Dickey, R., & Ben-Aron, M. (1987). Sex hormones in murderers and assaulters. *Behavioral Sciences and the Law, 5*(1), 95–101.

Bandura, A. (1978). Social learning theory of aggression. *Journal of Communication, 28*(3), 12–29.

Barnett, G. D., & Mann, R. E. (2013). Cognition, empathy, and sexual offending. *Trauma, Violence & Abuse, 14*(1), 22–33.

Baumeister, R. F., Catanese, K. R., & Wallace, H. M. (2002). Conquest by force: A narcissistic reactance theory of rape and sexual coercion. *Review of General Psychology, 6*(1), 92–135.

Beech, A., & Ward, T. (2004). The integration of etiology and risk in sexual offenders: A theoretical framework. *Aggression and Violent Behavior, 10*(1), 31–63.

Berger, P., Berner, W., Bolterauer, J., Gutierrez, K., & Berger, K. (1999). Sadistic personality disorders in sex offenders: Relationship to antisocial personality disorder and sexual sadism. *Journal of Personality Disorders, 13*(2), 175–186.

Blanchard, R., Watson, M. S., Choy, A. L., Dickey, R., Klassen, P., Kuban, M., & Ferren, D. J. (1999). Pedophiles: Mental retardation, maternal age, and sexual orientation. *Archives of Sexual Behavior, 28*(2), 111–127.

Bowlby, J. (1958). The nature of the child's tie to his mother. *International Journal of PsychoAnalysis, 39*(5), 350–373.

Bowlby, J. (1977). The making and breaking of affectional bonds: I. Aetiology and psychopathology in light of attachment theory. *British Journal of Psychiatry, 130*(3), 201–210.

Bowlby, J. (1988). Developmental psychiatry comes of age. *American Journal of Psychiatry, 145*(1), 1–10.

Cann, J., Friendship, C., & Gonzna, L. (2007). Assessing crossover in a sample of sexual offenders with multiple victims. *Legal and Criminological Psychology, 12*(1), 149–163.

Choi, C. (2002, October 21, 2002). Brain tumour causes uncontrollable paedophilia. Retrieved January 10, 2016, from https://www.newscientist.com/article/dn2943-brain-tumour-causes-uncontrollable-paedophilia/

Cohen, L. E., & Felson, M. (1979). Social change and crime rate trends: A routine activity approach. *American Sociological Review, 44*(4), 588–608.

Colton, M., Roberts, S., & Vanston, M. (2010). Sexual abuse by men who work with children. *Journal of Child Sexual Abuse, 19*(3), 345–364.

English, K., Jones, L., Patrick, D., & Pasini-Hill, D. (2003). Sexual offender containment. *Annals of the New York Academy of Sciences, 989*(1), 411–427.

Felson, M., & Clarke, R. V. (1988). *Opportunity makes the thief.* London, UK: Policing and Reducing Crime Unit, Home Office Research, Development and Statistics Directorate.

Felson, M., & Eckert, M. (2015). *Crime and everyday life.* Thousand Oaks, CA: Sage.

Felson, R. B., & Lane, K. J. (2009). Social learning, sexual and physical abuse, and adult crime. *Aggressive Behavior, 35*(6), 489–501.

Finkelhor, D. (1984). *Child sexual abuse: New theory and research.* New York: Free Press.

Fiske, S. T., & Taylor, S. E. (1991). *Social cognition, 2nd ed.* New York: McGraw-Hill.

Fox, K. A., Gover, A. R., & Kaukinen, C. (2009). The effects of low self-control and childhood maltreatment on stalking victimization among men and women. *American Journal of Criminal Justice, 34*(3–4), 181–197.

Franklin, C. A., Bouffard, L. A., & Pratt, T. C. (2012). Sexual assault on the college campus: Fraternity affiliation, male peer support, and low self-control. *Criminal Justice and Behavior, 39*(11), 1457–1480.

Franklin, C. A., Franklin, T. W., Nobles, M. R., & Kercher, G. (2012). Assessing the effect of routine activity theory and self-control on property, personal, and sexual assault victimization. *Criminal Justice and Behavior, 39*(10), 1296–1315.

Freud, S. (1962). *Three essays on the theory of sexuality.* New York: Basic Books.

Galski, T., Thornton, K. E., & Shumsky, D. (1990). Brain dysfunction in sex offenders. *Journal of Offender Rehabilitation, 16*(1–2), 65–79.

Gibbs, J. P. (1972). *Sociological theory construction.* Hinsdale, IL: Dryden Press.

Gottfredson, M. R., & Hirschi, T. (1990). *A general theory of crime.* Stanford, CA: Stanford University Press.

Hall, G. C. N., & Hirschman, R. (1991). Toward a theory of sexual aggression: A quadripartite model. *Journal of Consulting and Clinical Psychology, 19*(5), 8–23.

Hanson, R. K., & Bussière, M. T. (1998). Predicting relapse: A meta-analysis of sexual offender recidivism studies. *Journal of Consulting and Clinical Psychology, 66*(2), 348–362.

Hanson, R. K., Gizzarelli, R., & Scott, H. (1994). The attitudes of incest offenders: Sexual entitlement and acceptance of sex with children. *Criminal Justice and Behavior, 21*(2), 187–202.

Harris, D. A., Mazzerolle, P., & Knight, R. A. (2009). Understanding male sexual offending: A comparison of general and specialist theories. *Criminal Justice and Behavior, 36*(10), 1051–1069.

Harrison, L. E., Clayton-Smith, J., & Bailey, S. (2001). Exploring the complex relationship between adolescent sexual offending and sex chromosome abnormality. *Psychiatric Genetics, 11*(1), 5–10.

Hendricks, S. E., Fitzpatrick, D. F., Hartmann, K., Quaife, M. A., Stratbucker, R. A., & Graber, B. (1988). Brain structure and function in sexual molesters of children and adolescents. *Journal of Clinical Psychiatry, 49*(3), 108–112.

Hirschi, T. (1969). A control theory of delinquency. In T. Hirschi (Ed.), *Causes of delinquency* (pp. 289–305). CA: University of California Press.

Knight, R. A., & Prentky, R. A. (1990). Classifying sex offenders: Issues, theories and treatment of the offender. In Marshall, W. L., Laws, D. R., Barbaree, H. E. (Eds.), *Handbook of sexual assault.* New York: Springer US.

Lang, R. A. (1993). Neuropsychological deficits in sexual offenders: Implications for treatment. *Sexual and Marital Therapy, 8*(2), 181–200.

Loeber, R. (1990). Development and risk factors of juvenile antisocial behavior and delinquency. *Clinical Psychology Review, 10*(1), 1–41.

Lussier, P. (2005). The criminal activity of sexual offenders in adulthood: Revisiting the specialization debate. *Sexual Abuse: A Journal of Research and Treatment, 17*(3), 269–292.

Lussier, P., LeBlanc, M., & Proulx, J. (2005). The generality of criminal behavior: A confirmatory factor analysis of the criminal activity of sex offenders in adulthood. *Journal of Criminal Justice, 33*(2), 177–189.

Lussier, P., Leclerc, B., Healey, J., & Proulx, J. (2008). Generality of deviance and predation: Crime-switching and specialization patterns in persistent sexual offenders. In M. DeLisi and P. J. Conis (Eds.), *Violent offenders: Theory, public policy and practice* (pp. 97–140). Boston, MA: Jones and Bartlett.

Marieb, E. N. (2001). *Human anatomy and physiology, 5th ed.* New York: Addison Wesley Longman.

Marshall, W. (1989). Intimacy, loneliness, and sexual offenders. *Behavior Research and Therapy, 27*(5), 491–503.

Marshall, W. L. (1993). The role of attachments, intimacy, and loneliness in the etiology and maintenance of sex offending. *Sexual and Marital Therapy, 8*(1), 109–121.

Marshall, W. L. (2010). The role of attachments, intimacy, and loneliness in the etiology and maintenance of sexual offending. *Sexual and Relationship Therapy, 25*(1), 73–85.

Marshall, W. L., Anderson, D., & Champagne, F. (1997). Self-esteem and its relationship to sexual offending. *Psychology, Crime & Law, 3*(3), 161–186.

Marshall, W. L., & Barbaree, H. E. (1990). Outcome of comprehensive cognitive-behavioral treatment programs. In W. L. Marshall, D. R. Laws & H. E. Barbaree (Eds.), *Handbook of sexual assault: Issues, theories, and treatment of the offender* (pp. 363–385). New York: Plenum Press.

Marshall, W. L., Hudson, S. M., Jones, R., & Fernandez, Y. M. (1995). Empathy in sex offenders. *Clinical Psychology Review, 15*(2), 99–113.

Marshall, W. L., & Mazzucco, A. (1995). Self-esteem and parental attachments in child molesters. *Sexual Abuse: A Journal of Research and Treatment, 7*(4), 249–252.

McKay, M. M., Chapman, J. W., & Long, N. R. (1996). Causal attributions for criminal offending and sexual arousal: Comparison of child sex offenders with other offenders. *British Journal of Criminology, 35*(1), 63–75.

Miethe, T. D., Olson, J., & Mitchell, O. (2006). Specialization and persistence in the arrest histories of sex offenders: A comparative analysis of alternative measures and offense types. *Journal of Research in Crime and Delinquency, 43*(3), 204–229.

Mouilso, E., Calhoun, K. S., & Rosenbloom, T. (2013). Impulsivity and sexual assault in college men. *Violence and Victims, 28*(3), 429–442.

O'Callaghan, D. (1998). Practice issues in working with young abusers who have learning disabilities. *Child Abuse Review, 7*(6), 435–448.

Pavlov, I. (1927). *Conditioned reflexes.* Oxford: Clarendon Press.

Pedneault, A., Beauregard, E., Harris, D. A., & Knight, R. A. (2015). Rationally irrational: The case of sexual burglary. *Sexual Abuse: A Journal of Research and Treatment, 27*(4), 376–397.

Porter, S., Campbell, M. A. W. M., & Birth, A. R. (2001). A new psychological conceptualization of the sexual psychopath. In F. Columbus (Ed.), *Advances in psychology research* (pp. 21–36). Huntington, NY: Nova Science.

Quinsey, V. L., Lalumière, M. L., Rice, M. E., & Harris, G. T. (1995). Predicting sexual offenses. In J. C. Campbell (Ed.), *Assessing dangerousness: Violence by sexual offenders, batterers, and child abusers* (pp. 114–137). Thousand Oaks, CA: Sage.

Raine, A., & Buchsbaum, M. S. (1996). Violence, brain imaging, and neuropsychology. In D. M. S. R. B. Cairns (Ed.), *Aggression and violence: Genetic, neurobiological, and biosocial perspectives* (pp. 195–217). Mahwah, NJ: Erlbaum.

Sample, L. L., & Bray, T. M. (2003). Are sex offenders dangerous? *Criminology & Public Policy, 3*(1), 59–82.

Saunders, E., Awad, G. A., & White, G. (1986). Male adolescent sexual offenders: The offender and the offense. *Canadian Journal of Psychiatry, 31*(6), 542–549.

Seto, M. C., & Lalumière, M. L. (2010). What is so special about male adolescent sexual offending? A review and test of explanations through meta-analysis. *American Psychological Association, 136*(4), 526–575. doi: 10.1037/a0019700

Simon, L. M. J. (1997). Do criminal offenders specialize in crime types? *Applied and Preventative Psychology, 6*(1), 35–53.

Skinner, B. F. (1932). On the rate of formation of a conditioned reflex. *Journal of General Psychology, 7*(2), 274–286.

Smallbone, S. W., Wheaton, J., & Hourigan, D. (2003). Trait empathy and criminal versatility in sexual offenders. *Sexual Abuse: A Journal of Research and Treatment, 15*(1), 49–60.

Soothill, K. L., Francis, B., Sanderson, B., & Ackerly, E. (2000). Sex offenders: Specialists, generalists - or both? *British Journal of Criminology, 40*(1), 56–67.

Stinson, J. D., Sales, B. D., & Becker, J. V. (2008). *Sex offending: Causal theories to inform research, prevention, and treatment.* Washington DC: American Psychological Association.

Sullivan, C. J., Mcgloin, J. M., Pratt, T. C., & Piquero, A. (2006). Rethinking the "norm" of offender generality: Investigating specialization in the short-term. *Criminology, 44*(1), 199–233.

Sullivan, J., & Beech, A. (2004). A comparative study of demographic data relating to intra- and extra-familial child sexual abusers and professional perpetrators. *Journal of Sexual Aggresssion, 10*(1), 39–50.

Terry, K. J., & Ackerman, A. (2008). Child sexual abuse in the Catholic Church: How situational crime prevention strategies can help create safe environments. *Criminal Justice and Behavior, 35*(5), 643–657.

Thornhill, R., & Palmer, C. T. (2000). *A natural history of rape: Biological bases of sexual coercion.* Massachusetts: The MIT Press.

Tingle, D., Barnard, G. W., Robbins, L., Newman, G., & Hutchinson, D. (1986). Childhood and adolescent characteristics of pedophiles and rapists. *International Journal of Law and Psychiatry, 9*(1), 103–116.

Ward, T. (2000). Sexual offenders' cognitive distortions as implicit theories. *Aggression and Violent Behavior, 5*(5), 491–507.

Ward, T., & Hudson, S. M. (1998). A model of relapse process in sexual offenders. *Journal of Interpersonal Violence, 13*(6), 700–725.

Ward, T., & Hudson, S. M. (2000). A self-regulation model of ralapse prevention. In S. M. H. D. R. Laws, and T. Ward (Eds.), *Remaking relapse prevention with sex offenders: A sourcebook* (pp. 79–101). New York: Sage.

Ward, T., Polaschek, D. L. L., & Beech, A. R. (1995). Attachment style and intimacy deficits in sexual offenders: A theoretical framework. *Sexual Abuse: A Journal of Research and Treatment, 7*(4), 317–335.

Warr, M. (1988). Rape, burglary, and opportunity. *Journal of Quantitative Criminology, 4*(3), 275–288.

Widom, C. S. (1995). Victims of childhood sexual abuse: Later criminal consequences. *National Institute of Justice: Research in Brief.*

Wortley, R. K., & Smallbone, S. W. (2006). Applying situational principles to sexual offending against children. In R. Wortley and S. Smallbone (Eds.), *Situational prevention of child sexual abuse. Crime prevention studies* (pp. 7–35). Monsey, NY: Criminal Justice Press.

Zimring, F. E., Piquero, A. R., & Jennings, W. G. (2007). Sexual delinquency in Racine: Does early sex offending predict later sex offending in youth and young adulthood. *Criminology and Public Policy, 6*(3), 507–534.

Zion, D. (2000, April 3, 2000). To put the ape back into rape. Retrieved from http://www.theage.com.au

## DEFINITIONS

**Attachment**: One of four principal types of bonds identified in Hirschi's (1969) social control theory. Attachment involves the extent to which people have strong affectional ties to other people. (See, Belief, Commitment, and Involvement.)

**Attachment Theory:** An explanation of dysfunctional adulthood behavior proposed by Bowlby that has been relied upon to explain sexual offending.

**Belief:** One of four principal types of bonds identified in Hirschi's (1969) social control theory. Belief refers to an endorsement of conventional norms, including laws. (See, Commitment, Attachment, and Involvement).

**Callousness:** A personality trait that involves blunted emotional response to others.

**Castration Anxiety:** A concept identified by Freud. It refers to boys around the ages of three to five years becoming fearful of losing or having damage done to their penis.

**Classical Conditioning:** A learning principle identified by Ivan Pavlov in which a neutral stimulus (bell ringing) is successively paired with a potent stimulus (dog food) to eventually cause a known and predictable response (dog salivating) with only the neutral stimulus (bell ringing).

**Cognitive Biases:** Illogical thoughts that skew one's perception of the world.

**Cognitive Distortions:** Minimize or deny the dangerousness of the behavior, justify it, and relieve the offender of responsibility. (Examples: children need to be taught about sex; children are very seductive; the child is too young to know what is happening.)

**Cognitive Schemas:** Basic building blocks that help individuals organize information and make sense of the world. They involve organized patterns of previous experiences, which are relied upon to interpret new information.

**Commitment:** One of four principal types of bonds identified in Hirschi's (1969) social control theory. Commitment refers to the extent to which individuals have an investment (a "stake in conformity") in conventional goals, such as education and employment. (See, Attachment, Belief, and Involvement.)

**Crossover:** Describes sex-offender behavior that involves a variety of victims who vary in their characteristics (e.g., male and female victims, old and young, commit rape and child molestation, etc.).

**Deterministic Cause:** The relationship between a stated cause and effect is deterministic when the cause *always* leads to a specified effect. (See Probabilistic Cause.)

**Ego:** A concept identified by Freud. The ego acts as a mediator between the id and superego. (See Id and Superego.)

**Experiential Learning:** A type of learning that occurs through personal direct experience. (See Vicarious Learning.)

**Grooming:** The process of befriending and establishing an emotional connection with children for the purpose of sexually abusing them.

**Hormones:** Chemical secretions in the the body that affect a wide range of bodily functions.

**Id:** A concept identified by Freud. The id is one of three parts of one's personality that is responsible for pleasure seeking. (See Ego and Superego.)

**Impulsivity:** A personality trait that involves a need for instant gratification and an inability to control impulses.

**Involvement:** One of four principal types of bonds identified in Hirschi's (1969) social control theory. Involvement pertains to the amount of time spent in conventional activities. (See Attachment, Belief, and Commitment.)

**Lack of Empathy:** A personality trait that involves an inability to respond to someone else with appropriate emotions.

**Narcissism:** a personality trait that involves an overwhelming sense of self-love, grandiose perceptions of one's self, and a sense of entitlement.

**Neurotransmitters:** Chemicals in the brain that affect brain function, mood, and autonomic reactions (heart rate, breathing, and other bodily functions that respond in anxiety-provoking situations).

**Operant Conditioning:** A learning principle identified by B. F. Skinner that explains acquiring and maintaining new behaviors through a process of reinforcement and punishment.

**Penis Envy:** A concept identified by Freud. It refers to a feeling of anxiety experienced by girls between the ages of three to five years that occurs when they realize they do not have a penis.

**Personality Pathology:** A set of personality disorders that have been identified by the American Psychiatric Association. They involve a set of emotional and behavioral characteristics that cause maladaptive behaviors.

**Probabilistic Cause:** The relationship between a stated cause and effect is probabilistic when the cause increases the chances that a specified effect will occur. (See Deterministic Cause).

**Psychosexual Development:** Five stages of human development identified by Freud that occur from birth to adulthood: (1) oral, (2) anal, (3) phallic, (4) latency, and (5) genital.

**Rape Myths:** Falsely held beliefs regarding rape (e.g., all women secretly desire to be raped).

**Sadism:** A personality trait that is associated with deriving sexual pleasure from inflicting pain or humiliation on another person.

**Self-Regulation Model of Sexual Offending:** A theory developed by Ward and Hudson explaining sexual offending that is based on behavioral theory concepts. They proposed that people behave in goal-directed ways and there are four paths that can lead to sexual offending.

**Superego:** A concept identified by Freud. The superego is associated with one's moral principles, acting as one's conscience. (See Id and Ego.)

**Vicarious Learning:** A type of learning where people learn from what they observe has happened to others. (See Experiential Learning.)

# CHAPTER 3

# *Rape*

## CHAPTER OBJECTIVES

- Identify situational rape myths.
- Identify attitudinal rape myths and their link to commission of rape.
- Describe the legal and social evolution of rape as a crime.
- Define and identify the primary risk factors for committing rape.
- Summarize rapist typologies.
- Describe the criminal justice response to rape, from police reporting to court adjudication.

When the topic of sex crimes is brought up, the terms "rape," "sexual assault," "sexual battery," "criminal sexual abuse," and many other comparable terms often come to mind. As stated previously, the purpose of this textbook is to demonstrate that a vast spectrum of sex crimes exists, as do the offenders who commit them. Crimes of rape and sexual assault are central to this topic.

The number of reported rapes has decreased since the early 1990s, but it is important to remember from Chapter 1 that the majority of sex crimes go unreported. Further, it is believed that rape and sexual assault are among the least reported sex crimes. It is currently estimated that as many as 1 in 6 women in the U.S. has been a victim of a completed or attempted rape at some point (Truman, Langton & Platy, 2013). The likelihood of experiencing rape can increase because of poverty, living in a more isolated, rural community, or being from a racial/ethnic minority. Native American Indian women, for example, suffer the highest rape rates in the U.S.

In this chapter, we begin with a discussion of common misconceptions about rape, including a thorough overview of rape myths. This overview will dovetail into subsequent sections, including a discussion of the historical and legal context of rape and sexual assault, particularly highlighting how public opinion and the law have evolved over time. We will then move on to discussing various types of rape and sexual assault, along with typologies of offenders and victims of rape and sexual assault. Criminal justice responses to rape and sexual assault, including police and judicial processing of rape cases, are also addressed. Finally, this chapter closes with a brief examination of current rape and sexual-assault issues in an international context to demonstrate how key issues discussed in this chapter play out beyond domestic borders in rape cases.

"Rape" and "sexual assault" are often used synonymously. They can be used to describe the same act in some instances, but there are important differences in how the two terms are historically and legally defined. The word "rape" dates back to late fourteenth century France, where it meant "to seize property, abduct, or take by force." Prior to this, the Latin word *rapere* was infused with similar meaning and was defined as "to seize, carry off by force, or abduct" (Burgess-Jackson, 1999, p. 16). Sexual violation rarely entered into historical connotations of rape, which focused more on issues of force and power. Under ancient Roman law, *raptus* referred primarily to acts of kidnapping and abduction, with sexual violation as a peripheral issue (Moses, 1993). Today, **rape** refers to any sexual penetration (vaginal, anal, or oral) of a person without his or her consent (Federal Bureau of Investigation, 2016). Prior to recent changes in the legal definition, the crime of rape was much more limited in scope—this will be discussed later. **Sexual assault** is a much broader term that encompasses a variety of behaviors that can be considered sex crimes, including voyeurism, exhibitionism, and even sexual harassment in some cases. To put it concisely: all rapes are considered sexual assault, but not all sexual assaults are considered rape. The differences between defining rape versus defining sexual assault can become quite complex, particularly when charging and prosecuting offenders—an idea to which we will return later. Apart from definitional differences, the terms rape and sexual assault are used interchangeably in this chapter.

## RAPE MYTHS

This chapter begins with an overview of common misconceptions and myths about rape. Given the misconceptions about the offenders who commit rape and the victims who suffer its consequences, it is important to present this information in the beginning. As the chapter progresses, note how a number of these misconceptions and myths are still very much embedded in current rape laws and policies, prevention efforts, typologies of rapists and rape victims, and criminal justice responses, including police investigation and judicial processing of rape. Two types of rape myths are discussed—situational rape myths and attitudinal rape myths.

### Situational Rape Myths

*Situational rape myths* refer to misconceptions about the crime of rape, including who commits it, its victims, and when/where it happens. These myths are born primarily out of biased media coverage of rape, as well as inaccurate reporting and record keeping of rape statistics. These myths are summarized in Table 3.1.

**TABLE 3.1**   *Summary of Situational Rape Myths*

| RAPE MYTH | REALITY |
|---|---|
| Rape only happens to young, attractive women. | All segments of the population can be and are raped. Rape has less to do with physical and sexual attraction, and more to do with power. |
| Rape only happens to "bad" women. | Anyone can be a victim of rape. Certain segments of the population are more vulnerable to rape than others, but it is not exclusive to these segments. |
| The majority of rape claims are false. | False rape allegations are rare. It is also important to differentiate between false allegations (which prove that the event did not happen) and unsubstantiated allegations (which fail to prove the event did happen). Unsubstantiated allegations are more common than false allegations. |
| Rapists are mentally ill monsters. | The majority of rapes are committed by men who do not suffer from a severe mental illness. |
| Only men can rape and only women can be victims. | The most common rape scenario involves a male offender and a female victim, but females can be offenders and men can be victims of rape. |
| Unsafe, unmonitored places are breeding grounds for rape and sexual assault. | Most rapes happen in the home or behind closed doors and are committed by people known to the victim. |

### Rape only happens to young, attractive women

While it is true that about 80% of rape victims are under the age of 30, and that 9 out of 10 rape victims are female (Rape Abuse and Incest National Network (RAINN), 2009), rape is not exclusively limited to this population. In 2014, victims of reported rape ranged from 93-year-olds to infants as young as a few weeks. Anyone can be raped, including men, the elderly, people with disabilities, lesbian, gay, bisexual, transgender (LGBT) populations, and people from every racial, ethnic, religious, and socioeconomic group. While rape affects all segments of the population, research has revealed a systemic bias in the judicial processing of sex crimes, with physically attractive victims being viewed as more credible and, therefore, less responsible, compared to physically unattractive victims. This will be discussed in greater detail later.

### Rape only happens to "bad" women

The belief that we live in a fair world where good things happen to good people and bad things happen to bad people (***Just world hypothesis***) is prevalent (Strömwall,

Alfredsson, & Landström, 2013). Victims of crime are, therefore, responsible for their own fate. This belief pins the blame on rape victims for not adhering to society's rules (Belknap, 2015) and suggests that only certain kinds of women are vulnerable to rape and sexual assault. Women seen as promiscuous, having prior sexual experiences, drinking alcohol, or engaging in activities at inappropriate places and/or times are labeled as deviant. Sex workers (or prostitutes) are an example.

This myth is most likely perpetuated by evidence that certain groups are more vulnerable to rape and sexual assault. Female street prostitutes experience high rates of violence. In one study, it was found that about 40% of Chicago street prostitutes had been raped at some point, and 22% had been raped more than ten times (Raphael & Shapiro, 2002). Because street prostitutes violate gender norms by selling sex, they are viewed as "loose," "immoral," or "of low moral character." Because of these labels, the violence perpetrated against them has become normalized. Some male customers (or "Johns") believe raping a prostitute does not constitute rape (Oselin & Blasyak, 2013).

Even women who do not explicitly violate rules and norms through risky behaviors, but are perceived as "other" because of their minority or socioeconomic status, can be seen as "bad girls." The reasons are linked to the legacies of racism, colonialism, and imperialism. In the antebellum South, sexual victimization of enslaved women was a common method for replenishing the slave workforce. This socially-approved sexual abuse led to Black female rape victims' portrayal as loose and immoral sexual temptresses who led men astray, rather than as victims of sex abuse (Collins, 2000). These portrayals equate women of color with "bad." Race, therefore, becomes another means for victim blaming.

### Most rape claims are false

In 1680, Sir Matthew Hale (Hale, 1972, p. 635) observed that "rape ... is an accusation easily to be made and hard to be proved, and harder to be defended by the party accused, though never so innocent." Hale's critique of the justice system regarding rape victims under English common law—where the victim is on trial, not the defendant—reflects a common view that female rape victims routinely make false allegations of rape. This view implies that women claim rape as an act of revenge, fantasy, or deceit to hide their own sexual appetites or deviance. Early research to determine the extent of false rape allegations concluded the following:

> False accusations of ... rape in particular are generally believed to be much more frequent than untrue charges of other [types of] crimes. A woman may accuse an innocent man of raping her because she is mentally sick or given to delusions ... or because, having consented to intercourse, she is ashamed of herself and bitter at her partner; or because she is pregnant and prefers a false explanation to a true one.
>
> (Corroborating Charges of Rape, 1967 as cited in Cuklanz, 1996, p. 22)

A review of studies and reports of false rape allegations listed over 20 sources with estimates ranging from 1.5% to 90% (Rumney, 2006). Unfortunately, many published reports of false rape allegations suffer from measurement problems. Reports have either failed to explicitly define what constitutes a false rape allegation or have included cases outside the parameters of accepted definitions. The International Association of Chiefs of Police (IACP) clearly articulated this definition in its comprehensive model policy:

> The determination that a report of a sexual assault is false can be made only if the evidence establishes that no crime was committed or attempted. *This determination can be made only after a thorough investigation.* This should not be confused with an investigation that fails to prove a sexual assault occurred. In that case the investigation would be labeled unsubstantiated. *The determination that a report is false must be supported by evidence that the assault did not happen.*
>
> (IACP, 2005, p. 13)

Research regarding false rape allegations is discussed in more detail in Chapter 9.

### People who rape are mentally ill or psychotic

For decades, a commonly accepted myth has been that all rapists are psychotic, insane, or otherwise mentally ill. Similar to the myth that only "bad"women are raped, the belief that all rapists are mentally ill provides a false sense of security that "normal" people cannot commit such atrocious crimes. The vast majority of rapes are committed by people who do not suffer from a severe mental illness. In one of the most comprehensive studies analyzing psychiatric diagnoses of 535 rapists from a Swedish prison, it was determined that only 2.6% suffered a personality disorder and only 1.7% were deemed clinically psychotic (Långström, Sjöstedt & Grann, 2004).

Despite these findings, there is a tendency, especially in the U.S. among forensic mental-health specialists, to use the residual, paraphilia-not-otherwise-specified (PNOS) diagnosis in assessing and recommending treatment for convicted rapists. Given that a psychiatric diagnosis is required for civil commitment of rapists, such residual diagnoses have been used to detain rapists beyond their sentences (Frances, Sreenivasan & Weinberger, 2008). A great deal of controversy surrounds the notion of "inventing diagnoses" as a basis for further confining rapists when the research does not support it (Zander, 2008).

### Only men can rape and only women can be raped

The belief that only men can rape and only women can be raped reflects a broader and more engrained belief that men are aggressive and women are passive. It bears repeating that *anyone* can be a victim of rape. In 2010, the CDC estimated that 1 in 71 men in the U.S. had been raped (Centers for Disease Control and Prevention, 2011). It is further estimated that men are significantly less likely to report a rape, due to a number of barriers, including lack of social services and support mechanisms. Examples are that rape crisis centers and hospitals often lack the in-depth knowledge and skills to adequately assist male victims of sex crimes, and there are also inadequacies in the legal system. Additionally, the potential stigma of being perceived as weak and having one's sexual identity/orientation questioned is another reason for underreporting.

Similarly, there is a widely held belief that women cannot commit rape. Statements such as "women don't do such things" (Wijkman, Bijleveld & Hendriks, 2010) or "what harm can be done without a penis" (Hislop, 2001) serve to minimize the significance of female sex offenders. Female sex offenders are more thoroughly explored in Chapter 7.

### Unsafe, unmonitored places are breeding grounds for rape and sexual assault

By and large, current sex-crime policies, educational efforts, and primary prevention strategies portray rape and sexual assault as "stranger-danger" offenses that occur in public places, such as parks, bus stops, and dark alleys. Only a very small percentage of sex crimes occur in such places, however, with the vast majority occurring in the home and between acquaintances or family members (Colombino, Mercado, Levenson, & Jeglic, 2011).

There has been little effort to identify ways that public-education campaigns and community strategies can help to deter or prevent rapes in non-public places. As a result, sex-crime policy has been largely criticized for implementing little more than "feel-good" measures that account for a very small percentage of rapes and sexual assaults committed each year. Consequently, policies that embrace the "stranger-danger, dark-alley" scenario do little to reduce rape and sexual assault (Ewing, 2011) and may even increase the risk of recidivism by undermining offender re-entry and stability (Calkins, Colombino, Matsuura & Jeglic, 2015).

### Attitudinal Rape Myths

Whereas situational rape myths are concerned with the who, what, where, and when of rape, ***attitudinal rape myths*** explain (incorrectly) why rapes occur. At their core, attitudinal rape myths are stereotypical, false beliefs about rape, rape victims, and rapists that create a hostile social climate toward rape victims, are sympathetic of rapists, and somewhat forgiving of the rape. Several rape-myth scales have been developed to gauge these beliefs. For example, an early rape-myth acceptance scale consisted of various statements divided into four categories: (1) victim responsible for rape, (2) rape only happens to certain kinds of women, (3) rape reports as a form of manipulation, and (4) disbelief of rape claims (Burt, 1980). Table 3.2 presents

**TABLE 3.2** *Bumby RAPE Scale*

| EXCUSING RAPE | JUSTIFYING RAPE |
|---|---|
| Women generally want sex no matter how they can get it. | Women who get raped probably deserve it. |
| If a woman does not resist strongly to sexual advances, she is probably willing to have sex. | Since prostitutes sell their bodies for sexual purposes, it is not as bad if someone forces them into sex. |
| Women often falsely accuse men of rape. | If women did not sleep around so much, they would be less likely to get raped. |
| A lot of women who get raped had "bad reputations" in the first place. | If a man has had sex with a woman before, then he should be able to have sex with her any time he wants. |
| If a woman gets drunk at a party, it is really her own fault if someone takes advantage of her sexually. | Just fantasizing about forcing someone to have sex isn't all that bad since no one is really being hurt. |
| When women wear tight clothes, short skirts, and no bras or underwear, they are just asking for sex. | A lot of times, when women say "no," they are really just playing hard to get and really mean "yes." |
| A lot of women claim they were raped just because they want attention. | Part of a wife's duty is to satisfy her husband sexually whether or not she is in the mood. |
| Victims of rape are usually a little bit to blame for what happens. | As long as a man does not slap or punch a woman in the process, forcing her to have sex is not as bad. |
| Women who go to bars a lot are mainly looking to have sex. | When a woman gets raped more than once, she is probably doing something to cause it. |
| Often, a woman reports a rape long after the fact because she gets mad at the man she had sex with and is trying to get back at him. | Women who get raped will eventually forget about it and move on with their lives. |
| Before the police investigate a woman's claim of rape, it is a good idea to find out what she was wearing, if she had been drinking, and what kind of person she is. | On a date, when a man spends a lot of money on a woman, the woman ought to at least give the man something in return sexually. |
| Generally, rape is not planned—a lot of times it just happens. | If a woman lets a man kiss her and touch her sexually, she should be willing to go all the way. |
| If a person tells himself he will never rape again, then he probably won't. | When women act like they are too good for men, most men probably think about raping the women to put them in their place. |

*(Continued)*

**TABLE 3.2** (Continued)

| EXCUSING RAPE | JUSTIFYING RAPE |
| --- | --- |
| A lot of men who rape do so because they are deprived of sex. | Society and the courts are too tough on rapists. |
| The reason a lot of women say "no" to sex is because they don't want to seem loose. | Most women are sluts and get what they deserve. |
| If a woman goes to the home of a man on the first date, she probably wants to have sex with him. | Any woman can prevent herself from being raped if she really wants to. |
| Many women have a secret desire to be forced into having sex. | |
| Most of the men who rape have stronger sexual urges than other men. | |
| Most of the time, the only reason a man commits rape is because he was sexually assaulted as a child. | |
| Men who commit rape are probably responding to a lot of stress in their lives, and raping helps reduce that stress. | |

Source: (Bumby, 1996)

one of the most comprehensive and reliable rape-myth acceptance scales, known as the Bumby RAPE Scale (Bumby, 1996), a self-report tool consisting of 36 statements reflective of attitudinal rape myths. There are two broad categories of rape myths: Excusing Rape (beliefs that minimize rapists' responsibility or guilt of rape through questioning victim credibility or deficits on the rapist's part) and Justifying Rape (beliefs that minimize the wrongfulness and harmfulness of rape).

For the past 40 years, researchers have sought to determine how rape myths are connected to the commission of rape. It is argued that acceptance of attitudinal rape myths has two different kinds of effect. First, it promotes various types of aggressive behavior. There is an association between such beliefs and sexual aggressiveness. One study concluded that subscribing to these rape myths, commonly termed "rape-supportive cognition," facilitates rape because it allows rapists to misinterpret victims' intentions, beliefs, or behaviors (Polascheck & Ward, 2002, p. 402). Other studies have shown that rape-supportive cognition, together with other factors, such as sexual arousal to rape depictions, the inability to control emotions, and personality problems, promotes rape (Hall & Hirschman, 1991). It has also been shown that a decrease in rape-supportive cognitions reduces aggressive sexual behavior (Lanier, 2001).

The second effect of acceptance of attitudinal rape myths is that it promotes tolerance of sexual abuse. Those who accept these myths perceive rape as something positive, compared to those who do not accept such myths. Morry and Winkler (2001) showed that acceptance of rape myths increases acceptance of coercive behavior. Rape victims with rape-supportive attitudes (e.g., in the form of self-blaming) have extended recovery times when compared to those without rape-supportive attitudes (Ruiz & Escursell, 2000).

This does not imply, however, that only rapists subscribe to rape myths. Researchers have sought to determine how acceptance of rape myths is tied to broader cultural beliefs. Several studies have examined what accounts for rape-myth acceptance by some people and not by others. One of the earliest studies found that men and women with strong beliefs about sex-role stereotyping (i.e., beliefs that assign specific, exclusive, and usually outdated gender roles to women and men), strong adversarial beliefs about sex (i.e., beliefs that refer to the expectation that sexual relationships are exploitative and that each party in the relationship is manipulative, sly, cheating, and not to be trusted), and strong acceptance of interpersonal violence (i.e., force and coercion are legitimate, acceptable, or normal methods to gain compliance) also demonstrated considerable rape-myth acceptance (Burt, 1980).

More recent research reveals a strong correlation between rape-myth acceptance and endorsement of racism, classism, ageism, homophobia and religious intolerance (Aosved & Long, 2006). One study found that endorsement of the "just world hypothesis" (discussed earlier) is correlated with rape-myth acceptance (Hayes, Lorenz, & Bell, 2013). Finally, a meta-analysis of 37 studies assessing rape-myth acceptance found that men display a significantly higher endorsement of rape-myth acceptance compared to women, and that these beliefs are highly correlated with hostile attitudes toward women, in addition to heterosexism, ageism, racism, and classism (Suarez & Gadalla, 2010).

Acceptance of rape myths has also been compared across various cultures. One study presented a sample of Australians and White South Africans with a series of rape scenarios that varied in how the victim was portrayed. Scenarios included whether the victim fought her attacker; did not resist at all; was portrayed as sober; was intoxicated. Regardless of how a victim was portrayed, Australians were less likely than White South Africans to blame the victim. This suggests that victim blame may not only be a function of how the victim is perceived, but is also linked to broader cultural beliefs (Heaven, Connors, & Pretorius, 1998). More recent studies have found regional variation in rape-myth acceptance in the U.S. A study of college students revealed that Appalachian students were less likely than non-Appalachian students to condemn or blame rape victims (Haywood & Swank, 2008).

To summarize, the explanations surrounding the context and rationale of rape and sexual assault are plagued by fallacies, stereotypes, and a general misunderstanding of the facts, despite decades of research disentangling myth from truth. These faulty beliefs not only encourage excuses and justifications for rape, but also result in ill-informed policy decisions, poor prevention planning, and injustice for victims. In the next section, we delve into the history of rape law, which has been shaped historically and recently by many of the situational and attitudinal rape myths discussed.

# RAPE LAW IN THE U.S.

Rape, or forcible rape, to be more precise, currently stands as one of the eight Part I index crimes of the UCR. Along with murder, robbery, and aggravated assault, it is classified as a violent crime. While rape has been a crime with severe punishments for offenders, it has not always been classified as a violent crime. This section presents a survey of the history of rape law to demonstrate how rape and the attendant social and legal reactions to it have changed over time (Federal Bureau of Investigation, 2016).

## Women as Property

Throughout most of recorded human history, women have been treated as property. They were the property of their fathers until marriage, at which point ownership was transferred to their husbands. Because women did not exist as independent beings and carried no status independent of their fathers or husbands, rape of a woman was not predicated on a lack of female consent or refusal to engage in sex, nor her right to bodily integrity. Rape, therefore, whether against a man's daughter or a man's wife, was treated as a man-on-man crime; it was a property crime committed by one man against another man's property. These principles dominated from the early codes of Ancient Babylon through the early twentieth century.

No property was valued more than a betrothed virgin. Rape of virgin women was treated as a capital offense, with offenders facing a death penalty and the victimized girl considered guiltless. Married women who were raped did not fare as well. According to the Code of Hammurabi (approximately 4,000 years ago), a man would be killed if he raped a betrothed virgin; the victim suffered no consequence. A married woman who experienced the same crime, however, had to share the blame equally with her attacker. The crime was labeled "adultery" and both parties were thrown into the river. The remnants of these policies and practices are evident in some of the rape myths discussed earlier.

## Rape Reform Movement

Until the early 1970s, little had changed with respect to how rape was handled by criminal justice officials. Rules of evidence required a victim to physically resist her attacker, and the victim's testimony often required corroboration. Evidence of the victim's prior sexual history was admissible during trial proceedings. Traditional rape law made it "easy to commit rape and get away with it" (Rodabaugh & Austin, 1981, p. 17). Critics argued that these rules and laws had serious consequences for both the victims and the criminal justice system. They were partially responsible for the unwillingness of victims to report rape, which accounted for low rates of arrest, prosecution, and conviction for rape. Critics charged that the criminal justice response to rape was predicated on rape myths, and the most serious dispositions were reserved for "real" rapes with "real" victims (Spohn & Horney, 1992). This approach clearly reflected several situational and attitudinal rape myths, particularly that rape only happens to "young, attractive women" or to "bad girls."

The feminist movement of the 1960s and 1970s was a major catalyst of change for women's rights. It was in the midst of the feminist movement in 1975 that Susan Brownmiller published *Against our Will: Men, Women and Rape.* This seminal book characterized rape as a tool of male dominance over women. Rape is a political act, and Brownmiller emphasized the need of making rape a "speakable crime" that is open and can be discussed. This book also led to the much publicized maxim that rape is a violent crime, and not a product of men's natural sexual desires. It was against this backdrop that numerous initiatives were born, such as speak-outs, rape crisis centers, self-defense classes, and new rape legislation.

By the 1990s, all 50 U.S. states either revised or repealed traditional rape laws and evidentiary standards. Although the exact nature of reform varied across and within states, there were four common reform themes (Spohn & Horney, 1992):

1. The single crime of rape was replaced with a series of offenses graded by seriousness. The traditional definition of rape excluded male victims, acts other than vaginal intercourse, sexual assaults with an object, and rapes committed by a spouse. The language was written in a gender-neutral fashion.

2. The consent standard was changed by modifying or eliminating the requirement that a victim resist her attacker. Traditional rape laws required that a victim resist to the utmost (Schwartz, 1983) to demonstrate her lack of consent. Reformers challenged these standards, arguing that such resistance could lead to serious injury to the victim and that the focus should be placed on the offender, not the victim.

3. The corroboration requirement (the rule prohibiting conviction for forcible rape on the unsupported testimony of the victim) was eliminated. Given the private nature of most rapes, critics cited the immense difficulty in obtaining evidence to corroborate victim testimony.

4. Most states enacted ***rape shield laws*** that placed restrictions on introducing evidence of a victim's sexual history during trial proceedings.

Clearly, the rape-law reform movement signaled a rapid shift in how rape was defined and handled by criminal justice officials. Advocates, feminists, and reformers hoped that the movement would lead to improved treatment of rape victims, which would increase victim reporting. They also expected an increase in the arrest, conviction, and imprisonment for all types of rape, including date rape and spousal rape.

One of the first comprehensive studies assessing the impact of the rape-law reform movement (Spohn & Horney, 1992) assessed its impact in six jurisdictions (Detroit, Michigan; Chicago, Illinois; Philadelphia, Pennsylvania; Houston, Texas; Atlanta, Georgia; and Washington, D.C.). All jurisdictions varied in the extent to which they enacted the four reforms described above. On the positive side, the researchers concluded that judges, prosecutors, and defense attorneys in all jurisdictions expressed support for the reforms, adding that the treatment of rape victims had improved in their jurisdiction. Officials in all jurisdictions also noted that the rape shield laws were implemented appropriately and that the victim's sexual history was unlikely to be admitted at trial.

Despite these successes, there were several shortcomings. Despite the elimination of legal requirements surrounding resistance by the victim, as well as corroboration of testimony, criminal justice officials in every jurisdiction still held these elements as critical indicators of whether a rape case would result in a conviction. Additionally, although rape shield laws effectively barred a victim's sexual history in a rape trial, officials in each of the jurisdictions noted exceptions. If there was a prior sexual relationship between the victim and defendant, this type of evidence would likely be introduced without challenge. Most disappointing was the limited effect on reporting and processing of rape cases. The reforms did not increase the likelihood of conviction in any of the six jurisdictions, and increased the reporting rate and likelihood of indictment in only one jurisdiction.

A recent review demonstrates there is still considerable heterogeneity in rape laws and legal standards in the U.S. (Decker & Baroni, 2011). For example, 28 states can convict a defendant of rape by showing that the victim did not consent to the sexual act.[1] There is no requirement for the prosecution to show that the defendant used force or threat of force. Conversely, 16 states require "forcible compulsion" or "incapacity to consent" to prosecute a rape case.[2] The rape-law reform movement changed the resistance requirement such that the burden was no longer on the victim to "resist to the utmost." Today, eight states still require the victim to resist his/her attacker.[3] In these states, the victim's behavior is more determinative than the defendant's actions. West Virginia, for example, defines resistance as physical resistance or any clear communication of the victim's lack of consent. Fourteen states do not require resistance on the part of the victim.[4] Specifically, the victim is not required to resist to establish a lack of consent. In New Mexico physical or verbal resistance is required to prove force or coercion by the defendant.

The extensive grassroots efforts of the 1970s, 1980s and the early 1990s led to the passage of the Violence Against Women Act (VAWA) as a federal law in 1994. VAWA provides $1.6 billion toward investigation and prosecution of violent crimes against women (including sexual assault, domestic violence, and most recently, dating violence and stalking), imposes restitution requirements on individuals con-victed of such crimes, and provides opportunities for civil remedies for criminally un-prosecuted cases. VAWA was reauthorized in 2000, 2005, and most recently in 2013. VAWA laws provide numerous programs and services, including community prevention programs, funding for victim-assistance services (e.g., rape crisis centers, shelters, and hotlines), and legal aid for victims.

## Current Rape Law

Until recently, the legal definition of rape was very limited in scope. The U.S. Depart-ment of Justice (DOJ) defined rape as: "The carnal knowledge of a female forcibly and against her will."

In this fairly abstract definition, there are three necessary components. First, "carnal knowledge" refers to the act of a man having sexual bodily connection with a woman (i.e., sexual intercourse). Carnal knowledge exists, therefore, if there is the slightest penetration of the female sexual organ (vagina) by the male sexual organ (penis). Second, force is also a necessary condition and is usually established through threats of physical violence or if the female believes resistance would not prevent the rape. Third, "against her will" indicates that the female is incapable of giving consent due to a temporary or permanent mental or physical incapacity. The ability of the victim to provide consent can be a very complicated matter and is usu-ally decided by the police officer responding to a rape call. The following scenarios would constitute rape under this definition:

- A woman is returning to her car after work and is threatened at knifepoint by a man who forces her to have vaginal sex with him.

- A young girl is attacked, assaulted, and forced to have vaginal sex by two boys on her way home from school.

This definition of rape effectively excludes other types of sexual violence, including statutory rape, incest, forcible sodomy, sexual assault with an object, and forcible fondling. Moreover, any sexual assaults against male victims were not considered rape in accordance with this definition, nor were assaults that involved oral or anal penetration of either gender. The following scenarios would *not* constitute rape under this definition:

- An 18-year old male and his 16-year old girlfriend engage in a mutually agreed upon sexual relationship in a state where the legal age of consent is 18 (this would be considered statutory rape).

- An adult male is sodomized by his adult male co-worker (this would be con-sidered forcible sodomy).

---

*Focus Box 3.1    The New Summary Rape Definition (FBI Uniform Crime Reporting Program, 2014)*

*Penetration, no matter how slight, of the vagina or anus with any body part or object, or oral penetration by a sex organ by another person, without the consent of the victim*

The revised definition:

- Includes male and female victims and offenders
- Includes instances in which the victim is incapable of giving consent because of a temporary or permanent mental or physical incapacity (e.g., age, intoxication, etc.)
- Reflects various forms of sexual penetration understood to be rape

---

To counter some of the problems inherent with this narrow definition, many states adopted gender-neutral guidelines for forcible rape (i.e., "carnal knowledge of a *person*" instead of "carnal knowledge of a female"), while others defined rape in terms of the seriousness of the offense (penetration vs. other sexual contact), the amount of coercion used by the offender, and the degree of injury to the victim. Most states redefined "penetration." The Michigan statute, for example, defined sexual penetration as "sexual intercourse, cunnilingus, fellatio, anal intercourse, or any other intrusion, however slight, of any part of a person's body or any object into the genital or anal opening of another person's body, but emission of semen not required" (Mich. Comp. Laws Ann. §750.520(a)(r)).

In 2012, the U.S. Attorney General, Eric Holder, announced revisions to the UCR's definition of rape, stating:

> These long overdue updates to the definition of rape will help ensure justice for those whose lives have been devastated by sexual violence and reflect the Department of Justice's commitment to standing with rape victims ... This new, more inclusive definition will provide us with a more accurate understanding of the scope and volume of these crimes.
>
> (Department of Justice, 2012)

The new definition of forcible rape is:

> The penetration, no matter how slight, of the vagina or anus with any body part or object, or oral penetration by a sex organ of another person, without the consent of the victim.

The primary goal of the revision was to ensure that the data reported on rape would better reflect state criminal codes, as the new definition did not change federal or state criminal codes or impact prosecutorial decision-making at the local level. Moreover, there was also an attempt to better acknowledge and reflect victim experiences. The former definition only applied to male penile penetration of a vagina. The new definition widens the net by including oral and anal penetration, rape of males, penetration of the vagina and anus with an object or body part other than a penis, rape of females by females, and non-forcible rape. This is not to say that these were not considered sex crimes previously—indeed they were.

## RAPISTS

As discussed earlier, rape seldom fits the stereotype in a fictional book or movie. Rapists are very rarely strangers jumping from the bushes or from dark alleys and assaulting females they do not know. Furthermore, rape, contrary to popular opinion, is not motivated solely by sexual desire. These misunderstandings of rape, and the offenders and victims, have resulted in two common rapist stereotypes that are still dominant in the U.S. (Laufersweiler-Dwyer & Dwyer, 2009). Note how these two stereotypes reflect the attitudinal rape myths discussed previously:

(1) Misunderstood Offender: An offender becomes involved in an allegation of coerced sex because of circumstances beyond his control, misunderstandings, or defective communication.

(2) Sex-Starved Offender: An offender's insatiable sexual needs drive him to commit acts that could provide sexual gratification. These offenders are often portrayed as sex fiends, sex maniacs, or sex psychopaths.

Knowing the numerous myths and stereotypes regarding rape and rapists, we now focus our attention on offenders' risk factors, which are observed characteristics and/or behaviors of people who commit rape/sexual assault. Risk factors are determined from research examining large samples (hundreds, or potentially thousands) of offenders. Although there are numerous risk factors for committing rape, we focus on five that have been well-documented in the clinical and social science literature. They are:

(1) Hostile masculinity.

(2) Aggressive sexual beliefs.

(3) Physical and psychological aggression

(4) History of violence.

(5) Alcohol use and abuse.

These risk factors do not operate independently of each other, but are often strongly interrelated. A challenge in providing treatment and rehabilitation for rapists (and sex offenders, generally) is that in many cases, all of these risk factors may be present, and determining their relationship to rape/sexual assault is not easy. Details of this are discussed in Chapter 10.

## Hostile Masculinity

Hostile masculinity, often referred to as ***hostile masculinity syndrome***, often manifests in rapists via two primary sets of attitudes and emotions (Malamuth, 2013). The first consists of hostile, distrustful, insecure feelings toward people, especially women. These feelings are accompanied by misogynous (i.e., woman-hating) attitudes. These attitudes include attitudinal rape myths, including a belief that women secretly desire to be raped. The second set of attitudes/emotions involves a desire to control and dominate women. These desires fuel sexual arousal and sexual gratification. It has been shown repeatedly that hostile masculinity is a strong predictor of sexual assault (e.g., Wheeler, George & Dahl, 2002).

## Aggressive Sexual Beliefs

Closely related to hostile masculinity are aggressive sexual beliefs. These include any attitudes supportive of aggression, use of force, coercion, humiliation, or violence and sexuality. Agreement to such statements as "Get a woman drunk, high, or hot and she'll let you do whatever you want" may be indicative of aggressive sexual beliefs. Aggressive sexual beliefs are often linked to pedophilic acts, including sadism and masochism (discussed in Chapter 1). Recall that sexual sadism takes place when an individual receives sexual pleasure or excitement from the psychological or physical suffering of another person. Sexual masochism, on the other hand, involves sexual pleasure and gratification as a result of *receiving* psychological or physical suffering and pain. Much research has shown that people subscribing to such beliefs are more likely to commit sexual assault (e.g. Abbey, McAuslan, Zawacki, Clinton-Sherrod & Buck, 2003; Bernat, Wilson & Calhoun, 1999).

Some researchers have even argued that viewing adult pornography may be symptomatic of aggressive sexual beliefs. Evidence for this relationship, however, is mixed. Early researchers claimed that pornography predisposes some men to want to rape women or intensifies that predisposition in men already inclined to rape, as well as overriding internal and social inhibitions against acting out rape desires (Russell, 1988). A recent evaluation, however, revealed that consumption of pornography is negatively associated with rape victimization rates (i.e., the greater the consumption of pornography, the lower the rape victimization rate), both in the U.S. and other countries (Ferguson & Hartley, 2009). This suggests that the presumed pornography-rape connection is questionable and may be a product of exaggerated claims by politicians, pressure groups, and even some social scientists.

Finally, engaging in frequent casual sex or expectancy of impersonal sex is associated with sexual aggression. One study of college men found that high levels of impersonal sex, as well as hostile masculinity, strongly predict sexual aggression (Wheeler et al., 2002). Another study revealed that sexual-assault offenders were more likely than non-offenders to have high expectations for having sex earlier in a romantic relationship, as well as have more positive attitudes about casual sex (Abbey, Parkhill, Clinton-Sherrod & Zawacki, 2007).

## Physical and Psychological Aggression

Physical aggression occurs in approximately 25% to 50% of dating, cohabiting, and married couples. It includes such behaviors as grabbing, pushing, slapping, biting, and more serious physical acts that result in serious injury or death. Physical aggression is strongly associated with rape and sexual assault. One study of married couples found that husbands' use of physical aggression strongly predicted forced sex (Marshall & Holtzworth-Munroe, 2002). Another study of male rapists found that 120 men who reportedly committed rape were also responsible for 1,225 different acts of physical aggression. In this same study, repeat rapists (those who committed multiple rapes over time) were responsible for 85% of the total acts of physical aggression (Lisak & Miller, 2002).

Psychological aggression is the most common form of aggression in intimate relationships, including dating relationships (Shorey, Cornelius & Bell, 2008). It encompasses a wide range of verbal and behavioral acts intended to humiliate, criticize, blame, dominate, isolate, intimidate, and threaten one's partner. Some research has concluded that the consequences of psychological aggression are more severe and long-lasting than those of physical aggression (Murphy & Hoover, 1999).

Psychological aggression consists of two highly related components: expressive aggression, such as name calling, insulting or humiliating an intimate partner, and coercive control, which includes behaviors intended to monitor and control or threaten an intimate partner (e.g., isolating an intimate partner from family and friends, deciding what clothes an intimate partner should wear, limiting access to money and other financial resources, and threatening to hurt an intimate partner). Psychological aggression has been linked to aggressive sexual beliefs (Marshall & Holtzworth-Munroe, 2002).

## History of Violence

Research has revealed that the childhood histories of rapists include risk factors for violence. One study found that rapists frequently report experiences of physical abuse, parental violence, emotional abuse, and cruelty to animals (Simons, Wurtele & Durham, 2004). Researchers contend that physical abuse, parental violence, and emotional abuse result in externalizing behaviors when they occur in combination. For example, one study found that physical and verbal abuse during childhood led to antisocial behavior and callous personality traits, both of which led to aggressive sexual fantasies (Beauregard, Lussier & Proulx, 2004).

Likewise, research has shown that the combination of physical violence, domestic violence, emotional abuse, and neglect predict subsequent sex offending. Researchers explain that a person who has been raised in an emotionally impoverished environment is often unable to identify his emotions and, as a result, likely to become confused when in emotionally-charged situations (e.g., Craissati, McClurg, & Browne, 2002). These people often react to confusing situations with overt aggression and violence.

### Alcohol Use and Abuse

Alcohol use/abuse increases the likelihood of violence. The relationship between alcohol and rape, however, is often oversimplified by the public and the media (e.g., "alcohol abuse causes rape"), but the relationship is actually more complex. One study assessed whether the amount of alcohol consumed increased the severity of the sexual assault and the aggression involved. The results showed that while increased alcohol use increased aggression, moderate alcohol use was associated with the most severe sexual assaults (Abbey et al., 2003).

Several experiments have assessed the effects of alcohol on expectancies and attitudes about sexual intent. In one experiment, participants who were assigned to drink alcohol while reading a fictional scenario were more likely to perceive the woman in the scenario as more sexually aroused and the man's coercive behavior as more appropriate, compared to participants who read the same scenario but did not drink alcohol while reading it (Abbey, Buck, Zawacki & Saenz, 2003). Also, it is important to note that the effects of alcohol abuse are not the same for all people equally. Some evidence suggests that for people who already have a propensity to sexually abuse, alcohol abuse can provide an impetus for it (English, 2004). In other words, alcohol may cause sexual assault by people already likely to commit such acts, even without alcohol. Another study revealed that alcohol consumption (by both the offender and the victim) is more strongly associated with sexual assaults between strangers than those occurring between acquaintances and family members (Ullman & Brecklin, 2000).

In addition to the individual risk factors identified above, research has shown that numerous relational, community, and societal factors also contribute to the commission of rape. Everyone who abuses alcohol or exhibits hostile masculinity does not commit rape. The CDC's multi-level framework suggests that these individual risk factors are driven by broader factors. Understanding these broader factors is important for identifying opportunities for intervention and prevention. Figure 3.1 displays this framework.

## TYPOLOGIES OF RAPISTS

*Typologies*—or classification systems—are often utilized to categorize individuals who are alike into distinct categories. Ideally, a typology consists of any number of categories where individuals within each category are very similar (or even

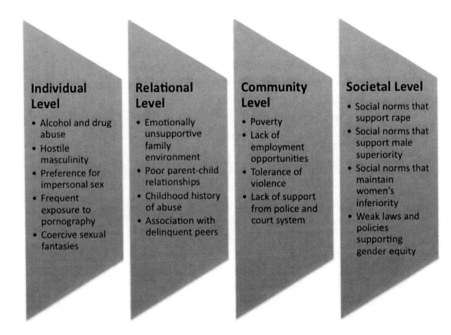

**Individual Level**

- Alcohol and drug abuse
- Hostile masculinity
- Preference for impersonal sex
- Frequent exposure to pornography
- Coercive sexual fantasies

**Relational Level**

- Emotionally unsupportive family environment
- Poor parent-child relationships
- Childhood history of abuse
- Association with delinquent peers

**Community Level**

- Poverty
- Lack of employment opportunities
- Tolerance of violence
- Lack of support from police and court system

**Societal Level**

- Social norms that support rape
- Social norms that support male superiority
- Social norms that maintain women's inferiority
- Weak laws and policies supporting gender equity

**FIGURE 3.1** *Social-Ecological Model for Understanding Rape*

identical), and each category consists of individuals who are different from the individuals in all other categories (i.e., individuals in Category A are different from individuals in Category B). Typologies have been utilized in criminological research to make diverse crimes and offenders more manageable. Development of typologies for rapists has many practical uses, including aiding the criminal investigation process, informing decisions within the criminal justice system, treatment planning, and understanding the causes of rape. It is important to understand, however, that rapists do not always fit neatly into a single category; they only approximate the characteristics of people in that category. Sometimes, rapists may fit into more than one category, while others may not fit into any category. In order to be considered reliable and accurate, typologies must withstand the test of time. That is, follow-ups must be conducted on a regular basis to see if offenders continue to fall into the categories based on the criteria originally used to develop them.

Caution must be exercised, therefore, in interpreting rapist typologies. Rape is a behavior reflecting multi-dimensional needs. Using typologies to "diagnose" a rapist as a certain type can have limiting effects on an investigation. It can ignore other offender motivational patterns and ultimately overlook physical and behavioral evidence. More on investigations will be discussed in Chapter 9. In this section, three of the most common rapist typologies are presented. These typologies were constructed using a male rapist/female victim dyad. Other typologies representing different dyads (e.g., female rapist/male victim) also exist and will be covered in Chapter 7.

## Groth's Typology

In 1979, Groth and Birnbaum developed a typology of rapists, derived from their work with people who had been arrested, convicted, and imprisoned for sex crimes. Factors that were considered to construct their typology included the offender's motivation and the degree of aggression exhibited by the offender. Victim/witness statements, responding-officer statements, *modus operandi* of offenders, and prior criminal histories informed these factors. It is important to recognize the limitations of this typology as it is based on data acquired from imprisoned sex offenders. As we have learned, most sex crimes are never reported to police, and there are likely systematic differences between imprisoned and non-imprisoned rapists.

Groth's Typology consists of three primary categories: the power rapist, the anger rapist, and the sadistic/ritualistic rapist.

### *Power Rapist*

As the name suggests, power rapists are primarily motivated by power. Men in this category are interested more in having control over their victims and "possessing" them than they are interested in causing physical harm to the victim. They do not use force beyond what is necessary to commit the rape. They exhibit anger only in response to victim resistance/fighting back, but will use any amount of force necessary to accomplish their goal, including verbal intimidation, use of a weapon, or actual physical force. Power rapists will sometimes flee the scene if a victim fights back. Power rapists often feel inadequate, controlled by others, or insecure about their masculinity, so they use rape as a means of feeling more powerful, strong, or in control. Power rapists have sometimes been divided further into two sub-categories:

#### Power Reassurance Rapist (also known as the Gentleman Rapist)

This offender can be complimentary to the victim in an attempt to sexually satisfy her. The style of attack is often premeditated and preceded by a fantasy that the victim sexually desires him (he may instruct the victim to state so during the attack). After the attack, these offenders may give victims information about themselves, such as their cell phone number or email address, in order to arrange for another "consensual" sexual encounter. Limited force or threats are utilized, and weapons are employed usually only as a means of intimidation and are seldom used for injury. This offender usually spends a short amount of time with his victim, as he lacks the social skills to interact with his victim for a long period. However, offenders may engage in "pillow talk" with "compliant" victims after the assault in the hope that a friendship develops. The offender may also have the victim undress herself, and he may have the victim undress him to fuel the fantasy of a consensual sexual relationship. This offender is often described as having low self-esteem, underachieving, employed in menial work, passive, non-athletic, and living a solitary lifestyle. Prior arrests, if any, may include minor sex offenses, such as indecent exposure or peeping.

**Power Assertive Rapist**

This offender commits rapes that are more impulsive, spontaneous, and unplanned. Victims are often met through chance encounters, such as meetings at bars, clubs, or parties. Their style of attack involves a moderate level of force of relatively short duration. Unlike the power reassurance rapist, the power assertive rapist aims to prove his virility to women, seeing himself as a "macho man." His language is abusive and full of obscenities. He may commit multiple assaults in the same evening to prove his masculinity. This offender is more likely to have an athletic build and to be involved in work that plays to this image (e.g., heavy equipment operator, police officer, or construction worker). Prior arrests, if any, may include aggressive crimes, such as reckless driving, assault, and breach of the peace.

## Anger Rapist

The men in this category are believed to commit rape in part to express anger and hostility that has built up over time, not for sex. This type of rapist is considered the most unpredictable, with the rage exhibited during the assault ranging from verbal abuse to homicide. Whereas the assaults are brief relative to those of other rapists in this typology, they are often the most severe as evidenced by the serious physical injuries to the victim. These rapists wish to humiliate and degrade their victims, thinking that women are "dirty" and cannot be trusted.

In general, anger rapists have intimate relationships that are marked by conflict, and they direct their hostility and resentment to their targeted victims. It is believed that these rapes are more spontaneous and impulsive, rather than carefully planned, and they are often preceded by some type of precipitating life stressor, such as an argument with a girlfriend or wife, or a serious conflict at work. Anger rapists' targets, therefore, are often symbolic of someone with whom the offender wishes to get even or settle a score. Unlike the power rapist, the anger rapist's approach is usually a **blitz attack**—they strike at any time, day or night. Alcohol and other substance abuse are likely with the anger rapist. Personal acquaintances often report a "dark side" to the offender. Prior arrests, if any, may include aggressive crimes, such as reckless driving, assault, and breach of peace.

## Sadistic/Ritualistic Rapist

A rare and extreme category of sadistic rapists displays sexual aggression fueled by destructive sexual fantasies. These men experience a great deal of pleasure and excitement, including sexual arousal, from inflicting harm on their victims, and enjoy watching the victim's fear and suffering. During the rapes, these men are extremely abusive. Rape with objects and anal rape are common with sadistic rapists, as are acts of bondage (e.g., tying the victim up). In extreme cases, offenders kill their victims and commit other bizarre acts, including dismemberment and postmortem coitus (i.e., necrophilia: having sex with dead bodies). These crimes tend to be the product of considerable planning and premeditation. Victims are often targeted and then stalked because of specific physical or other attributes.

The sadistic rapist usually has above-average intelligence and is a white-collar professional. Unlike the anger rapist who lacks control, the sadistic rapist avoids situations where losing control is possible. Drug and alcohol abuse, therefore, is usually avoided. They are often happily married and otherwise well-liked by others. Despite their compulsive and bizarre behavior, there is usually no history of mental health care, making their detection difficult. Unlike other rapists, sadistic rapists usually have no criminal record, but those who do usually have prior arrests for other ritualistic or violent crimes. Although it has been reported in only 5% of rapists (Craissati, 2005), sexual sadism is a strong predictor of both sexual and violent recidivism (Hanson & Morton-Bourgon, 2005).

## Massachusetts Treatment Center Rapist Typology, Version 3 (MTC: R3)

Later research by Knight and Prentky (1990) led to a more comprehensive typology of male rapists. *The Massachusetts Treatment Center Rapist Typology* (MTC: R3) is similar to Groth's typology, and is largely based on what Knight and Prentky believed to be four primary motivations to commit rape: opportunity, pervasive anger, sexual gratification, and vindictiveness. Within each category of motivation, rapists are further categorized based on developmental, biological, and environmental factors that result in different degrees of antisocial behavior, sexual aggression, impulsivity, cognitive distortions, and deviant sexual arousal. Nine different subtypes of rapists are identified (see Figure 3.2).

The MTC: R3 typology represents the third version of ongoing empirical research in this area. Thus, it is to be interpreted as a "working document" that will undergo revisions from results of future research.

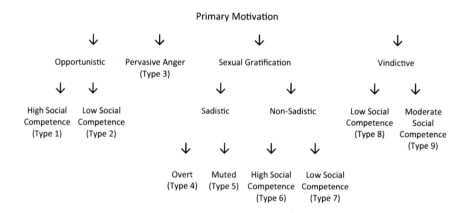

**FIGURE 3.2** *MTC Rapist Typology, Version 3*
*Source: (Knight and Prentky, 1990)*

## *Opportunistic Rapists (Types 1 and 2).*

Offenders in this category commit offenses that are typically impulsive, unplanned, and driven by opportunity as a means of seeking immediate gratification. While they do not exhibit gratuitous violence or aggression during the rape, they may use whatever force is necessary (e.g., when the victim resists or fights back), with little to no regard for the victim. Rapists in this category are further categorized by their degree of social competence—high (Type 1) or low (Type 2).

Broadly speaking, social competence refers to the social, emotional, and intellectual skills and behaviors needed to succeed as a member of society. In this typology, social competence is defined by the degree of stability and quality of interpersonal relationships with peers, family members, and romantic partners, as well as job stability and vocational achievement. Individuals with high social competence are more likely to have effective interpersonal relationship skills, high social awareness, and more self-confidence, compared to those with low social competence.

## *Pervasively Angry Rapists (Type 3)*

These offenders represent a category of their own (i.e., no sub-categories) and are characterized by impulsive behaviors, low social competence, and longstanding aggression and hostility toward men and women. There is no history of antisocial behavior. Rapes are primarily driven by anger, and rapists are likely to use excessive force and gratuitous violence, often causing significant bodily or even lethal harm to the victims.

## *Sexual Gratification Rapists (Types 4, 5, 6, and 7)*

This category is comprised of men who have extensive sexual perversions, many of which are incorporated into the rapes. If rapists in this category have sadistic tendencies (e.g., sexual pleasure from aggressive sex acts), they are further categorized into one of two types based on the extent to which they actually display those tendencies—overt sadists (Type 4) or muted sadists (Type 5). Type 4 rapists are characterized by high levels of aggression and gratuitous violence, whereas Type 5 offenders are less violent and their crimes tend to be more symbolic than injurious. Non–sadistic rapists in this category are further differentiated according to their level of social competency—non-sadistic high (Type 6) and non-sadistic low (Type 7).

## *Vindictive Rapists (Types 8 and 9)*

Unlike Type 3 rapists, anger among men in this category is not directed at people in general. Rather, vindictive rapists' anger is aimed primarily towards women (i.e., hostile masculinity). Their rapes are characterized by humiliating, degrading, and physically harmful behavior. This runs the gamut from verbal abuse to brutal murder. Vindictive rapists differ from Type 4 and Type 5 rapists in that their aggression is usually not eroticized, and they generally do not have preoccupations with sadistic fantasies. They also differ from Type 3 rapists in that they demonstrate relatively low levels of impulsivity. Men in this group can be further subdivided based on either low (Type 8) or moderate (Type 9) social competence.

## VICTIMS

In 2013, 173,610 people reported rape/sexual assault victimization in the U.S. (Langton & Truman, 2013). Though the accurate reporting of rape statistics is a complicated task (due to definitional issues, less-than-perfect data collection strategies, and gross underreporting), it is estimated that 1 in 6 women and 1 in 33 men annually are the victim of a completed or attempted rape. As research continues to address risk factors related to rape, factors pertaining to the risk of victimization have also been identified. It is controversial to discuss risk factors for rape victimization, as it may be perceived as blaming the victim. In no way do these factors imply that an "at-risk" rape victim is in any way responsible for his or her victimization. Rapists are 100% responsible for the crimes they commit. Understanding risk factors related to victimization is important as it allows for the development of tailored, victim-centered intervention and prevention strategies.

As discussed previously, there is a long-held belief that rape only happens to certain types of people. We know better, that *anyone* (regardless of gender, race, sexual orientation, religious beliefs, or socioeconomic status) can be a victim. It is also true, however, that certain segments of society are more at risk for experiencing rape. As Brownmiller (1975) reminds us, rape is a tool of power, an agent of fear, and a weapon of force against women and people with less power. Therefore, it stands to reason that vulnerable populations (i.e., those at a particular power disadvantage) are more likely to experience victimization. For example, racial minorities have a greater risk of victimization. The proportion of Black/African American women experiencing rape at some point in their lives is 18.8%, compared to 17.7% for White women. Mixed race women's lifetime rape rate is 24.4%. American Indian/Alaska Native women are the highest-risk racial group in the U.S. with a rate of approximately 34%. That is, 1 in 3 American Indian/Alaska Native women experience rape in their lifetime (Ruggiero & Kilpatrick, 2003). There is also an association between low socioeconomic status and sexual violence. People living in poverty and lacking economic power and resources are at greater risk for sexual violence compared to their better-off counterparts. Persons with a household income under $7,500 per annum are twice as likely as the general population to experience rape and sexual assault (Bassuk et al., 2004).

There are also risk factors among specific segments of the population. Given that women are particularly at risk for rape during young adult years, researchers have sought to determine risk factors within this group. For example, Krebs, Lindquist, Warner, Fisher, and Martin (2007) found the following interrelated factors to be associated with rape on college campuses:

- **Alcohol Use.** This was most commonly associated with campus rape. At least half of rapes occurred when the victim, offender, or both consumed alcohol.

- **Sorority Membership.** Almost 25% of all rape victims were sorority members, whereas only 14% of non-victims were sorority members.

- **Numerous Sexual Partners.** Women who reported having multiple sexual partners since entering college were more likely to have reported a forced-rape victimization.

- **Freshman or Sophomore Status.** The first two years of college were identified as the highest-risk years. Furthermore, the first few months of the school year were identified as the highest risk time of the academic year.

- **Day and time of the week.** Like all crime, more than half of rape crimes take place on the weekend. More than half of these crimes occur between the hours of midnight and 6 a.m.

- **Off-campus parties.** More than half of rapes against college women took place in off-campus settings.

## Effects of Rape on Victims

The most common barriers for reporting rape include feelings of guilt, shame and embarrassment, concerns of confidentiality, fear of not being believed, and fear of sexual re-victimization (Classen, Palesh, & Aggarwal, 2005). Apart from causing physical trauma to victims, rape can lead to serious mental-health scarring. In many cases, victims suffer from post-traumatic stress disorder, including negative social reactions and avoidance coping, and increased psychiatric disorders, such as depression (Ullman, Filipas, Townsend, & Starzynski, 2007). Support services, along with proper reporting processes, are important factors that can help to mitigate the consequences of rape for victims.

---

*Focus Box 3.2    Effects of Rape on the Victim*

According to the World Health Organization, victims of rape and sexual assault are:

- 1.5 times more likely to have a sexually transmitted infection (including HIV)
- 3 times more likely to suffer from depression
- 6 times more likely to suffer from post-traumatic stress disorder
- 13 times more likely to abuse alcohol
- 26 times more likely to abuse drugs
- 4 times more likely to contemplate suicide

Source: (World Health Organization, 2002)

---

### Male Rape Victims

In 2013, approximately 11% of all rape victims in the U.S. were men. In fact, some studies have shown that certain men, such as veterans and gay and bisexual men, report higher rates of rape and sexual assault than the general population (Peterson, Voller, Polusny, & Murdoch, 2011). Until recently, scientific studies had failed to fully recognize the experiences of male rape victims. Cultural stereotypes, such as rape against males only occurs in prison, or male victims are less affected by rape than female victims, have also led to a widespread misunderstanding of male victims (Polusny & Murdoch, 2005).

Myths and stereotypes not only lead to a lack of understanding of male victims, but also underreporting of sex crimes against men. Davies (2002) found that male rape victims tend to report or seek medical attention only when physical injuries are severe. Additionally, service providers' views are often dependent upon the victim's sexual orientation and the offender's gender (Davies, 2002). Given the unique experiences and needs of male victims, targeted intervention and prevention efforts must be predicated on a gender-responsive paradigm.

Current research shows that male sexual-assault victims experience similar negative mental and physical health consequences as female victims (Weiss, 2010). Men also experience a number of psychological effects that differ from women. For males, sex-role confusion and fears about sexuality are commonly cited psychological effects of rape. Walker, Archer, and Davies (2005) found that 68% of male rape victims in their sample reported long-term effects on their sense of masculinity, and 70% reported long-term problems with sexual identity. Men with untreated trauma have increased alcohol consumption, rape-related phobias, suicidality, sleep disturbances, difficulties in interpersonal relationships, fear of men, and social isolation.

## CRIMINAL JUSTICE RESPONSE TO RAPE

As discussed previously, there have been significant changes in U.S. rape and sexual-assault laws over the past 40 years. The scope of these changes varies across jurisdictions, but the legal definition of rape, formerly narrow and restrictive, has been replaced by a series of more inclusive, gender-neutral crimes graded by seriousness. Requirements pertaining to consent, corroboration, resistance, and marital-rape exemptions also were loosened to encourage victim reporting. Rape shield laws were enacted to prevent a victim's sexual history from being introduced as evidence against the victim's credibility during court proceedings. One goal of these changes was to improve the treatment of rape victims and, thus, help them to report sexual victimization to the police. Reducing *case attrition* (i.e., the failure of a case to advance to the next phase of the criminal justice process) and increasing successful prosecution of offenders were related goals.

Rape is still characterized by underreporting, as well as case attrition (see Figure 3.3 for the estimated attrition rate of rape cases in the U.S.). Therefore, it is

**FIGURE 3.3** *Attrition of Rape Cases in the United States (2009)*
*Source: Rape, Abuse and Incest National Network (RAINN)*

important to understand the dynamics of police and prosecutorial decision-making and responses to rape. Victims of rape who decide to report their victimization often embark on a long, drawn-out process that involves ongoing inter-actions with various criminal justice officials, including law enforcement officials, medical personnel, social service providers, and prosecuting and defense attorneys. Throughout the process, victims may confront officials who are skeptical about their claims, question their credibility, and sometimes minimize the extent of the harm caused by the offender.

During this process, victims often experience what is known as ***secondary victimization***, which refers to the attitudes and behaviors of criminal justice officials who are blameful, insensitive, minimizing, and dismissive of the victim. Disregard of victims' needs often so closely mirrors disregard of the victim by their own assailant that secondary victimization has also come to be known as "the second rape" or "the second assault" (Campbell & Raja, 1999, p. 261).

## Police Reporting and Response

It should be clear by now that rapes are underreported. Only about 26% to 36% of rapes are reported to police (Rennison, 2002). One study using the National Violence Against Women Survey found that only 19% of women who were raped since their eighteenth birthday reported the crime (Tjaden & Thoennes, 2006). Reasons for non-reporting are many and vary from victim to victim, but research has identified self-blame and guilt, shame and embarrassment, fear of the offender, and lack of faith in the criminal justice system as reasons for most victims (Du Mont, Miller, & Myhr, 2003). Studies of the factors related to police reporting reveal that victims are more likely to report if they experience what Williams (1984) referred to as the ***classic rape***—when the crime fits within the stereotype of rape (e.g., victim was assaulted by a stranger, had visible injuries that could corroborate allegations of forced sexual intercourse, the offender used a weapon or physical force, etc.). Conversely, victims are less likely to report if they were drinking alcohol or using drugs at the time of the rape or if they knew the offender (Felson & Paré, 2007). Victims, in other words, report the crime to the police when they believe that the probability of conviction is high. This belief may be arrived at independently or as a result of previous interactions with criminal justice officials who imply that the victim's character, reputation, or behavior at the time of the victimization is questionable. These findings suggest that, despite legal changes that have shifted from victim blaming, rape victims still believe they must conform to stereotypes of "real" rape victims.

For victims who do decide to report their victimization, the process almost always begins with law enforcement officials. They serve an important function in the reporting process and assume many "gatekeeping" roles. They decide whether a crime has occurred, the amount of investigative resources to devote to identifying and apprehending the suspect (more on this in Chapter 9), whether to make an arrest (and if so, what type of charges to press), and whether to refer the case to the prosecutor's office. One of the most important and most criticized law enforcement decisions is whether to **unfound** the case. Unfounding occurs when the responding official does not believe the victim's story and, therefore, concludes that the rape did not occur. Technically, cases can be unfounded only if it is determined that a crime did not occur. A case with a victim who makes a rape charge and later recants could be unfounded. Unfounding of cases is affected by a combination of legal and extralegal factors, including the victim's ability to identify the suspect, the victim's willingness to prosecute, the promptness of the victim's report, whether the victim was assaulted by an acquaintance rather than a stranger, and the suspect's use of a weapon.

In reality, however, law enforcement officials may also unfound a case when they believe the likelihood of arrest or prosecution is low. They are often evaluated in terms of *clearance rates*, which is the percentage of crimes that are cleared by an arrest. Because of the pressure to perform well in the eyes of management, they may unfound ambiguous or difficult cases. Such cases vary from the victim having a seemingly ulterior motive for pressing a rape charge, such as covering up for infidelity or getting pregnant, to the victim being compromised in some way, such as being under the influence of alcohol or another drug or having a previous consensual sexual relationship with the alleged rapist (Martin, 2005).

An early study by the Law Enforcement Assistance Administration (1977) found that the two most important predictors of whether cases would be founded or unfounded were proof of penetration and the suspect's use of physical force. Despite changes in the definition of rape, these predictors are still relevant today. Law enforcement officials may also unfound a case when the victim fails to strike the correct emotional balance (Venema, 2014). Victims who provide short answers and are "too matter of fact" are viewed as hiding something or not being completely truthful. On the other hand, highly emotional and distraught victims are seen as too unstable and unlikely to provide accurate, logical accounts of the crime. Law enforcement officials may also unfound a case on discriminatory grounds, such as socioeconomic status ("she was poor"), race or ethnicity ("she was a Black, Hispanic, or Native American woman"), or previous criminal history ("she was a prostitute" or "she has a record"). These views, reflective of the situational rape myth that rape only happens to "bad" girls, assume that the victim somehow precipitated her attack and that there is no way her story would hold up in court.

## Prosecutorial Decision Making

If a victim has made the decision to report a rape and that charge was cleared by arrest, the next phase involves prosecuting the suspect. Out of all the decision-makers in the criminal justice system, the prosecutor has the most discretion. Prosecutors decide who will be charged and who will not, what charge will be filed, who will be offered a **plea bargain**—an agreement between the prosecutor and defendant where the defendant enters a guilty plea for a particular charge in exchange for some concession from the prosecutor—and what the nature of the plea bargain will be. This is usually a lesser charge, a reduced sentence, or both.

The initial decision of whether to prosecute a rape is the most critical phase of the process. As "gatekeepers of justice," prosecutors have considerable discretion, and there are neither legislative nor judicial guidelines that prosecutors must follow in reaching their decisions. These decisions are also not subject to review by the courts. Only 22% to 25% of all reported rapes are prosecuted (Spohn, Beichner, & Davis-Frenzel, 2001).

Research on prosecutors' charging decisions reveals they are strongly influenced by legally relevant factors, such as the seriousness of the crime, the offender's criminal record, and the strength of the evidence (Frazier & Haney, 1996). A number of studies, however, also point to the powerful influence of victim characteristics (Frohmann, 1997; Beichner & Spohn, 2012). Similar to decision-making by law enforcement officials in unfounding a case, prosecutors may consider the victim's age, occupation, and education; "risk-taking" behavior, such as hitchhiking, drinking alcohol or using other drugs; and the character or reputation of the victim, despite rape shield laws that prohibit consideration of these factors (Kerstetter, 1990).

## Case Adjudication

In the event a prosecutor decides to try a case, extralegal characteristics of the offender and the victim often come into play in rape trials. Physical appearance and the attractiveness of both parties is often linked to trial outcomes. In the judicial context, research has shown a **good-looking effect** where physically attractive defendants, as well as victims, tend to fare more favorably compared to their less attractive counterparts. One experiment by Vrij and Firmin (2001) found that physically attractive victims made a more credible impression and were assigned less responsibility for their victimization than physically unattractive victims. Evidence against the defendant was deemed more powerful when the victim was considered beautiful. Sensitivity to good looks was conditioned by acceptance of rape myths. Those who accepted certain attitudinal rape myths were more likely to associate beauty with credibility, compared to those who did not accept such myths. These findings underscore the importance of screening potential jurors to assess their rape-myth acceptance.

The relationship between the victim and the offender also affects case outcome. The *intimacy effect* is such that rapes between intimates (e.g., spouses, partners, and friends) are treated as lesser offenses than those between strangers and are less likely to result in guilty verdicts. There is a perception that persons who victimize strangers are predators. Their threats and attacks are perceived as random, thus posing a larger future threat to the community. Those who victimize intimates, conversely, are perceived as inflicting less harm on their victims. The stereotype of marital rape characterizes this crime as involving little actual violence, minimal pain, and less suffering (Finkelhor & Yllo, 1985). Rapists who target their spouses are viewed as less likely to commit future crimes against random people. Following this stereotype, rape between intimates should be treated as a less serious offense than rape between strangers, despite the fact that research has shown that sex forced upon an intimate partner meets, and often surpasses, the harm to victims of stranger rapes (Bennice, Resick, Mechanic, & Astin, 2003).

## CURRENT ISSUES IN RAPE: CORRECTIVE RAPE

As discussed extensively in this chapter, legal remedies to rape have undergone extensive change, evolving from a crime against another man's property to a serious violent offense. The U.S. is not alone in this effort. In many countries, not just the U.S., national governments and organizations have adopted various measures to address the longstanding crisis of violence against women, including rape (Htun & Weldon, 2012). Although these well-intentioned changes appear effective on the surface, rapes persist.

---

*Focus Box 3.3    Corrective Rape in South Africa*

*The Rape of Mvuleni Fana*: In 1999 in Springs (a city on the East Rand in the Gauteng province of South Africa—approximately 30 miles east of Johannesburg), Mvuleni Fana was on her way home from football practice when four men Fana knew surrounded her, seized her, and raped and beat her unconscious. The last thing Fana remembered was being told: "After everything we're going to do to you, you're going to be a real woman, and you're never going to act like this again." Fana's experience was different from the majority of cases in two ways. First, she survived. At least 31 women in the past 15 years died as a result of their attacks. Her case was also unusual in the fact that, unlike

24 out of every 25 South Africa rapes, her case made it to trial. Two of her rapists were sentenced to prison for 25 years. The other two remain at large.

*The Rape of Pearl Mali*: In 2004, 12-year-old Pearl Mali was correctively raped by an elderly man whom her mother brought home from church. Mali's mother had deduced she was a lesbian based on her "tomboy" appearance and personality. Mali does not know much about the arrangement between her mother and the elderly man, only that there was money involved. Over the next four years, the man regularly raped Mali, as her "de facto husband," in order to make her straight. Mali attempted to contact the police, only to be laughed at for not "turning" sooner. When Mali became pregnant by her rapist at the age of 16, she was able to obtain a restraining order against him. However, Mali's mother and the man took the baby away when he was seven months old for fear that Mali would "turn him gay" if she touched or fed him. Three years later, Mali is still trying to win custody of her child and is only allowed weekend visitation.

Source: (New York Times, 2013)

Internationally, South Africa is celebrated for its transformation to a peaceful democratic society that embraces principles of human dignity, freedom, and equality. South Africa adopted one of the most progressive and inclusive constitutions in the world and was the first to legitimize gay, lesbian, and transgender rights. Discrimination on the grounds of sexual orientation is condemned and prohibited. Despite these legislative protections, however, pervasive homophobia, hate, and violence against LGBT populations continue.

Black lesbian women, in particular, have become the primary targets of *corrective rape*. Corrective rape refers to rape of lesbian women by men to "cure" them of their sexual orientation. In South Africa (and other African nations, as well), some believe that homosexuality is an imported White disease (Mittelstaedt, 2008) that is curable through heterosexual contact. Funeka Soldaat, founder of Free Gender, a Black lesbian activist group in the Khayelitsha township, stated "the community thinks homosexuality is un-African" (Carter, 2013). Determining the true extent of this problem is nearly impossible, although it is estimated that at least 500 lesbian women are victims of corrective rape each year and that 86% of Black lesbian women in the Western Cape live in fear of it (Di Silvio, 2011). Reporting of corrective rape is expected to be rare, as victims are likely to face greater trauma and secondary victimization if their sexual orientation became known. Focus Box 3.3 outlines two noteworthy cases of corrective rape in South Africa.

## CONCLUSION

Despite the prevalence of rape, as well as considerable research on its causes, numerous myths and stereotypes have clouded our understanding of it. As we have discussed, these misunderstandings lead to ill-informed policy decisions and misdirected intervention and prevention strategies at both the individual and community levels. Research on rape and the individuals who commit it is plentiful. Research has identified various risk factors associated with rape, such as hostile masculinity, alcohol abuse, and history of violence and victimization. However, these risk factors are not deterministic; they are probabilistic (see Chapter 2). Not everyone who abuses alcohol commits rape, and not all males who experience sexual abuse as children will grow up to commit rape. These factors only increase the likelihood of rape. Many typologies have been developed to identify and categorize rapists based on motivational and offending patterns, demonstrating the heterogeneity of rapists. Rapes are largely underreported, and reported cases suffer from a high degree of attrition, resulting in the conviction of a very small percentage of rapists.

## REVIEW POINTS

- Rape is a crime involving anger, aggression, and power. Rarely is rape solely motivated by sexual desire.

- Until recently, rape was narrowly defined and only included offenses involving vaginal penetration of a female by a male. Today, the definition of rape allows for any form of penetration (vaginal, oral, or anal). The revised definition also is not gender-specific and considers males as potential victims.

- Attitudinal rape myths are beliefs/statements that incorrectly explain or rationalize rape, including beliefs about the offender and the victim. In general, rape myths serve to blame the victim and excuse or minimize the behaviors of the offender. Studies of rapists indicate that rapists frequently accept rape myths.

- Numerous risk factors have been identified in people who commit rape, including hostile masculinity, aggressive sexual beliefs, physical and psychological aggression, history of violence, and alcohol use and abuse.

- It is estimated that 1 in 6 women and 1 in 33 men annually are the victim of a completed or attempted rape.

- Rape is an underreported crime, with only 26% to 36% of rapes reported to law enforcement officials each year.

- Very few rapes (about 2%) result in conviction due to underreporting to law enforcement officials, unfounding of rape cases, refusal of prosecutors to accept cases for prosecution, and the influence of extralegal case characteristics.

## REFERENCES

Abbey, A., Buck, P. O., Zawacki, T., & Saenz, C. (2003). Alcohol's effects on perceptions of a potential date rape. *Journal of Studies on Alcohol, 64*(5), 669–677.

Abbey, A., Clinton-Sherrod, A. M., McAuslan, P., Zawacki, T., & Buck, P. O. (2003). The relationship between the quantity of alcohol consumed and the severity of sexual assaults committed by college men. *Journal of Interpersonal Violence, 18*(7), 813–833.

Abbey, A., Parkhill, M. R., Clinton-Sherrod, A. M., & Zawacki, T. (2007). A comparison of men who committed different types of sexual assault in a community sample. *Journal of Interpersonal Violence, 22*(12), 1567–1580.

Aosved, A. C., & Long, P. J. (2006). Co-occurrence of rape myth acceptance, sexism, racism, homophobia, ageism, classism, and religious intolerance. *Sex Roles, 55*(7–8), 481–492.

Bassuk, E., Browne, A., Bassuk, S. S., Dawson, R., & Huntington, N. (2004). *Secondary data analysis on the etiology, course, and consequences of intimate partner violence against extremely poor women.* US Department of Justice.

Beauregard, E., Lussier, P., & Proulx, J. (2004). An exploration of developmental factors related to deviant sexual preferences among adult rapists. *Sexual Abuse: A Journal of Research and Treatment, 16*(2), 151–161.

Beichner, D., & Spohn, C. (2012). Modeling the effects of victim behavior and moral character on prosecutors' charging decisions in sexual assault cases. *Violence and Victims, 27*(1), 3–24.

Belknap, J. (2015). *The invisible woman: Gender, crime, and justice, 4th ed.* Belmont, CA: Cengage Learning.

Bennice, J. A., Resick, P. A., Mechanic, M., & Astin, M. (2003). The relative effects of intimate partner physical and sexual violence on post-traumatic stress disorder symptomatology. *Violence and Victims, 18*(1), 87–94.

Bernat, J. A., Wilson, A. E., & Calhoun, K. S. (1999). Sexual coercion history, calloused sexual beliefs and judgments of sexual coercion in a date rape analogue. *Violence and Victims, 14*(2), 147–160.

Brownmiller, S. (1975). *Against our will: Men, women and rape.* New York: Simon and Schuster.

Bumby, K. M. (1996). Assessing the cognitive distortions of child molesters and rapists: Development and validation of the MOLEST and RAPE scales. *Sexual Abuse: A Journal of Research and Treatment, 8*(1), 37–54.

Burgess-Jackson, K. (1999). *A most detestable crime: New philosophical essays on rape.* New York: Oxford University Press.

Burt, M. R. (1980). Cultural myths and supports for rape. *Journal of Personality and Social Psychology, 38*(2), 217.

Calkins, C., Colombino, N., Matsuura, T., & Jeglic, E. (2015). Where do sex crimes occur? How an examination of sex offense location can inform policy and prevention. *International Journal of Comparative and Applied Criminal Justice, 39*(2), 99–112.

Campbell, R., & Raja, S. (1999). Secondary victimization of rape victims: Insights from mental health professionals who treat survivors of violence. *Violence and Victims, 14*(3), 261–275.

Carter, C. (2013) "The Brutality of "Corrective Rape."" Retrieved June 12, 2015 from *www.nytimes.com.*

Centers for Disease Control and Prevention. (2011). National intimate partners violence survey: 2010 survey report. Washington DC: Government Printing Office.

Classen, C. C., Palesh, O. G., & Aggarwal, R. (2005). Sexual revictimization: A review of the empirical literature. *Trauma, Violence, & Abuse, 6*(2), 103–129.

Collins, P. H. (2000). Black feminist thought: Knowledge, consciousness, and the politics of empowerment. New York: Routledge.

Colombino, N., Mercado, C. C., Levenson, J., & Jeglic, E. (2011). Preventing sexual violence: Can examination of offense location inform sex crime policy? *International Journal of Law and Psychiatry, 34*(3), 160–167.

Craissati, J. (2005). Sexual violence against women: A psychological approach to the assessment and management of rapists in the community. *Probation Journal, 52*(4), 401–422.

Craissati, J., McClurg, G., & Browne, K. (2002). The parental bonding experiences of sex offenders: A comparison between child molesters and rapists. *Child Abuse & Neglect, 26*(9), 909–921.

Cuklanz, L. M. (1996). *Rape on trial: How the mass media construct legal reform and social change*. Philadelphia: University of Pennsylvania Press.

Davies, M. (2002). Male sexual assault victims: A selective review of the literature and implications for support services. *Aggression and Violent Behavior, 7*(3), 203–214.

Decker, J. F., & Baroni, P. G. (2011). "No" still means" yes": The failure of the "non-consent" reform movement in American rape and sexual assault law. *The Journal of Criminal Law and Criminology, 101*(4), 1081–1170.

Di Silvio, L. (2011). Correcting corrective rape: Carmichele and developing South Africa's affirmative obligations to prevent violence against women. *The Georgetown Law Journal, 99*, 1469–1515.

Du Mont, J., Miller, K. L., & Myhr, T. L. (2003). The role of "real rape" and "real victim" stereotypes in the police reporting practices of sexually assaulted women. *Violence Against Women, 9*(4), 466–486.

English, K. (2004). The containment approach to managing sex offenders. *Seton Hall Law Review, 34*, 1255–1272.

Ewing, C. P. (2011). *Justice perverted: Sex offense law, psychology, and public policy*. Oxford: Oxford University Press.

Federal Bureau of Investigation. (2016). *Crime in the United States: 2014*. Washington DC: Government Printing Office Retrieved February 15, 2016 from https://www.fbi.gov/about-us/cjis/ucr/crime-in-the-u.s/2014/crime-in-the-u.s.-2014.

Felson, R. B., & Paré, P. P. (2007). Does the criminal justice system treat domestic violence and sexual assault offenders leniently? *Justice Quarterly, 24*(3), 435–459.

Ferguson, C. J., & Hartley, R. D. (2009). The pleasure is momentary… the expense damnable? The influence of pornography on rape and sexual assault. *Aggression and Violent Behavior, 14*(5), 323–329.

Finkelhor, D., & Yllo, K. (1985). *License to rape: Sexual abuse of wives*. New York: Holt, Rinehart & Winston Inc.

Frances, A., Sreenivasan, S., & Weinberger, L. E. (2008). Defining mental disorder when it really counts: DSM-IV-TR and SVP/SDP statutes. *Journal of the American Academy of Psychiatry and the Law Online, 36*(3), 375–384.

Frazier, P. A., & Haney, B. (1996). Sexual assault cases in the legal system: Police, prosecutor, and victim perspectives. *Law and Human Behavior, 20*(6), 607–628.

Frohmann, L. (1997). Convictability and discordant locales: Reproducing race, class. *Law & Society Review, 31*(3), 531–555.

Groth, A. N., & Birnbaum, A. H. (1979). *Men who rape: The psychology of the offender*. New York: Plenum.

Hale, M. (1972). *Pleas of the crown: A methodical summary, 1678*. London: Professional Books.

Hall, G. C. N., & Hirschman, R. (1991). Toward a theory of sexual aggression: a quadripartite model. *Journal of Consulting and Clinical Psychology, 59*(5), 662.

Hanson, R. K., & Morton-Bourgon, K. E. (2005). The characteristics of persistent sexual offenders: a meta-analysis of recidivism studies. *Journal of Consulting and Clinical Psychology, 73*(6), 1154.

Hayes, R. M., Lorenz, K., & Bell, K. A. (2013). Victim blaming others: rape myth acceptance and the just world belief. *Feminist Criminology, 8*(3), 202–220.

Haywood, H., & Swank, E. (2008). Rape myths among Appalachian college students. *Violence and Victims, 23*(3), 373–389.

Heaven, P. C., Connors, J., & Pretorius, A. (1998). Victim characteristics and attribution of rape blame in Australia and South Africa. *The Journal of Social Psychology, 138*(1), 131–133.

Hislop, J. (2001). *Female sex offenders: What therapists, law enforcement and child protective services need to know*. Idyll Arbor.

Htun, M., & Weldon, S. L. (2012). The civic origins of progressive policy change: Combating violence against women in global perspective, 1975–2005. *American Political Science Review, 106*(03), 548–569.

International Association of Chiefs of Police (2005). *Investigating Sexual Assaults: Model Policy and Concepts and Issues Paper.* Published by the IACP National Law Enforcement Policy Center, Alexandria, VA.

Kerstetter, W. A. (1990). Gateway to justice: Police and prosecutorial response to sexual assaults against women. *Journal of Criminal Law and Criminology, 81*(2), 267–313.

Knight, R. A., & Prentky, R. A. (1990). Classifying sexual offenders. In W. L. Marshall, D. R. Laws, & H. B. Barbaree (Eds.), *Handbook of sexual assault* (pp. 23–52). Springer US.

Krebs, C. P., Lindquist, C. H., Warner, T. D., Fisher, B. S., & Martin, S. L. (2007). *The campus sexual assault (CSA) study.* Washington, DC: National Institute of Justice, US Department of Justice.

Krug, E. T., Dahlberg, L. L., Mercy, J. A., Zwi, A. B., & Lozano, R. (2002). *World report on violence and health.* Geneva, Switzerland: World Health Organization.

Långström, N., Sjöstedt, G., & Grann, M. (2004). Psychiatric disorders and recidivism in sexual offenders. *Sexual Abuse: A Journal of Research and Treatment, 16*(2), 139–150.

Langton, L., & Truman, J. (2013). *Criminal Victimization 2013.* Accessed November 1, 2015 from http://www.bjs.gov/content/pub/pdf/cv13.pdf.

Lanier, C. A. (2001). Rape-accepting attitudes precursors to or consequences of forced sex. *Violence Against Women, 7*(8), 876–885.

Laufersweiler-Dwyer, D. L., & Dwyer, G. (2009). Sex offenders and child molesters. In Reddington, F. P. & Kreisel, B. W. (Eds.) *Sexual assault: The victims, perpetrators, and the criminal justice system* (pp. 239–265). Durham, NC: Carolina Academic Press.

Law Enforcement Assistance Administration. (1977). Forcible rape: A national survey of responses by prosecutors. Washington, DC: U.S. Government Printing Office

Lisak, D., & Miller, P. M. (2002). Repeat rape and multiple offending among undetected rapists. *Violence and Victims, 17*(1), 73–84.

Malamuth, N. (2013). Hostile masculinity. In Baumester, R. F. & Vohs, K. K. (Eds.) *Encyclopedia of social psychology.* Thousand Oaks: Sage.

Marshall, A. D., & Holtzworth-Munroe, A. (2002). Varying forms of husband sexual aggression: predictors and subgroup differences. *Journal of Family Psychology, 16*(3), 286.

Martin, P. Y. (2005). *Rape work: Victims, gender and emotions in organization and community context.* Psychology Press.

Mich. Comp. Laws Ann. §750.520(a)(r)).

Mittelstaedt, E. (2008). Safeguarding the rights of sexual minorities: The incremental and legal approaches to enforcing international human rights obligations. *Chicago Journal of International Law, 9*(1), 353–685.

Morry, M. M., & Winkler, E. (2001). Student acceptance and expectation of sexual assault. *Canadian Journal of Behavioural Science/Revue canadienne des sciences du comportement, 33*(3), 188.

Moses, D. C. (1993). Livy's Lucretia and the validity of coerced consent in Roman Law. In A. Laiou (Ed.) *Consent and coercion to sex and marriage in ancient and medieval societies* (pp. 39–81). Washington, D.C.: Dumbarton Oaks Research Library.

Murphy, C. M., & Hoover, S. A. (1999). Measuring emotional abuse in dating relationships as a multifactorial construct. *Violence and Victims, 14*(1), 39–53.

New York Times. (2013). Retrieved from http://www.nytimes.com/interactive/2013/07/26/opinion/26corrective-rape.html?_r=0)

Oselin, S. S., & Blasyak, A. (2013). Contending with violence: female prostitutes' strategic responses on the streets. *Deviant Behavior, 34*(4), 274–290.

Peterson, Z. D., Voller, E. K., Polusny, M. A., & Murdoch, M. (2011). Prevalence and consequences of adult sexual assault of men: Review of empirical findings and state of the literature. *Clinical Psychology Review, 31*(1), 1–24.

Polaschek, D. L., & Ward, T. (2002). The implicit theories of potential rapists: What our questionnaires tell us. *Aggression and Violent Behavior, 7*(4), 385–406.

Polusny, M. A., & Murdoch, M. (2005). Sexual assault among male veterans. *Psychiatric Times, 22*(4), 34–38.

Rape, Abuse, and Incest National Network (RAINN) (2009). *Reporting rates.* Retrieved November 1, 2015 from www.rainn.org/statistics/ index.html.

Raphael, J., & Shapiro, D. L. (2002). *Sisters Speak Out: The Lives and Needs of Prostituted Women in Chicago: A Research Study.* Center for Impact Research.

Rennison, C. M. (2002). *Rape and sexual assault: Reporting to police and medical attention, 1992–2000.* Washington, DC: US Department of Justice, Office of Justice Programs.

Rodabaugh, B. J., & Austin, M. (1981). *Sexual assault: A guide for community action.* Garland STPM Press.

Ruggiero, K. J., & Kilpatrick, D. G. (2003). *Rape in Alaska: A Report to the State.* Charleston, SC: National Violence Against Women Prevention Research Center, Medical University of South Carolina.

Ruiz, P. T., & Escursell, M. R. I. (2000). Variables socioculturales en la atribución de culpa a las víctimas de violación. *Psicothema, 12*(2), 223–228.

Rumney, P. N. (2006). False allegations of rape. *The Cambridge Law Journal, 65*(01), 128–158.

Russell, D. (1988). Pornography and rape: A causal model. *Political Psychology, 9*(1), 41–73.

Schwartz, S. (1983). An argument for the elimination of the resistance requirement from the definition of forcible rape. *Loyola of Los Angeles Law Review, 16*(3), 567–602.

Shorey, R. C., Cornelius, T. L., & Bell, K. M. (2008). A critical review of theoretical frameworks for dating violence: Comparing the dating and marital fields. *Aggression and Violent Behavior, 13*(3), 185–194.

Simons, D. A., Wurtele, S. K., & Durham, R. L. (2008). Developmental experiences of child sexual abusers and rapists. *Child Abuse & Neglect, 32*(5), 549–560.

Spohn, C., & Horney, J. (1992). *Rape law reform: A grassroots movement and its impact.* Plenum Press.

Spohn, C., Beichner, D., & Davis-Frenzel, E. (2001). Prosecutorial justifications for sexual assault case rejection: Guarding the "gateway to justice." *Social Problems, 48*(2), 206–235.

Strömwall, L. A., Alfredsson, H., & Landström, S. (2013). Rape victim and perpetrator blame and the Just World hypothesis: The influence of victim gender and age. *Journal of Sexual Aggression, 19*(2), 207–217.

Suarez, E., & Gadalla, T. M. (2010). Stop blaming the victim: A meta-analysis on rape myths. *Journal of Interpersonal Violence, 25*(11), 2010–2035.

Tjaden, P. G., & Thoennes, N. (2006). *Extent, nature, and consequences of rape victimization: Findings from the National Violence Against Women Survey.* Washington, DC: US Department of Justice, Office of Justice Programs, National Institute of Justice.

Truman, J., Langton, L., & Planty, M. (2013). *Criminal Victimization, 2012. Bulletin.* NCJ 243389, Washington, DC: United States Department of Justice, Office of Justice Programs, Bureau of Justice Statistics.

Ullman, S. E., & Brecklin, L. R. (2000). Alcohol and adult sexual assault in a national sample of women. *Journal of Substance Abuse, 11*(4), 405–420.

Ullman, S. E., Filipas, H. H., Townsend, S. M., & Starzynski, L. L. (2007). Psychosocial correlates of PTSD symptom severity in sexual assault survivors. *Journal of Traumatic Stress, 20*(5), 821–831.

U.S. Department of Justice. (2012). Attorney general Eric Holder announces revisions to the uniform crime report's definition of rape [Press release]. Retrieved from https://www.fbi.gov/news/pressrel/press-releases/attorney-general-eric-holder-announces-revisions-to-the-uniform-crime-reports-definition-of-rape.

Venema, R. M. (2014). Police officer schema of sexual assault reports: Real rape, ambiguous cases, and false reports. *Journal of Interpersonal Violence,* DOI: 10.1177/0886260514556765

Vrij, A., & Firmin, H. R. (2001). Beautiful thus innocent? The impact of defendants' and victims' physical attractiveness and participants' rape beliefs on impression formation in alleged rape cases. *International Review of Victimology, 8*(3), 245–255.

Walker, J., Archer, J., & Davies, M. (2005). Effects of rape on men: A descriptive analysis. *Archives of Sexual Behavior, 34*(1), 69–80.

Weiss, K. G. (2010). Male sexual victimization examining men's experiences of rape and sexual assault. *Men and Masculinities, 12*(3), 275–298.

Wheeler, J. G., George, W. H., & Dahl, B. J. (2002). Sexually aggressive college males: Empathy as a moderator in the "Confluence Model" of sexual aggression. *Personality and Individual Differences, 33*(5), 759–775.

Wijkman, M., Bijleveld, C., & Hendriks, J. (2010). Women don't do such things! Characteristics of female sex offenders and offender types. *Sexual Abuse: A Journal of Research and Treatment.*

Williams, L. S. (1984). The classic rape: When do victims report? *Social Problems, 31*(4), 459–467.

Zander, T. K. (2008). Commentary: Inventing diagnosis for civil commitment of rapists. *Journal of the American Academy of Psychiatry and the Law Online, 36*(4), 459–469.

# DEFINITIONS

**Attitudinal Rape Myths:** Faulty explanations of why rape occurs. These explanations operate to excuse rape, as well as justify it (also known as rape-supportive cognition).

**Blitz Attack:** Generally unplanned, spontaneous attacks that occur at any time.

**Case Attrition:** The failure of a criminal case to advance to the next phase of the criminal justice process.

**Classic Rape:** A rape that fits within the stereotypical rape: victim was assaulted by a stranger, had visible injuries that could corroborate allegations of forced sexual intercourse, and the offender used a weapon or physical force.

**Clearance Rate:** Percentage of reported crimes that are cleared by arrest.

**Corrective Rape:** Rape of lesbian women with the purpose of "curing" them of their sexual orientation.

**Good-Looking Effect:** Courtroom phenomenon whereby physically attractive individuals tend to fare better than their non-attractive counterparts.

**Hostile Masculinity Syndrome:** A common profile of sexually aggressive men involving (1) a desire to be in control, particularly in relationships with women, and (2) an insecure, defensive, and distrustful reaction to women.

**Intimacy Effect:** Court phenomenon whereby rape and sexual assaults between intimates are viewed as less severe than those occurring between strangers.

**Just World Hypothesis:** The belief that we live in a just and fair world where good things happen to good people and bad things happen to bad people.

**Massachusetts Treatment Center Rapist Typology, Version 3 (MTC: R3):** A typology of rapists developed by Knight and Prentky that includes nine categories of rapists. They are based on the offender's motivation, developmental, biological, and environmental factors. (See also: Opportunistic Rapists, Pervasively Angry Rapists, Sexual Gratification Rapists, and Vindictive Rapists.)

**Opportunistic Rapists (Type 1 and 2):** A category of rapists identified in the MTC: R3 classification of rapists developed by Knight and Prentky. They commit rapes that are typically impulsive, unplanned, and driven by opportunity as a means of seeking immediate gratification. Opportunistic rapists include two subtypes: those who have high social competence (Type 1) and low social competence (Type 2). (See also: Massachusetts Treatment Center Rapist Typology, Pervasively Angry Rapists, Sexual Gratification Rapists, and Vindictive Rapists.)

**Pervasively Angry Rapists (Type 3):** A category of rapists identified in the MTC: R3 classification of developed by Knight and Prentky. They are rapists who are characterized by impulsive behaviors, low social competence, and longstanding aggression and hostility toward men and women. (See also: Massachusetts Treatment Center Rapist Typology, Opportunistic Rapists, Sexual Gratification Rapists, and Vindictive Rapists.)

**Plea Bargain:** Agreement between the prosecutor and defendant where the defendant enters a guilty plea in exchange for some concession from the prosecutor.

**Rape:** Any sexual penetration (vaginal, anal, or oral) of a person without his or her consent.

**Rape Shield Laws:** Trial rules that limit a defendant's ability to introduce evidence or cross-examine rape victims about their past sexual behavior.

**Secondary Victimization:** Attitudes and behaviors of criminal justice officials who are blameful, insensitive, minimizing, and dismissive of rape victims.

**Sexual Assault:** Sex crimes involving any unwanted sexual contact.

**Sexual Gratification Rapists (Type 4, 5, 6, and 7):** A category of rapists identified in the MTC: R3 classification of developed by Knight and Prentky. They are rapists who have extensive sexual perversions, many of which are incorporated into the rapes. It includes four subtypes: (Type 4) overt sadists, who are characterized by high levels of aggression and gratuitous violence; (Type 5) muted sadists, who are less violent and their crimes tend to be more symbolic than injurious; (Type 6) non-sadistic high, who do not exhibit sadistic characteristics and have high social competence; and (Type 7) non-sadistic low, who also do not exhibit sadistic characteristics and have low social competence. (See also: Massachusetts Treatment Center Rapist Typology, Opportunistic Rapists, Pervasively Angry Rapists, and Vindictive Rapists.)

**Situational Rape Myths:** Misunderstandings and misconceptions of the crime of rape.

**Typologies:** Used to place people into distinct categories. Each category includes people who are similar to each other, yet different from people in other categories.

**Unfound:** A decision by law enforcement officials to not proceed with formal charging of a crime.

**Vindictive Rapists (Type 8 and 9):** A category of rapists identified in the MTC: R3 classification of developed by Knight and Prentky. They are rapists who direct anger towards women and often humiliate, degrade, and physically harm their victims. They also include two subtypes based on their level of social competence: (Type 8) low social competence and (Type 9) high social competence. (See also: Massachusetts Treatment Center Rapist Typology, Opportunistic Rapists, Pervasively Angry Rapists, and Sexual Gratification Rapists.)

## CHAPTER 4

# *Child Sexual Abuse*

## CHAPTER OBJECTIVES

- Define child sexual abuse and differentiate child sexual abuse from pedophilia.
- Identify the common myths associated with child sexual abuse.
- Describe the societal reaction to child sexual abuse crimes throughout American history.
- Describe child sexual-abuser typologies.
- Identify the medical, psychological, and legal consequences of child sexual abuse for victims.

*Child sexual abuse* refers to a broad spectrum of behaviors in which an adult (and sometimes an older adolescent) engages in inappropriate sex acts with a child. All crimes that involve sexually touching a child, as well as non-contact offenses and sexual exploitation, constitute child sexual abuse. Forms of child sexual abuse include child molestation, child rape/sexual assault, child incestuous abuse, child sexual exploitation (including engaging minor children in child prostitution and child pornography), and indecent exposure to a child (see Focus Box 4.1). Similar to rape, the sexual exploitation of children and young people appears to be a universal phenomenon. Evidence shows that *any* child or adolescent can be a victim of child sexual abuse (Lalor & McElvaney, 2010). Child sexual abuse often co-occurs with other forms of child maltreatment, including physical abuse, emotional abuse, and neglect (Vachon, Krueger, Rogosch, & Cicchetti, 2015).

As we learned in Chapter 3, sex acts between adults do not constitute a crime, provided that both parties have consented to the activity. The sex acts become criminal (as with rape or sexual assault) when at least one of the parties does not consent to it. In contrast, sex acts with children or adolescents are illegal regardless of the minor's seeming consent, compliance, or cooperation. Just as children (in most jurisdictions) are deemed to lack the capacity to make a contract, they also cannot legally consent to sex acts. An adult who engages in sex acts with a minor below the legal age of consent (between 16 and 18, depending on the state), therefore, has committed a crime of child sexual abuse.

---

*Focus Box 4.1   Child Sexual Abuse Offenses*

**Contact sexual offenses against children include:**

- Fondling a child
- Making a child touch an adult's sexual organs
- Penetrating a child's mouth, anus, or vagina no matter how slight with any human organ or object that does not serve a valid medical purpose

**Non-contact sexual offenses against children include:**

- Child peeping (voyeurism)
- Engaging in indecent exposure to a child (exhibitionism)
- Exposing children to pornographic materials
- Masturbating in front of a child

**Sexual exploitation includes:**

- Soliciting a child for purposes of prostitution
- Using a child to photograph, film, or model pornography

---

Thousands of children are victims of child sexual abuse each year. In 2013, 60,956 child sexual abuse incidents were reported in the U.S., representing 9% of the total number of reported child maltreatment cases that year (U.S. Department of Health and Human Services, Administration for Children and Families, 2015). Research conducted by the Centers for Disease Control and Prevention (CDC) estimates that approximately one in four girls and one in six boys is sexually abused before age 18. Whether the amount of child sexual abuse has changed over time is a matter of debate; some researchers report a decrease from the mid-1990s to 2005 (Gilbert et al., 2009), while others do not find much variation over time (Goldman & Padayachi, 2000).

In this chapter, we begin with a discussion of common myths and misconceptions surrounding child sexual abuse. Many result from the moral panic and misinformation since the increased attention and heightened concern over sex crimes and sex offenders in the U.S. Next, a brief history of the evolution of social and legal reactions to child sexual abuse in the U.S. is discussed. Situated within this history are a number of public myths and misconceptions that still exist today. We then delve into some of the prominent theories of child sexual abuse and present a sample of the dominant child sexual-abuser typologies that describe how and why offenders do what they do. A description of child sexual abuse victims follows, with particular emphasis on short- and long-term effects and outcomes. Finally, this chapter concludes with an examination of the criminal justice response to child sexual abuse, focusing on investigative procedures, child-testimony issues, and sentencing of convicted offenders.

There are many different types of child sexual abuse: contact offenses, non-contact offenses, and sexual exploitation. Each type certainly warrants individualized attention, but it is beyond the scope of this textbook to thoroughly discuss each type. Instead, the focus of this chapter is primarily upon contact sex crimes against children, as non-contact sex crimes against children are customarily not accounted for in estimates of incidence and prevalence of sexual abuse against children (Finkelhor, 1984). Throughout the chapter, there is some discussion of certain types of sex crimes when referencing particular studies, but in general, the term "child sexual abuse" is relied upon.

## MYTHS ON CHILD SEXUAL ABUSE

### Child Sexual Abusers Target Any and All Children

Like their non-offending counterparts, child sexual abusers do not tend to engage in sexual acts with anyone and everyone. They tend to have sexual tastes and preferences, and are aroused by certain types. Many child molesters and other sex offenders who abuse children carefully select their targeted victims. For example, many male child molesters have reported that they often choose children who have family problems, are alone, lack confidence, and are indiscriminate in their trust of others—especially when the child is also perceived as pretty, provocatively dressed, young, or small (Elliott, Browne, & Kilcoyne, 1995). Sexual abuse against children may not happen instantaneously. It is often the result of an extensive process where the offender psychologically manipulates the child (and sometimes the child's family) into trusting him or her, thereby diminishing the child's resistance. This process, known as *grooming*, is discussed later.

### Children Who Are Sexually Abused Will Sexually Abuse Others When They Grow up

There is a widespread belief in the "cycle" of sexual abuse whereby childhood sexual victimization *inevitably* leads to committing sexual abuse during adulthood. This is a myth, and it is particularly damaging as it assigns the label of "predator" or "sex offender" to an abused child (especially boys) and takes the focus off their needs for help. The evidence of a link between childhood sexual victimization and later commission of sexual abuse is mixed, at best. One meta-analysis reported a 3.4 times greater likelihood of sexual abuse in childhood in adult sex offenders, compared to adult non-sex offenders (Jespersen, Lalumière, & Seto, 2009). Another study found that sexually abused children were almost eight times more likely to be charged for a sex crime in later life, compared to their non-abused counterparts (Ogloff, Cutajar, Mann, & Mullen, 2012).

Although child sexual abuse is an important risk factor for later commission of sex crimes (this is known as the ***abused-abuser hypothesis*** or the ***cycle of child sexual abuse***), not all victims go down this path. In fact, research suggests that the majority of child sexual-abuse victims do *not* commit sex crimes later in life. One study found that 12% of sexually abused boys went on to commit contact sex crimes, mostly against children (Salter et al., 2003). A more recent meta-analysis of 89 studies similarly concluded that most individuals who are sexually abused as children do not later commit child sexual abuse (Whitaker et al., 2008). Critics of the abused-abuser hypothesis take issue with its simplicity. Researchers have found that child sexual abuse is a strong predictor of other negative outcomes, such as depression and substance abuse, which are also strongly associated with committing sex crimes in adulthood (Aebi, Landolt, Mueller-Pfeiffer, Schnyder, Maier, & Mohler-Kuo, 2015). Similarly, Burton (2008) noted that researchers have rarely examined the history of sexual victimization alongside personality factors in evaluating the causes of sexual abuse in adulthood. Moreover, Widom and Maxfield (2001) reported that child physical-abuse history better predicts later violent crimes than sex crimes among male offenders. Recall from the introduction to this chapter, however, that sexual abuse in childhood often co-occurs with other types of child abuse. Therefore, in assessing the unique role of child *sexual* victimization in later adult offending, there are several factors that need to be assessed individually and collectively. Reckdenwald, Mancini, and Beauregard (2014) considered the role of self-image in the abused-abuser hypothesis, finding that sexually abused children may experience developmental deficiencies, specifically poor sense of self, and it is these deficiencies that predict onset of future adult sexual offending. Studies such as this show that the link between childhood experiences and adult behavior is not necessarily direct, but instead is influenced by intervening mechanisms.

Many ***protective factors*** (those that minimize or eliminate risk) have been identified that call into question the seemingly strong association between sexual abuse as a child and sex offending later in life. Research has indicated that if children disclose an act of sexual abuse early and are supported by people close to them, they have a much lower likelihood of subsequently committing a sex crime (Alaggia, 2010). Prendergast (1993) identified several factors that safeguard sexually abused male victims from later becoming sex offenders: good self-esteem, availability of emotional support, and a solid knowledge of human sexuality at the onset of their childhood sexual victimization.

## All Child Sexual Abusers Are Pedophiles

It is important to de-link an adult's sexual attraction to a child from his or her sexual contact with a child. Growing use of the terms "pedophilia" and "pedophile" has come from expanded publicity and awareness concerning the sexual abuse of children. Just as we may casually refer to someone as neurotic, paranoid, or delusional without necessarily assuming psychiatric expertise or implying a psychiatric diagnosis, it is increasingly common among laypeople to consider someone who has sexually victimized a child as a pedophile. Labeling all child molesters as pedophiles, however, is incorrect.

*Pedophilia* consists of a sexual attraction to children that may or may not lead to child sexual abuse, whereas child sexual abuse involves sexual contact with a child that may or may not be due to pedophilia (Camilleri & Quinsey, 2008). Sometimes there is overlap between pedophilia and child sexual abuse; but in many cases, there is not. According to the DSM–5 (American Psychiatric Association, 2013), a diagnosis of pedophilia requires an individual to:

(1)  Have recurrent, intense, and sexually arousing fantasies, urges, or behaviors directed toward a prepubescent child over a period of at least 6 months.

(2)  Have acted on these urges *or to be distressed by them.*

(3)  Be at least 16 years old and at least 5 years older than the child victim.

Some pedophiles are exclusively attracted to children, while others are aroused by both adults and children. Are all child sexual abusers pedophiles? No. In fact, research overwhelmingly indicates that the majority of individuals who engage in sex acts with children are not pedophiles.

One study concisely summarized that "pedophilia is neither a necessary nor a sufficient condition for child sex offenses" (Jahnke & Hoyer, 2013, p. 171). Are all pedophiles child sexual abusers? It is true that pedophilia is a predictor of child sexual abuse (Hanson & Morton-Bourgon, 2005). But remember that pedophilia is clinically defined as a sexual attraction to children. Some pedophiles may elect to view sexually explicit (as well as non-sexually explicit) images of children, an issue we will explore in Chapter 5. Some pedophiles may engage in overt strategies to avoid having sexually deviant thoughts. A study by Amelung et al. (2012) suggests that "self-motivated" pedophiles using Androgen Deprivation Therapy (ADT) may benefit from decreased deviant sexual behaviors and an increase in empathy for potential victims. The confusion surrounding pedophilia is most likely a product of sensationalism in mass media, in which people with pedophilic interests are stereotypically portrayed as violent predators (Kitzinger, 2004).

Increasingly, there is evidence that these two groups of sex offenders against children differ in a number of important ways. For example, compared to non-pedophiles, pedophiles tend to have more victims (Abel & Harlow, 2001), respond more poorly to treatment, and are more likely to re-offend (Hanson & Bussiere, 1998; Seto, 2008). Biologically, differences have been identified between pedophiles and child sexual abusers with regard to executive function in the brain, with child sexual abusers demonstrating greater cognitive deficits, compared to pedophiles (Schiffer & Vonlaufen, 2011). In summary, from clinical, legal, and policy perspectives, pedophilia must be carefully distinguished from child sexual abuse. Table 4.1 summarizes these differences.

**TABLE 4.1**   *Characteristics of Pedophiles versus Child Sexual Abusers*

| PEDOPHILES | CHILD SEXUAL ABUSERS |
|---|---|
| • May abuse family members, but the majority of offenses are extra-familial<br>• Have high recidivism rates after incarceration and treatment<br>• May have hundreds of victims over their lifetimes<br>• Are uncomfortable with and reject adult intimacy<br>• Pedophilia is adult sexual attraction/orientation to children. | • Primary sexual attraction/orientation is to adults<br>• More likely to commit intra-familial abuse<br>• Lower number of victims<br>• Lower rates of recidivism<br>• Abuse of children is generally committed to fulfill an emotional need, such as powerlessness or loneliness, and not sexual arousal<br>• More severe cognitive deficits |

### If We Protect Our Children from Strangers, Child Sexual Abuse Will Not Be a Problem

Most sex-offender legislation and public policy (discussed in greater detail in Chapter 11) is based on the notion of stranger danger. Pinning the problem of child sexual abuse on strangers and formulating strategies to safeguard our children from the "bad guys" provide a sense of security and quell fears that our children could become potential targets. But stranger danger is a red herring. As discussed in this chapter, the overwhelming majority of sex crimes against children are not committed by strangers, but by those who are close to them. Often, child sexual abusers are related to their victims. Furthermore, those who are not related become intimately attached to their victims, effectively becoming "like a member of the family."

### Child Sexual-Abuse Cases Are Wrought with False Accusations and Exaggerated Accounts

It is true that not all statements made by children are true. It is true that a range of factors, such as types of questions asked, the sorts of ancillary aids used, and the characteristics of interviewers, can seriously decrease the accuracy of children's statements and even lead to entirely false accounts (see generally: Bruck, Ceci, & Hembrooke, 2002). Very few child sexual-abuse prosecutions and convictions, however, come from false allegations. There are low rates of false accusations in child sexual-abuse cases. Jones and McGraw (1987) found that only 1% of a sample of 576 social service referrals for child sexual abuse was based on fictitious accounts. Likewise, a more recent study found a false allegation rate of 2.5% (Oates et al., 2000).

In many cases, false allegations do not originate with the children. Maltreated children (particularly younger children) actually demonstrate a greater sensitivity to lying, in that they display a better understanding of "truth" and "lies," compared to non-maltreated children (Lyon, Carrick, & Quas, 2010). Rather, it has been found that parents are more likely to falsely claim child sexual abuse, often in divorce proceedings and child-custody battles (Trocmé & Bala, 2005). This finding, however, must be interpreted with caution because of the danger that it could be used to protect sexual abusers at the expense of children's safety (Jenkins, 2002).

More often, the opposite holds true. Children are more likely to minimize and/or deny sexual abuse than exaggerate or falsely report it. Studies have repeatedly shown that sexually abused children questioned for the first time are likely to deny the abuse (Lyon, 2007). Moreover, the frequency with which children take back allegations of sexual abuse also confounds this problem. The rate that children take back allegations of sexual abuse varies from study to study—from 4% at the low end (Bradley & Wood, 1996), up to 23% on the high end (Malloy, Lyon, & Quas, 2007). Many factors are associated with why a child might take back an allegation of sexual abuse. For example, it is more likely among children abused by a parent or caretaker, and this is made worse when the child's non-offending caregiver is unsupportive (Malloy et al., 2007). Such cases, therefore, are said to be **unsubstantiated**, meaning that there is insufficient legal evidence to determine that a crime has occurred. Taken together, the evidence suggests that child sexual-abuse cases are much more likely to be unsubstantiated than they are to be false. Of the 3.8 million children considered in a child maltreatment report in 2012, 58% were unsubstantiated versus 0.2% that were classified as intentionally false reports (U.S. Department of Health and Human Services, Administration for Children and Families, 2013).

## All Child Sexual Abusers Are Monsters

Any mention of child molesters usually elicits images of society's lowest rung. They are creeps, perverts, monsters—and not our family members, neighbors, friends, or co-workers. They lack traditional values, have no work ethic, and have low moral turpitude—they are not upstanding members of our community. They come from neighborhoods and communities with violence, poverty, and inequality. They are not in our communities.

It is misleading to suggest that child sexual abusers are somehow different from the general population. In one of the most comprehensive studies of child sexual abusers, Abel and Harlow (2001) compared a sample of over 4,000 admitted child molesters to the general U.S. population on a number of characteristics, including education, employment status, marital status, and religious observance. The results were clear—when compared to the general population of U.S. men, child molesters were no different. Table 4.2 displays an overview of male child-molester characteristics, compared to the general population of American men.

What do these numbers mean? Is it simply that the typical child sexual abuser is married, educated, employed and religious? In a way, the answer is "yes," but with

**TABLE 4.2** *Profile of Admitted Child Molesters Compared to U.S. Male Population*

| | ADMITTED CHILD MOLESTERS | U.S. MEN |
|---|---|---|
| Married or formally married | 77% | 73% |
| Some college education | 46% | 49% |
| High school only | 30% | 32% |
| Employed | 69% | 64% |
| Religious observance | 93% | 93% |

Source: (Abel and Harlow, 2001)

an important caveat. Education, employment and religion do not cause individuals to commit sex crimes against children. Do parents and caretakers need to be aware of what a child sexual abuser looks like? To an extent yes, but the reality is that they look a lot like the rest of us. In equating abusers with society's rejects, we create a false sense of security that our families and children are insulated from child sexual abuse. To reiterate, the only obvious thing that sets child sexual abusers apart from the general population is that they abuse children.

The myths surrounding child sexual abuse did not emerge spontaneously at a specific point in time, but rather, have been conditioned by social, legal, and political forces that have shaped public opinion on child sex-abuse crimes, the offenders that commit them, and the victims that are targeted. Next, we discuss this history, focusing on the evolution of the societal responses to child sexual abuse.

## HISTORICAL TRENDS IN CHILD SEXUAL-ABUSE LAWS, POLICIES, AND SOCIETAL RESPONSES

Sexual abuse of children is far from new. Family historians have discovered that adults in fifteenth century elite households sometimes treated children as sexual playthings. In New York, during the late 1700s and through the 1800s, between one-third and one-half of rape victims were younger than 18 years old (Sacco, 2009). Public attention to child sexual abuse has waxed and waned repeatedly throughout U.S. history. Historical research has shown that concern was at its greatest following the Civil War, during the Progressive Era, during and immediately after World War II, and in our own time (Gordon, 1988; Pleck, 1987). Interestingly, this concern did not reflect a sudden spike in reported instances of child sexual abuse, but rather evolved from broader social anxieties.

During the Reconstruction Period, after the U.S. Civil War (1865–1877), rapid urbanization, a massive influx of immigrants, and a sharp rise in divorce rates provoked fears about the future of the family. New York City, for example, was flooded with destitute war widows, orphans, crippled veterans, and immigrants, giving visibility to poverty, crime, and disorder. In 1874, the first Society for the Prevention of Cruelty to Children was formed to address child abuse. Within the next 40 years, about 500 such organizations were established throughout the U.S. By and large, these anti-cruelty organizations acted as moral agents. The focus was on urging women to be diligent mothers and men to be good providers. By 1890, the focus on child abuse shifted to child neglect (Myers, 2008).

The Progressive Era (1890–1920) was marked by anxieties over mass immigration, divorce, child labor, and juvenile delinquency. Similar to reform efforts during Civil War Reconstruction, family professionals and court officials during this era focused on changing the values and behaviors of the poor. Child neglect remained the focus of intervention efforts, and single mothers were disproportionately targeted. Shortly thereafter, Sigmund Freud's *theory of infantile sexuality* (discussed in Chapter 1), which claimed that children who reported sexual abuse by adults had imagined or fantasized the experience, diffused the moral outrage about child neglect and maltreatment.

From the Progressive Era through the 1950s, concern over child abuse largely retreated from the public conscience. Social service agencies coming across such cases usually classified them as problems of economic strain, family maladjustment, genetic inferiority, or mental pathology. During the Great Depression, child abuse was attributed to economic hardship. During and shortly following World War II, concerns about working mothers, latchkey children, and absent fathers sparked anxieties about child abuse and neglect. Still, however, these were viewed as manifestations of family problems or mental illness and not as a widespread social epidemic (Gordon, 1988).

A focus on family violence in the early 1960s generated interest in the study of child abuse. This is largely credited to the work of pediatric physicians and medical providers. In 1946, pediatric radiologist John Caffey published a case study of six young children with subdural hematomas, as well as arm and leg fractures. Though he did not explicitly use the term "child abuse," it was certainly implied in his conclusions (Caffey, 1946). Building on the momentum of this study, physicians and medical providers also began to examine questionable childhood injuries. This culminated in the landmark publication of the *battered child syndrome* by Kempe et al. (1962), which established the duty and responsibility of physicians to fully evaluate injured children and guarantee non-recurrence of "expected repetition of trauma" (p. 143).

The combined efforts of physicians, medical providers, and others increased interest in criminalization of child abuse. By 1967, every state had enacted laws requiring physicians to report child abuse to law enforcement officials or social service agencies. In 1974, Congress passed the *Child Abuse Prevention and Treatment Act (CAPTA)*, which authorized funds to improve states' investigation and reporting of physical abuse, neglect, and sexual abuse.

While many sexually abused children were protected prior to the 1970s, recognition of, and genuine concern for, child sexual abuse lagged behind that of physical abuse. Early scholars noted the virtual absence of literature and discussion of child sexual abuse (Walters, 1975), attributing the void to the taboo nature of it

(Sgroi, 1975). The sexual revolution in the U.S. in the 1960s, typified by a change in beliefs about sex and sexuality, fueled speculation that the taboo of engaging in sexual acts with children would soon dissipate. According to Rush (1980), this sparked a movement in which child molesters claimed sex with children was a civil right and even encouraged practitioners and professionals to defend it. Indeed, the inclination to view child-adult sex as a harmless, victimless crime is not too distant of a memory in the history of child sexual abuse.

Awareness of the deleterious effects of sexual abuse evolved from the observations of medical providers and pioneering researchers. One surgeon issued the following statement to the National Commission on Pornography and Obscenity in 1970:

> Lately, I've been in gynecology and obstetrics. It's absolutely frightening to see what's going on. The wards and private rooms are filled with young girls. Their insides are torn to pieces. It is impossible to describe the repair jobs we do. These girls suffer from every kind of sexual abuse. It used to be that doctors treated prostitutes in such condition but now we have to treat young girls from the best of families. Every day we see girls in their teens with disease and infection.
>
> (United States, 1970, p. 611)

Prior to the 1970s, there was little research on the scope and effects of child sexual abuse. De Francis' (1969) study of 250 sexual-abuse cases in Brooklyn underscored the need for systematic inquiries into child sexual-abuse issues. De Francis concluded that "the problem of sexual abuse of children is of unknown national dimensions, but the findings strongly point to the probability of an enormous national incidence many times larger than the reported incidence of physical abuse of children" (De Francis, 1969, p. vii). De Francis further concluded that victims of child sexual abuse were the least protected children, emphasizing that communities had, at the time, failed to acknowledge the problem.

Within a decade, much had changed. An explosion in interest was accompanied by an increase in knowledge of child sexual abuse. Research began to reveal its widespread prevalence. One of the most influential studies was Finkelhor's (1979) pioneering work, which estimated that one in four females and one in five males had experienced forced sexual contact before age 18 (Finkelhor, 1979). This burgeoning research, combined with an emergence of strong state-reporting laws, increased the number of cases of suspected child sexual abuse reported to officials and prosecuted (Beckett, 1996). Not surprisingly, media coverage on child sexual abuse increased in the 1970s and 1980s. As newspapers and television news headlined stories of child sexual abuse, moral panic and sex-abuse hysteria followed. Notable during this period was alleged child sexual abuse in daycare centers. Perhaps the most well-known example of this was the McMartin Preschool Trial, where employees of a family-operated preschool in California were accused of hundreds of acts of child sexual abuse. The abuse allegations were extremely graphic and bizarre, involving torture, Satanism, and witchcraft. After six years of criminal trials, no convictions were obtained, and all of the charges were dropped in 1990. Some of the accusing parties have since come forward to admit the allegations were false. At a cost of approximately $15 million, this case remains one of the most expensive trials in U.S. history (this case and other daycare-abuse cases are discussed in Chapter 8).

Cases such as these undoubtedly contributed to the backlash against rigorously prosecuting child sexual-abuse cases in the early 1990s. Some researchers equated the mass hysteria surrounding child sexual abuse with the Salem witch trials. In seventeenth century Salem, a group of young girls were found to have what medical professionals referred to as hysterical outbursts. Having no medical reasons to explain the causes of these outbursts (which included episodic fits associated with screaming, speechlessness, physical aggression, epileptic-like seizures, and unintelligible utterances), doctors attributed them to demonic possession. Between June and September of 1692 (note the relatively short time frame!), many individuals were accused of witchcraft from every strata of society. By September 1692, 27 were convicted, and 19 were hanged. During the early 1990s, social critics observed an uncanny parallel between seventeenth century Salem and the present.

The backlash in the early 1990s was short-lived as Americans began to embrace the "get-tough" criminal justice policies in the late 1990s (Garland, 2001). During this period, concerns about increasing crime rates and failed rehabilitation efforts resulted in broad-sweeping reform to "crack down on crime" by using harsher punishments for convicted offenders (Mauer, 2002). In the early 1990s, the federal and state governments enacted new laws and policies targeting sex offenders. These included registries, residence-restriction laws, and civil commitment and castration statutes (discussed in more detail in Chapter 11). Part of the "get-tough" policy was the revision of death-penalty statutes in some states to include convicted child rapists (LaFond, 2005). In 1995, Louisiana became the first state to execute child rapists. Other states soon adopted similar statutes (Bell, 2008). In 2008, the U.S. Supreme Court ruled in *Kennedy v. Louisiana*, however, that such statutes were unconstitutional under the Eighth and Fourteenth Amendments. The Court also concluded that execution of child rapists could increase harm to children, and may encourage non-disclosure by victims.

Public attention to child sexual abuse has ebbed and flowed throughout U.S. history. Indeed, child sexual-abuse law and policy in the U.S. is a product of political, social, and cultural forces, as well as research exploring the underpinnings of this crime. Child sexual abuse is taken very seriously today, as evidenced by a potpourri of federal and state legislation aimed at prevention and a burgeoning research agenda focusing on child sexual abusers, their tactics, their victims, and the societal response to these crimes. The remainder of this chapter covers these topics.

# GROOMING TACTICS

Child sexual abuse usually does not occur between strangers. For example, one survey of 182 child sexual abusers found that only 6.5% victimized children they did not know (Smallbone & Wortley, 2001). Child sexual abusers become personally and emotionally invested in their victims through a process where trust and confidence are built through emotional manipulation. This process is known as grooming. Grooming generally involves an abuser skillfully manipulating a child into situations where he or she can be more readily sexually abused and less likely to disclose the incident. This process is quite detailed and lengthy and requires patience on the offender's part to maximize the child's trust and confidence in the offender. Grooming sometimes is a well-organized, long-term activity. It is carried out in a series of steps that build up to sexual abuse of a child. In order, these steps are: target selection, befriending the target, desensitizing the target, and maintenance.

## Target Selection

Many child sexual abusers have acknowledged that they carefully select victims by their perceived vulnerability. Offenders consider many factors in selecting a potential target, including the child's status (e.g., age, physical disability, living in a divorced or broken family, and living in poverty), as well as the child's emotional/ psychological state (e.g., a needy child, a depressed child, or a lonely child). One study, for example, found that child sexual abusers often target children from dysfunctional families, without supervision, and with physical signs of neglect (Beauregard, Rossmo, & Proulx, 2007). Accordingly, one offender in this study offered the following scenario to illustrate how he selected his child targets:

> "When I saw a kid that always had a key around his neck and who was badly dressed, I knew that his parents didn't take care of him and that I could easily approach him to offer him things... I knew that he'd accept because he had nothing."
> (Beauregard, Rossmo & Proulx, 2007, p. 455)

Child sexual abusers may also use their work environment to victimize children. The **sophisticated rape track** consists of offenders who work with or are involved with children, including teachers, daycare providers, after-school activity leaders, clergy, and others in authoritative positions (Beauregard, Proulx, Rossmo, Leclerc, & Allaire, 2007). Because of their position and status, they appear nonthreatening to their victims and can easily create situations that allow them to be alone with them (e.g., staying after class/school, and camping trips). One study of 41 child molesters who targeted children with whom they worked found that 15% chose their profession *solely* on the basis that it provided them access to children. Also, 42% revealed that this arrangement partially motivated their career choice (Sullivan & Beech, 2004). Beauregard, Proulx et al. (2007) also identified **family infiltrators**—offenders who become acquainted with families with children (especially single-mother families) and assume a role as surrogate parent or friend to the child.

## Befriending the Target

The second step of grooming involves gaining the child's and family's trust and gaining access to the target. The offender may observe the child and assess his/her vulnerabilities to learn how to approach and interact with the child. Offenders may offer their targets special attention, which may consist of talking with them and offering a sympathetic ear, playing games with them, offering transportation, and giving them gifts and/or treats. Eventually, the offender will begin to play a significant role in the child's life. Offenders sometimes have a remarkable ability to manipulate the relationship so that it appears he or she is the only one who fully understands the child or meets the child's needs. During the process of befriending the target, the offender will also create opportunities to isolate him/her. For example, the offender will babysit the child, take him/her out of town for weekend getaways, or have the child accompany them on daily errands (Craven, Brown, & Gilchrist, 2006).

## Desensitizing the Target

Until this point, all behaviors initiated by the offender are "positive" and do not involve any sexually abusive elements. During the desensitization phase, offenders will interweave abuse into their day-to-day interactions with the child to gradually sexualize the relationship (Berliner & Conte, 1990). Abuse does not proceed immediately to a high level, but is started at low levels. Slowly, abusive acts progress in a systematic, yet subtle, fashion. Because the victim does not understand the intention of their new "friend," he or she becomes desensitized to seemingly harmless acts that an objective observer might view as danger signals. Offenders might desensitize a child to physical touching by beginning first with non-sexual touching, such as tickling or stroking the child's head. Conversations may also become more sexual. The aim is to progress to sexual touching, first on top of clothes and then under or without clothes (van Dam, 2001).

## Maintenance

Child sexual abuse is rarely an isolated event. Offenders often take great strides to maintain their relationships with victims. Maintenance activities include reassuring the victim that no harm (physical, emotional, moral, or otherwise) has been done. Statements such as "this is a way we show our love for each other" or "I am trying to teach you" are examples of how offenders mask their behavior.

Sex offenders rely on secrecy not only to maintain the relationship, but also to prevent the child from disclosing the abuse. Offenders will engage in myriad tactics, from instilling shame, blame, or guilt to shifting responsibility to the child. The offender may also threaten disclosure of the relationship, self-harm, or physical harm to the child or loved ones.

# CHILD SEXUAL-ABUSE TYPOLOGIES

The concept of typologies was introduced in Chapter 3. Recall that the purpose of typologies is to classify sex offenders into distinct categories based on their motivation or proclivity to commit sex crimes, as well as their style or method of carrying them out. This section provides an overview of some of the typologies of child sexual abusers. Individuals who sexually abuse children are diverse in their motivations to sexually offend and their patterns of offending.

## Groth, Hobson, and Gary (1982) Typology

One of the earliest and most influential typologies was created by Groth, Hobson, and Gary (1982). They suggested there are two types of child sexual offenders: fixated and regressed. The distinction involves the degree to which deviant sexual behavior exists and the basis for psychological and emotional needs. As our discussion of rapist typologies in Chapter 3 warned, offenders may not necessarily fall "neatly" into one category. Sometimes, they may fall along a continuum, with the categories representing the polar extremes.

Child sexual abusers in the fixated category are characterized by persistent, continuous, and compulsive sexual desire and attraction to children. They are unlikely to have healthy sexual and/or emotional relationships with age-appropriate partners. They are unable to attain any degree of psychosexual maturity, tend to be emotionally immature, and have an intense preoccupation with children. As such, many fixated child sexual abusers are often diagnosed with pedophilia. Holmes and Holmes (2008) point out that these offenders are not fully emotionally developed, and they go to great lengths to establish "relationships" with vulnerable children. They tend to target young male children who are not related to them, and their actions are often premeditated, as evidenced by lengthy grooming. Fixated offenders are considered to be high-risk for sexual recidivism because of their primary deviant sexual interests in children and because they target male victims. They also average the greatest number of victims and offenses, most of which go unreported (Elliot et al., 1995).

Offenders who are categorized as regressed abusers primarily have "normal" sexual interests toward and relationships with age-appropriate partners. Generally, they tend not to be sexually interested in children, and they may choose sexual contact with children as a means of coping with external stressors. These stressors can be situational, such as unemployment, divorce, alcoholism and substance abuse. Negative emotions, such as loneliness, depression, anxiety, and isolation, may also trigger the child sexual abuse. Because abuse is more situational, opportunistic, and impulsive, it is more a temporary departure from the offender's attraction to age-appropriate adults. While the fixated offender's primary motivation is sexual attraction to children, the regressed offender's motivation is situational. The victim profile of regressed offenders is also very different from their fixated counterparts.

Their victims are often adolescent girls and are more likely to be children with whom they are related or they know well.

Research evaluating the validity of this typology has yielded mixed results. The results of one study of 94 child molesters were generally supportive (Johnston & Johnston, 1997). Fixated molesters were more likely to be child-centered, to molest male children outside the family, to come from "broken" homes, and to use alcohol less frequently than regressed child sexual abusers. Regressed abusers, on the other hand, were likely to be better adjusted, to molest female children outside the family, and to come from intact homes. Some critics contend that this model is too simplistic and disregards important factors. Some researchers, for example, suggest that child molesters who are younger, related to their victims, and have arrests for previous non-sexual offenses are more likely to appear on the regressed end of the Groth et al. (1982) continuum (Simon, Sales, Kaszniak, & Kahn, 1992). There are also methodological limitations identified with this typology, in that it was developed using an incarcerated sample of child sexual abusers, and thus is not generalizable to non-incarcerated abusers.

Finally, some have noted that the primary problem with this typology is that it is often unclear just how many factors are either necessary or sufficient before one can assign an offender to a particular category or if any one factor should be considered more important than another (Bickley & Beech, 2001). Consequently, it is argued that neither a truly fixated nor a truly regressed child sexual abuser exists, but that they all fall somewhere in between on the continuum.

## Federal Bureau of Investigation (FBI) Typologies (Lanning, 1986)

Recognizing the limits of the typology developed by Groth et al. (1982) and the need for a typology that would meet the investigative needs of law enforcement officials in handling child sexual-abuse cases (what evidence to look for, whether there are additional victims, how to interview a suspect, and so on), Lanning (1986) expanded Groth et al.'s typology. Unlike the previous typology, which was predicated on understanding *why* child molesters have sex with children in order to treat them, this typology focuses on the need to recognize and evaluate *how* child molesters have sex with children in order to identify, arrest, and convict them. This typology considers a *modus operandi* continuum distinguishing between situational and preferential offenders (somewhat resonating with regressed and fixated offenders, respectively). Seven distinct categories of offenders are identified in Table 4.3.

The FBI typology has undergone extensive revision. In the fourth edition (Lanning, 2001), the sexually indiscriminate sub-category was dropped from the situational-offender category, and the fixated sub-category was dropped from the preferential-offender category. The introverted and diverse categories were added to the latter classification. Introverted offenders prefer children, but lack the interpersonal

**TABLE 4.3** *FBI Typology of Situational and Preferential Child Molesters (Lanning, 1992)*

| TYPE OF OFFENDER | OFFENDER CHARACTERISTICS |
| --- | --- |
| **Situational Offenders** | |
| Regressed | Offenders have poor coping skills, target victims who are easily accessible, abuse children as a substitute for adult relationships. |
| Morally Indiscriminate | Offenders do not prefer children over adults and tend to use children (or anyone accessible) for their own interests (sexual or otherwise). |
| Sexually Indiscriminate | Offenders are mainly interested in sexual experimentation, and abuse children out of boredom. |
| Inadequate | Offenders are social misfits who are insecure, have low self-esteem, and see relationships with children as their only sexual outlet. |
| **Preferential Offenders** | |
| Seductive | Offenders "court" (i.e., groom) children and give them affection, love, praise, and gifts to carry on a "relationship." |
| Fixated | Offenders have poor psychosexual development, desire affection from children, and are compulsively attracted to children. |
| Sadistic | Offenders are aggressive, sexually excited by violence, target stranger victims, and are extremely dangerous. |

Source: (Holmes and Holmes, 1996)

skills necessary to seduce them. This sub-category somewhat reflects the widespread stereotype of child molesters, in that they are likely to be seen in playgrounds or other areas where children congregate. The diverse sub-category describes offenders who often appear to be discriminating in their behavior, except when it comes to sex. The basic motivation of this offender in victimizing children is often sexual experimentation. The latest iteration of the FBI typology (Lanning, 2010) places all sex offenders (not just child sexual abusers) along a situational-preferential continuum, instead of discrete categories. Motivation is a difficult construct to evaluate, and several indicators and behavioral patterns are considered (see Table 4.4).

**TABLE 4.4**  *Revised FBI Typologies*

| MOTIVATION CONTINUUM | |
|---|---|
| BIOLOGICAL/PHYSIOLOGICAL SEXUAL NEEDS | PSYCHOSEXUAL/DEVIANT |
| \|=====\|=====\|=====\|=====\|=====\|=====\|=====\|=====\|=====\|=====\|=====\| | |
| POWER/ANGER NONSEXUAL NEEDS | SEXUAL NEEDS |
| (NOT ONE OR THE OTHER, BUT A CONTINUUM) | |

| SITUATIONAL SEX OFFENDER (> MORE LIKELY) | PREFERENTIAL SEX OFFENDER (> MORE LIKELY) |
|---|---|
| Less Intelligent | More Intelligent |
| Lower Socioeconomic Status | Higher Socioeconomic Status |
| Personality Disorders, including:<br>• Antisocial/Psychopathy<br>• Narcissistic<br>• Schizoid | Paraphilias, including:<br>• Pedophilia<br>• Voyeurism<br>• Sadism |
| Varied Criminal Behavior (Generalist) | Focused Criminal Behavior (Specialist) |
| Uses Violent Pornography | Theme (i.e., child) Pornography |
| Impulsive | Compulsive |
| Considers Risk | Considers Need |
| Sloppy Mistakes | Needy Mistakes |
| Thought-Driven | Fantasy-Driven |
| Spontaneous or Planned:<br>• Availability<br>• Opportunity<br>• Tools<br>• Learning | Scripted:<br>• Audition<br>• Rehearsal<br>• Props<br>• Critique |
| Method of Operation (MO) Patterns of Behavior<br>• Works<br>• Dynamic | Ritual Patterns of Behavior<br>• Need<br>• Static |

Source: (Lanning, 2010)

## Massachusetts Treatment Center: Child Molester Typology, Version 3 (MTC:CM3)

Knight, Carter, and Prentky (1989) used statistical procedures to explore and refine Groth et al. (1982) and Lanning's (1986) typologies of child sexual abusers. Unlike the previous two typologies, the MTC:CM3 treats child sexual abuse as multi-dimensional, involving two axes. Axis I addresses the degree to which the offender is fixated on children, which is further broken down to consider the offender's level of social competence. Offenders whose sexual interests are primarily limited to children are considered high fixation. Those with primarily age-appropriate sexual interests are considered low fixation. As discussed in Chapter 3, social competence refers to the degree of stability and quality of interpersonal relationships with peers, family members, and romantic partners, as well as job stability and vocational achievement. Four subtypes comprise Axis I:

(1) High fixation/high social competence.

(2) High fixation/low social competence.

(3) Low fixation/high social competence.

(4) Low fixation/low social competence.

Axis II evaluates the degree of contact an offender has with a child, the meaning of the contact (e.g., interpersonal and sexual), as well as the presence of threats and/or physical injury involved in the contact. For individuals with high contact with children, two subtypes are identified:

(5) High contact/interpersonal: High amount of contact is perceived to be meeting social, emotional, and sexual needs as if they were attempting to have a "relationship."

(6) High contact/narcissistic: High amount of contact is considered to be for purely selfish reasons, in that they are attempting to meet their own needs for sexual gratification without consideration for the victim.

For individuals who have low amounts of contact with children (often, victims are strangers to the offenders), the extent to which they cause physical injury and whether they are considered to be sadistic or non–sadistic forms the basis for four more Axis II subcategories:

(7) Low contact/low physical injury/non–sadistic (Exploitative): Physical injury is only utilized to the extent necessary to gain victim compliance. Generally, the level of planning of the offenses is low.

(8) Low contact/low physical injury/sadistic (Muted Sadistic): Engages in "sham" sadism (i.e., behaviors and fantasies that reflect sadist acts, but do not result in serious injury), but again, physical injury is only utilized to the extent necessary to gain victim compliance. Generally, the level of planning of the offenses is moderate.

(9) Low contact/high physical injury/non–sadistic (Non-sadistic Aggressive): Offenders inflict serious injury to their victims, but do not show a preference for sadism. Generally, the level of planning of the offenses is low.

(10) Low contact/high physical injury/sadistic (Sadistic): Engages primarily in sadistic acts with victims, often resulting in a serious physical injury. Sexual acts are often symbolic and, as a result, require a high degree of planning.

Pragmatic issues with this typology have also been identified. Findings from one study, for example, suggest that such statistically-derived typologies can often yield certain categories that are not clinically meaningful (Hall, 1996). Furthermore, it has been noted that the detailed information required to assign offenders to various categories is often not available to clinicians (Fisher & Mair, 1998). Finally, the exclusion criteria for this typology, which eliminate offenders who have committed incest-only offenses, greatly reduce the utility of this model to clinicians who deal regularly with such offenders (Bickley & Beech, 2001).

# VICTIMS

It should be clear by now that the sexual abuse of children is a serious social problem. The purpose of this section is to discuss child sexual abuse from the victim's perspective, specifically focusing on the myriad of consequences facing child sexual-abuse victims. Research shows that the consequences of child sexual abuse are far reaching, often extending into the child's adult life.

## Consequences of Child Sexual Abuse

In the late 1970s, a national conference on the sexual abuse of children was held in Washington D.C. The conference consisted of professionals from different disciplines, including medicine, psychiatry, children's advocacy, and social work. One speaker, a professional who had worked on issues of child sexual abuse (incest specifically), reported that according to his unpublished evidence, "some incest may be a positive, healthy experience or at worst dull and neutral" (Green, 1980, p. 1). This statement reveals another common myth pertaining to child sexual abuse victims—that harm done to the victim is minimal.

Much clinical and empirical research has overwhelmingly pointed to a multitude of negative effects of child sexual abuse. The extent and magnitude to which children are affected by abuse varies based on many factors, including the age of abuse onset, the relationship of the child to the offender, the duration of the abuse (e.g., one-time-only versus chronic), the child's support system, and whether the child disclosed the incident(s). As Briere and Elliott (1994) observed, "there is no single universal or uniform impact of sexual abuse, and no certainty that any given person will develop a posttraumatic response to sexual abuse" (p. 62).

Researchers and clinicians have long noted the emotional distress felt by many victims of child sexual abuse. Depression is the most commonly reported consequence, with one study finding that abused patients were four times more likely to have depressive symptoms, compared to non-abused patients (Browne & Finkelhor, 1986). Sexually victimized children are also at high risk of developing anxiety disorders (including panic attacks, phobias, and post-traumatic stress disorder) immediately following their abuse, as well as years later (Valente, 2005). In an attempt to cope with the chronic trauma of sexual abuse, victims may engage in avoidant behaviors, including:

- **Substance abuse and addiction**: Many studies have tested the association between sexual abuse during childhood and later substance abuse during adolescence and adulthood. One study found that adults who reported child sexual abuse were 1.5 to 2 times as likely to have alcohol problems, severe alcohol dependence, drug problems, or severe drug dependence, compared to adults who did not experience child sexual abuse (Molnar, Buka, & Kessler, 2001). Research has also underscored the importance of addressing unresolved traumas involving child sexual abuse with substance-abuse treatment patients. Not addressing the abuse is associated with rapid substance-abuse relapse (Rohsenow, Corbett, & Devine, 1988).

- **Suicide**: Victims of child sexual abuse are at increased risk for self-injury and suicide. Research has revealed that the frequency of suicidal ideation and actual attempts are significantly greater for child sexual-abuse victims during adolescence and young adulthood, compared to non-victims (Silverman, Reinherz, & Giaconia, 1996). Recent estimates reveal that those with histories of victimization are approximately 2.5 times more likely to attempt suicide than those not victimized (Devries et al., 2014).

- **Tension-reducing behaviors**: Certain behaviors reported by victims of child sexual abuse can be seen as fulfilling a need to numb the pain of unresolved trauma. Such activities are often characterized as "acting out," and can include risky sexual behaviors, eating disorders, and self-mutilation. Adolescents with a history of child sexual abuse often report inconsistent condom use, less impulse control, and less knowledge of HIV/AIDS than their non-abused counterparts, effectively putting them at greater risk of HIV infection (Brown, Lourie, Zlotnick, & Cohn, 2000). Studies that have examined the association between child sexual abuse and eating disorders (e.g., anorexia nervosa, bulimia, and binge eating) have found an association, although studies have generally reported the associations are weak, at best (Smolak & Murnen, 2001).

Researchers have found that child sexual abuse predicts a host of psychological problems during adulthood for both male and female victims, including anxiety, depression, dissociation, and anger/irritability (Briere & Elliott, 2003). Additionally, situational characteristics of the abuse were found to intensify the symptoms. Sexual abuse that occurred at a later age, involved multiple incidents and/or multiple abusers, and involved oral, anal, or vaginal penetration led to even more severe negative consequences during adulthood.

Research has also demonstrated that early child sexual abuse can shape dysfunctional sexual behaviors later in life. One study showed that child sexual abuse predicted dysfunctional sexual behaviors during adulthood, such as using sex as a bargaining/negotiating tool, having multiple sexual partners, and sex with strangers (Briere & Runtz, 1990). There is also evidence for the *revictimization hypothesis*, which predicts that individuals (namely, women) who are child sexual abuse victims have an increased risk of assaults during adulthood.

One study of adult, female child sexual-abuse victims found support for the revictimization hypothesis. Child sexual-abuse victims were significantly more likely than their non-victim counterparts to have experienced unwanted sexual experiences (from fondling to violent sexual assault), minor and severe physical abuse, and psychological maltreatment (Messman-Moore & Long, 2000).

## Barriers to Disclosure

Almost all published studies on disclosure of child sexual abuse show that the vast majority of victims who disclose their abuse to officials delay the disclosure, and many children do not disclose their abuse at all. Summit's (1983) *child sexual abuse accommodation syndrome* provides one of the earliest explanations for delays in disclosing child sexual abuse, and there are five highly inter-related dynamics:

1) **Secrecy**: The abuse occurs when the victim and offender are alone, and the offender encourages the victim to maintain secrecy.

2) **Helplessness**: Children are obedient to adults and are naturally inclined to obey an offender who insists on secrecy.

3) **Entrapment and Accommodation**: Once the child is helplessly entrenched in an abusive situation, he or she assumes responsibility for the abuse and begins to dissociate (i.e., mentally disconnect or "check out") from it.

4) **Delayed Disclosure**: Due to lengthy periods between initial abuse and disclosure to authorities, many victims' disclosures are subsequently questioned and scrutinized.

5) **Retraction**: Facing disbelief, lack of emotional support, and sometimes disappointment and anger from officials, family members, and peers, victims might retract their disclosures.

Summit's work was met with initial criticism in that it was based on anecdotal rather than systematic evidence. Recent research, however, has acknowledged that closer relationships between child sexual-abuse victims and offenders are associated with longer delays in reporting and lower disclosure rates (London, Bruck, Wright, & Ceci, 2008). Children who are abused by parents are more likely to have lower disclosure rates and higher recantation rates than other abuse victims (Lippert, Cross, Jones, & Walsh, 2010). Grooming by child sexual abusers also allows for delayed disclosure and non-disclosure. As discussed previously, sex offenders who commit crimes against children have emphasized that they do not commit isolated assaults against their victims, but rather, seduce their victims over time (Smallbone & Wortley, 2001). Abuse can be a process that requires careful planning and preparation to establish trust and gain cooperation of the victims.

Some researchers have speculated that delayed disclosure and nondisclosure are rooted in victims' beliefs that they have granted permission for more intrusive sexual contact after offenders begin the process of desensitization (Kaufman et al., 1998). It is also argued that reasons for non-disclosure do not vary much for victims of familial abuse and extra-familial abuse. In cases of intra-familial abuse, offenders exploit family loyalties, whereas in extra-familial abuse cases, offenders take steps to become like a family member (Lyon & Ahern, 2010). Regardless of the relationship, the victim feels helpless in reporting the abuse.

It is a common myth that when children disclose sexual abuse, they will provide a clear, detailed account of the incident(s). This is not consistent with research on disclosure. Similar to the grooming process, a victim's disclosure unfolds gradually and may be presented as a series of hints (Canadian Centre for Child Protection, 2014). Children may begin by implying that something *may* have happened to them without directly stating they were sexually abused. This is a method of testing the reaction of the child's confidante. The child is ready, and depending on the initial reaction of the confidante, he or she might follow up with a larger hint.

## CRIMINAL JUSTICE RESPONSE TO CHILD SEXUAL ABUSE

### Reporting Child Sexual Abuse

It has been estimated that approximately 60% to 70% of adults who experienced child sexual abuse never reported their abuse when they were children. Only a small minority (10% to 18%) *ever* reported their abuse to officials (London, Bruck, Ceci & Shuman, 2005). Therefore, what is known about the criminal justice response to child sexual abuse, from reporting to investigation to prosecution, is based on a minority of all cases. All U.S. states have statutes identifying persons who are required to report suspected sexual abuse to an appropriate agency, such as Child Protective Services (CPS), law enforcement, or a state-operated child abuse reporting hotline. Mandatory reporters are customarily individuals who are in frequent contact with children, including social workers, school personnel, medical examiners, mental health professionals, and law enforcement officials. Other professionals are also identified as mandated reporters in certain states. For example, film processors and developers are mandated to report child sexual abuse in 12 states. Animal control and humane officers are mandated reporters in seven states, and members of the clergy are required to report in 27 states (Child Welfare Information Gateway, 2014). In 18 states, *any person* who suspects child sexual abuse is required to report, regardless of their profession.

The requirement for mandated reporters to report a suspected case of child sexual abuse varies from state to state and depends on a number of factors, including the ages of both parties involved in the sexual act and indications of coercion, bribery and/or intimidation. For example, in California, if a child is 14–15 years of age and the sexual partner is 13 years of age or younger, a report is mandated. If a child is 14–15 years old and the sexual partner is 14–20 years old *and* there is no indication of abuse *and* there is no evidence of an exploitative relationship (i.e., coercion, bribery and/or intimidation has not occurred), this is not a mandatory report, and reporters have the latitude to exercise clinical judgment as to whether they will inform the authorities. Reports of child sexual abuse are generally made to law enforcement officials or CPS. Generally, CPS handles child sexual-abuse issues occurring within the home, and law enforcement officials work on extra-familial cases.

An investigation is conducted once a report has been filed. States, counties, and even cities and townships vary considerably in how investigations are structured. They may involve CPS caseworkers, law enforcement officials, physicians, mental health providers, victim advocates and other professionals. Many state statutes require a joint CPS–law enforcement investigation for child sexual-abuse cases. *Joint investigations*, which involve inter-agency cooperation and shared information between law enforcement and child protective services, have become increasingly common in child sexual-abuse investigations. In comparison to independent investigations, which consist of various agencies working separately from one another, the benefits of joint investigations are many, including more offender confessions, more victim corroboration, more substantiated reports, more criminal prosecutions, and more guilty pleas (Tjaden & Anhalt, 1994). More detail on investigative and forensic procedures is discussed in Chapter 11.

## Prosecutorial Issues: The Role of Child Testimony

Similar to rape and sexual assault, child sexual abuse mostly occurs behind closed doors and without any eyewitnesses. Because of the secretive nature of child sexual abuse, successful prosecution often rests solely on the testimony of the child victim. The role of the child victim providing testimony in court has become especially important in the past ten years in light of the U.S. Supreme Court case *Crawford v. Washington* (2004), which altered prosecution of child sexual-abuse cases. The decision effectively barred **testimonial hearsay** (evidence that is gathered or collected by state agents for the purpose of prosecution) from entering into criminal trials as evidence. For example, if a law enforcement officer interviews a child sexual-abuse victim and that child becomes unavailable for a trial, calling in the officer to court to report to the jury what was said would constitute testimonial hearsay. The *Crawford* decision, therefore, requires the physical presence of child victims in court proceedings, making it difficult, if not impossible, to prosecute cases in which the child witness initially reported the crime, but later is afraid or intimidated by the prospect of testifying.

This has led to the reversal of some convictions for sex crimes committed against children. In *Pitts v. State* (2005), the four-year-old victim made consistent statements to a physician, a psychologist, and a forensic interviewer in videotaped interviews revealing sexual abuse. The child also disclosed having seen the defendant sexually abuse the child's cousin, who herself confirmed abuse in a videotaped interview. The state presented both girls at trial, but they appeared too upset and frightened to answer questions and were declared unavailable. The videotaped interviews of both children were admitted, and the conviction was reversed on appeal because the interviews were deemed testimonial hearsay.

Similarly, in *People v. Sharp* (2005), a five-year-old victim was unavailable to testify in court because she suffered enduring trauma from her abuse. The trial court admitted a videotaped statement in which the child disclosed to a forensic interviewer that her father sexually abused her, which was consistent with what she previously told her mother. Again, the appellate court reversed the conviction because the statement was testimonial hearsay. The issue is not that victims are viewed as somehow less credible or believable unless they testify in person. Rather, the issue is procedural in that defendants accused of child sexual abuse are denied their constitutional right to confront and cross-examine witnesses.

Although experienced prosecutors have acknowledged that convictions can be obtained solely on the testimony of child victims (American Prosecutors Research Institute, 2004), the testimony is less persuasive without corroborating evidence, such as developmentally unusual sexual behavior by the victim, unusual psychological symptoms (e.g., severe and recurrent nightmares), medical evidence indicative of sexual abuse, eyewitnesses to the alleged crime, offender confessions, or additional complaints against the suspect that confirm the victim's testimony. Nevertheless, research has shown that child sexual-abuse cases with no evidence supporting the child's testimony can and do result in successful prosecution of offenders (Walsh, Jones, Cross, & Lippert, 2010). There are many barriers—legal, social, and cultural—that preclude acceptance of child testimony in court proceedings. This especially affects very young victims of sexual abuse.

## Very Young Victims

Research has consistently shown that child sexual-abuse victims' first unwanted sexual experiences occur around age ten (Finkelhor, 1979; Godbout, Briere, Sabourin, & Lussier, 2010). Child sexual abuse, however, involves victims of all ages. Very young children, from infancy to approximately age six, are at a significant disadvantage with respect to successful prosecution and adjudication of suspected sexual abuse. These reports are by far the least likely to be substantiated. One clinician provides the following example to demonstrate the difficulty in substantiating a child sexual-abuse case involving a two-year-old female victim:

A two-year-old child was in a domestic violence shelter with her mother. The mother was badly beaten by an alcoholic father. When the mother changed the child's diaper, she grabbed her vulva and cried "Daddy hurt butt! Daddy hurt butt!" The child was also observed to be nervous and anxious around her father and had trouble sleeping after a visit. Law enforcement officers and child protective services conducted a joint investigation but could not substantiate sexual abuse. The child was eventually returned to the father for unsupervised visitation.

(Hewitt, 1999, p. 1)

Scenarios like this are all too common for very young victims of sexual abuse. The difficulties in substantiating sexual abuse of very young victims point to several legal and extralegal factors. First, the likelihood of detecting diagnostic physical evidence in these cases is low (Heger, Ticson, Velasquez, & Bernier, 2002). Many types of sexual abuse do cause injuries, but such injuries can heal completely by the time the child is brought for a medical examination (McCann, Miyamoto, Boyle, & Rogers, 2007). Second, very young children may have difficulty in communicating abusive situations. Preverbal children, for example, may use what few verbal skills they have in combination with other gestures and behaviors that are suggestive of abuse (American Prosecutors Research Institute, 2004). There is a low likelihood that such communications will withstand legal scrutiny. Third, it has been argued that very young children are unduly suggestive, meaning they may be misled to report inaccurate information. Some earlier critics portrayed the prosecution of child sexual-abuse cases as an unethical process, led by corrupt professionals on a witch-hunt for false allegations (Gardner, 1991). There has never been evidence of such a witch-hunt. There is evidence, however, that some well-intentioned therapists, law enforcement officials, attorneys, and social workers have used interview techniques that could distort children's memories. Proper interviewing of vulnerable victims is explored further in Chapter 9.

By and large, successful prosecution, specifically in cases involving the youngest victims, depends on the quality of the verbal evidence and the effectiveness of the child victim's testimony (De Jong & Rose, 1991). It has been established that older children are more likely to disclose sexual abuse, as well as provide a more detailed disclosure of it, compared to younger children (London et al., 2005). Before a child can testify in court, the judge must be convinced that the child possesses *testimonial competence*. Testimonial competence requires basic cognitive and moral capacities. The child must be able to understand the difference between a lie and the truth and appreciate the need to tell the truth in court. Moreover, usable testimony also depends on a child's understanding and memory of the abuse, ability to describe what happened, and concerns about the consequences.

In most states, attorneys and judges can inquire about children's understanding of truth and lies (Myers, 2005). For example, in California, witnesses are disqualified from testifying if they are "incapable of understanding the duty of a witness to tell the truth" (California Evidence Code, 2010, § 701, subds. (a)(2)). As a result, child witnesses are likely to confront questions about their understanding of truth and lies and the importance of telling the truth. Their responses may be used as a prerequisite to allowing their testimony or as a means of evaluating their credibility. For school-age children and adolescents, this is usually not a serious barrier to prosecution. For very young victims with limited verbal communication abilities, however, this can be an insurmountable obstacle.

In the past ten years, the U.S. Supreme Court has increased the significance of oath-taking competency requirements for child witnesses. Under the law in most jurisdictions, children demonstrate oath-taking competency if they understand that "truth" refers to factual statements and that one ought to tell the truth. The ways young children understand abstract concepts, such as truth and honesty, often belie some jurisdictions' strict-oath competency requirements. Research has shown that young children conceptually understand notions of "truth" and "lie," despite their inability to successfully articulate them. Researchers have found that maltreated preschool-aged children (ages four to six years) successfully accepted true statements and rejected false statements before they were able to label true and false statements as "truth" and "lie" or as "good" and "bad" (Lyon, Carrick, & Quas, 2010). This finding is in line with previous research that has found that young children were able to label statements as "truth" or "lie" before they were able to provide a definition or explain the difference between the two (Lyon & Saywitz, 1999). Taken together, this means that children can and do accept true propositions and reject false ones even though they are incapable of articulating their understanding of truth and lies.

If some form of an oath is required, many children who reliably accept true statements and reject false statements will nevertheless be incapable of promising to "tell the truth" because they lack a technical understanding of the kinds of statements to which "the truth" refers. These children appreciate the importance of speaking truthfully but are unable to comment prospectively on whether they would do so and thus would be incapable of promising to tell the truth (Lyon et al., 2010).

Another significant barrier to prosecution of child sexual-abuse cases is the common belief that a child will be further traumatized by the legal process which, depending on the nature of the charges, can be a lengthy process, requiring the child to repeatedly face and relive trauma (Walsh et al., 2008). This is intensified when the child victim is related to his or her offender and may lack familial support. Though some evidence suggests that longer court processes increase anxiety and distress in child victims, thereby hindering their recovery process (Runyan et al., 1988), the negative effects appear to be short-lived. By the time child sexual-abuse cases are resolved, behavioral adjustment of children who testify is similar to that of children who do not testify (Goodman et al., 1992).

## Factors Affecting Criminal Trial Proceedings

Child sexual-abuse cases have one of the lowest conviction rates of all types of crime. There are many factors that can influence whether a prosecutor will accept a case for prosecution, as well as verdict decisions. In this section, we examine the impact of medical and behavioral evidence on prosecutorial and jury decision-making in child sexual-abuse cases.

## Medical Evidence

Next to an offender's confession, medical evidence of physical markers of abuse is considered one of the best forms of evidence. Often, jurors enter into a sexual abuse criminal trial with the expectation that some form of medical evidence will be presented (Werner & Werner, 2008). Such evidence is not available in most cases. When evidence is available, it may not prove whether a child was abused. In a study of 236 sexually abused children, researchers reviewed medical records to determine the frequency of abnormal findings (e.g., absence of hymenal tissue, hymenal lacerations, scarring of anal sphincter tissue) as a result of genital or anal penetration. Examination findings revealed that 28% of cases were rated as normal, 49% were nonspecific, 9% were suspicious, and 14% were rated as abnormal or indicative of abuse/penetration (Adams, Harper, Knudson, & Revilla, 1994).

The association between the presence of medical evidence in child sexual-abuse cases and the case outcome is disputable, with evidence on both sides. In one of the first studies of decision-making in child sexual-abuse cases, researchers concluded that medical evidence nearly doubled the chances of a conviction (Bradshaw & Marks, 1990). Subsequent research has shown that the presence of physical evidence can impact prosecutorial decision-making, in that cases with medical evidence of abuse are more likely to be prosecuted than cases without medical evidence (Brewer, Rowe, & Brewer, 1997). In other recent research, physical evidence was found to be neither predictive, nor essential, for conviction of 115 child sexual-abuse cases that went to criminal trial (De Jong & Rose, 1991). Furthermore, other researchers found that medical evidence was not a significant predictor of whether a prosecutor would accept a child sexual-abuse case for prosecution (Walsh et al., 2008). Unlike medical evidence, behavioral evidence has demonstrated a strong and consistent association with trial outcomes.

## Behavioral Evidence

The way victims behave in the courtroom may have a substantial impact on the trial outcome. One study found that too little or too much emotion from the alleged child victim negatively affected credibility in the eyes of the mock jurors (Golding, Fryman, Marsil, & Yozwiak, 2003). In this study, the alleged offender was more likely to be convicted when the child was teary-eyed versus when the child was calm or hysterical. The age of the victim is important. Research has found that older child victims (12–17) appear to be most emotionally impacted by the court process, followed by 7–11-year olds, then 4–6-year olds. In one study of juror perceptions of child sexual-abuse victims, 7 to 11-year olds were seen as more sexually naïve and, therefore, more credible, compared to victims ages 12 and older (Bottoms, Davis, & Epstein, 2004). Taken together, this suggests that mid-adolescent children are likely to be viewed as most credible to jurors, provided that they present as emotional, but still in control. Certain victim behavioral indicators (such as sleeping difficulties, social withdrawal, depression, and suicidal ideation) also have been found to increase the chances of a guilty verdict (Lewis, Klettke, & Day, 2014), while simultaneously finding that medical evidence did not impact case dispositions.

Earlier, we discussed the many impacts of sexual abuse on child victims. Tension-reducing activities, such as self-injury, running away, risky sexual behaviors, and engaging in criminal activity, have been well documented in studies investigating the effects of child sexual abuse. Victims who engage in such activities may be viewed as less credible to jurors. One study found that when child victims showed evidence of destructive behavior or acting in a way that ran counter to social norms, a jury was more likely to discredit their allegations and return a not-guilty verdict (Lewis et al., 2014).

## CONCLUSION

Child sexual abuse is a serious social problem that can have serious lifelong consequences. Although concern over the issue has ebbed and flowed, contemporary awareness of widespread sexual abuse of children dates back to the late 1970s. Victims of child sexual abuse vary greatly with respect to the effect these experiences have on them. Some victims do not suffer any immediate or long-term consequences, while others suffer a host of short- and long-term negative physical and mental-health problems, substance abuse, and possible revictimization later in life. Similar to rape and sexual assault, child sexual abuse is underreported, and many factors affect trial proceedings for cases that are prosecuted.

## REVIEW POINTS

- Not all child sexual abusers are pedophiles. Child sexual abuse is legally defined as engaging in inappropriate sexual acts with a child, whereas pedophilia is based on clinical diagnosis.

- Most victims of childhood sexual abuse do not go on to become child molesters. However, sexual victimization as a child, if accompanied by other factors, such as the co-occurrence of other types of abuse, may contribute to a victim's later emergence as a child sexual-abuse offender.

- Often, the successful investigation, prosecution, and conviction of guilty child sexual abusers depends on the child's testimony. It is estimated that a small minority of victimizations (10%–18%) is reported to officials.

- Many factors may account for child sexual-abuse case dispositions. Behavioral evidence appears to be a better predictor of case outcome compared to medical/physical evidence.

## REFERENCES

Abel, G. G., & Harlow, N. (2001). *The stop child molestation book: What ordinary people can do in their everyday lives to save three million children*. Xlibris Corporation.
Adams, J. A., Harper, K., Knudson, S., & Revilla, J. (1994). Examination findings in legally confirmed child sexual abuse: It's normal to be normal. *Pediatrics, 94*(3), 310–317.

Aebi, M., Landolt, M. A., Mueller-Pfeiffer, C., Schnyder, U., Maier, T., & Mohler-Kuo, M. (2015). Testing the "sexually abused-abuser hypothesis" in adolescents: A population-based study. *Archives of Sexual Behavior, 44*(8), 2189–2199.

Alaggia, R. (2010). An ecological analysis of child sexual abuse disclosure: Considerations for child and adolescent mental health. *Journal of the Canadian Academy of Child and Adolescent Psychiatry, 19*(1), 32–39.

Amelung, T., Kuhle, L. F., Konrad, A., Pauls, A., & Beier, K. M. (2012). Androgen deprivation therapy of self-identifying, help-seeking pedophiles in the Dunkelfeld. *International Journal of Law and Psychiatry, 35*(3), 176–184.

American Prosecutors Research Institute. (2004). *Investigation and prosecution of child abuse.* Thousand Oaks, CA: Sage.

American Psychiatric Association. (2013). *Diagnostic and Statistical Manual of Mental Disorders (DSM-5®).* American Psychiatric Publishing.

Beauregard, E., Proulx, J., Rossmo, K., Leclerc, B., & Allaire, J. F. (2007). Script analysis of the hunting process of serial sex offenders. *Criminal Justice and Behavior, 34*(8), 1069–1084.

Beauregard, E., Rossmo, D. K., & Proulx, J. (2007). A descriptive model of the hunting process of serial sex offenders: A rational choice perspective. *Journal of Family Violence, 22*(6), 449–463.

Beckett, K. (1996). Culture and the politics of signification: The case of child sexual abuse. *Social Problems, 43*(1), 57–76.

Bell, M. C. (2008). Grassroots death sentences? The social movement for capital child rape laws. *Journal of Criminal Law and Criminology, 98*(1), 1–30.

Berliner, L., & Conte, J. R. (1990). The process of victimization: The victims' perspective. *Child Abuse & Neglect, 14*(1), 29–40.

Bickley, J., & Beech, A. R. (2001). Classifying child abusers: Its relevance to theory and clinical practice. *International Journal of Offender Therapy and Comparative Criminology, 45*(1), 51–69.

Bottoms, B. L., Davis, S. L., & Epstein, M. A. (2004). Effects of victim and defendant race on jurors' decisions in child-sexual abuse cases. *Journal of Applied Social Psychology, 34*(1), 1–33.

Bradley, A. R., & Wood, J. M. (1996). How do children tell? The disclosure process in child sexual abuse. *Child Abuse & Neglect, 20*(9), 881–891.

Bradshaw, T. L., & Marks, A. E. (1990). Beyond a reasonable doubt: Factors that influence the legal disposition of child sexual-abuse cases. *Crime & Delinquency, 36*(2), 276–285.

Brewer, K. D., Rowe, D. M., & Brewer, D. D. (1997). Factors related to prosecution of child sexual-abuse cases. *Journal of Child Sexual Abuse, 6*(1), 91–111.

Briere, J. N., & Elliott, D. M. (1994). Immediate and long-term impacts of child sexual abuse. *The Future of Children/Center for the Future of Children, the David and Lucile Packard Foundation, 4*(2), 54–69.

Briere, J., & Elliott, D. M. (2003). Prevalence and psychological sequelae of self-reported childhood physical and sexual abuse in a general population sample of men and women. *Child Abuse & Neglect, 27*(10), 1205–1222.

Briere, J., & Runtz, M. (1990). Differential adult symptomatology associated with three types of child abuse histories. *Child Abuse & Neglect, 14*(3), 357–364.

Brown, L. K., Lourie, K. J., Zlotnick, C., & Cohn, J. (2000). Impact of sexual abuse on the HIV-risk-related behavior of adolescents in intensive psychiatric treatment. *The American Journal of Psychiatry, 157*(9), 1413–1415.

Browne, A., & Finkelhor, D. (1986). Impact of child sexual abuse: A review of the research. *Psychological Bulletin, 99*(1), 66–77.

Bruck, M., Ceci, S. J., & Hembrooke, H. (2002). The nature of children's true and false narratives. *Developmental Review, 22*(3), 520–554.

Burton, D. L. (2008). An exploratory evaluation of the contribution of personality and childhood sexual victimization to the development of sexually abusive behavior. *Sexual Abuse: A Journal of Research and Treatment, 20*(1), 102–115.

Caffey, J. (1946). Multiple fractures in the long bones of infants suffering from chronic subdural hematoma. *The American Journal of Roentgenology and Radium Therapy, 56*(2), 163–173.

California Evidence Code. (2010) § 701, subds. (a)(2)

Camilleri, J. A., & Quinsey, V. L. (2008). Pedophilia: Assessment and treatment. In D. R. Laws & W. O'Donohue (Eds.), *Sexual deviance: Theory, assessment, and treatment*, vol. 2 (pp. 183–212). New York: Guilford Press.

Canadian Centre for Child Protection, Inc. (2014). Child sexual abuse: It is your business. Winnipeg, Manitoba, Canada: Canadian Centre for Child Protection, Inc. Retrieved January 1, 2016 from https://www.cybertip.ca/pdfs/C3P_ChildSexualAbuse_ItIsYourBusiness_en.pdf

Child Welfare Information Gateway. (2014). Mandatory reporters of child abuse and neglect. Washington, DC: U.S. Department of Health and Human Services, Children's Bureau.

Craven, S., Brown, S., & Gilchrist, E. (2006). Sexual grooming of children: Review of literature and theoretical considerations. *Journal of Sexual Aggression, 12*(3), 287–299.

De Francis, V. (1969). *Protecting the child victim of sex crimes committed by adults: Final report*. The American Humane Association, Children's Division.

De Jong, A. R., & Rose, M. (1991). Legal proof of child sexual abuse in the absence of physical evidence. *Pediatrics, 88*(3), 506–511.

Devries, K. M., Mak, J. Y., Child, J. C., Falder, G., Bacchus, L. J., Astbury, J., & Watts, C. H. (2014). Childhood sexual abuse and suicidal behavior: A meta-analysis. *Pediatrics, 133*(5), e1331-e1344.

Elliott, M., Browne, K., & Kilcoyne, J. (1995). Child sexual abuse prevention: What offenders tell us. *Child Abuse & Neglect, 19*(5), 579–594.

Finkelhor, D. (1979). *Sexually victimised children*. New York: Free Press.

Finkelhor, D. (1984). *Child sexual abuse: New theory and research*. New York: Free Press.

Fisher, D., & Mair, G. (1998). *A review of classification systems for sex offenders*. London: Great Britain Home Office Research Development and Statistics Directorate.

Gardner, R. A. (1991). *Sex abuse hysteria: Salem witch trials revisited*. Cresskill, NJ: Creative Therapeutics.

Garland, D. (2001). *The culture of control: Crime and social order in contemporary society*. Chicago: University of Chicago Press.

Gilbert, R., Kemp, A., Thoburn, J., Sidebotham, P., Radford, L., Glaser, D., & MacMillan, H. L. (2009). Recognising and responding to child maltreatment. *The Lancet, 373*(9658), 167–180.

Godbout, N., Briere, J., Sabourin, S., & Lussier, Y. (2014). Child sexual abuse and subsequent relational and personal functioning: The role of parental support. *Child Abuse & Neglect, 38*(2), 317–325.

Golding, J. M., Fryman, H. M., Marsil, D. F., & Yozwiak, J. A. (2003). Big girls don't cry: The effect of child witness demeanor on juror decisions in a child sexual-abuse trial. *Child Abuse & Neglect, 27*(11), 1311–1321.

Goldman, J. D., & Padayachi, U. K. (2000). Some methodological problems in estimating incidence and prevalence in child sexual-abuse research. *Journal of Sex Research, 37*(4), 305–314.

Goodman, G. S., Taub, E. P., Jones D. P. H., England, P., Port, L. K., Rudy, L., Prado, L., Myers, J. E. B., & Melton, G. B. (1992). Testifying in criminal court: Emotional effects on child sexual assault victims. *Monographs of the Society for Research in Child Development, 57*(5), i–159. http://doi.org/10.2307/1166127

Gordon, L. (1988). *Heroes of their own lives: The politics and history of family violence: Boston 1880–1960*. Penguin Group USA.

Green, A. H. (1980). *Child maltreatment: A handbook for mental health and child care professionals*. Jason Aronson.

Groth, A. N., Hobson, W. F., & Gary, T. S. (1982). The child molester: Clinical observations. *Journal of Social Work & Human Sexuality, 1*(1–2), 129–144.

Hall, G. C. N. (1996). *Theory-based assessment, treatment, and prevention of sexual aggression*. Oxford: Oxford University Press.

Hanson, R. K., & Bussiere, M. T. (1998). Predicting relapse: a meta-analysis of sexual offender recidivism studies. *Journal of Consulting and Clinical Psychology, 66*(2), 348–362.

Heger, A., Ticson, L., Velasquez, O., & Bernier, R. (2002). Children referred for possible sexual abuse: Medical findings in 2384 children. *Child Abuse & Neglect, 26*(6), 645–659.

Hewitt, S. K. (1999). *Assessing allegations of sexual abuse in preschool children: Understanding small voices* (No. 22). Thousand Oaks, CA: Sage.

Holmes, S. T., & Holmes, R. M. (2008). *Sex crimes: Patterns and behavior.* Sage.

Jahnke, S., & Hoyer, J. (2013). Stigmatization of people with pedophilia: A blind spot in stigma research. *International Journal of Sexual Health, 25*(3), 169–184.

Jenkins, S. (2002). Are children protected in the family court? A perspective from Western Australia. *Australian and New Zealand Journal of Family Therapy, 23*(3), 145–152.

Jespersen, A. F., Lalumière, M. L., & Seto, M. C. (2009). Sexual abuse history among adult sex offenders and non-sex offenders: A meta-analysis. *Child Abuse & Neglect, 33*(3), 179–192.

Johnston, F. A., & Johnston, S. A. (1997). A cognitive approach to validation of the fixated–regressed typology of child molesters. *Journal of Clinical Psychology, 53*(4), 361–368.

Jones, D. P., & McGraw, J. M. (1987). Reliable and fictitious accounts of sexual abuse to children. *Journal of Interpersonal Violence, 2*(1), 27–45.

Kaufman, K. L., Holmberg, J. K, Orts, K. A., McCrady, F. E., Rotzien, A. L., Daleiden, E. L, & Hilliker, D. R. (1998). Factors influencing sexual offenders' modus operandi: An examination of victim-offender relatedness and age. *Child Maltreatment, 3*, 349–361.

Kempe, C. H., Silverman, F. N., Steele, B. F., Droegemueller, W., Silver, M. K. (1962). The battered-child syndrome. *Journal of the American Medical Association, 181*(1), 17–24.

Kitzinger, J. (2004). Media coverage of sexual violence against women and children. In K. Ross & C. M. Byerly (Eds.), *Women and media: International perspectives* (pp. 13–38). Malden, MA: Blackwell.

Knight, R. A., Carter, D. L., & Prentky, R. A. (1989). A system for the classification of child molesters: Reliability and application. *Journal of Interpersonal Violence, 4*(1), 3–23.

LaFond, J. Q. (2005). *Preventing sexual violence: How society should cope with sex offenders.* Washington, DC: American Psychological Association.

Lalor, K., & McElvaney, R. (2010). Child sexual abuse, links to later sexual exploitation/high-risk sexual behavior, and prevention/treatment programs. *Trauma, Violence, & Abuse, 11*(4), 159–177.

Lanning, K. V. (1986). *Child molesters: A behavioral analysis for law enforcement.* Quantico, VA: U.S. Department of Justice, Federal Bureau of Investigation.

Lanning, K. V. (1992). *Child molesters: A behavioral analysis* (3rd ed.). Alexandria, VA: National Center for Missing & Exploited Children.

Lanning, K. V. (2001). *Child molesters: A behavioral analysis* (4th ed.). Washington, DC: National Center for Missing & Exploited Children.

Lanning, K. V. (2010). *Child molesters: A behavioral analysis for professionals investigating the sexual exploitation of children.* National Center for Missing & Exploited Children with Office of Juvenile Justice and Delinquency Prevention.

Lewis, T. E., Klettke, B., & Day, A. (2014). The influence of medical and behavioral evidence on conviction rates in cases of child sexual abuse. *Journal of Child Sexual Abuse, 23*(4), 431–441.

Lippert, T., Cross, T. P., Jones, L., & Walsh, W. (2010). Suspect confession of child sexual abuse to investigators. *Child Maltreatment, 15*(2), 161–170.

London, K., Bruck, M., Ceci, S. J., & Shuman, D. W. (2005). Disclosure of child sexual abuse: What does the research tell us about the ways that children tell? *Psychology, Public Policy, and Law, 11*(1), 194–226.

London, K., Bruck, M., Wright, D. B., & Ceci, S. J. (2008). Review of the contemporary literature on how children report sexual abuse to others: Findings, methodological issues, and implications for forensic interviewers. *Memory, 16*(1), 29–47.

Lyon, T. D. (2007). False denials: Overcoming methodological biases in abuse disclosure research. In M. Pipe, M. Lamb, Y. Orbach, & A. Cederborg (Eds.), *Disclosing abuse: Delays, denials, retractions and incomplete accounts* (pp. 41–62). Mahwah, NJ: Erlbaum.

Lyon, T. D., & Ahern, E. C. (2010). Disclosure of child sexual abuse. In J. Myers (Ed.), *The APSAC handbook on child maltreatment* (3rd ed., pp. 233–252). Newbury Park, CA: Sage.

Lyon, T. D., & Saywitz, K. J. (1999). Young maltreated children's competence to take the oath. *Applied Developmental Science, 3*(1), 16–27.

Lyon, T. D., Carrick, N., & Quas, J. A. (2010). Young children's competency to take the oath: Effects of task, maltreatment, and age. *Law and Human Behavior, 34*(2), 141–149.

Malloy, L. C., Lyon, T. D., & Quas, J. A. (2007). Filial dependency and recantation of child sexual abuse allegations. *Journal of the American Academy of Child & Adolescent Psychiatry, 46*(2), 162–170.

Mauer, M. (2002). State sentencing reforms: Is the "get tough" era coming to a close? *Federal Sentencing Reporter, 15*(1), 50–52.

McCann, J., Miyamoto, S., Boyle, C., & Rogers, K. (2007). Healing of hymenal injuries in prepubertal and adolescent girls: A descriptive study. *Pediatrics, 119*(5), e1094-e1106.

Messman-Moore, T. L., & Long, P. J. (2000). Child sexual abuse and revictimization in the form of adult sexual abuse, adult physical abuse, and adult psychological maltreatment. *Journal of Interpersonal Violence, 15*(5), 489–502.

Molnar, B. E., Buka, S. L., & Kessler, R. C. (2001). Child sexual abuse and subsequent psychopathology: Results from the National Comorbidity Survey. *American Journal of Public Health, 91*(5), 753–760.

Myers, J. E. B. (2005). *Myers on evidence in child, domestic, and elder abuse cases.* Aspen Publishers.

Myers J. E. B. (2008). A short history of child protection in America. *Family Law Quarterly, 42*(3), 449–463.

Oates, R. K., Jones, D. P., Denson, D., Sirotnak, A., Gary, N., & Krugman, R. D. (2000). Erroneous concerns about child sexual abuse. *Child Abuse & Neglect, 24*(1), 149–157.

Ogloff, J., Cutajar, M., Mann, E., & Mullen, P. (2012). Child sexual abuse and subsequent offending and victimisation: A 45 year follow-up study. *Trends & Issues in Crime and Criminal Justice [P], 2012*(440), 1–6.

Pleck, E. H. (1987). *Domestic tyranny: The making of social policy against family violence from colonial times to the present.* New York: Oxford University Press.

Prendergast, W. E. (1993). *The merry-go-round of sexual abuse: Identifying and treating survivors.* Haworth Press.

Reckdenwald, A., Mancini, C., & Beauregard, E. (2014). Adolescent self-image as a mediator between childhood maltreatment and adult sexual offending. *Journal of Criminal Justice, 42*(2), 85–94.

Rohsenow, D. J., Corbett, R., & Devine, D. (1988). Molested as children: A hidden contribution to substance abuse? *Journal of Substance Abuse Treatment, 5*(1), 13–18.

Runyan, D. K., Everson, M. D., Edelsohn, G. A., Hunter, W. M., & Coulter, M. L. (1988). Impact of legal intervention on sexually abused children. *The Journal of Pediatrics, 113*(4), 647–653.

Rush, F. (1980). *The best kept secret: Sexual abuse of children.* Englewood Cliffs, NJ: Prentice-Hall.

Sacco, L. (2009). *Unspeakable: Father-daughter incest in American history.* Johns Hopkins University Press.

Salter, D., McMillan, D., Richards, M., Talbot, T., Hodges, J., Bentovim, A., Hastings, R., Stevenson, J., & Skuse, D. (2003). Development of sexually abusive behaviour in sexually victimised males: A longitudinal study. *The Lancet, 361*, 471–476.

Schiffer, B., & Vonlaufen, C. (2011). Executive dysfunctions in pedophilic and nonpedophilic child molesters. *The Journal of Sexual Medicine, 8*(7), 1975–1984.

Seto, M. C. (2008). *Pedophilia and sexual offending against children: Theory, assessment, and intervention.* American Psychological Association.

Sgroi, S. M. (1975). Sexual molestation of children. *Children Today, 4*(3), 18–21.

Silverman, A. B., Reinherz, H. Z., & Giaconia, R. M. (1996). The long-term sequelae of child and adolescent abuse: A longitudinal community study. *Child Abuse & Neglect, 20*(8), 709–723.

Simon, L. M., Sales, B. D., Kaszniak, A., & Kahn, M. (1992). Characteristics of child molesters: Implications for the fixated-regressed dichotomy. *Journal of Interpersonal Violence, 7*(2), 211–225.

Smallbone, S. W., & Wortley, R. K. (2001). *Child sexual abuse: Offender characteristics and modus operandi* (Vol. 193). Australian Institute of Criminology.

Smolak, L., & Murnen, S. K. (2001). Gender and eating problems. In R. H. Striegel-Moore & L. Smolak (Eds.), *Eating disorders: Innovative directions in research and practice* (pp. 91–110). Washington, DC American Psychological Association

Sullivan, J., & Beech, A. (2004). A comparative study of demographic data relating to intra- and extra-familial child sexual abusers and professional perpetrators. *Journal of Sexual Aggression, 10*(1), 39–50.

Summit, R. C. (1983). The child sexual-abuse accommodation syndrome. *Child Abuse & Neglect, 7*(2), 177–193.

Tjaden, P. G., & Anhalt, J. (1994). The impact of joint law enforcement-child protective services investigations in child maltreatment cases. *Final report for Grant* (90-CA), 1446.

Trocmé, N., & Bala, N. (2005). False allegations of abuse and neglect when parents separate. *Child Abuse & Neglect, 29*(12), 1333–1345.

United States. (1970). *Technical report of the commission on obscenity and pornography.* Washington, D.C.: U. S. Government Printing Office.

U.S. Department of Health and Human Services, Administration for Children and Families, Administration on Children, Youth and Families, Children's Bureau. (2013). *Child maltreatment 2013.* Available from http://www.acf.hhs.gov/programs/cb/research-data-technology/statistics-research/child-maltreatment.

U.S. Department of Health and Human Services, Administration for Children and Families, Administration on Children, Youth and Families, Children's Bureau. (2015). *Child maltreatment* 2013. Available from http://www.acf.hhs.gov/programs/cb/research-data-technology/statistics-research/child-maltreatment

Vachon, D. D., Krueger, R. F., Rogosch, F. A., & Cicchetti, D. (2015). Assessment of the harmful psychiatric and behavioral effects of different forms of child maltreatment. *JAMA Psychiatry, 72*(11), 1135–1142.

Valente, S. M. (2005). Sexual abuse of boys. *Journal of Child and Adolescent Psychiatric Nursing, 18*(1), 10–16.

van Dam, C. (2001). *Identifying child molesters: Preventing child sexual abuse by recognizing the patterns of the offenders.* Binghamton, NY: Haworth Maltreatment and Trauma Press/The Haworth Press, Inc.

Walsh, W. A., Lippert, T., Cross, T. P., Maurice, D. M., & Davison, K. S. (2008). How long to prosecute child sexual abuse for a community using a children's advocacy center and two comparison communities? *Child Maltreatment, 13*(1), 3–13.

Walsh, W. A., Jones, L. M., Cross, T. P., & Lippert, T. (2010). Prosecuting child sexual abuse: The importance of evidence type. *Crime & Delinquency, 56*(3), 436–454.

Walters, D. R. (1975). *Physical and sexual abuse of children: Causes and treatment.* Bloomington: Indiana University Press.

Werner, J., & Werner, M. C. M. (2008). Child sexual abuse in clinical and forensic psychiatry: A review of recent literature. *Current Opinion in Psychiatry, 21*(5), 499–504.

Whitaker, D. J., Le, B., Hanson, R. K., Baker, C. K., McMahon, P. M., Ryan, G., Klein, A., & Rice, D. D. (2008). Risk factors for the perpetration of child sexual abuse: A review and meta-analysis. *Child Abuse & Neglect, 32*(5), 529–548.

Widom, C. S., & Maxfield, M. G. (2001). An update on the "cycle of violence": Research in brief. Washington, DC: National Institute of Justice.

## Court Cases

*Crawford v. Washington*, 541 U.S. 36 (2004).

*Kennedy v. Louisiana*, 554 U.S. 407 (2008).

*People v. Sharp*, 2005 WL 583755 (111. App. 4 Dist. 2005).
*Pitts v. State*, 2005 WL 127049 (Ga. App. 2005).

## DEFINITIONS

**Abused-Abuser Hypothesis:** Widespread belief that sexually abused children and adolescents who are sexually abused are at risk of themselves committing sexual abuse (see also Cycle of Child Sexual Abuse).

**Battered Child Syndrome:** A clinical condition in young children who have received repeated serious physical abuse, including bone fractures, subdural hematomas, failure to thrive, or sudden death, and repetition of that abuse is likely to reoccur without intervention.

**Child Abuse Prevention and Treatment Act (CAPTA):** Key legislation passed in 1974 (and reauthorized by the federal government several times since then) that addressed child abuse and neglect and authorized funds to improve states' investigation, reporting, assessment, prosecution, and treatment of physical abuse, neglect, and sexual abuse of children.

**Child Sexual Abuse:** When an adult (and sometimes an older adolescent) engages in inappropriate sexual acts with a child. This may include contact and non-contact offenses, as well as exploitative offenses.

**Child Sexual Abuse Accommodation Syndrome:** Theory describing how children respond to and internally resolve experiences of sexual abuse. Also accounts for why children fail to disclose or delay the disclosure of these experiences.

**Cycle of Child Sexual Abuse:** Widespread belief that sexually abused children and adolescents who are sexually abused are at risk of themselves committing sexual abuse (see also Abused-Abuser Hypothesis).

**Family Infiltrators:** Child sexual-abuse offenders who become acquainted with families with children and assume a role as surrogate parent or friend.

**Grooming:** The process of befriending and establishing an emotional connection with children for the purpose of sexually abusing them.

**Joint Investigations:** Investigations of child sexual-abuse incidents involving interagency cooperation and shared information between law enforcement officials and child protective services.

**Pedophilia:** Psychiatric disorder in which an adult or older adolescent experiences a primary or exclusive sexual attraction to prepubescent children (generally age 11 years or younger).

**Protective Factors:** Conditions or attributes that, when present, serve to minimize, reduce, or eliminate risk of maladaptive behaviors.

**Revictimization Hypothesis:** Theory linking child sexual-abuse experiences to increased vulnerability to subsequent abusive experiences later in life.

**Sophisticated Rape Track:** Child sexual-abuse offenders who work with or are involved regularly with children, including teachers, daycare providers, after school activity leaders, clergy, and others in authoritative positions.

**Testimonial Competence:** The mental capacity of individuals to provide testimony in legal proceedings.

**Testimonial Hearsay:** Evidence collected or gathered by state agents (e.g., law enforcement officials, social workers, child protective services professionals) for the purpose of a prosecution.

**Theory of Infantile Sexuality:** Theory of sexual development in children (developed by Sigmund Freud) that argues that human sexuality begins at birth. At one point, Freud argued that children who had claimed sexual experiences with adults had imagined the experience.

**Unsubstantiated:** Claims that lack sufficient evidence that a crime has occurred.

# Child Pornography

## CHAPTER OBJECTIVES

- Describe how child pornography laws have evolved in the U.S. legal system.
- Describe the characteristics and offending patterns of child pornography offenders.
- Compare and contrast child pornography crimes with other types of sex crimes.
- Identify criminal justice responses to child pornography crimes, including response by police and courts.

Thus far, it has been emphasized that sex offenders are a heterogeneous group of offenders who commit various types of sex crimes. As will be discussed in Chapter 5, child sexual abusers Chapter 4 may utilize the Internet to establish contact with children and facilitate victim *grooming*. The Internet can also be relied upon to commit other sex crimes that do not involve the direct targeting and contact of children by sex offenders. Recently, the U.S. Subcommittee on the Oversight and Investigation of the Committee on Energy and Commerce made the following statement regarding sex offenders who use the Internet to commit sex crimes:

> With the growing use of the Internet, the number of child predators who seek to make, distribute, and view images of children being sexually abused continues to skyrocket. This is due to the anonymity, accessibility, and ease with which child predators can operate on the Internet. The extent of the problem is staggering. Some examples of statistics that our witnesses today at the hearing will discuss more fully include: one in five children report being sexually solicited over the Internet and only 25% of those children that are sexually solicited online tell their parents; 3.5 million images of child sexual exploitation over the Internet have been identified in the U.S. alone. The commercial enterprise of online *child pornography* is estimated in 2005 to be approximately $20 billion, and it is an industry on the rise. The National Center for Missing and Exploited Children receives approximately 1,500 tips a week on its cyber tip line about suspected online child pornography.

> Child predators that are found in possession of child pornography typically have thousands of images of sexual abuse of children on their computers.
>
> (C-SPAN, 2012)

With regard to most sex crimes, there is a defined offender committing an illegal sexual act and a victim. A typical sexual assault, for example, involves a man victimizing a female without her consent. These are *predatory crimes*, which are violent crimes committed against a person. This chapter examines a relatively new sex crime that has garnered extensive attention and concern in recent years—one that does not necessarily require direct interaction with a victim. We turn our attention to child pornography, a serious sex crime for which arrests have been on the rise over the past 20 years (Walsh, Wolak, & Finkelhor, 2013). Many of us are familiar with the terms child exploitation, Internet offending, and production, distribution, and possession of child pornography. By the end of this chapter, however, you will have a basic knowledge of this type of sex crime, including the history of child pornography laws, the types of offenders who commit such offenses, and the criminal justice, legal, and political responses to them.

## DEFINING CHILD PORNOGRAPHY

*Child pornography* is most commonly defined as the visual depiction (including any photograph, film, video, picture, or computer-generated image or picture, as well as undeveloped film or data stored on computer storage devices) of sexually explicit conduct where (18 U.S.C. §2256(8)):

- the production of the visual depiction involves the use of a minor engaging in sexually explicit conduct; or

- the visual depiction is a digital image, computer image, or computer-generated image that is, or is indistinguishable from, that of a minor engaging in sexually explicit conduct; or

- the visual depiction has been created, adapted, or modified to appear that an identifiable minor is engaging in sexually explicit conduct.

Embedded within this definition is not only *actual child pornography*, which consists of images of real children engaged in real sexual acts, but also *virtual child pornography*, which consists of synthesized, manipulated images of children who appear to be engaged in sexual acts. Federal law (18 U.S.C. §1466A) also classifies such images in the forms of drawings, cartoons, sculptures, and paintings as pornographic as well. Images themselves (whether actual or virtual) may vary considerably in their sexual content. The legal definition of child pornography, therefore, does not capture all material that an adult with a sexual interest in children may consider sexualized or sexual. Researchers have identified ten levels of increasing image severity (Taylor, Holland, & Quayle, 2001):

1. **Indicative:** Non-sexualized pictures collected from legitimate sources (e.g., magazines, catalogs) showing children in undergarments, bathing suits, etc. from either commercial sources or family albums.

2. **Nudist:** Pictures of naked or semi-naked children in appropriate nudist settings (e.g., baby bathtub photographs).

3. **Erotica:** Surreptitiously taken photographs of children in appropriate nudist settings.

4. **Posing:** Deliberately posed pictures of children fully clothed, partially, clothed, or naked.

5. **Erotic Posing:** Deliberately posed pictures of children fully clothed, partially, clothed, or naked in sexualized or provocative positions.

6. **Explicit Erotic Posing:** Emphasizing genital areas where the child is either naked, partially clothed, or fully clothed.

7. **Explicit Sexual Activity:** Involves touching, mutual, or self-masturbation, oral sex, and intercourse by child, but not involving an adult.

8. **Assault:** Pictures of children being subject to a sexual assault, involving digital touching, and involving an adult.

9. **Gross Assault:** Grossly obscene pictures of sexual assault, involving penetrative sex, masturbation, or oral sex involving an adult.

10. **Sadism/Bestiality:** Pictures showing a child being tied, bound, beaten, whipped, or otherwise subject to something that implies pain; pictures where an animal is involved in some form of sex with a child.

Deciding which of these levels actually constitutes child pornography has become difficult, particularly in today's courts. It is arguable that images that fall under Levels 1 and 2 (i.e., indicative and nudist) are just as dangerous (if not more dangerous) than those images falling under Levels 9 and 10 (i.e, gross assault and sadism/bestiality). For example, research shows that pedophiles usually construct erotic fantasies *not* through the use of perverse, sexual material, but rather through innocuous, non-sexualized images of children, such as images from television advertisements, children's clothing catalogs, and even photographs of children at Disneyland (Howitt, 1995). This is discussed more in-depth after covering the child pornography laws. For now, the important take away is that the "legitimateness" of material or an image may be irrelevant to an offender given that sex offenders with interests in children may use perfectly legitimate material to satisfy sexual needs.

Child pornography exists in numerous formats, including printed media, film, CD-ROM, and DVD, to name a few. Today, it is most commonly transmitted on various platforms within the Internet, including email, websites, Internet chat rooms, Instant Message, File Transfer Protocol, and peer-to-peer technology. Child pornography is one of the fastest growing online businesses, with an estimated 9,550 child sexual-abuse webpages hosted by 1,561 individual domains detected in 2012 (Internet Watch Foundation, 2012). Of those, 54% were housed within the U.S. Worldwide, the production and distribution of child pornography has developed into a huge industry, with annual revenues estimated upwards of $20 billion. A study of arrested child pornography offenders revealed that 83% were in possession of images involving children between the ages of 6 and 12. Also, 39% had images of children between three and five years old. Another 19% had images of infants and toddlers under the age of three (Wolak, Finkelhor, & Mitchell, 2005).

## THE HISTORY OF CHILD PORNOGRAPHY LAW

Defining what child pornography is—where and how exactly does one draw the line between legal and illegal—is difficult. Federal law criminalizes knowingly producing, manufacturing, distributing, or accessing with intent to view child pornography (18 U.S.C. §2252). Additionally, all 50 U.S. states have enacted laws criminalizing the possession, manufacture, and distribution of child pornography. Violation of these laws may result in both state and federal charges. For the purpose of enforcing the federal law, "minor" is defined as a person under the age of 18. The development of law protecting children from sexual exploitation is relatively modern (Adler, 2001; Wortley & Smallbone, 2006). Unlike some other types of sex offending discussed in this textbook, the laws that have developed as a response to child pornography have a unique constitutional history. To trace the origins (and eventual tightening) of child pornography laws, it is important to first turn attention to the history of the related concept of obscenity.

### History of Obscenity

The concept of *obscenity* laid the groundwork for what would eventually shape the child pornography laws that emerged in the 1970s. Though the term "obscenity" varies between communities and cultures, it generally refers to what is offensive to decency, filthy, disgusting, or repulsive (Richards, 1974). Obscene materials can include books, photographs, films, paintings, music, press, speech, and even thought. The most common method of regulating obscenity is through censorship. Materials are not censored because of fear that they will incite crimes, but rather because they are offensive to others.

Sexual obscenity, therefore, was not banned, regulated or controlled for fear of inciting sex crimes, but because it offended the morals or values of the community. In short, obscenity is immoral, and individuals should not indulge in it, and the community should not tolerate it (Henkin, 1963). Despite the First Amendment protection of freedom of speech in the U.S. Constitution, this moral rule went largely unchallenged for the majority of the twentieth century. Also noteworthy, until the mid-1970s, there was no systematic method for determining what constituted obscene material and what was considered protected under the First Amendment.

In 1973, the landmark U.S. Supreme Court case, *Miller v. California*, established the standard of what constitutes unprotected obscenity for First Amendment purposes. In this case, the question before the Court was whether the sale and distribution of obscene material (in this case, sexually explicit illustrated books, labeled "adult material") was protected under the First Amendment's freedom of speech guarantee. The Court ruled that it was not a protected form of speech. The Court, however, also recognized the potential danger in regulating and limiting forms of creative expression. The Court, therefore, created a set of criteria, known as **The Miller Test** (also known as the Three-Prong Obscenity Test), which questionable material must meet in order to be legitimately regulated by the law. These criteria include:

(1) whether the average person, applying contemporary community standards, would find that the work, taken as a whole, appeals to **prurient interests** (i.e., interests in sexual matters);

(2) whether the work depicts or describes, in a patently offensive way, sexual conduct [or excretory functions] specifically defined by the applicable state law; and

(3) whether the work, taken as a whole, lacks serious literary, artistic, political, or scientific value.

This case provided individual states in the U.S. greater freedom in prosecuting individuals for the production and distribution of obscene materials. It is also important, however, to note that, despite the greater restrictions imposed as to what could be considered "obscene material," the law did not specifically target child pornography or child exploitation. A number of major motion pictures released after the ruling featured sexualized images of young children. Many movies, such as *Taxi Driver, Pretty Baby*, and *The Blue Lagoon*, featured adult themes involving sexually active children under the age of 18. Films such as these, although featuring child nudity, would have been able to pass the Miller Test of Obscenity, as they were produced and distributed for artistic value (see criterion 3). Also, note that at this time period, such laws only applied to *actual images*. Virtual images, including virtual photographs, were not considered under this early legislation.

## Growing Awareness of Child Exploitation

By the late 1970s through the early 1980s, awareness of the need to protect children from sexual exploitation was growing in the U.S. Even in nations hesitant to tolerate censorship of sexual materials, use of child subjects crossed a line. It was during this time that fears of child sexual abuse became linked to other social ills, including kidnapping, serial homicide, and organized sex trafficking and sex rings. This was the backdrop for the unanimous decision of *New York v. Ferber* (1982). This U.S. Supreme Court case held that states can prohibit the depiction of minors engaged in sexual conduct, and that the Miller Test for Obscenity need not be applied in cases of child pornography. The Court offered five reasons for its decision:

(1) Using children as subjects of pornography could be harmful to their physical and psychological well-being, and child pornography does not fall within the protection of the First Amendment.

(2) Application of the *Miller* standard for obscenity is not a satisfactory solution to the problem of child pornography.

(3) The financial gain involved in selling and advertising child pornography provides incentive to produce such material—and such activity is prohibited throughout the U.S.

(4) The value of permitting minors to perform/appear in lewd exhibitions is negligible at best.

(5) The distribution of photographs and films depicting sexual activity by children is intrinsically related to the sexual abuse of children, and is, therefore, within the state's interest and power to prohibit.

Examining the differences between the *Miller* decision and the *Ferber* decision, it should be noted that the *Ferber* case has essentially separated child pornography from obscene material and has labeled it as its own category (Wortley & Smallbone, 2006). This granted states more leeway in regulating material that involved sexual exploitation of children. The Court ruled that the values of free speech and freedom of expression in content involving child pornography were outweighed by these important social considerations (Akdeniz, 2013). As important as it was to addressing the problem of child victims, however, this decision still was limited to regulation of visual depictions of *actual* minors engaged in sexually explicit conduct (Burke, 1997). Also, this ruling only pertained to individuals who produced, promoted, or distributed such media.

As the Court was rendering decisions that shaped legal responses to child pornography, the U.S. legislature also began to demonstrate a shared interest in the issue. In 1977, Congress passed the Protection of Children Against Sexual Exploitation Act. This Act prohibited using children to make pornographic materials for financial gain. Later, in 1984, the Child Protection Act was passed, making it illegal to produce child pornography, regardless of commercial intent. In 1986, Congress also passed the Child Sexual Abuse and Pornography Act, which introduced mandatory sentencing for repeat offenders, in addition to civil remedies for victims.

The *Ferber* ruling was later extended when the U.S. Supreme Court ruled that the possession of child pornography was also illegal. The case, *Osborne v. Ohio* (1990), overturned an earlier decision that neither states nor the federal government could prohibit possession of obscene material in the privacy of one's home (*Stanley v. Georgia* (1969)). Consistent with *Ferber*, the Court upheld the protection of children against sexual exploitation as a top priority. According to Ohio, these additional provisions were set in place because it was not practical to solve the child-pornography problem by only attacking production and distribution. Three state interests supported Ohio's criminalization of possession of child pornography:

(1) Materials produced by child pornographers permanently recorded the victims' abuse, which would result in continuing harm to the child victims by haunting them for years to come.

(2) Because evidence suggested that child molesters use child pornography to seduce children, the Court reasoned that the state could legitimately encourage the destruction of child pornography by banning its possession.

(3) The Court found that it was reasonable for the state to conclude that production would decrease if demand decreased as a result of penalizing possession.

The state of Ohio's interest in criminalizing possession of child pornography was based on the observation that many child sexual abusers would not merely keep pornographic materials for themselves, but also would distribute them to other abusers, thus executing a never-ending cycle of distribution (Ost, 2002; 2009). As discussed in this chapter, recent research has suggested that child pornography possession is a strong predictor of pedophilia (Seto, Cantor, & Blanchard, 2006).

Through the mid-1980s and early-1990s, the trafficking of child pornography within the U.S. continued to decrease and had almost been eradicated because of the tightening of child exploitation laws and successful campaigns by police. Producing such material became difficult and expensive, and reproducing it was equally risky. Purchase, distribution, and receipt of child pornography also became impossible, as consumers of such material found it increasingly difficult to find a safe, discreet medium to interact with one another. The improvement of technology, however, has gravely revived it. Today, child pornography has not only resurged as a serious crime in the U.S., but it is also a multi-billion-dollar business.

## How the Internet Changed the Child Pornography Industry and Law

The Internet is, at its core, a worldwide network of smaller computer networks connected by cable, telephone lines, or satellite links. It is decentralized, timeless, and spaceless. It is impossible to determine the size of the Internet at any moment, as it continuously grows. While the Internet has proved invaluable as a communication and educational tool, particularly in the twenty-first century, this same technological wonder has also proved to be a grave threat to children.

The Internet has served as a major catalyst for the accelerated production, distribution, and purchase of child pornography. Today, pornographic images and films of children have flooded the Internet, and are easily accessible to anyone with access to a computer. The Internet has allowed the distribution of child pornography to be conducted at an extremely low cost, with virtual anonymity, and at extraordinary speed. Additionally, the technology makes constant updating relatively easy (e.g., some distributors claim to update their material bi-weekly or, in some cases, daily). Furthermore, material that is downloaded from the Internet has a unique advantage over other types of media (e.g., film and photographs) in that it does not deteriorate with age or with transfer to other electronic devices. The Internet provides a safe, easily accessible, distribution medium that operates on at least three levels simultaneously (O'Connell, 2001):

(1) The technology facilitates the anonymous, rapid dissemination of an immediate and constant supply of illegal child pornography.

(2) It enables creation and maintenance of deviant behavior (i.e., the Internet offers a medium through which child pornography consumers can interact at a social organizational level as "colleagues").

(3) It provides supportive context in that depictions of sexualized children often appear to be designed to provide a sense of justification (i.e., "the pictures are on a professional-looking website, so it must not be wrong").

Along with easier production and distribution of, and access to, child pornography, the Internet also became a medium through which virtual child pornography (also known as pseudo child pornography) began to flourish. Virtual child pornography refers to simulated representations, as well as computer-generated or morphed images of children engaged in pornographic, sexual, or other lewd acts. This material takes on two forms: (1) computer-generated images in which a child's head is digitally placed onto the body of an adult who is involved in some form of sexually explicit conduct, and (2) depictions of adults over the age of legal sexual consent (18 in the U.S.) who are portrayed as being a minor.

Prior to the heightened popularity and utility of the Internet, the law made no concession for virtual child pornography. Only images of real children engaged in real acts were considered unlawful. The basis for the *Osborne* ruling, however, partially rested on the assumption that child molesters might use child pornography as a tool to seduce other child victims into engaging in the same acts. As the use of the Internet, coupled with advanced imaging software, began to become a staple in the child pornography industry, new fears arose concerning virtual child pornographic images as being equally damaging vis-à-vis their real image counterparts. This called for swift action that prosecuted the production, distribution, and possession of virtual child pornographic images in the same way that real ones were, thereby eliminating any distinction between the two. The first major court decision to arise in response to the Internet becoming a mechanism for easier access to child pornography was the Child Pornography Protection Act (1996) (CPPA).

The CPPA expanded the federal prohibition of child pornography to include not only real images involving the sexual abuse of children, but also "any visual depiction, including any photograph, film, video, picture, or computer or computer-generated image or picture that is, or appears to be, of a minor engaging in sexually explicit conduct" (18 U.S.C. §2256(8)). Therefore, not only were sexual images involving actual children to be criminalized, but also computer-generated images, the use of adult "body doubles," and sexual images that appeared to be minors or that were advertised as minors, even if minors were not actually involved (Akdeniz, 2013).

CPPA was met with extreme opposition and criticism, namely by individuals and organizations protesting the Act's infringement on constitutional protections. Some opponents, including the American Civil Liberties Union (ACLU), argued that because no actual victim existed in virtual child pornography, and the events in question were not "real events" with actual child endangerment or harm involved, such images should not be criminalized. Furthermore, the ACLU was able to defend its views with the *Ferber* (1982) decision. Recall that in *Ferber*, the U.S. Supreme Court decided that sexually abusive child images were not a guaranteed First Amendment protection, on the grounds that such materials were harmful to the physical and psychological well-being of children involved in their production. On this basis, the ACLU argued that it was clear from *Ferber* that the government's interest was in protecting children from *actual* harm, not shielding the general public from such images.

The U.S. Judiciary Committee rejected the ACLU's arguments, maintaining that the U.S. government also had a compelling interest in prohibiting computer-generated images due to the potential of future harm to children. Research on the issue has shown that exposure to virtual child pornography results in viewers being more likely to associate sex and sexuality with non-sexual depictions of minors (Paul & Linz, 2008). In other words, researchers were able to detect an association between viewing "barely legal" pornography and the attribution of sexuality to legal photos of real children. What is unknown, however, is whether viewing virtual child pornography whets the appetite for actual child pornography and child exploitation. It is possible that those viewing virtual child pornography may create a cognitive schema of children that people find disturbing, and thus, work hard to avoid making similar associations in the future.

Ultimately, the provisions under CPPA were overthrown by the U.S. Supreme Court in 2002 in *Ashcroft v. Free Speech Coalition*. The Free Speech Coalition initially challenged CPPA on the grounds that it was unconstitutionally vague and in violation of First Amendment protections. In the first case, *The Free Speech Coalition v. Reno* (1997), the plaintiffs charged that the CPPA "impermissibly suppresses material that is protected under the First Amendment" (U.S. Dist. LEXIS 12212, No C 97–0281). The District Court, however, continued to reaffirm that CPPA was neither vague, nor overly broad—that the law had been passed to suppress the secondary effects of child molesting and the broader child pornography industry. The Free Speech Coalition appealed the decision.

The decision of the District Court was reversed by the Ninth Circuit U.S. Court of Appeals. The Court held that the government could not prohibit forms of speech that had the potential to persuade consumers to commit illegal acts. It was determined that not only did the government ban materials that were not obscene (as defined under *Miller v. California*), but also materials that did not involve the sexual exploitation of real children (as set under *New York v. Ferber*). The Court also found that certain phrases, such as "appears to be a minor" and "conveys the impression that the depiction portrays a minor," were too vague and subjective (*Free Speech Coalition v. Reno* (1999)). Specifically, the Court stated:

> The two phrases in question are highly subjective. There is no explicit standard as to what the phrases mean. The phrases provide no measure to guide an ordinarily intelligent person about prohibited conduct and any such person could not be reasonably certain about whose perspective defines the appearance of a minor.
>
> (198 F3d 1083, 1097 (9th Cir. 1999))

Burke (1997) noted that words that advocate illegal activity are protected as long as they fall short of *incitement*. Therefore, virtual child pornography—although it may encourage, promote, persuade or influence child molesters to engage in illegal activity with children—is unlikely to incite sex offenders to abuse and molest children. It may "validate their illegal activity, and it may assist in their illegal activity, but the conduct is neither sufficiently imminent nor impelling to constitute incitement" (Burke, 1997 p. 461). In *Ashcroft v. Free Speech Coalition* (2002), the Court commented how digitally-created images that involved no *real* minor(s) did not have a victim and, therefore, produced no record of the crime.

The *Ashcroft* decision was arguably the most substantial setback for anti-child pornography law in the U.S. This decision meant that prosecutors of child pornography cases had to prove, beyond a reasonable doubt, that the sexually explicit material presented as evidence was indeed a *real* image of a minor, as opposed to one that was computer-generated. In response to this decision, President George W. Bush signed into effect the Prosecutorial Remedies and Other Tools to end the Exploitation of Children Today (PROTECT) Act (Pub.L. 108–21, 117 Stat. 650, S. 151) in 2003. Among many other provisions, the PROTECT Act criminalized the visual depiction (of any kind) of minors engaged in sexually explicit conduct or obscenity. These depictions were not limited to films or photographs, but also drawings, cartoons, paintings, sculptures and comic strips.

Since the passage of the PROTECT Act, there have been successful (albeit rare) prosecutions of individuals possessing animated media (including comic books and cartoons) that have depicted minors in sexually obscene situations. *United States v. Whorley* (4th Cir. 2008) involved the prosecution of a man who received sexually explicit **Manga** (Japanese comic books). In 2006, Dwight Whorley was arrested for using computers at the Virginia Employment Commission, a public resource, to download Manga depicting children in sexually-explicit situations. He was charged with knowingly receiving child pornography for printing out two comics and viewing others. Whorley was found guilty and sentenced under the same guidelines governing actual images of child pornography.

## DESCRIPTION OF CHILD PORNOGRAPHY OFFENDERS

Like all sex offenders, several emotional and wrenching questions arise with regard to child pornography offenders: Who would commit such a crime? Why would a grown adult produce, distribute, or view sexualized images of children? Are all offenders pedophiles? Have they experienced previous victimization by the child pornography industry? Are those who produce/distribute child pornography different from those who merely access/view it? In this section, we attempt to answer some of these questions using evidence, both empirical and anecdotal sources.

In preceding chapters, we have considered individuals who commit certain types of sex crimes and several theoretical explanations—biological, behavioral, social learning, and psychological. As Chapters 3 and 4 have indicated, offenders are sometimes organized by *typologies*. While typologies have the advantage of allowing us to categorize offenders with similar traits and characteristics, we must also recognize that the categories are not mutually exclusive (i.e., not every offender fits in a typology category, and some offenders may fit in many typology categories). One early profile of the child pornography perpetrator illustrates this:

> Usually a White male, 35–45 years old, well-off financially, and generally in a professional or white-collar occupation. He is married, may have a couple of children and is highly respected in the community. The perpetrator is usually a person who knows or is related to the victim.
>
> (Ayood, 1978, p. 19)

It should be noted how broad-sweeping and vague this description of the child pornography offender actually is. Not only does this description provide a probable likeness of other types of sex offenders (or any type of criminal offender, for that matter), but it also excludes other characteristics of individuals who may engage in child pornography crimes (e.g., women, juveniles and working-class individuals). Also, this profile is purely demographic—it does not take into account underlying mental pathology, prior criminal history, family background, or other risk factors.

While several typologies exist for rapists and child sexual abusers as discussed in Chapters 3 and 4, a limited number of comprehensive typologies have been developed for child pornography offenders. The use of the Internet as a tool to commit child pornography offenses further complicates profiling this group of offenders. Provided that child pornography offenders need not have direct contact with victims, a question has arisen about whether online offenders are a distinct type of sex offender, or if they are "typical" sex offenders who use technology to execute their crimes. It is clear, however, that not all child pornography offenders are alike, and our understanding of them has changed over the past 30 years.

## Early Perceptions of Child Pornography Offenders

For the most part, systematic research on child pornography offenders has only begun to appear in recent years (e.g., Lam, Mitchell, & Seto, 2010; Seto, Cantor, & Blanchard, 2006). Such research has focused on criminal history, clinical diagnoses, *static* (i.e., non-changing factors) and *dynamic risk factors* (i.e., changing factors), as well as *recidivism* risk. Recidivism refers to committing a crime again. Prior to studies of child pornography offenders, profiles of offenders were constructed largely on the experiences of police officials who arrested them or mental health practitioners who worked with them. In order to understand how we have arrived at a current understanding and conceptualization of child pornography offenders, it is necessary to examine some of the early views of them.

By the late 1970s, many myths of the child pornography industry and its associated victims and offenders had been identified. In particular, Groth, Burgess, Birnbaum, and Gary (1978) exposed a number of misconceptions (presented in Table 5.1) that previously dominated popular thought on the subject.

As the subject continued to garner attention and interest, progress was made to solve the problem through the creation of profiles, or composites. As mentioned earlier, these profiles were usually very vague and broad-sweeping, and were not informed by research. An important milestone was achieved, however, in that the scientific community began to realize that child pornography offenders, like rapists and child sexual abusers, actually mirrored mainstream society. An early composite described by O'Brien (1983) illustrates how child pornography consumers are not necessarily aberrant individuals:

1. **Ethnicity**—White. There are some minority-group offenders, but they do not make up a large percentage of offenders.

2. **Gender**—Male. Consumers of pornography are almost exclusively male. Adult and child pornography appeal primarily to male audiences.

3. **Age**—Usually 25 to 35 years old, but offenders can range in age from late adolescence to elderly.

4. **Income Level**—Middle class. Although earlier reports situated the offender as a "well-to-do" citizen, he is seen to also come from lower and middle socio-economic levels.

5. **Marital Status**—Married. The majority (at least 50%) of offenders are married.

6. **Children**—The majority of offenders have children.

7. **Community Standing**—Stable. The majority of offenders enjoy an average to high degree of community respect.

## Modern Perceptions of Child Pornography Offenders

As noted already, the number of child pornography-related arrests, investigations, prosecutions, and convictions has increased, especially since the advent of the Internet. For example, in 2006, there were an estimated 3,672 arrests for crimes involving possession of child pornography—more than twice the number of arrests made in 2000. Researchers have compared offender characteristics between both these time periods, finding a number of similarities (Wolak et al., 2011). During both time

**TABLE 5.1**    *Myths and Realities on Child Pornography Perpetrators*

| MYTH | REALITY |
| --- | --- |
| *The offender is a "dirty old man."* | *The perpetrator is neither "dirty" nor old.* |
| *The offender is a stranger to the child.* | *Most victims know the perpetrator.* |
| *The offender is an alcoholic or drug addict.* | *Alcohol and other drugs are not critical to the commission of the crime.* |
| *The offender is sexually frustrated.* | *The majority of offenders have normal sexual functioning and relationships with adult partners.* |
| *The offender is mentally ill.* | *Offenders rarely have mental impairments or low intelligence.* |

periods, most cases involved offenders who were non-Hispanic White males, with varying educational backgrounds, incomes, and geographic locations. Few had prior sexual-offense histories against children, and young adults (ages 18–25) made up less than 20% of those arrested.

With regard to demographic characteristics, we see that not much has changed with child pornography offenders since the late 1970s and early 1980s, with the notable exception of the sharp increase in the number of offenses. In light of the increased range, volume, and accessibility of sexually abusive imagery involving children, research has attempted to expand earlier views of offenders in an effort to inform policy and clinical decisions regarding risk, treatment, and supervision. To this end, more recent research has focused on criminal histories, clinical diagnoses, and risk factors of offenders to develop more in-depth, informative profiles.

## Heterogeneity among Child Pornography Offenders

One of the most widely contested debates in the characterization of child pornography offenders is whether they constitute a distinct, separate type of sex offender. In other words, are child pornography offenders the same as other sex offenders (e.g., rapists and child sexual abusers)? Child pornographers can be separated into four categories (Krone, 2004; Lanning, 2001):

(1)   Those who access child pornography to satisfy curiosity or impulse, without a particular sexual interest in children.

(2)   Those who access child pornography to satisfy sexual fantasies involving children, but do not commit actual contact offenses.

(3)   Those who utilize the Internet in order to execute contact sex crimes.

(4)   Those who create and distribute child pornography solely for the purpose of financial gain.

**TABLE 5.2** *Krone's Typology of Child Pornography Offending Behavior (2004)*

| INVOLVEMENT TYPE | FEATURES | NETWORKING LEVEL | NATURE OF ABUSE |
|---|---|---|---|
| Browser | Response to spam, accidental hit on suspect site—material knowingly saved | None | Indirect |
| Private Fantasy | Conscious creation of online text or digital images for private use | None | Indirect |
| Trawler | Actively seeking child pornography using openly available browsers | Low | Indirect |
| Non-Secure Collector | Actively seeking material often through peer-to-peer networks | High | Indirect |
| Secure Collector | Actively seeking material but only through secure networks | High | Indirect |
| Groomer | Cultivating an online relationship with one or more children. Pornography may be used to facilitate abuse | Varies—online contact with individual children | Direct |
| Physical Abuser | Abusing a child who may have been introduced to the offender online. Pornography may be used to facilitate abuse | Varies—physical contact with individual children | Direct |
| Producer | Records own abuse or that of others (or induces children to submit images of themselves) | Varies—may depend on whether individual becomes distributor | Direct |
| Distributor | May distribute at any one of the above levels | Varies | Indirect |

Source: (Krone, 2004)

In the following sections, we further explore heterogeneity in this population, focusing on these four categories. Though these categories do not constitute a typology, they incorporate categorizations from empirically-validated typologies. Krone's (2004) research of child pornography offenders in Australia yielded a typology comprised of nine different categories, with different degrees of child pornography utility, offending severity, and networking frequency. This typology is presented in Table 5.2. As we discuss the four groups of child pornography offenders below, reference is made to categories from this and other typologies.

### Impulsive Child Pornography Offenders

Some individuals who access and/or consume child pornography do it to satisfy curiosity or impulse, rather than acting from sexual desire or sexual fantasies about children. These offenders are not sexually preoccupied with children, and they do not commit contact offenses against children. These offenders generally act out of impulsivity and carry out this behavior sporadically, sometimes as part of a broader interest in pornography (Elliott & Beech, 2009). According to Krone's typology, browsers may fit this category of child pornography offenders. Browsers access child pornography unintentionally (e.g., receiving a spam email containing a link to child pornography), but knowingly save and keep the material. Research has shown that some child pornography offenders fit this description. For example, one study reported that a sizeable percentage of child pornography offenders scored highly on psychological measures of impulsivity, suggesting that they tended to act without thinking and had a lack of regard for future consequences for their crimes (Middleton, Elliott, Mandeville-Norden, & Beech, 2006).

As we have discussed, one of the features of the Internet is the perceived ease and anonymity with which one can navigate within and across different forums. Some researchers have observed that the perceived anonymity and the playful nature of the online environment can have a powerful disinhibiting effect on some users, and this diminished impulse control has been found to be a factor in problematic use of the Internet, including child pornography use (Danet, 1998).

## Child Pornography Offenders and Pedophiles: Cut From the Same Cloth?

Consumers of child pornography may also be motivated by sexual desires or sexual fantasies involving children. Offender types from Krone's typology fitting this category of child pornography offenders may include private fantasy collectors, non-secure collectors, and secure collectors. These categories include offenders who may hold sexual interests and attraction to children, as well as offenders who engage in high levels of networking (potentially with other like-minded offenders). A common societal reaction to individuals who commit a crime involving child pornography is to label them as a *pedophile*. Recall from Chapter 4 that in order to be labeled a pedophile, one must meet the diagnostic criteria of pedophilia, established by the American Psychiatric Association. To review, in order to meet the diagnostic criteria of pedophilia, a person must demonstrate the following as specified in *DSM-5* (American Psychiatric Association, 2013):

- Over a period of at least 6 months, recurrent, intense sexually arousing fantasies, sexual urges, or behaviors involving sexual activity with a prepubescent child or children (generally age 13 years or younger).

- The person has acted on these sexual urges, or the sexual urges or fantasies caused marked distress or interpersonal difficulty.

- The person is at least 16 years of age and at least five years older than the child or children.

Given this clinical definition, it is still difficult to determine: (1) whether child pornography offenders are also pedophiles and (2) whether child pornography serves to fuel the sexual appetites and desires of these offenders. The vast majority of research on this has indicated that use of child pornography *in some cases* is a predictor of pedophilia. Riegel (2004) found that 95% of 290 self-identified homosexual pedophiles acknowledged using child pornography at some point in their lives, while 59% acknowledged using it frequently. In this sample, respondents commonly stated that viewing prepubescent erotica was a useful substitute for actual sexual contact with young boys. Furthermore, recent analyses of child pornography images seized by police indicate that the most common image is that of a prepubescent girl.

Seto et al. (2006) found that viewing child pornography is a better predictor of pedophilia than contact crimes against children because the majority of child pornography offenders demonstrated greater sexual arousal (measured by ***phallometric assessment***—a method of detecting arousal through change in penile blood volume) in response to images of children compared to images of adults. In other words, those charged with child pornography offenses were more likely than those charged with sexual abuse or molestation of a child to manifest diagnostic criteria for pedophilia. Seto (2010, p. 592) offered the following explanation, stating that "some non-pedophilic men commit sexual offenses against children, such as antisocial men who are willing to pursue sexual gratification with girls who show some signs of sexual development but are below the legal age of consent."

Blanchard (2010) recommended that, for diagnostic purposes, digitally engineered, fictitious images of children should be treated the same as real photographs. The rationale is that the sexual arousal experienced by the individual does not discriminate between real and fictitious images. In addition to digitally-enhanced or photo-shopped sexualized images of children, anime, or Manga cartoon images, therefore, may also serve as relevant indicators of pedophilic interests. Recall that the provisions of the PROTECT Act criminalize this material today.

Although research has established an association between viewing child pornography and a pedophilic diagnosis, this does *not* establish a causal link that use of such images causes child sexual abuse. As discussed in Chapter 4, not all pedophiles engage in child sexual abuse. Likewise, it is important to exercise caution in equating child pornography offenders with pedophiles. Howitt's (1995) study of pedophiles concluded that they usually construct erotic fantasies *not* through the use of perverse, sexual material, but rather through innocuous, non-sexualized images of children, such as images from television advertisements, children's clothing catalogs, and even photographs of children at Disneyland. The law, however, obviously does not restrict availability of these types of materials. This indeed creates a quandary for authorities who attempt to rid communities of child pornography, as this material is certainly not the sole source of sexual incitement for offenders targeting children. Individuals wishing to view child pornography may never come in contact with, and offend against a living child, while active pedophiles who regularly abuse children may be content to view legal and commercially available images of children to incorporate into their fantasies (Miller, 2013).

In summary, the risk of actual offending posed by those in possession of child pornography is largely unknown. It is hypothesized, however, that child pornography offenders with a greater number of collected images, a higher ratio of child to adult images, images depicting younger children, and images including both male and female children are more likely to be at risk for eventually seeking live sexual contact with children (Seto, 2010).

## Concurrence of Child Pornography and Child Sexual-Abuse Crimes

The third grouping of child pornography offenders is comprised of individuals who concurrently access child pornography and sexually abuse children. Krone's typology, for example, notes the existence of groomers and physical abusers, both of whom inflict abuse on child victims. Online groomers expose their victims to child pornography to desensitize them and lower sexual inhibitions. Physical abusers initiate sex acts with children found online (e.g., chatrooms and social media websites) and may record their encounters with children for personal use after the crime has been committed. A content analysis of newspaper stories by Alexy, Burgess, and Baker (2005) revealed there may exist a group of Internet offenders, termed *combination trader-travelers*, who trade child pornography, as well as travel across state and/or national boundaries to sexually abuse or molest children. Examples of such offenders in this study included:

- An assistant principal was charged with having sex with a 15-year-old girl with whom he communicated in an Internet chatroom. The man also admitted to downloading and distributing child pornography over the Internet.

- A homeless offender maintained a child pornography website in a public library. When arrested, it was discovered that the man had been carrying condoms and KY Jelly for an impending sexual encounter with children.

- A Scottish university lecturer was caught sending child pornography, lewd photographs of himself, and traveling to the U.S. to have sex with a boy he met on the Internet (Alexy et al., 2005).

Wolak et al. (2011) also reported the existence of *dual offenders* who committed child pornography and child sexual abuse concurrently. This study found that dual offenders were more likely to live with children under age 18, to have access to children under age 18 through their employment, to have problems with drugs or alcohol, and to have prior arrests for sex crimes against children.

As emphasized throughout this textbook, one of the most problematic issues in sex-crimes research is that the vast majority of studies are limited to official data and reports, capturing only offenders who have been apprehended for their crimes. Largely absent from this research are self-reported data, which include information about crimes, not only those known to formal criminal justice authorities. Bourke and Hernandez (2009) addressed this gap by comparing two groups of child pornography offenders in a voluntary prison treatment program. One group's reported sex-offense history was limited to possession, receipt, and/or distribution of child pornography, while the other group, in addition to having similar child pornography criminal histories, also had a history of hands-on crimes. Offenders' self-reported sex-crime histories were assessed at two times—before and after the completion of an 18-month intensive treatment program. By the end of treatment, 91 of the "Internet only" offenders admitted to abusing an average of 8.7 child victims, including both pre- and post-pubescent children. This large number of contact sex crimes self-reported by child pornography offenders challenges the notion of the impulsive child pornography offender (someone who consumes out of curiosity or impulsively without a sexual interest in children). This study also demonstrates that child pornographers, like all sex offenders, do not "fit neatly" into the categories discussed in this chapter.

In addition to child pornography offenders who simultaneously commit child sexual abuse, there is also evidence that child pornography use may predict future sexual offending. One of the first studies examining recidivism of child pornography offenders was conducted by Seto and Eke (2005), who examined 201 adult male child pornography offenders. There were several important findings, including:

- 17% offended again *in some way* within an average of 2.5 years following their release from prison.

- 4% committed a *new contact sexual offense* within an average of 2.5 years.

- Offenders with prior criminal records were significantly more likely to offend again during the follow-up period.

- Offenders who committed prior and concurrent sex crimes were the most likely to offend again.

This study shows that although the risk of repeated sex offending among child pornographers is low, the risk is heightened for those offenders with prior criminal records, especially for those with prior sexual offenses. This study was replicated in 2011 to include a larger sample and a lengthier follow-up period (Eke, Seto, & Williams, 2011). In this study, 541 child pornography offenders were assessed over a 4.1-year period. The results from this study showed an alarming divergence from the previous study:

- 32% offended again *in some way* within an average of 4.1 years following release into the community.

- 4% committed a new contact sex crime within an average of 4.1 years, with an additional 2% charged with historical contact sex offenses (i.e., sexual offenses that occurred prior to the child pornography offense, but were not known to authorities until the follow-up period).

- 7% were charged with a new child pornography offense.

- Predictors of new violent offending included criminal history and (younger) offender age.

The results of this study illustrate the importance of lengthy follow-up periods, as well as large samples. They also shed light on important risk factors for recidivism (i.e., criminal history and younger offender age). Other important risk factors for recidivism among child pornographers are lower education, being single, consuming non-Internet child pornography, prior sex-offender treatment, and possessing collections of pornography involving prepubescent children (Faust, Bickart, Renaud, & Camp, 2014). Other research suggests, however, that while online offenders may display greater sexual deviancy, they may also exhibit certain psychological characteristics that buffer against sexual recidivism, including greater victim empathy, less emotional identification with children, and fewer cognitive distortions.

Generally speaking, sex offenders as a whole rarely re-offend by committing another sex offense. In the majority of cases, those who re-offend commit a wide range of offenses, from writing bad checks to motor vehicle theft to felony homicide. The research on child pornography offenders, specifically, suggests similar re-offending patterns.

## *Producers, Distributors, and Profiteers: Beyond Possession of Child Pornography*

Most of the discussion up to this point has focused on consumers of child pornography. Attention, however, must also be given to the child pornographers who produce and distribute it. This is the final group of child pornographers discussed in this chapter. Krone's typology identifies two examples of offenders in this category: producers and distributors. Producers of child pornography are involved with the recruitment/solicitation of child victims and the filming and/or photography of sexually explicit material. Distributors are generally not involved with production, instead distributing child pornography across networks of consumers. Both producers and distributors are motivated by profit (hence the term "profiteers") and do not necessarily have a sexual interest in children, although some studies have found that in some rare instances, profiteers may also consume child pornography (Mitchell & Jones, 2013).

## Child Pornography Offenders and Other Sex Offenders

In order to effectively identify, apprehend, and treat child pornography offenders, it is worth knowing how this group of sex offenders differs from other groups. This is of particular importance in identifying risk factors associated with victimization as well as recidivism. Webb, Craissati, and Keen (2007) compared a group of child pornography offenders to a group of child molesters, examining psychometric measures to determine risk and personality traits. The results were largely similar for the two groups. Both were similar in terms of ethnicity, child-abuse history, education, history of self-harm, and marital status. Child pornography offenders were more likely than child molesters to have previous convictions for a sex crime, but the difference was not statistically significant. Both groups scored similarly on both the Risk Matrix 2000/S and the Stable 2000 (instruments for assessing risk among sex offenders—discussed further in Chapter 10).

**TABLE 5.3**  *Differences between Child Pornographers and Child Sexual Abusers*

| CHILD PORNOGRAPHERS | CHILD SEXUAL ABUSERS |
|---|---|
| Offenses are more indicative of pedophilia compared to those of child sexual abusers. | Offenses are less indicative of pedophilia than those of child pornographers. |
| More likely to succeed in treatment. | Less likely to succeed in treatment. |
| Less likely to have intimate relationships. | More likely to maintain healthy, age-appropriate relationships. |
| Fewer substance abuse problems compared to child sexual abusers. | Greater substance abuse problems compared to child pornography users. |
| Greater reported psychological and mental health problems. | Fewer reported psychological and mental health problems. |

Child pornography offenders, however, were younger than child molesters, more likely to have had contact with mental health providers/services during adulthood, less likely to have healthy intimate relationships, and had fewer problems with substance abuse. Child pornographers were also less likely than child sexual abusers to fail in the community. For example, child molesters were more likely to miss treatment sessions, drop out of treatment altogether, and engage in sexually risky behaviors compared to child pornography offenders. Table 5.3 summarizes the differences between child pornographers and child sexual abusers.

## CRIMINAL JUSTICE RESPONSES TO CHILD PORNOGRAPHERS

Over the past 20 years, as awareness and reporting of child pornography crimes have increased, law enforcement agencies and courts have been tasked with identifying, investigating, and prosecuting individuals involved in the child pornography industry—from producers and distributors to collectors and consumers. Criminal justice officials have been forced to adapt to technological innovations that afford offenders greater, easier, faster, and more secretive access to child pornography. As offenders become more tech-savvy, law enforcement agencies must continuously fine-tune their investigative practices and procedures. As well, courts must engage in an ongoing review process to ensure the constitutionality of their procedures of search and seizure of evidence, standards of proof, and sentencing of offenders. In this section, the investigation, prosecution, and sentencing of child pornographers are examined more closely.

### Investigating Child Pornography

Prior to the advent of the Internet, policing authorities were able to investigate child pornography crimes similar to the investigation for other types of crime. Traditional search and seizure, sting operations, and child pornography busts were typical methods for managing this type of crime. U.S. Customs special agents were able to seize books and magazines with pornographic child images and prevent them from entering the country via U.S. mail and commercial parcel services. Police even were able to infiltrate offender networks using computers and modems to communicate and exchange information on victims. By the early 1990s, the threat of child pornography was believed to have been successfully contained. As we have learned, the Internet has facilitated the return and exponential expansion of child pornography.

Child pornography is now a largely digital and virtual industry both nationally and internationally. Offenders are no longer collecting and transmitting photographs, videotapes, and magazines, but rather sending virtual images through complex peer-to-peer networks. This crime now falls almost exclusively into the realm of *cyber crime*. The rapid evolution of child pornography crimes has required police to become more technologically savvy and adaptive. Policing child pornography is difficult for three primary reasons: (1) the sheer volume of available illegal material is so vast that it is nearly impossible to determine the full extent of the problem, (2) the lack of reporting limits the number of leads and clues available to initiate an investigation, requiring almost exclusively proactive measures, and (3) the advanced technological expertise necessary to target these crimes usually comes at a high price that is not within the limited resources of many police agencies. It has been found that setting up specialized task forces in police departments is crucial for targeting child pornography crimes (Marcum, Higgins, Ricketts, & Freiburger, 2011).

*Computer forensics*, which involves the assessment of computers and computer-related media for evidence of crimes, has become necessary for detecting child pornography crimes. This is a very complex and technical process, so we only cover a brief overview of the procedures employed in criminal investigations of child pornography crimes. Computer-forensic examinations involve three basic steps:

1. Acquisition: Investigators must acquire electronic information on a computer or computer media and make an exact physical copy (or "mirror image") of all data on the hard drive to preserve the data exactly as they existed at the time of seizure.

2. Authentication: Investigators must ensure that the mirrored image and the original computer media are identical. This is often accomplished using complex forensics software programs that can verify the precision of the mirrored content.

3. Recovery: Investigators view and analyze the acquired data, in addition to hidden files with renamed file extensions, deleted files, and temporary Internet files from the computer's cache. Additionally, investigators learn extensive information about a suspect's browsing history, including particular websites visited, the duration of those visits, and any downloading activity.

## Prosecuting Child Pornography

The child pornography prosecution rate has increased in recent years, likely as a result of advanced law-enforcement detection methods that have brought a greater number of offenders under criminal justice investigation. Charging decisions vary from case to case, and prosecutors often use a mix of complex strategies to try a case. Some prosecutors, for example, may charge one count per image (i.e., if a defendant is caught with ten illegal images, the prosecutor charges the defendant with ten counts of child pornography). Other prosecutors have described a saturation point, at which there is no reason to go beyond a certain number of images, while others have lumped images into categories based on image severity or access date. Some prosecutors base charges not on the number of images, but on the number of devices containing illegal images (computer, cell phone, flash drive, and CD-ROM), while others only charge for images with an identified victim. Needless to say, there is no single way to prosecute child pornography crimes.

Prosecuting child pornography crimes can be difficult, especially with respect to establishing *mens rea*. It is the duty of the prosecutor to prove that the defendant in question *knowingly* possessed the illegal images. The results of the National Juvenile Online Victimization (N-JOV) Prosecutor Study indicate that a number of defenses are encountered by prosecutors of child pornography (Walsh, Wolak, & Finkelhor, 2013). Most of these defenses align with Sykes and Matza's (1957) *techniques of neutralization*. These defenses (or neutralizations) include the following:

- Unknowing or unintentional download of illegal images.
- Someone else with physical access to defendant's computer downloaded the illegal images.
- Addiction or mental illness.
- Downloaded images were not construed as child pornography in the eyes of the defendant.
- Downloaded images were used for research purposes.

One way federal and state statutes have construed the knowing possession of child pornography has to do with images found on a defendant's computer cache. A cache is a storage mechanism designed to speed up the loading of Internet displays, including pictures and movies. When a webpage is viewed, the web browser saves a copy of the page in a folder on the computer's hard drive. This folder is known as the cache. The majority of courts take the position that the images or movies on a hard drive are sufficient evidence to demonstrate possession of child pornography.

In the landmark case *United States v. Tucker* (10th Cir. 2002), forensic examiners discovered child pornography located on the defendant's browser cache, recycle-bin, and C-drive. The defendant argued he did not knowingly possess child pornography, given that he did not actually download or copy any material and he deleted the content off his computer's cache. Nevertheless, the court rejected Tucker's defense on the basis that he was able to control the viewed images in many ways (for example, he could enlarge or "zoom in" on particular images, print them, or copy them to other directories). The court affirmed that the mere act of deleting one's cache is evidence enough of possession, because one cannot destroy what one does not possess and control.

Prosecutors also face challenges with regard to evidence from police investigations, particularly with computer forensics. In the N-JOV Prosecutor Study, 62% of polled prosecutors noted the following difficulties with computer forensics in child pornography cases:

- Timeliness of the forensics examination: This concerns the amount of time it takes for forensic investigators to provide computer-related evidence that is reliable and comprehensive. The amount of digital evidence submitted for analysis varies from one request to another. One investigation may result in the seizure of a single computer, while another may involve multiple computers. As such, cases are often backlogged.

- Chain-of-custody issues: Instances where there are charges of evidence tampering during transportation of evidence among multiple parties.

- Peer-to-Peer (P2P) investigations issues: P2P networks have become a common medium for transfer and sharing of child pornography. Given that these networks do not operate on a centralized server, no one person is responsible for the content of what is shared on them. This creates technical and legal difficulties for prosecutors, especially when deciding whether to try a defendant for dissemination/sharing of child pornography, and not just mere possession.

- Credentials of the forensic examiner or the forensic laboratory: Defense attorneys can question the credentials and qualifications of forensic investigators. In some cases, forensic investigators have been found to falsify their certifications, resumes, and professional references.

## Penalties and Sentencing for Child Pornographers

As mentioned earlier in this chapter, images of child pornography are not protected under the First Amendment, and are, therefore, considered illegal contraband under federal law. Also, we have established that the vast majority of child pornography offenses are committed using the Internet to view or transmit images. For these reasons, federal jurisdiction almost always applies to child pornography. Violations of federal child pornography laws are considered serious crimes, and convicted offenders face severe punishments. These punishments are largely dictated by the *Federal Sentencing Guidelines*, which determine sentences based on two factors: (1) the seriousness of the offense, and (2) the defendant's criminal history. Depending on the seriousness of the offense and the prior criminal history of the offender, these guidelines specify a sentencing range within which the court may sentence the defendant.

From the inception of the sentencing guidelines in 1987 until now, there have been significant revisions to make the penalties substantially more severe. Prior to

1990, simple child pornography possession was not a federal crime. When Congress criminalized possession of child pornography and possession with intent to sell child pornography, the guidelines were amended to impose harsher punishments. After the PROTECT Act was signed into effect, Congress directed the U.S. Sentencing Commission to reduce the frequency of **downward departures**, as well as add enhancements for crimes with aggravated situations, such as (i) the images are violent, sadistic, or masochistic in nature, (ii) the minor was sexually abused, or (iii) the offender has prior convictions for child sexual exploitation. There was a significant impact on punishments for offenders convicted of child pornography. From 1997 to 2007, the mean imprisonment sentence of child pornographers increased from 20.6 months to 91.3 months. The sentencing guidelines currently adhere to the following principles:

(1) Harsher punishments for trafficking (distribution, receipt, and production) than for mere possession.

(2) Harsher punishments if the material involves prepubescent children or sadomasochistic/violent material.

(3) Harsher punishments if material was distributed for financial gain.

(4) Harsher punishments for sending the material to minors or using the material to entice minors into sexual activity.

(5) Harsher punishments for use of a computer for activity.

(6) Harsher punishments for increased number of images.

(7) Minimum sentence of 20 years to maximum sentence of life imprisonment for exploitation of an actual child.

Much controversy surrounds the sentencing of child pornographers. In a survey of federal trial court judges, 70% deemed the guidelines as "too high" as they applied to those in possession of child pornography (U.S. Sentencing Commission, 2010). The Second Circuit Court noted that the guidelines do not do a good job of distinguishing between commercial distributors of child pornography and those merely in possession. As Steiker (2013) shows:

> "The guidelines for child pornography are so high that they treat an offender who never had any contact with a child more severely than the Guideline sentences for repeated sex with a child or for aggravated assault with a firearm that results in bodily injury."
>
> (Steiker, 2013, p. 42)

As a result, many judges have not adhered to these in sentencing child pornographers.

## CURRENT ISSUES IN CHILD PORNOGRAPHY: SEXTING

Recently, new forms of electronic communication (such as Facebook, Twitter, and text messaging) have generated concern among parents, educators, policy makers, and police with respect to how children use them. In particular, recent media coverage detailing the serious consequences of "sexting" has created a new public-safety concern.

Although no legal definition currently exists, sexting generally refers to the sending and/or receiving of sexually suggestive images or messages to peers through a cell phone (Agustina & Gomez-Duran, 2012). This can include nude images or nearly nude images (e.g. images with youths wearing bathing suits, posing provocatively with clothes on, or images that are focused on covered genitalia). Given the relative newness of this phenomenon, researchers have only begun to estimate the prevalence of sexting among today's youth. Some studies have shown that as little as 4% of today's youth have engaged in sexting at some point in their lives (Lenhart, 2009), while other studies estimate a prevalence rate as high as 30% (Martinez-Prather & Vandiver, 2014).

Given the legal definition of child pornography, and how the current law treats content such as this, the immediate reaction may be to assume sexting is a form of child pornography. Recent headlines of teenagers facing felony charges for child pornography offenses situate sexting as a serious crime deserving severe punishments. In October 2014, 30 high school students from a school in suburban Michigan were arrested and placed on felony trial for taking and sending sexually suggestive images of themselves and other students. Some may even be convicted and mandated to register as a sex offender (Jacques, 2014). Some researchers, however, remain skeptical about treating sexting as a form of child pornography. Some argue that the context of the images does not constitute legal child pornography and media coverage resulted in a moral panic (Mitchell, Finkelhor, Jones & Wolak, 2012). As discussed in the first chapter of this textbook, many laws and policies pertaining to sex crimes and sex offenders have been the result of moral panic, with little research or evidence to warrant them. With sexting being a relatively new sexual deviance issue, it will be interesting to see how the law, criminal justice policy, and the broader community treat it in the future.

## CONCLUSION

Child pornography offenses are sex crimes that involve the visual depiction of children involved in a sexual act. Once on the brink of eradication, the advent of the Internet signaled the return and proliferation of child pornography. Like other sex crimes, child pornography is a serious crime with the majority of cases going unreported and unknown to policing authorities. The link between possession/consumption of child pornography and actual sexual abuse of children is certainly more suggestive than it is causal, with research showing conflicting evidence as to whether child pornography causes actual abuse against children. As child pornography crimes have gone high technology, it has become imperative for police to adopt advanced methods of cyber crime investigation, including computer forensics examinations.

## REVIEW POINTS

- There is a range of child pornography crimes, from production and filming, to distribution and trafficking, to download and personal possession.

- Child pornography, once on the brink of eradication, has emerged as one of the fastest growing online enterprises, with an estimated value exceeding $20 billion.

- As child pornographers have relied on high technology, police, courts, and lawmakers have been required to adapt to apprehend offenders.

- Pedophiles use child pornography to satisfy sexual urges, but not all child pornographers are pedophiles by diagnostic measure. There is evidence that some pedophiles may prefer legal images of children to fuel sexual appetites.

- Similar to other sex offenders, child pornographers demonstrate a low rate of recidivism for the same crime.

- In the majority of cases, child pornography offenses are prosecuted as federal crimes, with convicted offenders sentenced under the Federal Sentencing Guidelines.

- Sexting has emerged as a new criminal justice concern about youth, although there is not a consensus about whether it constitutes child pornography.

## REFERENCES

18 U.S.C. §2256
18 U.S.C. §1466A
18 U.S.C. §2252
18 U.S.C. §2256(8)(B))
Adler, A. (2001). The perverse law of child pornography. *Columbia Law Review, 101*, 209–273.
Agustina, J., & Gomez-Duran, J. (2012). Sexting: Research criteria of a globalized social phenomenon. *Archives of Sexual Behavior, 41*(6), 1325–1328.
Akdeniz, Y. (2013). *Internet child pornography and the law: National and international responses.* Ashgate Publishing, Ltd.
Alexy, E. M., Burgess, A. W., & Baker, T. (2005). Internet offenders: Traders, travelers, and combination trader-travelers. *Journal of Interpersonal Violence, 20*(7), 804–812.
American Psychiatric Association. (2013). *Diagnostic and statistical manual of mental disorders, fifth edition.* Washington DC: American Psychiatric Publishing
Ayood, M. F. (1978). The littlest victims. *The Missouri Police Chief*, Winter: 19–22.
Blanchard, R. (2010). The DSM diagnostic criteria for pedophilia. *Archives of Sexual Behavior, 39*(2), 304–316.
Bourke, M. L., & Hernandez, A. E. (2009). The 'Butner Study' redux: A report of the incidence of hands-on child victimization by child pornography offenders. *Journal of Family Violence, 24*(3), 183–191.
Burke, D. D. (1997). Criminalization of virtual child pornography: A constitutional question. *The Harvard Journal on Legislation, 34*, 439–472.
C-SPAN. (2012). Exploitation of Children over the Internet, Day 1. Retrieved from https://www.c-span.org/video/?c3958421/clip-exploitation-children-internet-day-1

Child Pornography Prevention Act of 1996 (CPPA), Pub. L. No. 104–208 (1996)

Danet, B. (1998). Text as mask: Gender, play, and performance on the Internet. In S. G. Jones (Ed.) *Cybersociety 2.0: Revisiting computer-mediated communication and community* (pp. 129–158). Thousand Oaks, CA: Sage.

Eke, A. W., Seto, M. C., & Williams, J. (2011). Examining the criminal history and future offending of child pornography offenders. *Law and Human Behavior, 35*(6), 466–478.

Elliott, I. A., & Beech, A. R. (2009). Understanding online child pornography use: Applying sexual offense theory to internet offenders. *Aggression and Violent Behavior, 14*(3), 180–193.

Faust, E., Bickart, W., Renaud, C., & Camp, S. (2014). Child pornography possessors and child contact sex offenders: A multilevel comparison of demographic characteristics and rates of recidivism. *Sexual Abuse: A Journal of Research and Treatment*. OnlineFirst Version: DOI: 10.1177/1079063214521469.

Groth, A. N., Burgess, A. W., Birnbaum, H. J., & Gary, T. S. (1978). A study of the child molester: Myths and realities. *Journal of the American Criminal Justice Association, 41*(1), 17–22.

Henkin, L. (1963). Morals and the constitution: The sin of obscenity. *Columbia Law Review, 63*(3), 391–414.

Howitt, D. (1995). *Paedophiles and sexual offences against children.* Chichester: Wiley.

Internet Watch Foundation (IWF) (2012). *Annual and Charity Report,* Internet Watch Foundation, Cambridge, UK.

Jacques, I. (2014, October 17). Could your teen face child porn charges? *The Detroit News.* Retrieved December 20, 2014 from http://www.detroitnews.com

Krone, T. (2004). *A typology of online child pornography offending.* Australian Institute of Criminology.

Lam, A., Mitchell, J., & Seto, M. C. (2010). Lay perceptions of child pornography offenders 1. *Canadian Journal of Criminology and Criminal Justice/La Revue canadienne de criminologie et de justice pénale, 52*(2), 173–201.

Lanning, K. V. (2001). *Child molesters: A behavioral analysis.* National Center for Missing and Exploited Children. Washington, DC.

Lenhart, A. (2009). Teens and sexting: How and why minor teens are sending sexually suggestive nude or nearly nude images via text messages. Washington, DC: Pew Internet & American Life Project. Retrieved July 29, 2012 from http://www.pewinternet.org/Reports/2009/Teens-and-Sexting.aspx.

Marcum, C. D., Higgins, G. E., Ricketts, M. L., & Freiburger, T. L. (2011). An assessment of the training and resources dedicated nationally to investigation of the production of child pornography. *Policing, 5*(1), 23–32.

Martinez-Prather, K., & Vandiver, D. M. (2014). Sexting among teenagers in the United States: A retrospective analysis of identifying motivating factors, potential targets, and the role of a capable guardian. *International Journal of Cyber Criminology, 8*(1), 21–35.

Middleton, D., Elliott, I. A., Mandeville-Norden, R., & Beech, A. R. (2006). An investigation into the applicability of the Ward and Siegert Pathways Model of child sexual abuse with Internet offenders. *Psychology, Crime & Law, 12*(6), 589–603.

Miller, L. (2013). Sexual offenses against children: Patterns and motives. *Aggression and Violent Behavior, 18*(5), 506–519.

Mitchell, K. J., Finkelhor, D., Jones, L. M., & Wolak, J. (2012). Prevalence and characteristics of youth sexting: A national study. *Pediatrics, 129*(1), 13–20.

Mitchell, K. J. & Jones, L. M. (2013). Internet-facilitated commercial sexual exploitation of children. Crimes against Children Research Center, University of New Hampshire, Durham, NH.

O'Brien, S. (1983). *Child pornography.* Dubuque, IA: Kendall/Hunt Publishing Co.

O'Connell, R. (2001). Paedophiles networking on the Internet. In Arnaldo, C. A. (Ed.) *Child abuse on the Internet: Ending the silence* (pp. 65–79). UNESCO Publishing/Berghahn Books

Ost, S. (2002). Children at risk: Legal and societal perceptions of the potential threat that the possession of child pornography poses to society. *Journal of Law and Society, 29*(3), 436–460.

Ost, S. (2009). *Child pornography and sexual grooming: Legal and societal responses.* Cambridge: Cambridge University Press.

Paul, B., & Linz, D. G. (2008). The effects of exposure to virtual child pornography on viewer cognitions and attitudes toward deviant sexual behavior. *Communications Research, 35*(1), 3–38.

Richards, D. A. (1974). Free speech and obscenity law: Toward a moral theory of the First Amendment. *University of Pennsylvania Law Review, 123*(1), 45–91.

Riegel, D. L. (2004). Letter to the editor: Effects on boy-attracted pedosexual males of viewing boy erotica. *Archives of Sexual Behavior, 33*(4), 321–323.

Seto, M. C. (2010). Child pornography use and internet solicitation in the diagnosis of pedophilia. *Archives of Sexual Behavior, 39*(3), 591–593.

Seto, M. C., Cantor, J. M., & Blanchard, R. (2006). Child pornography offenses are a valid diagnostic indicator of pedophilia. *Journal of Abnormal Psychology, 115*, 610–615.

Seto, M. C., & Eke, A. W. (2005). The criminal histories and later offending of child pornography offenders. *Sexual Abuse: A Journal of Research and Treatment, 17*(2), 201–210.

Steiker, C. S. (2013). Lessons from two failures: Sentencing for cocaine and child pornography under the federal sentencing guidelines in the United States. *Law & Contemporary Problems, 76*, 27–52.

Sykes, G. M. & Matza, D. (1957). Techniques of neutralization: A theory of delinquency. *American Sociological Review, 22*(6), 664–670.

Taylor, M., Holland, G., & Quayle, E. (2001). Typology of pedophilic picture collections. *The Police Journal, 74*, 97–107.

U.S. Sentencing Commission (2010). Results of survey of United States district judges: January 2010 through March 2010. *Federal Sentencing Report, 23*, 296.

Walsh, W., Wolak, J., & Finkelhor, D. (2013). *Prosecution dilemmas and challenges for child pornography crimes: The Third National Juvenile Online Victimization Study (NJOV-3).* Durham, NH: Crimes Against Children Research Center.

Webb, L., Craissati, J., & Keen, S. (2007). Characteristics of Internet child pornography offenders: A comparison with child molesters. *Sexual Abuse: A Journal of Research and Treatment, 19*(4), 449–465.

Wolak, J., Finkelhor, D., & Mitchell, K. J. (2005). *Child-pornography possessors arrested in Internet-related crimes.* National Center for Missing & Exploited Children. Obtained on January 7, 2016 from http://www.missingkids.com.

Wolak, J., Finkelhor, D., & Mitchell, K. J. (2011). Child pornography possessors: Trends in offender and case characteristics. *Sexual Abuse: A Journal of Research and Treatment, 23*(1), 22–42.

Wolak, J., Finkelhor, D., & Mitchell, K. (2012). *Trends in arrests for child pornography possession: The Third National Juvenile Online Victimization Study (NJOV-3).* Durham, NH: Crimes against Children Research Center.

Wortley, R. K., & Smallbone, S. (2006). *Child pornography on the Internet.* US Department of Justice, Office of Community Oriented Policing Services.

## Court Cases

*Ashcroft v. Free Speech Coalition,* 535 U.S. 234 (2002).
*Free Speech Coalition v. Reno,* 98 F.3d 1083 (9th Cir. 1999).
*Miller v. California,* 413 U.S. 15 (1973).
*New York v. Ferber,* 458 U.S. 747 (1982).
*Osborne v. Ohio,* 495 U.S. 103 (1990).
*Stanley v. Georgia,* 394 U.S. 557 (1969).
The PROTECT Act of 2003 (Pub.L. 108–21, 117 Stat. 650, S. 151).
*United States v. Tucker,* 305 F.3d 1193 (2002).
*United States v. Whorley,* 550 F.3d 326 (4th Cir. 2008).

# DEFINITIONS

**Child Pornography:** Material visually depicting the sexual exploitation of children and adolescents. This can include photographic, film, or other visual representations.

**Combination Trader-Travelers:** Child pornographers who trade child pornography, as well as travel across state and/or national boundaries to sexually abuse or molest children.

**Computer forensics:** assessment of computers and computer-related media for evidence of crimes.

**Cyber Crime:** Any criminal act involving computers, networks, or the Internet.

**DSM-5 (Diagnostic and Statistical Manual of Mental Disorders, fifth edition):** A publication by the American Psychiatric Association that provides a list and diagnosis criteria of all the recognized mental disorders.

**Downward Departures:** Sentences issued by judges that are less severe than the recommended sentence under Federal Sentencing Guidelines.

**Dual Offenders:** Sex offenders who commit child pornography and child sexual abuse concurrently.

**Dynamic (Risk) Factors:** Factors that will change throughout one's life depending on one's situation. These include attitude towards work and employment status.

**Federal Sentencing Guidelines:** Rules that set uniform sentencing policy for defendants convicted of serious felonies.

**Grooming:** The process of befriending and establishing an emotional connection with children for the purpose of sexually abusing them.

**Manga:** A style of comic books created in Japan and developed prior to the twentieth century.

***Mens Rea:*** An element of criminal responsibility referring to a guilty mind or wrongful purpose.

**Miller Test:** A set of three criteria that material must meet in order for it to be considered pornography.

**Obscenity:** Any statement, act, or material which strongly offends against prevailing moral standards (though not necessarily legal standards) of that time.

**Pedophilia/Pedophile:** A psychiatric disorder where afflicted individuals exhibit primary or exclusive sexual attraction to prepubescent children (under the age of 12).

**Phallometric Assessment:** A method of measuring male sexual arousal to both legal and illegal sexual stimuli.

**Predatory Crime:** A broad range of violent crimes against another person, such as murder, robbery or sexual assault.

**Prurient Interests:** To have or to encourage excessive interest in sexual matters.

**Recidivism:** An individual's return or relapse into criminal behavior, often after having received sanctions or punishment for previous criminal behavior.

**Static Factors:** Factors that will remain stable throughout one's life. These include factors such as age at first sexual experience and whether one has been victimized as a child.

**Techniques of Neutralization:** Justifications or rationalizations for violating society's norms and/or committing crimes.

**Typology:** Classification system whereby similar individuals or observations are grouped together. Individuals within a group are considered to be very similar, while groups tend to be very distinct.

**Virtual Child Pornography** (also known as pseudo child pornography): Pornographic material that does not include actual images of children, but creates the illusion of sexual exploitation.

## CHAPTER 6

# Juvenile Sex Offenders

## CHAPTER OBJECTIVES

- Describe the number and characteristics of known juvenile sex offenders.
- Compare/contrast categories of juvenile sex offenders according to different typologies.
- Summarize explanations of juvenile sex crimes.
- Describe criminal justice responses to juvenile sex offenders.
- Distinguish various assessment and treatment techniques for juvenile sex offenders.
- Discuss recidivism rates of juvenile sex offenders.
- Describe rare groups of juvenile sex offenders.

When one thinks of a sex offender, a middle-aged or old man who lurks in the bushes waiting for his next victim might come to mind. As noted in previous chapters, however, sex offenders are a heterogeneous group. This is also true of *juvenile* sex offenders. They commit diverse sex crimes. In this chapter, we provide a summary of the theories, research, and realities of juveniles who commit sex crimes. Although the focus is on juvenile sex offenders, some researchers use the term *adolescents*; hence, both terms are used in this chapter. The purpose of this chapter is not to present all of the available information on juvenile sex offenders, as the scope of that information is too broad for this one chapter. Several authors have written entire books on this topic, which shows the amount of available information is vast.

Media often misrepresent this group of offenders by reporting only the most serious cases. For example, the following newspaper headlines have referred to juvenile sex offenders: "Juvenile Sex Offenders in School with Your Kids" and "Registered Juvenile Sex Offender in Brandenton Facing New Sexual Battery Charge." The public is often led to believe these offenders are poised to prey on schoolmates. There is an assumption in these headlines that juvenile sex offenders are predatory and often repeat their offenses. While some juvenile sex offenders may be predatory and some may be repeat offenders, the largest portion of juvenile sex offenders are neither predatory nor repeat offenders. One of the goals of this chapter is to dispel some of the myths and false assumptions about juvenile sex offenders.

Critical to dispelling these myths and identifying how heterogeneous this group of offenders is, this chapter presents the characteristics of juvenile sex offenders, including their family background, intelligence/academic abilities, substance abuse, *emotional intelligence*, range of abusive behaviors, victim characteristics, and extent of mental illness. The reader will find that juvenile sex offenders, as a group, are diverse on all of these characteristics.

Law enforcement officials and practitioners who work with juvenile sex offenders in developing treatment plans often rely on typologies. Thus, we discuss various typologies that have been developed from empirical studies. Typologies also serve as a way to describe the characteristics of juvenile sex offenders. They reveal how heterogeneous juvenile sex offenders are. For example, one way juvenile sex offenders differ is by the type of victim they choose—peers or other individuals, which is discussed in this chapter. One may notice in reading this chapter, however, that there is a relatively weak link between the typologies that have been developed and the explanations that have been proposed for them. Much of this is due to the state of the research on the topic—it is still relatively new, and many gaps exist in the topics presented here.

In Chapter 10, we discuss the various assessment tools that researchers have developed and practitioners use to evaluate juveniles, as many of those developed for adults cannot be applied to juveniles. While the literature on adults has existed for several decades, research on juvenile sex offenders did not begin until more recently. Nevertheless, the research that does exist sheds light on this population of offenders. A substantial amount of the research appeared in the 1990s and 2000s, which is relied upon for this chapter. Separate assessment tools have been developed because the factors that predict recidivism for juvenile sex offenders differ from those for adult sex offenders.

This chapter also provides a description of the treatment and the recidivism rates of juvenile sex offenders. With regard to treatment, despite the heterogeneity of juvenile sex offenders, cognitive-behavioral treatment is often used—similar to what is used for adult sex offenders. This type of treatment, however, does involve conducting thorough assessments, which allows for cognitive-behavioral treatment to take into consideration individual differences and tailor the treatment for individual offenders. Other types of treatments that have been used with some degree of success are also discussed.

A central myth regarding juvenile sex offenders is that they are all male, predatory, and dangerous. It is also assumed they will escalate over time to commit more serious offenses. Some research has been conducted on rare groups of sex offenders, such as female juvenile sex offenders and juveniles who not only rape, but also kill. Research relying on rare groups is also described to dispel this myth.

## OVERVIEW OF JUVENILE SEX OFFENDERS

There are many reasons why it is important to consider juvenile sex offenders: (1) a small, yet noteworthy, number of adults begin to sexually offend when they are juveniles; (2) juveniles account for a substantial portion of arrests for sex crimes; (3) some juveniles commit serious, violent sex crimes; and (4) sex-offender treatment may need to be modified to meet the specific needs of juveniles.

With regard to continued offending from adolescence to adulthood, it has been noted recently that juvenile sex offenders and adult sex offenders are distinct groups (Lussier & Blockland, 2014). A large percentage of juvenile sex offenders desist—that is, they do not continue offending into adulthood. Adult sex offenders, likewise, do not always begin offending during adolescence.

Knowing that some do begin to offend when they are young can have important implications. Early intervention can prevent future victimizations. If treatment can be provided, not only can the juvenile go on to a healthy and successful future; many victims can be spared.

It is also important to examine juvenile sex offenders because they account for a substantial portion of arrests for sex crimes. In 2014, the FBI reported 1,501 arrests of juveniles for forcible rape (Federal Bureau of Investigation, 2016). This accounted for 15% of the total estimated number of arrests for these offenses. With regard to other sex crimes (excluding prostitution and rape), juveniles accounted for 18% of the arrests in 2014. In 2005, they accounted for 21% of the arrests for other sex crimes. This is a critical point to note, as a perception of juvenile sex offenders is that they are accounting for an increasingly large percentage of sex crimes. This is not accurate.

An expert in the field, David Finkelhor, who is the Director of the Crimes Against Children Research Center at the University of New Hampshire, indicated that any increase in juvenile sex offending likely represents an increase in the *reporting* of sex crimes to legal officials rather than a true increase (Jones, 2007). This is worth noting. As reported in Chapter 1, official statistics on sex offenders are imperfect measures of the true number of sex offenders and may reflect more of what legal officials know than offenders actually do.

Juvenile sex offenders often commit crimes that go beyond "simply experimenting" and include violent crimes. For example, each year a few teenagers not only commit rape—they also commit sexual murders. Noted psychiatrist, Wade Myers, describes some of his encounters with them:

> I subsequently crossed paths with other juvenile murderers during my child psychiatry training. As a consultant to the local juvenile detention center, I had the opportunity to evaluate a variety of children charged with homicide … I was struck by how different these homicides were: each child had a unique story and set of life circumstances that set the stage for their crime. But without question, the most perplexing juvenile cases were the sexual murderers I began to see during my consultation work. My first encounter with this sort of offense involved a 13-year old boy with rape fantasies who clumsily committed his crime on the way home from school. I went to my textbooks and the scientific literature to learn what I could about this type of crime by youth. I came up nearly empty-handed aside from a few case reports, some decades old.
>
> (Myers, 2002, pp. 4–5)

Juvenile sexual murders are rare; thus, the research is limited.

# CHARACTERISTICS OF JUVENILE SEX OFFENDERS

One persistent question in the sex offending literature is whether juvenile sex offenders differ from other offenders. This question, however, is difficult to answer as research has only recently begun. As noted in Chapter 1, obtaining large enough samples of adult sex offenders is difficult. Given that there are even fewer juvenile sex offenders, the problem is magnified. Another problem is that the comparison group is often juveniles who have committed non-sex crimes. Thus, they are compared to another group of offenders rather than a community sample. Despite these obstacles, researchers have been able to garner some information that may shed light on distinguishing juvenile sex offenders from juvenile non-sex offenders.

## Family Dysfunction

Juvenile sex offenders have high rates of family problems (Righthand & Welch, 2004). They often grow up in dysfunctional families, including exposure to marital violence and parents who engaged in substance abuse and other crimes (Manocha & Mezey, 1998).

One study found that the parents of juvenile sex offenders are often disengaged, aloof, and emotionally inaccessible (Miner & Crimmins, 1995). Family conflict is pervasive (Lightfoot & Evans, 2000). One study found that juveniles who had committed sexual abuse, compared to those who had not, were more likely to have had a change in primary caretakers (Awad & Saunders, 1991). Other researchers have found that three-fourths of their sample of juvenile sex offenders were exposed to violence against a female victim (Hunter, Figueredo, Malamuth, & Becker, 2003). Ninety percent of the sample were exposed to a male who exhibited antisocial behavior. Fifty-four percent witnessed a male relative assault a woman. Also, 49% had witnessed a related male threaten another male. Sixty-three percent of the sample had experienced physical abuse by a father/stepfather. Seventy-five percent reported sexual victimization. Thus, the overwhelming portion of studies show that family dysfunction is common among this population of sex offenders.

## Academic Performance and Intelligence (IQ)

In regard to academic performance, the research suggests that juvenile sex offenders do poorly in school. Although a few studies show no significant difference between juvenile sex offenders and non-sex offenders with regard to academic tests and academic ability (Jacobs, Kennedy, & Meyer, 1997), more studies show that juvenile sex offenders have some sort of academic impairment. For example, Veneziano, Veneziano, and LeGrand (2000) report that juvenile sex offenders do not perform well in academic settings. Another study found that the majority of a sample of juvenile sex offenders had less than average intelligence and were more likely to experience school suspensions. Awad and Saunders (1991) found that almost half of juvenile sex offenders had diagnosable learning disorders, and 83% had academic difficulties. Even more alarming, one study found that almost one-third of juvenile sex offenders had some neurological impairment (Ferrara & McDonald, 1996).

In one study, juvenile sex offenders with low IQ were compared to juvenile non-sex offenders who also had low IQ. The juvenile sex offenders with low IQ performed significantly worse than juvenile non-sex offenders with low IQ on the following tasks: switching attention, processing speed, prospective memory, and working memory. Additionally no differences were found between juvenile sex offenders and juvenile non-sex offenders without low IQ. This suggests the "neuropsychological characteristics of juvenile sex offenders are related to their IQ level" (Miyaguchi & Shirataki, 2014, p. 253). Therefore, developmental deficits are potentially related to juvenile sexual offending (Miyaguchi & Shirataki, 2014).

Other studies have also found weaknesses in the executive functioning of juvenile sex offenders (Butler & Seto, 2002; van Wijk et al., 2006; Veneziano, Veneziano, LeGrand, & Richards, 2004). Executive functioning includes attention, cognitive flexibility, working memory, inhibition, and ability to self-monitor. Executive function impairment is relevant with regard to treating juvenile sex offenders. As noted in Chapter 10, the most common type of treatment for sex offenders is cognitive-behavioral treatment. Such treatment is likely to be ineffective for people with neurological impairments because it relies on the ability to process information.

## Substance Abuse

Another question examined in the existing research is whether juvenile sex offenders and their families engage in more substance abuse than juvenile non-sex offenders. It should be noted there is a paucity of research on this topic, and identifying such an association does *not* indicate that substance abuse causes sex crimes. Two factors can be associated (i.e., occur together), yet one may not cause the other.

Lightfoot and Barbaree (1993), in a brief summary of existing literature, said that substance abuse rates among juvenile sex offenders ranged from 3% to 72%. These researchers, however, also described the association between substance abuse and sex crimes as spurious, meaning that substance use does not cause sex crimes; instead substance use and sex crimes occur together because they are both caused by poor coping strategies.

The research on the co-occurrence of substance use and sex crimes among juvenile sexual offenders is unclear. Some studies show there is a co-occurrence (Hsu & Starzynski, 1990; Leibowitz, 2012), while other studies show that juvenile sex offenders have less substance abuse than juvenile non-sex offenders (Seto & Lalumière, 2010). Thus, the association between substance use and sex crimes is disputable, and no clear pattern has been identified.

## Emotional Intelligence

Emotional intelligence includes one's ability to perceive others' emotions and express one's own emotion. This includes one's ability to process emotional information and respond appropriately to different cues in one's social environment. These characteristics are associated with mental health, leadership skills, and employment performance. Existing studies have shown that emotional intelligence is often low for juvenile sex offenders (Bischof, Stith, & Whitney, 1995). Adolescent sex offenders scored higher than non-offending adolescents on an aggression scale and lower on attention to feelings. Furthermore, they were less able to prolong positive moods and less likely to be able to repair negative moods (Moriarty, et al. 2001).

## Behaviors and Victim Characteristics

Juvenile sex offenders commit a wide range of sex crimes. Approximately two-thirds of the sample in one study engaged in either penetration or oral-genital contact, or both (Ryan, Miyoshi, Metzner, Krugman, & Fryer, 1996). Approximately 70% of the victims were female in another study (Righthand & Welch, 2001).

When the victim is male, he is typically very young (Davis & Leitenberg, 1987). Victims of juvenile sexual offenders are often young—more than 60% were younger than 12; 63% were younger than nine; and 40% were younger than six (Ryan et al., 1996). Also, younger victims were more likely than older victims to be related to their offenders (Worling, 1995). The majority of victims are known to their offenders (i.e., acquaintance or relative) (Johnson, 1988). One study found that 39% of juvenile sex offenders were related to their victims (Ryan et al., 1996), while another study found that 46% of the victims were related to their offenders (Johnson, 1988).

Prior sexual victimization also occurs at high rates among juvenile sex offenders (Veneziano et al., 2000); however, this association is not well understood (Veneziano, 2012).[1] Adolescent sex offenders with a history of sexual abuse are more likely than adolescent sex offenders who do not have a history of sexual abuse to have an earlier onset of sex offending, have more victims, abuse both male and female victims, and exhibit more interpersonal problems (Cooper, Murphy, & Haynes, 1996).

## Mental Illness

Much of the literature has identified a high rate of mental illness among juvenile sex offenders. The types of mental illnesses identified among this population include *conduct disorders*, *depression*, and *attention deficit hyperactivity disorder* (ADD/ADHD) (Terry, 2006). One may believe that a juvenile who molests another child or sexually assaults an adult must be "sick" or somehow mentally ill. Are juvenile sex offenders more likely to suffer from mental illness compared to juvenile non-sex offenders? One study found that 70% of 78 juvenile male sex offenders in a residential treatment program specifically designed for those who had committed a sexual crime had a mental illness prior to admission (Kraemer, Salisbury, & Spielman, 1998). Thus, preliminary information regarding mental illness indicates it occurs at a high rate among juvenile sex offenders.

### Depression

Adolescent sex offenders have high rates of depression (Briere & Runtz, 1991; Browne & Finkelhor, 1986; Chaffin, 2008; Mash & Barkley, 1996) compared to juvenile non-sex offenders and non-delinquent juveniles (Katz, 1990), and this is especially true of juvenile sex offenders who have experienced child abuse and/or neglect (Becker, Kaplan, Tenke, & Tartaglini, 1991). Forty-two percent of the adolescent sex offenders in one study scored high on a depression inventory scale (Becker et al., 1991). It also was found that offenders who reported being sexually abused themselves had a higher rate of depression than those who had not been sexually abused. Juveniles who sexually offend often exhibit more withdrawn symptoms, compared to those who have not sexually offended (Katz, 1990).

### Conduct Disorder, ADD/ADHD and Impulsiveness

Another distinction between juvenile sex offenders and juvenile non-sex offenders is behavior problems, including conduct disorders (Terry, 2006). Researchers have found considerable impulsiveness and acting out among juvenile sex offenders (Smith, Monastersky, & Deisher, 1987).

The American Psychiatric Association has identified criteria for conduct disorders, as presented in Focus Box 6.1. Although several studies have found it is not uncommon for juvenile sex offenders to exhibit symptoms of conduct disorders, they do differ significantly on several factors when compared to those with conduct disorders who have not committed a sex crime. For example, families of juvenile sex offenders told more lies, had more family myths, and were more likely to engage in taboo behavior (Baker, Tabacoff, Tornusciolo, & Eisenstadt, 2004). Thus, the development of sex crimes appears to have a different etiology (i.e., causality) than development of conduct-disorder behaviors.

---

*Focus Box 6.1   Conduct Disorder/Antisocial Personality Disorder*

The American Psychiatric Association (2013) defined the criteria for a Conduct Disorder in the DSM-5. A Conduct Disorder involves a host of behaviors that occur consistently over an extended period of time (with at least three behaviors discussed here occurring during the previous year and with at least one symptom occurring within the previous six months). The problematic behaviors include four broad categories: (1) aggression to people or animals, (2) destruction of property, (3) deceitfulness or theft, and (4) serious violations of rules. Several examples are provided for each category (refer to DSM-5 for a complete list). Examples of aggression to people or animals include bullying, engaging in physical fights, cruelty to animals, and cruelty to people. Destruction of property includes physical damage and damage caused by intentional fire setting. Deceitfulness or theft involves breaking into someone else's property (e.g., house or car), shoplifting, and forgery. Serious violations of rules include violating a curfew, running away, and school truancy. This host of behaviors must cause impairment in one's work, school, or social functioning. This disorder can range in severity from "mild" to "severe." For those who are at least 18 years old, the disorder is referred to as Antisocial Personality Disorder.

Source: (American Psychiatric Association (2013): *Diagnostic and Statistical Manual of Mental Disorders, fifth edition*)

## Juvenile Sex Offenders Compared to Other Groups

Fagan and Wexler (1988) reported that juvenile sex offenders were more likely than violent offenders (non-sex offenders) to live with their birth parents and have family not involved in the criminal justice system. They also had fewer drug and alcohol problems and appeared to be more sexually and socially isolated—fewer girlfriends and less interest in sex.

When compared to adult sex offenders, juvenile sex offenders are less likely to commit sex crimes against strangers and less likely to be diagnosed with a *paraphilia* (any intense and persistent sexual interest in objects not normally associated with sexual arousal). They also have fewer victims, are less compulsive, and their patterns of arousal are more fluid, as measured by psychophysiological measures (Becker, 2007).

Although one study reported no substantial *psychopathological* differences between juvenile sex offenders and violent non-sex offenders (Fagan & Wexler, 1988), another study distinguished between adolescent sex offenders with and without a history of sexual abuse and found those with an abuse history had greater psychopathology (Cooper et al., 1996).

## JUVENILE SEX-OFFENDER DISTINCTIONS AND TYPOLOGIES

Typologies serve as a way to organize heterogeneous offenders into homogeneous categories. Typologies can assist in identifying the profile for a specific sex crime. Characteristics of a crime scene, for example, can reveal characteristics about the offender. It should be noted that not all offenders fit into a distinct classification scheme. Hence, multiple typologies have been developed based on various characteristics. This section presents typologies that have been developed for juvenile sex offenders. Typologies can also be useful for treatment purposes—as the motivation or trigger to commit a sex crime may vary among the categories.

### Distinction: Juveniles Who Abuse Peers vs. Juveniles Who Abuse Children

Although detailed typologies have been proposed, one group of researchers has argued that juveniles who sexually offend can be distinguished simply by (1) those who molest children, and (2) those who sexually abuse peers or adults (Barbaree & Cortoni, 1993). Other researchers have also made this simple distinction (e.g., Hsu & Starzynski, 1990; Hunter, 2000). Hunter et al. (2003) found those who molested prepubescent victims had greater psychosocial deficits than those who molested pubescent victims.

Juveniles who molest children report lower self-esteem, higher levels of social isolation, and more chaotic backgrounds than those who sexually abuse peers. Those who sexually abuse peers, however, are more likely to have witnessed family violence more frequently and have family members who have committed crimes. Also, during the offense, child molesters were less likely than peer abusers to use violence. The following variables were significant predictors of being either a child molester or a peer sexual abuser: knowing the victim, being the victim of bullying, and lacking age-appropriate friends. More specifically, child molesters had higher odds of knowing the victim, being the victim of bullying, and lacking age-appropriate friends. This research was based on a comparison of only 21 child abusers and 22 peer abusers. Thus, the results may not be applicable to all juvenile sex offenders (Gunby & Woodhams, 2010).

### Typologies

One researcher divided a group of juveniles into the following categories: child molesters, rapists, sexually reactive children, fondlers, paraphilic offenders, and "others" (Prentky, Harris, & Righthand, 2000). These categories were not based on any statistical analysis, but rather on the researchers' personal observations. The typology was based, specifically, on the juvenile's family characteristics, peer relationships, social skills, and other behaviors.

The typology developed by O'Brien and Bera (1986) had seven categories of juvenile sex offenders. The typology was based on the offender's behaviors, offense motivations, family characteristics, and personality factors. The details of the seven categories are presented in Table 6.1.

Långström, Grann, and Lindblad's (2000) typology yielded five clusters. These clusters were based on characteristics of the offense (e.g., relationship to the victim, where the offense occurred, level of violence, whether penetration occurred, etc.). One researcher relied upon the *Minnesota Multiphasic Personality Inventory*

**TABLE 6.1** *Overview of Juvenile Sex Offender Typologies*

**O'BRIEN & BERA (1986) TYPOLOGY: SEVEN CATEGORIES**

| | |
|---|---|
| Naïve experimenter | • Young (11–14 years old)<br>• Some history of behavior problems<br>• Adequate social skills/peer relationships<br>• Sexually naïve<br>• Most likely to engage in situational abuse, such as babysitting abuse, and camping/family outing |
| Undersocialized child exploiter | • Experiences chronic social isolation<br>• Few friends his own age<br>• Has younger friends (who admire him)<br>• Some history of acting out<br>• Over-involved mother and distant father are common |
| Pseudo-socialized | • Older adolescent<br>• Good social skills<br>• Little/no history of behavior problems<br>• May have been victimized when he was a child<br>• Above-average intelligence<br>• Offender rationalizes sexual abuse<br>• Shows little guilt/remorse<br>• Views the abuse as non-abusive (intimate, mutually consenting)<br>• Narcissistic |
| Sexual aggressive | • Abusive/disorganized family<br>• Good social skills with same age peers<br>• Antisocial or character-disorder personality<br>• Charming/gregarious personality<br>• Uses violence or forced threats<br>• Victimizes peers and/or adults<br>• Motivation of abuse is power, domination, express anger, and humiliate victim<br>• May be a learned sexual arousal response to violence |
| Sexual compulsive | • Rigid/enmeshed family structure<br>• Emotionally repressive parents<br>• Offender has difficulty expressing negative emotions<br>• Has paraphilias (that do not involve touch, such as voyeurism)<br>• Sexual abuse is planned |
| Disturbed impulsive | • History of psychological problems, learning disorders, family problems<br>• Impulsive sexual abuse<br>• Sexual abuse may be a single act or pattern of odd ritualistic abuse involving children<br>• Impaired inhibitions<br>• Complex motivation for abuse |

*(Continued)*

**TABLE 6.1** (Continued)

| Group influenced | <ul><li>Younger teen</li><li>No previous contact with criminal justice system likely</li><li>Abuse occurs in the context of a group setting</li><li>Victim is usually an acquaintance</li><li>Blame is placed on others in the group</li><li>Motivation is from either peer pressure or attempt to gain approval from peers</li></ul> |
|---|---|

**LÅNGSTRÖM ET AL. (2000): FIVE CATEGORIES**

| Cluster 1 | <ul><li>Molested one male child (public area)</li><li>Does not know victim</li><li>Low to moderate amount of violence</li></ul> |
|---|---|
| Cluster 2 | <ul><li>Non-contact (exhibitionism) type offense</li><li>Peers or adult female victim</li><li>Most offend more than once with multiple victims</li><li>Low level of violence</li></ul> |
| Cluster 3 | <ul><li>Commits contact offense; usually only one (in public area)</li><li>Penetration typically occurs during abuse</li><li>Juvenile or adult female victim</li><li>Moderate to high levels of violence</li></ul> |
| Cluster 4 | <ul><li>Known victim</li><li>Occurs in private location</li><li>Penetration usually occurs</li><li>Low levels of violence</li></ul> |
| Cluster 5 | <ul><li>Contact sexual crimes (in private location)</li><li>Known juvenile or adult female victim</li><li>Involves (at least) penetration</li><li>Moderate to high levels of violence</li><li>Slightly less than half used a weapon</li></ul> |

**SMITH ET AL. (1987): FOUR CATEGORIES**

| Group I | <ul><li>Normal range profile: shy, over-controlled, worrier, few friends</li></ul> |
|---|---|
| Group II | <ul><li>Most disturbed profile: demanding, narcissistic, relies on illness for attention, argumentative, insecure, relies on fantasy to problem solve</li></ul> |
| Group III | <ul><li>Normal range profile: frank and realistic (in describing self), outgoing, normal affect, no impaired judgment, emotionally over-controlled, possible violent outbursts</li></ul> |
| Group IV | <ul><li>Abnormal range profile: impulsive, poor self-control, poor judgment, distrustful, alienated, likely to strike out towards others, schizoid personality, and undersocialized</li></ul> |

| BECKER ET AL. (1986): THREE CATEGORIES | |
|---|---|
| Continued delinquency | • Commits additional non-sexual crimes after initial sex crime |
| Continued sexual offending | • Commits additional sexual crimes after initial sex crime |
| No further offending | • Commits no further crime after initial sex crime |
| GRAVES (AS CITED IN WEINROTT, 1996): THREE CATEGORIES | |
| Sexually assaultive | • Victims are peers or adults |
| Pedophilic | • Victims were at least three years younger than himself |
| Undifferentiated | • Commit sexual and non-sexual crimes |

(MMPI) assessment to identify four types of juvenile sex-offender categories (Smith et al., 1987). The four categories (as presented in Table 6.1) include two groups in the normal range, one in an abnormal range, and one presenting with the most disturbed range.

Similarly, Becker, Cunningham-Rathner, and Kaplan (1986) relied upon juveniles' offending patterns to develop a typology (continued sexual offending, continued non-sexual offending, and desistence) of three categories. Another researcher identified three categories of juvenile sex offenders, yet these were based on a limited number of factors: age of victim and whether the offender committed non-sexual crimes in addition to the sex crime (Graves as cited in Graves, Openshaw, Ascoine, & Ericksen, 1996).

## Typologies Based on Personality

Other researchers have also identified typologies based on different factors. For example, Richardson, Kelley, Graham, and Bhate (2004) and Oxnam and Vess (2006) relied on the Millon Adolescent Clinical Inventory and identified several categories of juvenile sex offenders based on personality characteristics. Richardson et al. (2004) identified five categories (normal, antisocial, submissive, dysthymic/inhibited, and dysthymic negativistic), whereas Oxnam and Vess (2006) identified three categories (antisocial/externalizing, withdrawn/socially inadequate, and those without clinical symptoms).

Another researcher (Worling, 2001) also used a personality inventory to construct a typology of juvenile sex offenders. His typology included four types of personalities: antisocial/impulsive, unusual/isolated, over-controlled/reserved, and confident/aggressive. Thus, what is clear from the various typologies is the lack of consistency, even among typologies generated by similar instruments. To improve typologies and perhaps to generate greater consistency, larger samples and consistent use of instruments are needed.

# EXPLANATIONS OF JUVENILES COMMITTING SEX CRIMES

Why do juveniles commit sex crimes? As presented in Chapter 2, many theories have been proposed to explain crimes in general, including sex crimes. Several researchers, however, have proposed specific explanations of why juveniles commit sex crimes, not crimes in general.

## Experimentation

A New York Times Magazine news article asked, "How can you distinguish a budding pedophile from a kid with real boundary problems?" (Jones, 2007). This is a complex question to answer, and in attempting to answer it, one researcher noted there are many "in-between" juveniles who are difficult to categorize:

> It's not hard to categorize an act in which a 12-year-old grabs a girl's rear end. And, on the other extreme, it's not difficult to classify a 17-year-old who rapes young children. But many juveniles adjudicated (a term used in juvenile court to indicate a determination of delinquency) for sex crimes fall somewhere in between, both in terms of ages and offenses. How, for instance, should we categorize a … 14-year-old who was sexually aroused and asked a kindergarten-age girl to lick his penis?
>
> (Jones, 2007, n.p.)

Over the past 40 years, perceptions of juvenile sex offenders have changed substantially. In the past, juveniles who acted out sexually often were perceived as merely "experimenting" (Reiss, 1960). In the 1980s, however, this perception changed (Lussier & Blockland, 2014) because of several findings, including (1) juvenile sex offenders accounted for a large percentage of sex crimes; (2) juvenile sex offenders committed up to hundreds of sex crimes during their lifetimes; and (3) clinicians and practitioners expressed concern about them—as adults beginning their sex offending during their adolescence (Barbaree & Cortoni, 1993). It was believed that today's juvenile sex offender is "tomorrow's adult sex offender" (Lussier & Blockland, 2014, p. 153). This belief, however, has been challenged. Many *prospective* and *longitudinal studies* show no continuation from juvenile sex crime to adult sex crime.

The belief that juveniles who sexually offend become adults who sexually offend was based on an overreliance on *retrospective studies*, which take adult sex offenders and examine their pasts. Retrospective studies fail to capture a sample of juveniles who desist from sex crimes after they become adults (Abel et al., 1987). Research that relies on a criminal-career approach, which is prospective, has shown that many juvenile sex offenders do not continue to commit sex crimes in adulthood and that many adult sex offenders did not begin to commit sex crimes during adolescence (Lussier & Blockland, 2014).

It should be noted, however, that those who begin offending when they are young (for crime in general, not just sex crimes) often continue to offend in adulthood (Moffitt, 1993). It has been noted that this is not a perfect association—some early starters do not continue to offend into adulthood (Piquero, Farrington, & Blumstein, 2003). Overall, a large portion of existing studies show that the percentage of juvenile sex offenders who continue to commit sex crimes into adulthood is low—less than 10% (Kemper & Kistner, 2007; Nisbet, Wilson, & Smallbone, 2004; Vandiver, 2006a; Zimring, Jennings, & Piquero, 2009). Some studies that have assessed a sample of juvenile sex offenders for a long period of time show a slightly higher rate of recidivism, between 10% and 15% (Lussier, Van den Berg, Bijleveld, & Hendriks, 2012). Another study, however, yielded a 30% recidivism rate for juvenile sex offenders (Rubinstein, Yeager, Yeager, Goodstein, & Lewis, 1993). Still another study reported that "… being a juvenile sex offender did not significantly increase the likelihood for an individual being an adult sex offender, nor did the frequency of sexual offending" (Zimring et al., 2009, p. 58).

Overall, prospective studies show the most promise in determining the actual offending patterns of juvenile sex offenders, and most of these studies show that a small percentage of juvenile sexual offenders continue to sexually offend in adulthood, while the majority do not continue to commit sex crimes. For example, Vandiver (2006b) reported only 4% of a sample of 300 juvenile sex offenders were arrested for a sex crime after they turned 17 years old. Research, however, has found that those who commit a sex crime during adolescence have high recidivism rates for crime in general.

## Exposure to Pornography

Exposure to pornography, especially at an early age, has been proposed as a possible explanation for juvenile sex offending (Zgourides, Monto, & Harris, 1997). In one study, for example, it was found that 90% of one sample had some exposure to pornography (Becker & Stein, 1991). In another study, it was found that 41% of juvenile sex offenders had looked at pornographic magazines, compared to only 16% of non-offenders (Zgourides et al., 1997). It was also found that, for some of the offenders, use of pornographic material occurred right before commission of the sex crime. The researchers speculate that the context of the viewing of the pornography may be an important factor. Juvenile sex offenders may be using pornography as a precursor to a sex crime, whereas a non-offender may be viewing it out of curiosity. Thus far, the finding is relatively consistent: juvenile sex offenders have a higher rate of exposure to pornographic material than non-offenders.

### Sexual-Abuse Cycle

Another researcher has proposed a sex-abuse cycle specific to child abuse. First, the juvenile has a negative self-image, possibly related to upbringing and caused by physical abuse, sexual abuse, and/or other factors, such as a chaotic, violent household (Becker, 2007). Subsequently, the juvenile develops low self-esteem and becomes socially isolated. This leads to poor coping strategies—especially when negative situations occur. The juvenile begins to predict negative reactions from others. This leads to more social isolation and fantasies stemming from lack of power and control. When a triggering event occurs, such as boredom, or a traumatic event, these fantasies can lead to the commission of a sex crime. This reinforces a poor self-image and creates a sex-abuse cycle. *Cognitive distortions* often facilitate the offending.

### An Extension of Antisocial Behavior

From a *meta-analysis*, researchers noted that adolescent sex crimes could not be explained simply as an extension of antisocial behaviors. It was noted that adolescent sex offenders, compared to adolescent non-sex offenders, have less extensive criminal histories, fewer antisocial peers, and fewer substance-abuse problems. They do appear to have more of an abuse history and more exposure to sexual violence. They also have more atypical sexual interests, anxiety, and low self-esteem when compared to adolescent non-sex offenders (Seto & Lalumière, 2010).

## CRIMINAL JUSTICE RESPONSE TO JUVENILE SEX OFFENDERS

*Adjudicated* juvenile sex offenders are processed by the juvenile justice system, which is required to balance the safety of the community with the nearly impossible task of identifying those who are most at risk for re-offending. One juvenile sex-offender expert, Mark Chaffin, noted:

> If someone says I want to protect the public from the very small number of individuals who are highly dangerous, but I don't want to put children in institutions for things they might have done, the reality is you cannot have it both ways.
>
> (Michels, 2012, n.p.)

He also explains that a very small number of juveniles are likely to do horrible things. Thus, we run the risk of overreacting and restricting too many juveniles—many of whom would not commit subsequent sex crimes—or underreacting and allowing those who are at high risk to commit future sex crimes or to live in the community with too few restrictions. In this section, we discuss the trends in the juvenile justice system's response to juvenile sex offenders.

## Juvenile Waivers to Adult Court

*Juvenile waivers* have affected the way juveniles are processed through the system by requiring a juvenile to be tried in an adult criminal court rather than juvenile court. Although very little has been written specifically on the waiver of juvenile sex offenders to adult court, much has been written about waiving juvenile offenders, in general, to adult court (not just juvenile sex offenders). In most states, a juvenile must be at least 17 years old to be waived out of juvenile court, but some states allow some as young as 15 and 16 to be waived to adult criminal court. Typical offenses for juvenile waivers include (but are not limited to) drug possession/distribution, crimes against persons, and to a lesser extent, property and public order crimes (Puzzanchera & Addie, 2014).

The use of juvenile waivers steadily increased from 1986 to 1994. Since then they have steadily decreased. The types of cases making up the majority of waivers have changed over time. Approximately half of the cases waived to adult court from 1993 to 2010 involved crimes against persons, which included sex crimes. Prior to that time, drug offenses made up the highest percentage of cases waived to adult criminal court. It should be noted that during this period, concern about juvenile sex crimes also increased. It is not known, however, how much of the increase in juvenile waivers involved sex crimes specifically. A Juvenile Court Statistics summary reported that, in 2010, for every 1,000 referrals to juvenile court for violent crimes (including murder, rape, robbery, and aggravated assault), 28% were waived to criminal court. Thus, a sizeable percentage of sex crimes committed by juveniles is probably processed in adult criminal court (Puzzanchera & Robson, 2014).

## Sentencing Outcomes for Juveniles

Juvenile sex offenders have been given lengthy sentences and strict probation conditions over the past decade (Jones, 2007). This is in spite of the U.S. Supreme Court setting limits on how juveniles processed in the criminal justice system. For example, the U.S. Supreme Court ruled that the death penalty for juveniles is unconstitutional (*Roper v. Simmons, 2005*). Aside from murder, juveniles cannot be given mandatory life sentences without parole (*Graham v. Florida, 2010*). Despite these limits, laws regulating sex offenders often combine juveniles with adults. Thus, as the Supreme Court sets limits on excessive punishments of juveniles, state and federal laws have increased restrictions on juvenile sex offenders.

Although Juvenile Court Statistics do not report information specifically for juvenile sex offenders, it does report on violent crimes committed by juveniles, which include murder, rape, robbery, and aggravated assault. Of 1,000 violent crime cases in 2010, approximately 38% resulted in probation (Puzzanchera & Robson, 2014). Many juvenile sex offenders are mandated to outpatient sex-offender treatment (Center for Sex Offender Management, n.d.). Only 17% of juveniles referred to court are sent to an out-of-home placement (Puzzanchera & Robson, 2014). Fourteen percent of the cases are dismissed, and 10% receive some "other" sanction.

Many juveniles who are adjudicated for a sex crime receive probation paired with mandatory sex-offender treatment. This likely includes **wraparound services**, **functional family therapy**, and **multisystemic therapy**, which are all described later in the treatment section of this chapter—this in addition to the punishment that a juvenile is given by the juvenile court (or adult court for those who are waived). Juvenile sex offenders can also be required to register as sex offenders.

### Requirement to Register: Adam Walsh Act

A recent federal law, the Adam Walsh Act, requires that certain juveniles register as a sex offender. The Act is also known as the Sex Offender Registration and Notification Act (SORNA). As a federal law, it establishes guidelines for all states to follow or risk losing certain federal funding. Each state, however, can establish stricter guidelines than are prescribed by the law. SORNA requires any juvenile who commits a sex crime against a child under the age of 12 to register as a sex offender. Additionally, any juvenile who is 14 years old or older and has committed any crime that is similar to or more serious than aggravated sexual assault, as defined by the federal law, is required to register as well. The only exception to these guidelines is a "Romeo and Juliet" clause, which includes instances in which the victim is at least 13 years old and no more than four years younger than the offender (discussed in greater detail in Chapter 11). SORNA essentially limits the discretion of judges and mandates juveniles who commit the offenses noted above to register as a sex offender for possibly the rest of their lives (McPherson, 2007).

### Civil Commitment

In 1997, the U.S. Supreme Court ruled that civil commitment for sex offenders is constitutional (Kansas v. Hendricks, 1997). Civil commitments involve **Sexually Violent Predator laws**. Thus, when sex offenders, including juveniles, have completed their prison sentence, yet are still considered to be a threat to society—based on their likelihood of committing a future sex act—the offender can be civilly committed. This means they can be required to remain in an in-patient facility until they are no longer deemed a threat. As one can imagine, these are highly controversial laws. At least ten states currently allow for a juvenile sex offender to be civilly committed. Pennsylvania, for example, has established a civil commitment program for juveniles who are aging out of the juvenile justice system (Michels, 2012). As they become too old to remain in juvenile justice custody, a petition is filed for their civil commitment.

The outcome for many juvenile sex offenders who are processed through the juvenile justice system is mandatory treatment. As part of many, if not all, treatment programs, the first step is a thorough assessment.

# JUVENILE SEX-OFFENDER ASSESSMENT

Researchers have identified at least seven reasons for assessing juvenile sex offenders: decisions regarding (1) prosecution; (2) sentencing and disposition; (3) supervision and case planning; (4) discharge from residential treatment; (5) admission into/discharge from community-based treatment; (6) community notification; and (7) out-of-home or in-home placement (Prentky et al., 2000).

Assessment tools for sex offenders are relied upon to identify whether they are at risk for committing additional sex crimes. Assessment tools are developed by examining factors that are correlated with sexual recidivism. In 1983, Ageton (1983) found that only one variable, out of many, predicted sexual recidivism: having delinquent peers. In a subsequent study comparing juvenile sex offenders with juvenile non-sex offenders, juvenile sex offenders appeared less defensive, more depressed, and less likely to deny sexual behavior (Smith & Monastersky, 1986). In a 1991 study, juvenile sex offenders who recidivated were compared to juvenile sex offenders who did not recidivate, and it was found that recidivists were more likely to have victims who were strangers, child victims, and deviant sexual arousal patterns, as determined by a therapist (Kahn & Chambers, 1991). Prentky et al. (2000) conducted a thorough review of the existing literature and noted that juvenile sex offenders have limited social and interpersonal skills and are often socially isolated.

In 1993, the National Task Force on Juvenile Sexual Offending stated, "Currently, there are no scientifically validated instruments or criteria to assess risk of re-offense" (National Task Force on Juvenile Sexual Offending, 1993, p. 29). Since then, however, several assessment tools have been developed for juvenile sex offenders. These include, but are not limited to: Juvenile Sex Offender Assessment Protocol-II (J-SOAP-II), Estimate of Risk of Adolescent Sexual Offender Recidivism (ERASOR) (Worling, Bookalam, & Litlejohn, 2012), and the Juvenile Sexual Offense Recidivism Risk Assessment Tool-II (JSORRAT-II). Empirical evidence for these assessment tools suggests they are able to accurately predict juvenile sexual recidivism (Viljoen et al. 2009). Another study later revealed the effectiveness of MEGA♪ (Multiplex Empirically Guided Inventory of Ecological Aggregates for Assessing Sexually Abusive Adolescents and Children) and its application to a broad range of youth, including those with low intellectual functioning. Each of these assessment tools is discussed below.

## Juvenile Sex Offender Assessment Protocol-II (J-SOAP-II)

Prentky, Harris, and Righthand developed J-SOAP in 2000. After a thorough review of the literature at the time, 23 potential correlates of juvenile sex-offender recidivism were identified (Prentky & Righthand, 2003). After several studies were conducted, the instrument was updated, which is the current version, J-SOAP-II. "The J-SOAP is ... a 'structured risk assessment guide' that uses instrument-informed clinical judgment to determine level of recidivism risk" (Center for Families, Children &

the Court, 2012, p. 11). It predicts sex and non-sex crimes. It was designed for juvenile male sex offenders between the ages of 12 and 18 who have already committed a sex crime or those who have a history of sexually coercing others.

The instrument includes a checklist of 28 items that comprise four scales. The first two scales, which measure *static factors* (factors that will remain stable throughout one's life), assess: (1) the youth's sexual drive or preoccupation, (2) the number of victims, (3) the youth's behavior problems, and (4) the history of prior offenses (Center for Families, Children & the Court, 2012).

The last two scales measure the following *dynamic factors* (factors that will change throughout one's life depending on one's situation): (1) the level of responsibility the youth accepts for his offense(s), (2) the level of empathy, (3) the ability to manage sexual urges, and (4) stability in school.

Each scale's score is totaled for an overall score. Higher scores indicate higher risk. The clinician, based on a comprehensive evaluation, determines the level of risk. The scores for the subscales can be used to make decisions regarding treatment, placement, level of supervision for those on probation/parole, and the youth's progress in treatment. The instrument, especially the dynamic scales, can be administered several times over an extended period of time to measure progress.

## Estimate of Risk of Adolescent Sexual Offense Recidivism (ERASOR)

The goal of the ERASOR is to predict short-term risk for male sex offenders ages 12 to 18 (Center for Families, Children and the Court, 2012; Worling & Curwen, 2001). It is considered an empirically-guided approach and should only be used on adolescents who have already committed at least one sexual assault. The factors included in the assessment tool are based on existing literature. The ERASOR assesses 25 risk factors in several areas, such as sexual attitudes and behavior, history of sexual assaults, psychosocial functioning, family/environmental functioning, and treatment.

Each item is scored with the following options: present, possibly or partially present, not present, or unknown. Not all of the factors included in the assessment tool have been validated. The authors, however, note that they have received support in the literature (adult sex-offender literature and juvenile recidivism literature in general) or that clinicians generally accept them. Like the J-SOAP-II, the clinician makes a final decision regarding risk level.

## Juvenile Sexual Offense Recidivism Risk Assessment Tool-II (JSORRAT-II)

The JSORRAT-II is also an empirically-based assessment tool that was developed to assess sexual recidivism risk for juvenile males who have already committed a sex crime (Center for Families, Children & the Court, 2012; Epperson, Ralston, Fowers, & DeWitt, 2006). JSORRAT focuses on male sex offenders ages 12 to 18. The tool was developed from an examination of 600 male juvenile sex offenders in Utah and has been validated on other samples. Seven categories (based on 12 items) comprise this tool: (1) sex offending history, (2) offense characteristics, 3) sexual crime treatment history, (4) abuse history, (5) special education history, (6) school discipline history, and (7) non-sexual offending behavior.

The tool includes only static factors, and an assessment is conducted from a thorough review of an offender's case file. The scores are totaled, and there are three risk groups: low, moderate, and high.

## Multiplex Empirically Guided Inventory of Ecological Aggregates for Assessing Sexually Abusive Adolescents and Children (MEGA♪)

MEGA♪ was developed in 2006 by Miccio-Fonseca and is appropriate for male and female sex offenders ages 4 to 19. It can be used for youth with low intellectual functioning. It provides an individualized risk assessment report according to the age and gender of the offender. Cut-off scores are provided. It includes four scales: risk, protective, estrangement, and persistent sexual deviancy. Seventy-five items assess a youth's sexual behavior, neuropsychological functioning, antisocial behaviors, and family-history factors related to sexuality and any history of child sexual abuse. Each item is scored as either "present" or "not present" (Center for Families, Children & the Court, 2012; Miccio-Fonseca, 2006).

## JUVENILE SEX-OFFENDER TREATMENT

Juvenile sex-offender treatment, by and large, is based upon adult sex-offender treatment (Lambie & Seymour, 2006), despite research indicating juvenile sex offenders may be different from adult sex offenders (Gunby & Woodhams, 2010). As described by a well-known therapist, Robert Longo, in a New York Times Magazine article, treatment for juvenile sex offenders has changed substantially in the past few years:

> As part of [adolescent boys' sex offender] treatment, the boys had to keep journals – which Longo read – in which they detailed their sexual fantasies and logged how frequently they masturbated to those fantasies. They created "relapse-prevention plans," based on the idea that sex offending is like an addiction and that teenagers need to be watchful of any "triggers" (pornography, anger) that might initiate their "cycle" of re-offending. And at the beginning of each group session, the boys introduced themselves much as an alcoholic begins an Alcoholics Anonymous meeting: "I'm Brian, and I'm a sex offender. I sexually offended against a 10-year old boy; I made him lick my penis three times." Sex-offender therapy for juveniles was a new field in the 1980s, and Longo, like other therapists was basing his practices on what he knew: the adult sex-offender-treatment models ... As it turns out, he went on to say, "much of it was wrong." There is no proof that ... using adult sex-offender

treatments on juveniles is effective. Adult models he noted don't account for adolescent development and how family and environment affect children's behavior.

(Jones, 2007, n.p.)

Treatment for juvenile sex offenders was first developed in 1975; yet it was not until the 1980s when more structured programs were created (Lab, Shields, & Schondel, 1993). In 1980, there were only 20 juvenile sex-offender treatment programs (National Adolescent Perpetrator Network, 1993). Also, at this time, the rate of adjudicated juvenile sex offenders had increased (Reitzel & Carbonell, 2006). Mandatory treatment was urged by the National Adolescent Perpetrator Network (1993). Researchers reported that by 1992, there were 750 outpatient and residential treatment programs for juvenile sex offenders (Burton & Smith-Darden, 2000).

Juvenile sex offenders are treated either in a residential or outpatient center. One study showed that of 20,000 juvenile sex offenders who received sex-offender treatment, half were treated in a residential center (Center for Sex Offender Management, n.d.). Many factors, many of those identified during the assessment phase, will determine whether a juvenile is treated in an inpatient or outpatient center. The following is an explanation provided by the Center for Sex Offender Management (n.d., p. 3) in a training manual regarding such decisions:

> To illustrate, a youth who evidences considerable behavioral disturbances or aggression, demonstrates longstanding or chronic patterns of sexual deviance, resides in a chaotic home environment, and has considerable treatment needs may be best served in a residential program. And if the youth suffers from significant mental health symptoms that cause him to be a danger to himself or others, an inpatient psychiatric setting may be warranted.
>
> Conversely, a juvenile who seems to be more stable overall, has a supportive and structured home environment, has demonstrated a limited number of sexual behavior problems, and is motivated to change will probably be considered appropriate for treatment in the community.

When treatment programs for juvenile sex offenders were being developed in the 1980s and later, they lacked a foundation of empirically-based findings to build for effective therapy (Reitzel & Carbonell, 2006). More recently, suggested treatment included wraparound services, functional family therapy, cognitive-behavioral approaches (Walker, McGovern, Poey, & Otis, 2004), and multisystemic therapy (Center for Sex Offender Management, n.d.).

Wraparound services involve assigning a juvenile sex offender a case manager who is responsible for coordinating services within the community. Thus, there is an attempt to manage the juvenile in the community as opposed to providing services in a residential treatment center. Services are provided for not only the youth, but also the family. The case manager takes on many roles, including mentoring, supportive, and supervisory roles. It is also common for wraparound services to include a multidisciplinary team approach. Initial research on wraparound services show promising results, with reduced recidivism rates among those who have received this type of treatment (Aos, Phipps, Barnoski, & Lieb, 2001; Center for Sex Offender Management, n.d.).

Functional family therapy, as the name suggests, focuses on the structure and dynamics of the family. The focus is to provide parents with the skills necessary to provide appropriate boundaries, discipline, and support for the child. This type of therapy has existed for several decades and has been used for families with and without a juvenile sex offender (Aos et al., 2001; Center for Sex Offender Management, n.d.).

Multisystemic therapy focuses on, "improving family functioning, enhancing parenting skills, increasing the youth's associations with prosocial peers, improving school performance, and building upon community supports" (Center for Sex Offender Management, n.d., p. 9). It is similar to functional family therapy in that it involves the whole family and addresses multiple factors associated with antisocial behavior. The family is involved in developing a treatment plan. Initial research studies showed that not only were recidivism rates lower for those who participated in the treatment, but other improvements were also made, such as family functioning, school performance, peer relationships, and prosocial behaviors (Center for Sex Offender Management, n.d.; Saldana, Swenson, & Letourneau, 2006).

Cognitive-behavioral treatment is defined by the National Alliance of the Mentally Ill as a form of treatment that examines the intersection of thoughts, feelings and behaviors. It involves the identification of thinking patterns that are precursors to problem behaviors, such as committing a sex crime. It also involves the client and therapist actively working together and includes the client taking an active role in their own treatment (NAMI, n.d.). Cognitive-behavioral treatment is the most common type of treatment for juvenile sex offenders, and positive results have been obtained (Center for Sex Offender Management, n.d.; Righthand & Welch, 2001).

The effectiveness of treatment for juvenile sex offenders has been assessed through a meta-analysis that included nine studies. This included a total of 2,986 juvenile sex offenders who were followed for an average of 59 months. The results showed that 13% sexually recidivated. Also, 25% recidivated for non-sexual violent crimes, 29% for non-sexual non-violent crimes, and 20% for unspecified non-sexual offenses. It also showed that juveniles who received treatment had significantly lower recidivism rates than those who did not receive treatment. Thus, treatment appears to reduce recidivism among juvenile sex offenders. The type of treatment varied substantially from individual treatment, group therapy, family therapy, cognitive-based treatment, and non-cognitive-based treatment, to combinations of these (Reitzel & Carbonell, 2006).

## JUVENILE SEX-OFFENDER RECIDIVISM

Although research shows that a relatively small number of juveniles who sexually offend are arrested for another sex crime when they reach adulthood, many of these juveniles do go on to commit a non-sexual crime. Research shows that juvenile sex offenders are not more likely than juvenile non-sex offenders to commit a subsequent sex crime. In a comparison of juveniles who had committed a sex crime to juveniles in a correctional treatment facility who had no history of committing a sex crime, 12% of the juvenile sex offenders had a new sex-crime charge, compared to 12% of the non-sex offending juveniles (Caldwell, Ziemke, & Vitacco, 2008). Other researchers have also noted that once juveniles have committed a sex crime, there will not necessarily be a pattern of sexual offending (Becker, 1998).

Research suggests that juvenile sex offenders with only one sex crime on their record have low rates of recidivism when they are in a community-based treatment program as compared to those in a more restrictive setting (Rasmussen, 1999). The following excerpt is from a New York Times Magazine article on juvenile sex offenders and discusses juvenile sex-offender recidivism:

> When I heard about these juveniles, I wondered … [w]ould they become adult offenders? I asked Mark Chaffin, one of the country's leading experts and the director of research at the Center on Child Abuse and Neglect at the University of Oklahoma Health Sciences Center. Chaffin notes that while most juveniles who have committed sex crimes are boys around 13 or 14, in other ways they are not a homogeneous population. Though a small percentage — no one knows how many — will become adult rapists or pedophiles, the vast majority, 90% or more, will not, Chaffin says. Most have not committed violent assaults or abused multiple children repeatedly. Usually they have had sexual contact — from fondling to oral sex to intercourse — with a child who is at least two years younger than they are. Also, many of the juveniles have been sexually abused themselves, and as a consequence, they act out sexually, typically for a transitory period.
>
> (Jones, 2007, n.p.)

Existing research shows that the age of the victim may be a relevant factor in the range of offense behaviors and whether a juvenile sexually recidivates. For example, one study assessed the sexual behavior during the offense and the recidivism rates of juvenile sex offenders who assaulted (1) peers, (2) children, and (3) both peers and children (i.e., mixed victims). Although the smallest number of offenders was in the mixed-victim category, they engaged in the most diverse and most intrusive sexual behavior. More specifically, those with mixed victims were more likely to assault multiple victims at one time, vaginally penetrate the victim(s), and engage in oral sex (Kemper & Kistner, 2007).

With regard to recidivism rates, the sample was followed for an average of 5.2 years. The recidivism rates for non-sexual offenses varied only slightly among the three groups: those who had peer victims had the highest rate of recidivism (46%), followed by those with mixed victims (43%) and those with child victims (41%). The recidivism rates for sexual offenses did vary among the groups, although the rates were, overall, low. Those who had child victims had an 8% sexual recidivism rate, while those who offended against mixed victims had a 5% sexual recidivism rate, and those who offended against peers had the lowest sexual recidivism rate of only 1% (Kemper & Kistner, 2007).

A meta-analysis conducted to examine the question, "how many juveniles who have been identified as a juvenile sex offender re-offend?" provides some answers. The rate of sexual recidivism among juvenile sex offenders was examined in 63 studies that included a very large sample of juvenile sex offenders: 11,219. On average, offenders were followed for approximately five years. Sexual recidivism was measured by using arrest or conviction information, depending on availability. The average sexual-recidivism rate was approximately 7%. Thus, only 7% of 11,219 juvenile sex offenders were re-arrested or re-convicted within an average follow-up period of five years. Recidivism for any offense (sexual or non-sexual) for the sample was 43%. The findings are consistent with those from previous studies: the sexual-recidivism rate of juvenile sex offenders is relatively low, yet the rate of general recidivism is higher. It was also found that studies of adolescents revealed much higher sexual-recidivism rates than studies that only examined adults in their follow-up period. Thus, it appears that once juveniles reach the threshold of "adult," their chances of sexually recidivating decrease substantially (Caldwell, 2010).

## RARE JUVENILE SEX OFFENDERS

Often unusual cases of juvenile sex offenders are reported in the media—they are rare events and become newsworthy. This can give the impression that these cases occur more frequently than they do. For example, the majority of juvenile sex offenders are male—very few are female. Sensational media accounts of juvenile female sex offenders, however, may leave one with the impression that there are more juvenile female sex offenders than there actually are. This section discusses the number of female sex offenders, as indicated by arrest data. It will also provide information regarding the number of crimes where juvenile sex offenders escalate to murder.

### Juvenile Female Sex Offenders

Juvenile female sex offenders account for a small number of juvenile arrests for sex crimes. According to arrest records compiled by the FBI, of the arrests for rape and other sex crimes in 2014, approximately 2% were juvenile females (FBI, 2016). Given their small numbers, few studies have been conducted on juvenile female sex offenders. Moreover, most of those studies have relied on sample sizes of less than 30 (Bumby & Bumby, 1993; Bumby & Bumby, 1997; Fehrenbach & Monastersky, 1988; Fehrenbach, Smith, Montastersky, & Deisher, 1986; Fromuth & Conn, 1997; Hunter, Lexier, Goodwin, Browne, & Dennis, 1993; Johnson, 1989; Miller, Trapani, Fejes-Mendoza, Eggleston, & Dwiggins, 1995). Only a few include larger samples (Mathews, Hunter, & Vuz, 1997; Vandiver, 2010; Vandiver & Teske, 2006), limiting their *generalizability*. Thus, the findings presented here should be interpreted with caution, as studies with larger samples may generate different results.

Most juvenile female sex offenders are, on average, between the ages of 12 and 15 and are White (Vandiver, 2010). The victims are typically *very* young, usually younger than 12 years old (Chasnoff et al., 1986; Fehrenbach & Monastersky, 1988; Fehrenbach et al., 1986; Fromuth & Conn, 1997; Johnson, 1989), and are typically younger than for juvenile male sex offenders (Ray & English, 1995; Vandiver & Teske, 2006). Reports of physical abuse occur at higher rates among juvenile female sex offenders compared to juvenile male sex offenders (Mathews et al., 1997). Girls were also more likely to have experienced emotional abuse and/or neglect (Ray & English, 1995). The girls were more likely than boys to exhibit more psychological problems (Bumby, 1996; Bumby & Bumby, 1997; Ray & English, 1995). Girls were also more likely than boys to act with a co-offender (Vandiver, 2010).

There is considerable evidence that juvenile female sex offenders typically know their victims and are often related to them. For example, one study found that half of the sample were related to the victim, and another showed that three-fourths were related to the victim (Bumby & Bumby, 1993; Hunter et al., 1993). Thus, juvenile female sex offenders most often choose victims they know, and often they are relatives.

## Juvenile Sex Offenders as Sexual Murderers

As noted in Chapter 1, one of the goals of this book is to dispel myths about sex offenders and present findings from empirical, research-based studies. As previously indicated, media attention is often focused on extraordinary cases, which often leads to the perception, or rather misperception, that such cases are frequent. Thus, a *moral panic* is created (Jenkins, 1998). Albeit rare, a few juvenile sex offenders develop severe pathologies and escalate from minor paraphilic behaviors to sex crimes, and subsequently commit a sexual murder.

A recent study that examined juveniles who committed sexual murders found the actual numbers are extremely low (Chan, Heide, & Myers, 2013; Myers, 2002; Myers & Chan, 2012). It has been well documented that sexual murder committed by juveniles account for less than 1% of all murders by juveniles (Chan & Heide, 2008). Juvenile sexual murders occur only 10 to 15 times a year in the U.S. (Myers, Chan, Vo, & Lazarou, 2010). Given the small number, very few studies have examined this group of offenders. One study assessed 22 juveniles who committed sexual murder and were released from prison. All of the offenders were tried in adult court, and 59% received at least one life sentence (Myers et al., 2010). The average IQ was 103, which is slightly above average (100). It was common for these offenders to have been diagnosed with conduct disorder, personality disorder, and *sexual sadism disorder*. A large number had psychopathic traits. Post-release information was available for 11 of the 22 offenders. Only five did not commit another offense over a follow-up period of an average of 8.9 years. Six recidivated, and on average, it took them approximately 4.5 years to commit another offense. Three did not recidivate until 5.3 years later, and interestingly, those three committed an additional sexual murder. Therefore, of those who were followed up (half of the original sample), approximately one-third (27%) escalated to *serial sexual murders.*

# CONCLUSION

Juvenile sex offenders, like adult sex offenders, are heterogeneous offenders. Substantive research on this group of offenders did not really begin until the 1980s. The research is constrained by small sample sizes in limited geographical areas. Much research has relied on meta-analyses, which combine the results from multiple studies. One must interpret this research with caution, as the studies that enter into the meta-analyses are themselves limited. Many of the studies reported in this chapter present conflicting findings, leading to unclear conclusions. The research is in its early stages and at this point is not as strong as the research on adults. It does, however, show some patterns for juvenile sex offenders. These are summarized in the Review Points.

# REVIEW POINTS

- Juvenile sex offenders should be examined because (1) many adults begin offending when they are juveniles; (2) juveniles account for many of the sexual crimes; (3) sex-offender treatment may need to be modified to fit juveniles' needs.

- Although many adult sex offenders report committing sex crimes when they were juveniles, juvenile sex offenders are unlikely to commit sex crimes in their adulthood.

- Juvenile sex offenders commit a wide range of sex crimes. In some ways, however, juvenile sex offenders are more similar to non-offending juveniles than juveniles who commit non-sex crimes. There is a wide range of mental disorders, however, among juvenile sex offenders.

- Several juvenile sex-offender typologies have been developed and range from two categories (i.e., simply distinguishing between those who abuse children and those who abuse peers) to seven categories of offenders. They are based on various psychological tests, criminal histories, social histories, and personality profiles.

- Explanations of why juveniles commit sex crimes include exposure to pornography, a cycle of sexual abuse based on one's perception of self, and other salient factors not explained by general criminogenic development.

- Many assessment tools have been developed specifically for juvenile sex offenders. These include (but are not limited to): J-SOAP-II, ERASOR, JSORRAT-II, and MEGA♪.

- Structured treatment programs for juvenile sex offenders did not begin until the 1980s. Cognitive-behavioral therapy is the most common type of treatment. Research shows treatment effectively reduces the likelihood of recidivism.

- Juvenile female sex offenders account for only about 9% of juvenile arrests for sex crimes.

- It is rare for juvenile sex offenders to commit sexual murder, with only 10 to 15 such crimes occurring in a given year.

# REFERENCES

Abel, G., Becker, J. V., Mittelman, M., Cunningham-Rathner, J., Rouleau, J. L., & Murphy, W. D. (1987). Self-reported sex crimes of nonincarcerated paraphiliacs. *Journal of Interpersonal Violence, 2*(1), 3–25.

Ageton, S. S. (1983). *Sexual assault among adolescents.* Lexington, MA: D. C. Heath and Company.

American Psychiatric Association. (2013). *Diagnostic and statistical manual of mental disorders, fifth edition.* Washington DC: American Psychiatric Publishing.

Aos, S., Phipps, P., Barnoski, R., & Lieb, R. (2001). *The comparative cost and benefits of programs to reduce crime.* Olympia, WA: Washington State Institute for Public Policy.

Awad, G. A., & Saunders, E. B. (1991). Male adolescent sexual assaulters: Clinical observations. *Journal of Interpersonal Violence, 6*(4), 446–460.

Baker, A. J. L., Tabacoff, R., Tornusciolo, G., & Eisenstadt, M. (2004). Family secrecy: A comparative study of juvenile sex offenders and youth with conduct disorders. *Family Process, 42*(1), 105–116.

Barbaree, H. E., & Cortoni, F. A. (1993). Treatment of the juvenile sex offender within the criminal justice and mental health systems. In H. E. Barbaree, W. L. Marshall & S. M. Hudson (Eds.), *The juvenile sex offender* (pp. 243–263). New York: Guilford Press.

Becker, J. V. (1998). What we know about the characteristics and treatment of adolescents who have committed sexual offenses. *Child Maltreatment, 3*(4), 317–329.

Becker, J. V. (2007). *A snapshot of sex offenders: Juveniles vs. adults.* Paper presented at the National Legislative Briefing Sex Offender Management Policy in the States, Washington DC. http://www.csg.org/knowledgecenter/docs/pubsafety/Becker.pdf

Becker, J. V., Cunningham-Rathner, J., & Kaplan, M. S. (1986). Adolescent sexual offenders: Demographics, criminal and sexual histories, and recommendations for reducing future offenses. *Journal of Interpersonal Violence, 1*(4), 431–445.

Becker, J. V., Kaplan, M. S., Tenke, C. E., & Tartaglini, A. (1991). The incidence of depressive symptomatology in juvenile sex offenders with a history of abuse. *Child Abuse & Neglect, 15*(4), 531–536.

Becker, J. V., & Stein, R. M. (1991). Is sexual erotica associated with sexual deviance in adolescent males? *International Journal of Law and Psychiatry, 14*(1–2), 85–95.

Bischof, G. P., Stith, S. M., & Whitney, M. L. (1995). Family environments of adolescent sex offenders and other juvenile delinquents. *Adolescence, 30*(117), 157–170.

Briere, J., & Runtz, M. (1991). The long-term effects of sexual abuse: A review and synthesis. *New Directions for Mental Health Services, 51*(3), 3–13.

Browne, A., & Finkelhor, D. (1986). Impact of child sexual abuse: A review of research. *American Psychological Association, 99*(1), 66–77.

Bumby, K. M. (1996). Assessing the cognitive distortions of child molesters and rapists: Development and validation of the MOLEST and RAPE scales. *Sexual Abuse: A Journal of Research and Treatment, 8*(1), 37–54.

Bumby, K. M., & Bumby, N. H. (1993). *Adolescent females who sexually perpetrate: Preliminary findings.* Paper presented at the 12th Annual Research and Treatment Conference of the Association for the Treatment of Sexual Abusers, Boston, MA.

Bumby, N. H., & Bumby, K. M. (1997). Adolescent female sexual offenders. In B. K. Schwartz & H. R. Cellini (Eds.), *The sex offender: New insights, treatment, innovations, and legal developments* (Vol. 2, pp. 10.11–10.16). Kingston, NJ: Civic Research Institute, Inc.

Burton, D. L. & Smith-Darden, J. (2000). 1996 nationwide survey: A summary of the past ten years of specialized treatment with projections for the coming decade. Brandon, VT: Safer Society Program & Press.

Butler, S., & Seto, M. C. (2002). Distinguishing two types of adolescent sex offenders. *Journal of American Child Adolescent Psychiatry, 41*(1), 83–90. doi: 10.1097/00004583-200201000-00015

Caldwell, M. F. (2010). Study characteristics and recidivism base rates in juvenile sex offender recidivism. *International Journal of Offender Therapy and Comparative Criminology, 54*(2), 197–212. doi: 10.1177/0306624X08330016

Caldwell, M. F., Ziemke, M., & Vitacco, M. (2008). An examination of the Sex Offender Registration and Notification Act as applied to juveniles: Evaluating the ability to predict sexual recidivism. *Psychology, Public Policy, and Law, 14*(2), 89–114.

Center for Families, Children & the Court. (2012). *AOC briefing December 2012 screenings and assessments used in the juvenile justice system: Tools for assessing sexual recidivism in juveniles*. San Francisco: AOC Center for Families, Children & the Courts. Retrieved January 15, 2016 from http://www.courts.ca.gov/cfcc-publications.htm.

Center for Sex Offender Management. (n.d.). The effective management of juvenile sex offenders in the community: A training curriculum. Retrieved November 1, 2014, 2014, from http://csom.org/train/juvenile/index.html

Chaffin, M. (2008). Our minds are made up—Don't confuse us with the facts: Commentary on policies concerning children with sexual behavior problems and juvenile sex offenders. *Child Maltreatment, 13*(2), 110–121.

Chan, H. C. O., & Heide, K. M. (2008). Weapons used by juveniles and adult offenders in sexual homicide: An empirical analysis of 29 years of US data. *Journal of Investigative Psychology and Offender Profiling, 5*(3), 189–208.

Chan, H. C. O., Heide, K. M., & Myers, W. C. (2013). Juvenile and adult offenders arrested for sexual homicide: An analysis of victim-offender relationship and weapon used by race. *Journal of Forensic Science, 58*(1), 85–89.

Chasnoff, I. J., Burns, W. J., Schnoll, S. H., Burns, K., Chisum, G., & Kyle-Spore, L. (1986). Maternal-neonatal incest. *American Journal of Orthopsychiatry, 56*(4), 577–580.

Cooper, C. L., Murphy, W. D., & Haynes, M. R. (1996). Characteristics of abused and non-abused adolescent sexual offenders. *Sexual Abuse: A Journal of Research and Treatment, 8*(2), 105–119.

Davis, G. E., & Leitenberg, H. (1987). Adolescent sex offenders. *Psychology Bulletin, 101*(3), 417–427.

Epperson, D. L., Ralston, C. A., Fowers, D., & DeWitt, J. (2006). Actuarial risk assessment with juveniles who offend sexually: Development of the Juvenile Sexual Offense Recidivism Risk Assessment Tool-II (JSORRAT-II). In D. S. Prescott (Ed.), *Risk assessment of youth who have sexually abused: Theory, controversy, and emerging strategies* (pp. 222–236). Oklahoma City, OK: Wood N' Barnes.

Fagan, J., & Wexler, S. (1988). Explanations of sexual assault among violent delinquents. *Journal of Adolescent Research, 3*(3–4), 363–385.

Federal Bureau of Investigation. (2016). *Crime in the United States: 2014*. Washington DC: Government Printing Office.

Fehrenbach, P. A., & Monastersky, C. (1988). Characteristics of female adolescent sexual offenders. *American Journal of Orthopsychiatry, 58*(1), 148–151.

Fehrenbach, P. A., Smith, W., Montastersky, C., & Deisher, R. W. (1986). Adolescent sexual offenders: Offenders and offense characteristics. *American Journal of Orthopsychiatry, 56*(2), 225–231.

Ferrara, M. L., & McDonald, S. (1996). *Treatment of the juvenile sex offender: Neurological and Psychiatric Impairments*. Northvale, NJ: Jason Aronson.

Fromuth, M. E., & Conn, V. E. (1997). Hidden perpetrators: Sexual molestation in a non-clinical sample of college women. *Journal of Interpersonal Violence, 12*(3), 456–465.

Graves, R., Openshaw, K., Ascoine, F., & Ericksen, S. (1996). Demographic and parental characteristics of youthful sexual offenders. *International Journal of Offender Therapy and Comparative Criminology, 40*(4), 300–317.

Gunby, C., & Woodhams, J. (2010). Sexually deviant juveniles: Comparisons between the offender and offence characteristics of 'child abusers' and 'peer abusers'. *Psychology, Crime & Law, 16*(1–2), 47–64.

Hsu, L. K. G., & Starzynski, J. (1990). Adolescent rapists and adolescent child sexual assaulters. *International Journal of Offender Therapy and Comparative Criminology, 34*(1), 23–30.

Hunter, J. A. (2000). Understanding juvenile sex offenders: Research findings and guidelines for effective management and treatment. *Juvenile Justice Fact Sheet.* Charlottesville, VA: Institute of Law, Psychiatry, and Public Policy.

Hunter, J. A., Figueredo, A. J., Malamuth, N. M., & Becker, J. V. (2003). Juvenile sex offenders: Toward the development of a typology. *Sexual Abuse: A Journal of Research and Treatment, 15*(1), 27–48.

Hunter, J. A., Jr., Lexier, L. J., Goodwin, D. W., Browne, P. A., & Dennis, C. (1993). Psychosexual, attitudinal, and developmental characteristics of juvenile female sexual perpetrators in a residential treatment setting. *Journal of Child and Family Studies, 2*(4), 317–326.

Jacobs, W. L., Kennedy, W. A., & Meyer, J. B. (1997). Juvenile delinquents: A between-group comparison study of sexual and nonsexual offenders. *Sexual Abuse: A Journal of Research and Treatment, 9*(3), 201–217.

Jenkins, P. (1998). *Moral panic: Changing concepts of the child molester in modern America.* New Haven, CT: Yale University Press.

Johnson, T. C. (1988). Child-perpetrators – Children who molest other children: Preliminary findings. *Child Abuse & Neglect, 12*(2), 219–229.

Johnson, T. C. (1989). Female child perpetrators: Children who molest other children. *Child Abuse and Neglect, 13*(4), 571–585.

Jones, M. (2007). How can you distinguish a budding pedophile from a kid with real boundary issues. Retrieved May 1, 2013, from http://www.nytimes.com/2007/07/22/magazine/22juvenile-t.html?pagewanted=all&_r=0

Kahn, T. J., & Chambers, H. J. (1991). Assessing reoffense risk with juvenile sexual offenders. *Child Welfare, 70*(3), 333–345.

Katz, R. (1990). Psychosocial adjustment in adolescent child molesters. *Child Abuse & Neglect, 14*(4), 567–575.

Kemper, T. S., & Kistner, J. A. (2007). Offense history and recidivism in three victim-age based groups of juvenile sex offenders. *Sexual Abuse: A Journal of Research and Treatment, 19*(4), 409–424. doi: 10.1007/s11194-007-9061-4

Kraemer, B. D., Salisbury, S. B., & Spielman, C. R. (1998). Pretreatment variables associated with treatment failure in a residential juvenile sex-offender program. *Criminal Justice and Behavior, 25*(2), 190–202.

Lab, S. P., Shields, G., & Schondel, C. (1993). An evaluation of juvenile sexual offender treatment. *Crime and Delinquency, 39*(4), 543–553.

Lambie, I., & Seymour, F. (2006). One size does not fit all: Future directions for the treatment of sexually abusive youth in New Zealand. *Journal of Sexual Aggresssion, 12*(2), 175–187.

Långström, N., Grann, M., & Lindblad, F. (2000). A preliminary typology of young sex offenders. *Journal of Adolescence, 23*(3), 319–329.

Leibowitz, G. (2012). Correlates of modus operandi (coercion and force) among male sexually victimized adolescent sexual abusers: An exploratory study. *Journal of Forensic Social Work, 2*(2–3), 94–107.

Lightfoot, L. O., & Barbaree, H. E. (1993). The relationship between substance use and abuse and sexual offending in adolescents. In H. E. Barbaree, W. L. Marshall & S. M. Hudson (Eds.), *The juvenile sex offender* (pp. 203–224). New York: Guilford Press.

Lightfoot, S., & Evans, I. M. (2000). Risk factors for a New Zealand sample of sexually abusive children and adolescents. *Child Abuse & Neglect, 24*(9), 1185–1198.

Lussier, P., & Blockland, A. (2014). The adolescence-adulthood transition and Robin's continuity paradox: Criminal career patterns of juvenile and adult sex offenders in a prospective longitudinal birth cohort study. *Journal of Criminal Justice, 42*(2), 153–163.

Lussier, P., Van den Berg, C., Bijleveld, C., & Hendriks, J. (2012). A developmental taxonomy of juvenile sex offenders for theory, research and prevention. *Criminal Justice and Behavior, 39*(12), 1559–1581.

Manocha, K. F., & Mezey, G. (1998). British adolescents who sexually abuse: A descriptive study. *Journal of Forensic Psychiatry, 9*(3), 588–608.

Mash, E. J., & Barkley, R. A. (1996). *Child psycopathology*. New York: Guilford Press.

Mathews, R., Hunter, J. A., Jr., & Vuz, J. (1997). Juvenile female sexual offenders: Clinical characteristics and treatment issues. *Sexual Abuse: A Journal of Research and Treatment, 9*(3), 187–199.

McPherson, L. (2007). Practitioner's guide to the Adam Walsh Act. *National Center for Prosecution of Child Abuse, 20*(9 & 10), 1–7.

Miccio-Fonseca, L. C. (2006). *Multiplex Empirical Guided Inventory of Ecological Aggregates for Assessing Sexually Abusive Children and Adolescents (Ages 19 and Under) – MEGA ♪* San Diego, CA: Author.

Michels, S. (2012). Juvenile sex offenders: Locked up for life? Retrieved October 31, 2014, from Juvenile Justice Information Exchange at http://jjie.org/juvenile-sex-offenders-locked-up-for-life/94942/

Miller, D., Trapani, C., Fejes-Mendoza, K., Eggleston, C., & Dwiggins, D. (1995). Adolescent female offenders: Unique considerations. *Adolescence, 30*(118), 429–435.

Miner, M. H., & Crimmins, C. L. S. (1995). Adolescent sex offenders: Issues of etiology and factors. In B. K. Schwartz & H. K. Cellini (Eds.), *The sex offender: Vol. 1. Corrections, treatment, and legal prctice* (pp. 9.1–9.15). Kingston: Civic Research Institute.

Miyaguchi, K., & Shirataki, S. (2014). Executive functioning of juvenile sex offenders with low levels of measured intelligence. *Journal of Intellectual & Developmental Disability, 39*(3), 253–260.

Moffitt, T. E. (1993). Adolescence-limited and life-course-persistent antisocial behavior: A developmental taxonomy. *Psychology Review, 100*(4), 674–701.

Moriarty, N., Stough, C., Tidmarsh, P., Eger, D., & Dennison, S. (2001). Deficits in emotional intelligence underlying adolescent sex offending. *Journal of Adolescence, 24*(6), 743–751. doi: 10.1006/jado.2001.0441

Myers, W. C. (2002). *Juvenile sexual homicide*. London: Academic Press.

Myers, W. C., & Chan, H. C. O. (2012). Juvenile homosexual homicide. *Behavioral Sciences and the Law, 30*(2), 90–102. doi: 10.1002/bsl.2000

Myers, W. C., Chan, H. C. O., Vo, E. J., & Lazarou, E. (2010). Sexual sadism, psychopathy, and recidivism in juvenile sexual murderers. *Journal of Investigative Psychology and Offender Profiling, 7*(1), 49–58.

National Adolescent Perpetrator Network. (1993). The revised report from the National Task Force on Juvenile Sexual Offending. *Juvenile and Family Court Journal, 44*, 5–120.

National Alliance for the Mentally Ill. (n.d.) Cognitive behavioral therapy. Retrieved July 24, 2016 from: http://www.nami.org/Learn-More/Treatment/Psychotherapy

National Task Force on Juvenile Sexual Offending. (1993). Preliminary report. *Juvenile and Family Court Journal, 44*(4), 1–120.

Nisbet, I. A., Wilson, P. H., & Smallbone, S. W. (2004). A prospective longitudinal study of sexual recidivism among adolescent sex offenders. *Sexual Abuse: A Journal of Research and Treatment, 16*(3), 223–234.

O'Brien, M., & Bera, W. (1986). Adolescent sexual offenders: A descriptive typology. *National Family Life Education Network, 1*(3), 1–4.

Oxnam, P., & Vess, J. (2006). A personality-based typology of adolescent sexual offenders using the Millon adolescent clinical inventory. *New Zealand Journal of Psychology, 35*(1), 36–44.

Piquero, A., Farrington, D. P., & Blumstein, A. (2003). The criminal career paradigm: Background and recent developments. In M. Tonry (Ed.), *Crime and justice: A review of research* (pp. 359–506). Chicago: University of Chicago Press.

Prentky, R., Harris, B., & Righthand, S. (2000). An actuarial procedure for assessing risk with juvenile sex offenders. *Sexual Abuse: A Journal of Research and Treatment, 12*(2), 71–93.

Prentky, R., & Righthand, S. (2003). Juvenile Sex Offender Assessment Protocol-II (J-SOAP-II). Retrieved January 15, 2016 from http://www.psicologiagiuridica.eu/files/didattica/jsoap2.pdf

Puzzanchera, C., & Addie, S. (2014). *Delinquency cases waived to criminal court, 2010.* Washington DC: Government Printing Office.

Puzzanchera, C., & Robson, C. (2014). *Delinquency cases in juvenile court, 2010.* Washington DC: Government Printing Office.

Rasmussen, L. A. (1999). Factors related to recidivism among juvenile sexual offenders. *Sexual Abuse: A Journal of Research and Treatment, 11*(1), 69–85.

Ray, J. A., & English, D. J. (1995). Comparison of female and male children with sexual behavior problems. *Journal of Youth and Adolescence, 24*(4), 439–451.

Reiss, I. L. (1960). *Premarital sexual standards in America.* New York: Free Press.

Reitzel, L. R., & Carbonell, J. L. (2006). The effectiveness of sexual offender treatment as measured by recidivism: A meta-analysis. *Sexual Abuse: A Journal of Research and Treatment, 18*(4), 401–421.

Richardson, G., Kelley, T. P., Graham, F., & Bhate, S. R. (2004). A personality-based taxonomy of sexually abusive adolescents derived from the Millon Adolescent Clinical Inventory (MACI). *British Journal of Clinical Psychology, 43*(3), 285–298.

Righthand, S., & Welch, C. (2001). Juveniles who have sexually offended: A review of the professional literature (pp. 1–59). Washington DC: Office of Juvenile Justice and Delinquency Prevention.

Righthand, S., & Welch, C. (2004). Characterisitcs of youth who sexually offend. *Journal of Child Sexual Abuse, 13*(3/4), 15–32.

Rubinstein, M., Yeager, C., Yeager, M. A., Goodstein, C., & Lewis, D. O. (1993). Sexually assaultive male juveniles: A follow-up. *American Journal of Psychiatry, 150*(2), 262–265.

Ryan, G., Miyoshi, T. J., Metzner, J. L., Krugman, R. D., & Fryer, G. E. (1996). Trends in a national sample of sexually abusive youths. *Journal of the American Academy of Child and Adolescent Psychiatry, 35*(1), 17–25. doi: 10.1097/00004583–199601000–00008

Saldana, L., Swenson, C., & Letourneau, E. J. (2006). Multisystemic therapy with juveniles who sexually abuse. In R. E. Longo & D. S. Prescott (Eds.), *Current perspectives: Working with sexually aggressive youth and youth with sexual behavior problems* (pp. 119–141). Holyoke, MA: NEARI Press.

Seto, M. C., & Lalumière, M. L. (2010). What is so special about male adolescent sexual offending? A review and test of explanations through meta-analysis. *Psychological Bulletin, 136*(4), 526–575.

Smith, W. R., & Monastersky, C. (1986). Assessing juvenile sexual offenders' risk for reoffending. *Criminal Justice and Behavior, 13*(2), 115–140.

Smith, W. R., Monastersky, C., & Deisher, R. M. (1987). MMPI-based personality types among juvenile sexual offenders. *Journal of Clinical Psychology, 43*(4), 422–430.

Terry, K. J. (2006). *Sexual offenses and offenders: Theory, practice, and policy.* CA: Wadsworth.

van Wijk, A., Vermeiren, R., Loeber, R., Hart-Kerkhoffs, L., Doreleijers, T., & Bullens, R. (2006). Juvenile sex offenders compared to non-sex offenders: A review of the literature. *Trauma, Violence & Abuse, 7*(4), 227–243.

Vandiver, D. M. (2006a). Female sex offenders. In R. D. McAnulty & M. M. Burnette (Eds.), *Sex and sexuality* (Vol. 3, pp. 47–80). Westport, CT: Praeger.

Vandiver, D. M. (2006b). A prospective analysis of juvenile male sex offenders: Characteristics and recidivism rates as adults. *Journal of Interpersonal Violence, 21*(5), 673–688.

Vandiver, D. M. (2010). Assessing gender differences and co-offending patterns of a predominantly "male-oriented" crime: A comparison of a cross-national sample of juvenile boys and girls arrested for a sexual offense. *Violence and Victims, 25*(2), 243–264.

Vandiver, D. M., & Teske, R., Jr. (2006). Juvenile female and male sex offenders: A comparison of offender, victim, and judicial processing characteristics. *International Journal of Offender Therapy and Comparative Criminology, 50*(2), 148–165. doi: 10.1177/0306624X05277941

Veneziano, C. (2012). Juvenile sex offenders. In F. Williams & M. McShane (Eds.), *Encyclopedia of Juvenile Justice*. New York: Garland Press.

Veneziano, C., Veneziano, L., & LeGrand, S. (2000). The relationship between adolescent sex offender behaviors and victim characteristics with prior victimization. *Journal of Interpersonal Violence, 15*(4), 363–374.

Veneziano, C., Veneziano, L., LeGrand, S., & Richards, L. (2004). Neuropsychological executive functions of adolescent sex offenders and nonsex offenders. *Perceptual and Motor Skills, 98*(2), 661–674.

Viljoen, J. L., Elkovitch, N., Scalora, M. J., & Ullman, D. (2009). Assessment of reoffense risk in adolescents who have committed sexual offenses: Predictive validity of the ERA-SOR, PCL: YV, YLS/CMI, and Static-99. *Criminal Justice and Behavior. 36*(10), 981–1000.

Worling, J. R. (1995). Adolescent sex offenders against females: Differences based on the age of their victims. *International Journal of Offender Therapy and Comparative Criminology, 39*(3), 276–293.

Worling, J. R. (2001). Personality-based typology of adolescent male sexual offenders: Differences in recidivism rates, victim-selection characteristics, and personal victimization histories. *Sexual Abuse: A Journal of Research and Treatment, 13*(3), 149–166.

Worling, J., & Curwen, T. (2001). Estimate of risk of adolescent sexual offense recidivism (The ERASOR—Version 2.0). In M. C. Calder (Ed.), *Juveniles and children who sexually abuse: Frameworks for assessment* (pp. 372–397). Lyme Regis, UK: Russell House Publishing.

Worling, J. R., Bookalam, D., & Litteljohn, A. (2012). Prospective validity of the Estimate of Risk of Adolescent Sexual Offense Recidivism (ERASOR). *Sexual Abuse: A Journal of Research and Treatment, 24*, 203–223.

Zgourides, G., Monto, M., & Harris, R. (1997). Correlates of adolescent male sexual offense: Prior adult sexual contact, sexual attitudes, and use of sexually explicit materials. *International Journal of Offender Therapy and Comparative Criminology, 41*(3), 272–283.

Zimring, F., Jennings, W. G., & Piquero, A. (2009). Investigating the continuity of sex offending: Evidence from the second Philadelphia birth cohort. *Justice Quarterly, 26*(1), 58–76.

## Court Cases

*Graham v. Florida*, 560 U.S. 48 (2010)

*Kansas v. Hendricks*, 521 U.S. 346 (1997)

*Roper v. Simmons*, 543 U.S. 551 (2005)

# DEFINITIONS

**Adjudicated:** An analogous term for "convicted" in an adult court proceeding. Convicted refers to what occurs in an (adult) criminal court; adjudicated refers to what occurs in a juvenile court.

**Adolescents:** Persons who have reached the developmental stage between childhood and adulthood that begins with puberty.

**Attention Deficit Hyperactivity Disorder (ADD/ADHD):** A childhood disorder characterized by an inability to maintain focus, pay attention, control behavior, and excess activity for a period of time exceeding six months.

**Cognitive Distortions:** Minimize or deny the dangerousness of the behavior, justify it, and relieve the offender of responsibility. (Examples: children need to be taught about sex; children are very seductive; the child is too young to know what is happening.)

**Conduct Disorder:** A behavioral and emotional disorder affecting children and teenagers, characterized by long-lasting disruptive behavior, violence, and an inability to follow rules. Behaviors can include aggressiveness, destructiveness, deceitfulness, and violation of rules and/or laws.

**Depression:** Also known as major depression or clinical depression. A mental health disorder characterized by long-lasting symptoms of loss of interest in activities that were once pleasurable, low self-esteem, and a pervasive low/depressed mood.

**Dynamic Factors:** Factors that will change throughout one's life depending on one's situation. These include attitudes towards work and employment status.

**Emotional Intelligence:** One's ability to perceive others' emotions and express one's own emotion. This includes one's ability to process emotional information and respond appropriately to different cues in one's social environment. These characteristics are associated with mental health, leadership skills, and employment performance.

**Functional Family Therapy:** A type of therapy provided to delinquent youths and their families. It addresses conduct problems and criminal behavior, including violent behavior.

**Generalizability:** Whether the findings from one study are applicable to other studies, persons, settings, or time periods.

**Juvenile:** Someone who is younger than the age of majority. The age of majority in most U.S. jurisdictions is 17.

**Juvenile Waiver:** When a juvenile meets the state requirements, which vary among states, to be tried in an (adult) criminal court rather than a juvenile court and a judge makes this recommendation.

**Longitudinal Study:** An empirical investigation that follows a sample or defined population over an extended period of time, usually several years or decades.

**Meta-analysis:** A type of study that involves gathering all past, relevant studies on a particular topic and analyzing all of the results to gain a more comprehensive answer to the research question posed.

**Minnesota Multiphasic Personality Inventory (MMPI):** The MMPI is one of the most frequently used personality tests. Although several versions of the test exist, it consists of several hundred true-false questions, and the purpose is to identify underlying psychopathology or mental aberration. It is often administered as part of a standard psychological evaluation.

**Moral Panic:** A collective response to a perceived threat from an individual or group. The response often exceeds the actual threat, and is manifested through an us-versus-them, do-something-about-them sentiment.

**Multisystemic Therapy:** A method of treatment for delinquent youth that involves the entire family. The focus is to address multiple factors: improve family functioning, enhance parenting skills, increase the youth's associations with prosocial peers, improve school performance, and build upon community supports.

**Paraphilia:** Any intense and persistent sexual interest in anything other than genital stimulation or preparatory fondling with physically mature, phenotypically normal, consenting human partners.

**Prospective Study:** An empirical investigation that begins with a sample or defined population and continues to follow it as subjects age over time.

**Psychopathology:** Manifestation of behavior indicative of a mental or behavioral disorder.

**Retrospective Study:** An empirical investigation that begins with a sample or defined population and assesses events that occurred previous to that time.

**Serial Sexual Murderers:** Individuals who commit more than one sexually-motivated murder over a period of time.

**Sexual Sadism Disorder:** A paraphilic disorder that involves deriving sexual pleasure from inflicting pain or humiliation of another person.

**Sexually Violent Predator Laws:** Laws in the U.S. that allow sexual predators to be civilly committed indefinitely after they have completed a prison sentence if they are considered likely to commit another sex crime.

**Static Factors:** Factors that will remain stable throughout one's life. These include factors such as age at first sexual experience and whether one has been victimized as a child.

**Wraparound Services:** A multi-disciplinary approach to manage delinquent juveniles in the community. It involves the juvenile and his/her family. It involves a case manager who is responsible for coordinating services within the community.

# CHAPTER 7

# *Female Sex Offenders*

## CHAPTER OBJECTIVES

- Describe the number and characteristics of known female sex offenders.
- Compare male and female sex offenders.
- Compare/contrast categories of female sex offenders according to different typologies.
- Summarize explanations of female sexual abuse.
- Identify and describe assessment and treatment efforts for female sex offenders.
- Describe known recidivism rates of female sex offenders.

Female sex offenders are often overlooked. One myth about sex offenders is that they are all male (Center for Sex Offender Management, 2000). One of the goals of this chapter is to dispel this myth by examining the number and characteristics of women who have committed sex crimes. Although male offenders commit the majority of sex crimes, female offenders commit a sizeable portion of them. This chapter presents data on the number of women who have been arrested for rape and other sexual offenses, along with the trend over a recent ten-year period. The characteristics of female sex offenders, including a comparison with male sex offenders, are also discussed.

Over the past decade, there have been many media reports of women who have committed sex crimes. A typical report involves a female teacher who has a sexual relationship with a young male student. For example, Mary Kay Letourneau had a sexual relationship with one of her students who, at the time, was only in the sixth grade. Later she divorced her husband, spent time in prison for her crime, and continued to have contact with the former student. She eventually married him and had two children with him (see Focus Box 7.1 for more information). Since then, many other women have made headlines, including Debra LaFave, for similar behavior. This category of sex offender, *teacher/lover*, is only one of several categories of female sex offenders that researchers have identified. This chapter discusses typologies created by different researchers. The typologies of two groups of researchers are highlighted, along with brief summaries of other researchers' typologies.

*Focus Box 7.1   A Case of a Female Sex Offender: Mary Kay Letourneau*

1996: Mary Kay Letourneau was 34 years old and married with four children when her husband found love letters from her student, 12-year-old Vili Fualaau. The relationship between the two had turned sexual. A divorce later occurred, and Mary Kay Letourneau moved to Alaska with the former husband's children.

1997–1998: Mary Kay Letourneau was arrested for her sexual relationship with Fualaau, and she was already pregnant with his daughter, their first child. She was jailed for six months. A month after release, she was caught having sex with Fualaau. This led to a subsequent sentence of seven and a half years in prison at the Washington Corrections Center. She delivered Fualaau's second child, another daughter, while in prison. The daughter was placed with Fualaau's mother.

2002: Fualaau's family sued the Des Moines Police Department for failure to protect Vili Fualaau. No damages were awarded to the Fualaau family.

2004 (August 3): Mary Kay Letourneau was 42 years old and was released from prison. Vili Fualaau was 21 years old. His attorney, Scott Stewart, filed a motion to vacate an existing no-contact order, stating, Fualaau "does not fear Mary K. Letourneau" and noted that he is an adult. A friend of Fualaau's reported that he was "relieved that she's out of prison and currently he can't wait to see her."

2005: Mary Kay Letourneau and Vili Fualaau were married.

Source: (Associated Press, 2005; "Letourneau marries Fualaau amid media circus," 2005)

Much of the initial research on female sex offenders was limited to mental health samples. Therefore, a false belief developed that mental illness caused female sex crimes. Examining other populations of female sex offenders (i.e., non–mental health samples) helped to dispel this belief. Alternate explanations have been proposed for female sex offenders. These explanations are discussed, along with evidence from empirically-based studies.

Unfortunately, there is a shortage of empirically-based information on the assessment and treatment of female sex offenders. As we will present in Chapter 10, all of the assessment tools have been developed for male sex offenders. Assessment guidelines, however, have been suggested for female sex offenders. They will be presented in this chapter. Similarly, formal treatment programs for female sex offenders are lacking because the majority of sex offenders are male. The treatment programs that do exist are discussed.

This chapter also addresses the myth that female sex offenders are merely one-time sex offenders. Although research shows the recidivism rate of female sex offenders is low, studies with longer follow-up periods and improved measures of recidivism reveal higher recidivism rates. These studies are reviewed.

This chapter, therefore, addresses the number and characteristics of known female sex offenders, presents an overview of the typologies of female sex offenders, identifies explanations of female sex offenders, summarizes assessment and treatment programs developed specifically for female sex offenders, and provides an overview of the most recent information about recidivism of female sex offenders. Similar to previous chapters, it is not intended to provide a comprehensive overview of female sex offenders, as several books have been written solely on the topic. The intent, rather, is to provide highlights of the research that provides key details about female sex offenders for the purpose of dispelling myths about them.

## NUMBER OF KNOWN FEMALE SEX OFFENDERS

How many sex offenders are female? The *UCR* includes annual arrest data compiled by the FBI. In 2014, 308 girls/women were arrested for forcible rape in the U.S. They accounted for approximately 3% of the 9,757 estimated number of arrests for forcible rape (Federal Bureau of Investigation, 2016). Female offenders, however, accounted for approximately 8% of arrests for "other" sexual offenses (excluding prostitution). Overall, of all of the arrests for sex crimes (rape and other sexual offenses), 7% were female. While this information does not fully capture the extent of female sex crimes, it suggests that female offenders make up only a small portion of all sex offenders. Whether they make up approximately 7% of sex offenders is questionable. As noted in Chapter 1, official arrest data are limited because many victims do not report sex crimes. Those victimized by female offenders are even less likely than those victimized by male offenders to report such offenses, resulting in disproportionately fewer arrests of female sex offenders. (Denov, 2004).

Additional information about the extent to which girls/women sexually offend comes from individual sex abuse studies. Although the percentage of sex offenders in these studies who are female ranges from 1 to 59 (see Table 7.1), it should be noted some of the studies were not specifically designed to address the prevalence of female

**TABLE 7.1**  *Overview of Research Indicating Prevalence of Female Sex Offenders*

| RESEARCHERS | PERCENTAGE OF OFFENDERS WHO ARE FEMALE | SAMPLE SIZE AND SOURCE |
|---|---|---|
| Travin, Cullen and Protter, 1990 | 1% | 515 sex offenders in a specialized sex offender treatment program |
| Finkelhor, Hotaling, Lewis and Smith, 1990 (female respondents) | 1% | Telephone survey of 1,481 women about their sexual victimization experiences |
| Rowan, Rowan and Langelier, 1990 | 1.5% | 600 sex offenders from the New Hampshire judicial system and Vermont social service agencies and courts |

*(Continued)*

**TABLE 7.1** (Continued)

| RESEARCHERS | PERCENTAGE OF OFFENDERS WHO ARE FEMALE | SAMPLE SIZE AND SOURCE |
| --- | --- | --- |
| Vandiver and Kercher, 2004 | 1.6% | 29,376 registered sex offenders in Texas |
| Sandler and Freeman, 2007 | 2% | Total number of registered sex offenders in New York in August 2005 not given |
| Vandiver and Walker, 2002 | 2.4% | 1,644 registered sex offenders in Arkansas |
| Sandler and Freeman, 2009 | 3.2% | 168,037 registered sex offenders in New York between 1986 and 2006 |
| Vandiver, 2010 | 3.1% | 7,385 adults arrested for a sex offense; all adults arrested for a sex offense in 2001 (NIBRS data, including 21 states) |
| Faller, 1987 | 14% | Child Abuse and Neglect Treatment Center in Michigan |
| Finkelhor et al., 1990 (male respondents) | 17% | Telephone survey of 1,145 men about their sexual victimization experiences |
| Finkelhor, Williams and Burns, 1988 | 40% | 271 child sexual-abuse cases occurring in daycare, nationwide |
| Petrovich and Templer, 1984 | 59% | 83 incarcerated rapists report of their childhood sexual victimization |

sex offenders. For example, Finkelhor, Williams and Burns (1988) reported that 40% of sex offenders in their study were female. The researchers, however, focused on sexual abuse in daycare facilities, where women likely made up the majority of employees. The studies listed in Table 7.1 include self-report information from known sex offenders, official data of known sex offenders, and surveys of the general population.

A few conclusions can be drawn. First, women do commit sexual offenses. Second, women comprise a small portion of sex offenders—less than 10% of the total number of sex offenders. And last, women who sexually offend are a heterogeneous group of offenders, like male sex offenders.

## CHARACTERISTICS OF FEMALE SEX OFFENDERS

Female sex offenders are typically young, in their 20s or 30s, and White. They often report a history of sexual victimization and substance abuse. Researchers have noted that although many female sex offenders report substance use, drugs and alcohol were not commonly used immediately prior/during the commission of their sex crime (Johansson-Love & Fremouw, 2009). Thus, women likely do not offend because of disinhibition (West, Friedman, & Kim, 2011). Their sex crimes have been described as "not due to impulsivity/poor response inhibition, cognitive rigidity or attention validity. Rather, female sex offending is planned, intentional and goal directed" (Pflugradt & Allen, 2010, p. 447). Although mental illness is evident in many female sex offender studies, many of the samples come from mental health clinics. Thus, mental illness may be reported at higher levels in these studies than occurs in the general population (Vandiver, 2006b).

Approximately half of female sex offenders commit sex crimes with a co-offender. Their co-offender is often a romantic partner. When women act in concert with another person, there are typically multiple victims, both male and female. The relationship between the female offender and her partner is usually an abusive one (Vandiver, 2006a).

## COMPARISON OF FEMALE AND MALE SEX OFFENDERS

The research on male/female differences among offenders, in general, is more developed than research specific to sex offenders. Explanations of variations in male/female offending rates have included socialization differences, gender inequality, and adherence to traditional gender roles (Bloom, Owen, & Covington, 2003). Female offenders may be more affected than male offenders by self-esteem issues, depression, and a history of victimization (Hardyman & Van Voorhis, 2004). In one study, approximately one-third had at least one psychiatric hospitalization (West et al., 2011). Female offenders also pose less of a danger to society and commit fewer violent offenses than male offenders. Female offenders are more likely than male offenders to have substance abuse and mental health problems (Hardyman & Van Voorhis, 2004) and to have experienced physical and sexual abuse (Bloom et al., 2003). Moreover, female sex offenders report more severe abuse when compared to male sex offenders (Oliver, 2007).

There are few studies about male/female differences among sex offenders. It has been found, however, that female sex offenders are more likely than male sex offenders to have reported a history of sexual victimization (Allen, 1991), come from dysfunctional homes (Mathews, Hunter, & Vuz, 1997), have more psychological problems (Johanson-Love & Fremouw, 2009), and have more suicide attempts (Miccio-Fonseca, 2000). With regard to criminal histories, female sex offenders have significantly fewer prior arrests than male sex offenders (Freeman & Sandler, 2008). Female sex offenders are also less likely to have prior drug-, violent-, and sexual-offense arrests. Also, female sex offenders are less likely than male sex offenders to have a prior incarceration and probation sentence (Freeman & Sandler, 2008). Female sex offenders are more likely than male sex offenders to have a male victim (Freeman & Sandler, 2008).

Similarities between male and female sex offenders have also been found. Male and female sex offenders have been found in at least one study to be similar in age, race, ethnicity, education level, and life stressors, including job stressors (Miccio-Fonseca, 2000). Also noteworthy, the types of sex crimes committed by women and men are similar (Allen, 1991).

Female and male sex offenders appear to have different pathways to sex crimes (Freeman & Sandler, 2008), which may require different assessment tools and, most importantly, different treatment plans when compared to male sex offenders. In the next section we discuss typologies that have been identified, which again highlight the need to assess female sex offenders differently from male sex offenders.

## TYPOLOGIES OF FEMALE SEX OFFENDERS

Female sex offender typologies have only recently emerged and, unfortunately, are limited in that they are constructed using small sample sizes. With the exception of two studies, the typologies were based on samples of less than 30. Several researchers have proposed typologies of female sex offenders (see Table 7.2), several of which have received considerable attention in the literature. One of the earliest typologies, developed by Mathews, Matthews, and Speltz (1989), includes five categories. This typology was based on case histories of female sex offenders receiving psychological treatment.

More recently, Vandiver and Kercher (2004) developed a typology that provides another perspective on female sex offenders. This typology was developed from

**TABLE 7.2**  *Description and Source of Female Sex Offender Typologies*

| AUTHOR | CLASSIFICATIONS |
|---|---|
| Sarrel & Masters, 1982 | • Forced assault<br>• Babysitter abuse<br>• Incestuous abuse<br>• Dominant woman abuse |
| McCarty, 1981; 1986 | • Independent offenders of males (1986)<br>• Independent offenders of females (1986)<br>• Co-offenders and accomplices (1986)<br>• Severely psychologically disturbed abuser (1981) |
| Mathews, Matthews and Speltz, 1989 | • Teacher/lover<br>• Predisposed<br>• Male-coerced molester<br>• Exploration/exploitation<br>• Psychologically disturbed |

| AUTHOR | CLASSIFICATIONS |
|---|---|
| Mayer, 1992 | • Female rapist<br>• Female sexual harassment<br>• Mother molester<br>• Triads<br>• Homosexual molestation |
| Syed & Williams, 1996 (building on Mathews et al.'s (1989) categories) | • Teacher/lover (Mathews et al., 1989)<br>• Male-coerced (Mathews et al, 1989)<br>• Angry-impulsive<br>• Male-accompanied, familial<br>• Male-accompanied, nonfamilial |
| Vandiver & Kercher, 2004 | • Heterosexual nurturers<br>• Non-criminal homosexual offenders<br>• Female sexual predators<br>• Young adult child exploiters<br>• Homosexual criminals<br>• Aggressive homosexual offenders |

criminal histories and information from sex-offender registries. In this section, these two typologies are presented, along with brief summaries of other typologies that have been developed to identify unique categories of female sex offenders. When possible, examples of women who fit the various categories are provided.

## Mathews et al.'s (1989) Typology of Female Sex Offenders

One of the categories Mathews et al. (1989) identified is the ***Teacher/Lover*** category. Examples of this are often reported in the media. The case detailed in Focus Box 7.1 of Mary Kay Letourneau is an example of this category of offender.

A second category these researchers identified is ***Predisposed*** female sex offenders (Mathews et al., 1989). This category of offender typically chooses a family member as a victim; thus, incest is highly prevalent. The offender is typically sexually abused during childhood. Her relationship with her family members is strained (for example, one woman indicated that when it was discovered that her uncle was sexually abusing her, she was blamed for the victimization). Furthermore, these women report having difficulty establishing positive relationships with men their own age. Most report negative sexual experiences—not enjoying it, yet being promiscuous. Several cases were identified in which women acted alone in the abuse of daughters, sons, and nephews. These women often developed an unhealthy reliance on food, alcohol, and cigarettes.

One of the characteristics of this category of offender is that the sex crime is intrafamilial (within the same family). Other researchers have also identified categories of female sex offenders where the sex crime involves incest. For example, Sarrel and Masters (1982) reported the case of a 30-year-old man who indicated to his therapist that his mother who had been divorced since he was two years old began playing with his genitals when he was 13. The sexual activity later included her performing oral sex on him and having sex with him. They had sex two to three times a week until he left for college. When he went home on the weekends and holidays, he continued having sex with his mother. His mother died during his senior year of college. He reported that he never approached his mother; she always approached him. The researchers noted, "He felt strongly devoted to her, stating that he enjoyed her obvious pleasure during their sexual encounters far more than his own" (Sarrel & Masters, 1982, p. 124). After he left for college, he reported he was not able to achieve an erection when he attempted to have sex with a girl his own age. He felt guilty and unfaithful to his mother. Once, he became so nauseated after foreplay with a girl that he threw up. He resumed dating but was not able to have sex. He later married and entered therapy.

This case is unusual in that it is from the perspective of the victim. It is typical, however, in that it exemplifies a specific category of female sex offender—one who relies on children to whom she has access as her victim of choice.

A third category of female sex offender, **Male-Coerced** offenders, typically marries at a young age, has few job skills, and adopts a traditional view of the husband as the head of household and breadwinner (Mathews et al., 1989). Most of the women who fit into this category were abused in some way—verbally, physically, and/or sexually. The women attempted to avoid antagonizing their husbands to avoid such abuse. The relationships with their spouses typically deteriorated from bad to worse. The women were typically passive and dependent on their spouses. Most believed they had no alternative but to preserve the current marriage, as they felt they could not attract a better partner. In all of these cases, the husband initiated the abuse, and the women follow their husband's directives. Very few women willingly participated, while the rest struggled or resisted to some degree. Most reported feelings of turmoil. A few of the women later initiated sexual abuse on their own. One woman, for example, reported that having sex with her son was more enjoyable than having sex with her husband because she had some degree of control over her son. This category of offender often sexually abuses her own children.

An example of this includes Mathews et al.'s (1989) description of a husband and wife who molested a pair of 13-year-old twins who lived in the same apartment complex. The details are:

> [The woman] lived in an apartment building in an urban area. Her husband was unemployed, and she worked many hours to provide for their needs. [The woman's] husband developed a friendship with a pair of 13-year-old twins ... He liked to have them come to the apartment to play video games, watch television, and talk. [The woman] was nervous about her husband's interest in these twins, very insecure and jealous of the attention he was showing them, and suspicious of his motive ... At a later date [the woman] returned home early from an outing with her sister. When

she entered the living room, the male twin was watching television. She found his sister and her husband in the bedroom. The girl was on the bed, her husband was sitting on a chair, and both were nude. [The woman] … began screaming and crying … she again insisted that the children never come back … [her husband] blamed her for his actions … [he] "bugged" her about changing her mind and allowing the children to visit again … [she] finally relented, and the sexual abuse occurred almost as soon as the children started frequenting their home again … [the female victim] threatened to tell about her previous sexual contact with [the woman's] husband if [the woman] did not join in … she performed oral sex on [the female victim] … [the woman] and her husband also engaged in sexual behaviors in front of the children … A few days later [her] husband was again involved with the girl. [The woman] reported that she felt sorry for the boy because he was left out, so she performed oral sex on him. The sexual contact was very stressful for her.

(Mathews et al., 1989, pp. 19–20)

The woman was arrested after the female victim's boyfriend reported the sexual abuse. The woman was described as cooperative with law enforcement. She spent time in jail and participated in a sex-offender treatment program.

It has been speculated that the category of women who abuse in concert with a partner is one of the most common categories of female sex offenders (Vandiver, 2006a). Many co-offending situations involve women acting with male significant others with whom they are romantically involved, such as husbands or boyfriends. It is unclear, however, how much these women participate in the sexual abuse. Furthermore, it is suggested that women who act in concert with another person typically have multiple victims and other non-sexual arrests in their criminal histories.

In addition to these three categories of female sex offenders, Mathews et al. (1989) acknowledged a category identified by Sarrel and Masters (1982). This *Exploration/Exploitation* offender typically abuses in a babysitting situation. Sarrel and Masters (1982) defined this category as *babysitter abuse*. Two cases of babysitter abuse were described by Sarrel and Masters (1982). In one case, a 25-year-old man reported his babysitter sexually abused him when he was ten years old. The young man described the event as pleasurable and reported it had occurred for approximately one year. The young man reported "she frequently manipulated his penis and that sometimes there was an erection, but he had no ejaculatory experience" (p. 122). The boy later told his family about the experience. His father whipped him severely. He then took his son to a priest and a psychiatrist. The father often referred to his son's "shameful conduct" and told his son that he should have reported the sexual activity sooner. He did not know what happened to the babysitter. The young boy reported that afterwards he never masturbated and had overwhelming feelings of guilt. He did not date regularly and was not receptive to sexual advances by women. The man, after establishing a platonic relationship with a young woman at the age of 24, discussed his fears regarding sex and the incidents that occurred with the babysitter. He then began psychiatric treatment.

In another case a 16-year-old babysitter molested an 11-year-old boy. The babysitter undressed the boy and put his penis inside her vagina. He was confused about the incident. Later he did not masturbate and did not have sexual contact with anyone else. When he was 19, he married a young woman, but was unable to perform sexually on their wedding night. He had been in therapy for two years before he was married, but never mentioned the abuse to either his therapist or his future wife (Sarrel & Masters, 1982).

Both of these sexual-abuse incidents indicate the effects can be long-term and profound. Many may think babysitter abuse is not serious. In fact, it may even be interpreted (wrongly) as a pleasurable experience where a young boy is allowed to explore sex at an early age with someone who is more experienced than himself (see Hetherton, 1999). Psychologically disturbed offenders (the last category in the Mathews et al., (1989) typology) include people experiencing mental-health difficulties at the time of their sex crimes.

## Vandiver & Kercher's (2004) Typology

In 2004, Vandiver and Kercher examined one of the largest samples of female sex offenders that has appeared in the literature. Their research examined all registered female sex offenders in Texas. Albeit a large sample, it was limited in that it relied solely on factors found in the state's sex-offender registration dataset and criminal histories; diagnostic characteristics typically associated with clinical samples were not included.

The analysis is based on statistical analysis that essentially places like-offenders in the same category. Yet each category is very different from the others. This analysis yielded six categories of female sex offenders. These categories are presented here, beginning with the largest.

One of the most prominent characteristics of the largest category of female sex offenders that Vandiver and Kercher (2004) identified, **Heterosexual Nurturers**, is that these women likely were in a position of authority and formed a bond with a teenage male, which led to a sexual relationship.[1] The women in this study had an average age of 30, and their victims were relatively young boys with an average age of 12. Vandiver and Kercher noted that this category of female sex offender is comparable to Mathew et al.'s (1989) *teacher/lover* category. The researchers, however, suggested broadening the category to include women in any caregiving role (babysitter, mentor, neighbor, etc.), given that not all of the women are teachers.

An example of this category of sex offender has been described in a case study report, which included a woman who worked at a youth facility and "fell in love" with a young teenage boy. Thus, a mentor-mentee relationship existed (Vandiver, Cheeseman, & Worley, 2006). She was divorced with two children. She indicated that the victim was a 14-year-old teenager she met through her work. She described the sexual act between her and the teenager as consensual, but followed up by stating that she knew it was wrong and did not want to make an excuse for it. She indicated that the male teenager came from a "bad family." He did not know his father and had been sexually abused by his grandfather.

The relationship began at a youth recreational facility, and the boy began to come over to her residence to talk and get something to eat. The relationship progressed into a sexual one after he kissed her once. She had sex with him approximately seven times over a six-month period. She stated "When it happened it seemed natural—but I shouldn't say natural because it's not natural to have sex with a teenage boy. He kissed me and I didn't stop it."

The woman was with the boy when she had a car accident, which led to her arrest when police suspected the abuse. After she was arrested, she still tried to contact the young boy and was "taken in [by the police] several times." At the time of the interview, she had not seen the boy in several years.

One noteworthy point about this situation is that the woman described the young boy as having nowhere else to go and having no one else for support. He was *"social junk."* She could not do anything to harm him—he was already damaged goods. Mary Kay Letourneau also took a young boy under her wing who was in a similar situation (Focus Box 7.1).

The most prominent characteristic of the second largest category of female sex offenders, ***Non-Criminal Homosexual Offenders***, is that they did not act alone. They were offending with someone else—most likely a male with whom they had a romantic relationship (Vandiver & Kercher, 2004). Additionally, these women were the least likely of all the categories to have an arrest (for any type of crime) after the arrest that led to their registration. They also had the lowest average number of arrests, overall. The women had an average age of 32, and their victims had an average age of 13. The majority, 92%, of the victims were female. Although their data did not include the absence/presence of a co-offender, the authors speculated that this category of women may have been acting with a male accomplice. In a subsequent study, Vandiver (2006a) found female victims were often present when female sex offenders were co-offending with male sex offenders.

Researchers reported co-offenders were significantly different from those who acted alone. Co-offenders had more victims per incident. They were more likely to have both male and female victims and to abuse a relative. The type of behavior the women exhibited, however, included a broad continuum from passive to active, with more cases of passive participation (Vandiver, 2006a).

Characteristics that vary among co-offenders are their relationships to their victims and their co-offenders, their motivation (e.g., revengeful), whether they were coerced, and level of contact with the victim during abuse (i.e., hands-off or hands-on) (Vandiver, 2006a). Researchers have relied more on the relationship between the women and the victims (related or unrelated) and the motivation for engaging in the sexual abuse (e.g., feelings of rejection and revenge) in developing categories of co-offending women.

***Female Sexual Predators*** were the most likely to have a re-arrest after their sex-offense arrest that led to their registration. Thus, offenders in this category may have been part of a "criminal" group that committed various crimes, and the sex crime was simply part of their criminal lifestyle. These were relatively young women, with an average age of 29. Their victims had an average age of 11; 60% of the victims were male.

The most prominent characteristic of **Young Adult Child Exploiters** is that one-half of them were related to their victim. Thus, there was a large number of incest cases. Also, this category had the youngest average age (28), and they were also the most likely to have a previous arrest for sexual assault. Their victims had an average age of seven.

**Homosexual Criminals** had a high proportion of "forcing" offenses, such as sexual performance of a child (i.e., forcing a child to take nude pictures/videos, engage in specific sexual behavior) and forced prostitution. The authors note this category of offender may be motivated by economic gain, rather than sexual gratification. Also, these offenders commit hands-off offenses. The sexual abuse does not involve direct contact (e.g., sexual assault) between the female offender and the victim; rather the offender arranges for abuse to occur. This category also had the highest average number of arrests and had a high number of subsequent re-arrests (for any type of offense). Thus, they also had a criminal lifestyle, and the sex crime was one of many crimes. The average age of the offender was 32, and their victims had an average age of 11.

An article appearing in the Houston Chronicle provides an example of such incidents:

> A woman and her boyfriend, convicted of making her 12 year-old daughter perform sexual favors for strangers for money, have each been sentenced to 40 years in prison … the mother arranged for men to have sex with the … daughter. The 12-year-old testified concerning two occasions. On one, she did know how much money was given to her parents, she said, but they received $100 on the other.
>
> (Teachey, 2000, p. A 40)

Such reports are not uncommon. A recent news article, for example, reports both men and women being arrested for human trafficking and running a prostitution ring in Florida (Cardona, 2016).

This category of offender can also include having children pose nude for photographs to be sold privately or made available on websites for money. This offender, therefore, typically commits hands-off offenses. She is likely to already have a criminal record and use the sexual abuse as a method for obtaining money. The payoff is economic rather than sexual. It should also be noted these women are usually acting in concert with another person, usually a man. Sometimes they are part of a "ring" that involves many co-offenders. This category, therefore, overlaps with those who co-offend (i.e., Non-Criminal Homosexual Offenders).

The authors speculate that the most prominent characteristics of **Aggressive Homosexual Offenders** involve rape scenarios among female offenders and victims. Given that a small portion of the victims were male, it could also involve a rape scenario in which a female offender rapes a male victim. This category includes adult women with adult victims as well. The average age of the victims is 31, and most victims are female. A small number of the victims were male. This category of offender is similar to one identified by Sarrel and Masters. In their research four cases came from 11 male victim reports of female sexual abuse. The male is described as being fearful, not enjoying the experience. One of the victims was a truck driver who was 27 years old. After meeting a woman he had known previously, he went to a motel with her and the following occurred:

> [H]e was given another drink and shortly thereafter fell asleep. He awoke to find himself naked, tied hand and foot to a bedstead, gagged, and blindfolded. As he listened to voices in the room, it was evident that several women were present ... he was told that he had to "have sex with all of them." He thinks that during his period of captivity four different women used him sexually, some of them a number [of] times. Initially he was manipulated to erection and mounted ... He believes that the period of forcible restrained and repeated sexual assaults continued for more than 24 hours.
>
> (Sarrel & Masters, 1982, pp. 120–121)

After the incident, the man sought therapy. He never reported the incident to police. He suffered from psychological distress and was not able to complete sexual intercourse. He married later, but still was unable to engage in sexual intercourse. His wife was unaware of the rape he endured (Sarrel & Masters, 1982).

## Summary of Female Sex Offender Typologies

Several researchers have developed their own unique typologies, and it should be noted in some instances an offender may not fit into just one category. For example, a female sex offender may act with a co-offender and commit incest. These have been proposed as separate categories, yet the offender meets many of the criteria for both. Also, it should be noted that different researchers have proposed similar or identical categories, but labeled them differently. For example, Mayer (1992) identified *Female Rapist*, and Sarrel and Masters (1982) identified *Dominant Woman Abuse* offenders. These categories have different names, yet they describe the same offender.

Other similarities exist among the identified categories of female sex offenders. Incestuous relationships have been identified in many typologies. Research has found women have abused in the capacity of a relative, a mother, and an older sister (Mathews et al., 1989; Sarrel & Masters, 1982).

Mathews et al. (1989) identified a broad category of offenders, *predisposed*, who sexually abused relatives and were not limited to just their own children. Several cases were identified in which women acted alone in the abuse of daughters, sons, and nephews. A history of sexual abuse appeared to be prevalent in the families. While Mathews et al. adopted a general incest category, other researchers have identified the victim in more specific terms: mother-son incest, and mother-daughter incest.

A case of sister-brother incest was discussed in Sarrel and Masters' (1982) research. A 14-year-old girl began molesting her 10-year-old brother, and the abuse occurred for two years. The researchers describe the abuse:

> She stimulated him manually and orally and then inserted his penis into her vagina. At first he only felt frightened and did not understand what was happening. She usually threatened to beat him or attack him with a knife if he told anyone. He does not recall if he ejaculated. He was too frightened to tell his parents.
>
> (Sarrel and Masters, 1982, p. 125)

Later his sister entered psychiatric treatment. The victim later became suicidal, and he too was placed in psychiatric treatment. He subsequently married later and was unable to consummate his marriage.

Several researchers have reported instances of mother-son incest (Lawson, 1993; Mayer, 1992). Researchers have also identified accounts of mothers abusing their own daughters as a unique category of female sex offenders. Mathews et al. (1989) identified a mother whose husband had passed away and the mother began first physically abusing her four-year-old daughter and then sexually abusing her.

> When feeling alone and wanting to be close, "I would go into the bedroom and touch [her daughter]." The abuse consisted of kissing and fondling the child, usually over her pajamas or underwear. Initially the abuse occurred when her daughter was awake. As the child grew older, however, [the mother] would wait for [her daughter] to fall asleep before touching her.
>
> (Mathews et al., 1989, p. 15)

The mother was abused by her own father when she was a child. After the mother entered substance-abuse treatment, she reported the sexual abuse she had with her daughter. She was referred to sex-abuse treatment.

Many other similarities exist among the categories. Vandiver & Kercher's (2004) *young adult child exploiters* are comparable to the *predisposed offenders* Mathews et al. (1989) identified in their research.

The take-away message here is relatively simple: while the names are different, the offender characteristics are similar. From the various typologies that have been developed, it appears that the most common categories of women who sexually offend are:

(1) Women in a position of authority (e.g., teacher, caretaker, etc.) who engage in a sexual relationship with a teenage male.

(2) Women who co-offend with a male sex offender.

(3) Women who molest a relative, usually her own child.

(4)   Women who force others into prostitution

(5)   Women who rape either a male or female victim.

In all of the situations presented above, it should be noted that the women sexually abused someone they knew. Women, like men, typically do not engage in sexual abuse with strangers.

Women, as shown in these typologies, engage in diverse behaviors, many of which are hands-on offenses. They also commit hands-off offenses (e.g., forced prostitution) that also cause serious harm. Women who commit sex crimes can be dangerous in that they cause harm. The effects of sex abuse are long-lasting. The harm caused by sex offenders, regardless of their gender, can affect victims for the rest of their lives.

---

*Focus Box 7.2   A Case of a Violent Female Sex Offender*

Laura Faye McCollum is one of approximately 300 sex offenders who have been committed to McNeil Island, a secure treatment facility located approximately one hour from Seattle, Washington (Anderson, 2010). She is the only female among the residents. The sex offenders who reside here are considered the worst of the worst, Level 3 offenders. The facility resembles a prison, with its razor wire encasing the facility. Laura agreed to an interview with journalist Lisa Ling from Inside Edition (Ling, 2010). In a five-minute edited clip, Laura provides information that reveals the seriousness of the offenses she committed over a lengthy period of time along with the predatory features of her behavior. Laura, somewhat disheveled, appears in a prison cell-like room, wearing a "Jesus" t-shirt and sheepishly answers questions asked of her. She begins by explaining that she has already served a prison sentence for raping a child. Laura acknowledges that she "should be here" (meaning in a secure treatment facility without access to society). She finds it difficult to answer whether she would be a danger to children, if released to society—noting she still has things to work on. Laura recounts her extensive history of raping children. She indicates 15 are "accounted for," yet she emphasizes she had repeatedly admitted to 100 or more victims. Her offenses took place while she was a caretaker for babies and young children. She noted that she was not aroused by *all* children—she didn't want to hurt them all. Interestingly, she does pair sexual molestation with causing harm to them—characteristics of sadism. Laura notes that she bathed and clothed the babies/children and committed her offenses while this occurred. She explains that she tried to kill one of her victims, by placing a pillow over the baby's head, but was interrupted. Thus, she was a violent sex offender. Laura notes that she did not groom the victims because they were too young, but she did groom their parents. She often raped children who had parents who were vulnerable—had alcohol/drug problems, low income, showed a low stress tolerance for their child, and had difficulty caring for their child. Laura expresses some degree of remorse, claiming that she prays for her victims. Laura is the mother of four children and notes that none of them lived with her. She indicated that she was raped when she was seven years old.

It may be wrongly believed that women who commit sex crimes do not cause harm to their victims. Most female sex offenders portrayed in the media, for example, involve young female teachers who molest teenage boys. Although minor boys cannot legally consent, they often engage in the sexual activity without objection. It should be recognized this is only one type of female sex offender and that (1) the effects of this type of abuse have not been fully explored in the literature, and (2) there are other types of female sex offenders who cause obvious harm to their victim. As noted in Focus Box 7.2, one female sex offender admitted to raping approximately 100 children, including babies. Thus, the seriousness of sex crimes committed by women cannot be overstated.

## EXPLANATIONS OF FEMALE SEX OFFENDERS AND OFFENDING

As seen in the typologies presented above, the dynamics of sex offenses take on many different forms, and their explanations are just as varied. Existing research, specifically, has identified the following motivations for female sex offending:

- Reenactment of sexual abuse (Mayer, 1992; Saradjian & Hanks, 1996).
- Women acting out feelings, narcissistic women abusing their own daughters (Mayer, 1992).
- Extension of **battered woman syndrome**, socialization to follow male accomplices and to please male partners (Davin, Hislop, & Dunbar, 1999).
- Desire for intimacy (Mayer, 1992).
- Economic gain (Vandiver & Kercher, 2004).
- An interaction among cognitive, behavioral, affective (i.e., emotional), and contextual factors (Gannon, Rose, & Ward, 2008).

Reenactment of early sexual abuse has been proposed as an explanation of female sex crimes (Mayer, 1992; Saradjian & Hanks, 1996). It is proposed that the victim experiences displaced anger and, thus, identifies with the aggressor. The victim later becomes an offender and acts out her experiences on another person. Typically, researchers will cite the high rates of abuse that many sex offenders experienced themselves to support this notion. The extent that one affects the other, however, is questionable (Salter, 2003). Although a strong *correlation* between early abuse and later abusing is cited in many studies (see Knopp, 1984), this does not necessarily translate into *causation*. In fact, as noted by Salter (2003), studies including more objective measures (i.e., polygraph) report 50% fewer victims-turned-victimizer. Many sex offenders who reported being sexually abused as a child had not been sexually abused. Many of those who were sexually abused as a child did not go on to become sex offenders.

*Narcissism* has also been proposed as a possible cause of female sexual offending (Mayer, 1992). One researcher relied upon an example described by Foward and Buck (1978) of a mother who molested her daughters. She perceived the daughter as simply an extension of herself. The need to be nurtured, coupled with the need to nurture, resulted in a narcissistic mother with poor boundaries. Another researcher described a similar situation of a woman with severe nurture deprivations (Groth, 1982).

While sexual gratification has been explored as a possible cause of female sexual offending, it does not appear to be a sole motivating factor (Davin et al., 1999). It is proposed that instead of a sexual motivation, a need exists to connect with other persons. A sex crime is just one avenue for meeting this need.

Several theories have been explored specifically for women who have co-offenders. For example, battered woman syndrome may lead a woman to sexually abuse (Davin et al., 1999). Many women who were coerced into a sex crime have a history of physical abuse by a male partner (Davin et al., 1999). Many women who are victims of abuse, however, do not sexually offend. Davin et al. (1999) relied on sex-role theories in exploring other possible explanations. The authors note that these theories describe women as passive. Thus, their male counterparts initiate the sexual abuse, and the women follow. One researcher described the abuse as "an emotional process rooted out of fear, coercion, loneliness, and a perceived societal need to please a male partner" (Crawford, 2012, abstract).

A desire for intimacy has been proposed as a cause for adult women "falling in love" with younger boys (i.e., *heterosexual nurturer* and *teacher/lover*) (Vandiver & Kercher, 2004). Many of these women describe their actions as the outcome of having feelings of "love" for their victims (see Vandiver, 2003). The behavior is not necessarily associated, in the minds of the offenders, with crime. Additionally, economic gain has been proposed as a possible motivating factor for women who engage in hands-off offenses, such as forcing a child into prostitution or posing for pornographic pictures that are later sold (Vandiver & Kercher, 2004).

A more descriptive explanation of female sexual offending, the **Descriptive Model of Female Sexual Offending** (DMFSO), was proposed recently. It includes cognitive, behavioral, affective (i.e., emotional), and contextual factors that lead to women committing sex crimes. More specifically it identifies three factors that potentially distinguish female sex offenders from male sex offenders. First, physically, sexually and emotionally abusive childhood experiences occurred more frequently and more severely than has been reported in the literature for male sex offenders. This is speculated to cause vulnerability factors (low self-esteem, passivity or aggression traits, and early mental health problems) and major life stressors (abusive intimate relationships), which lead to the second factor identified among female sex offenders: abusive relationships (Gannon et al., 2008).

Abusive relationships appear to lead to further vulnerability that places women in risky situations that could lead to sexual offending (Gannon et al., 2008). Such abusive relationships were associated with social isolation, poor coping strategies, passive or aggressive traits, and mental health problems.

The third factor identified among female sex offenders includes co-offender influences. Co-offenders of female sex offenders seem to assist in planning, establishing a goal, and offense planning. Some co-offenders engaged in grooming the female sex offender—to engage in sexual behavior with children. Thus, this research identifies unique factors and suggests unique pathways for females who commit sexual abuse as compared to male sex offenders.

## ASSESSMENT OF FEMALE SEX OFFENDERS

Establishing empirically-based assessments for female sex offenders is difficult, as the research on female sex offenders is at least 20 years behind that of male sex offenders (Cortoni, 2010). This makes it difficult to establish assessment and treatment approaches, as research has found some differences between male and female sex offenders. Thus, it is safe to assume the assessment approaches for men may not be fully applicable to female sex offenders.

With regard to assessments of female sex offenders, there are no standard assessment tools tailored to the specific needs of women. As will be discussed in Chapter 10, many assessment tools have been developed, yet they are tailored specifically to men and developed from empirically-based research findings from the male sex-offender literature, which may not apply to female sex offenders. Recommendations for conducting assessments of female sex offenders, however, have been made.

Although there are no standard assessment tools, it has been established in the literature that women in the criminal justice system require a gender-based response to meet their needs (Bloom et al., 2003). Research has shown female offenders have different profiles than male offenders, suggesting a need for varying criminal justice policies and responses to female offenders. Incarcerated women are more likely than incarcerated men to have an immediate family member incarcerated. Women are more likely than men to come from a single-parent household. Also, women have high rates of physical abuse and substance abuse in the household and are likely to be in need of physical and mental health services. They also are in need of education and vocational skills. Fewer women were employed at the time of arrest compared to incarcerated men. Seventy percent of incarcerated women have at least one child under the age of 18.

Assessments for female sex offenders should follow accepted practices that have been established in the research literature (Cortoni, 2010). Assessments should examine the following (Craig, Browne, & Beech, 2008):

- Dispositional factors (e.g., antisocial personality characteristics).
- Historical factors (e.g., adverse developmental experiences and prior criminal history).
- Contextual elements (e.g., details and circumstances of the offense).

- Available support from social networks.

- Personal life circumstances (e.g., marital and parental status, educational, work, and social functioning).

- Clinical factors (e.g., mental-health and substance-use issues).

Cortoni (2010) recommends consideration of additional factors, including assessing co-offending, sexuality, cognitions, problematic relationships, and victimization. She also emphasizes the need to assess general antisocial tendencies. With regard to co-offending, she notes that whether the offender willingly participated or was coerced should be examined. Sexuality assessment should include an evaluation of the presence of deviant sexual interests, as these have been found to be significant predictors of recidivism among male sex offenders. For women, they may be significant predictors as well. A history of sexual development should also be assessed, including any history of sexual abuse. All of these may be related to female sex offending and should be taken into consideration.

Cognitions also have been correlated with sexual abuse. Pro-offending attitudes are correlated with core beliefs regarding relationships and children (Beech, Parrett, Ward, & Fisher, 2009). Denial and minimization-cognitive patterns need to be assessed for women who have committed sex crimes, as this may be critical to the abuse behavior. Also, intimate deficits and problematic relationships are essential to an assessment of female sex offenders (Cortoni, 2010). This is an area that is quite different for women who sexually offend, compared to men who sexually offend. For female offenders, abuse in relationships appears to be common. Researchers have found, for example, that women become overly dependent on the men in their lives (Eldridge & Saradjian, 2000). Researchers also have found that women who sexually offend often lack emotional support from friends and family. Thus, the assessment of women should include an assessment of social and family support (Cortoni, 2010).

With regard to past victimization, the victimization in and of itself may not be a cause of female sex crimes. Rather, it may be more symptomatic of a dysfunctional pattern women have developed. Also, antisocial tendencies should be assessed. It should be noted, however, that not all women who sexually offend present with these symptoms. It is not known at this time to what extent antisocial characteristics play a role in female offending (Blanchette & Brown, 2006).

## TREATMENT OF FEMALE SEX OFFENDERS

Treatment efforts for sex offenders have been based primarily on male sex offender samples and with a focus on treating male sex offenders, with little attention given to female sex offenders. As the research regarding treatment efforts of female sex offenders increases, the knowledge to develop treatment efforts for female sex offenders also increases.

Treatment programs that have been developed for females include cognitive-based programs. Examples can be found in Canada, where the federal system offers sex-offender therapy to women who are incarcerated and in the community under supervision. The treatment provided is based on a thorough review of the literature and sex-offender files of female sex offenders. The therapy involves five components with up to 70 treatment sessions. The components include (1) self management, (2) deviant arousal, (3) cognitive distortions, (4) intimacy, relationships, and social functioning, and (5) empathy and victim awareness (Blanchette & Taylor, 2010; Correctional Services Canada, 2001).

The self-management component focuses on each female offender's history and identifies alternative ways of coping. It also focuses on understanding offense progression, involving feelings, thoughts, and behaviors that led to the sex crime. The second component, deviant arousal, focuses on reducing deviant sexual interests that may have contributed to the sex offending. The cognitive-distortion component involves resolution of cognitive distortions through a cognitive restructuring process. The intimacy, relationships, and social-functioning component takes into account that many of the women co-offended with a partner. This component focuses on developing healthy relationships and enhancing self-esteem. The empathy and victim-awareness component focuses on developing generalized empathy skills and also empathy skills specific to understanding the effects of sexual offending on victims (Blanchette & Taylor, 2010; Correctional Services Canada, 2001).

## RECIDIVISM OF FEMALE SEX OFFENDERS

Only a few studies have been conducted on recidivism rates of female sex offenders. A recent study of 390 female sex offenders in New York found only six (1.5%) were rearrested for a sexual offense, and 89 (21%) were rearrested for a nonsexual offense (Freeman & Sandler, 2008). The women were followed for an average of 48 months. This study involved one of the largest samples of female sex offenders. Other studies have yielded similar results, although they have relied on smaller samples. For example, Peterson, Colebank, and Motta (2001), relied on a sample of 115 female sex offenders from Kentucky and reported that none recidivated sexually, yet 30 had committed another criminal offense (26%). The sample was followed for approximately five and a half years. Similarly, in 2003, two other researchers found that none of the 43 female sex offenders in Western Australia committed another sex offense, and four (9.3%) committed another violent offense (Broadhurt & Loh, 2003). General offense recidivism was not reported in this study. This sample was also followed for approximately five and a half years.

Also, Williams and Nicholachuk (as cited in Cortoni & Hanson, 2005) reported that of 61 female sex offenders in Canada, only two sexually recidivated (2.3%), seven (11.5%) had a violent re-offense, and 20 (32.8%) had a general re-offense over a period of 7.6 years. In a 2005 executive summary, Cortoni and Hanson reviewed previous studies of recidivism among a combined sample of 380 and after weighting the recidivism rates found that 1% sexually recidivated, 6.3% had violent recidivism, and 20.2% recidivated for any offense. Their review relied not only on published studies, but also included several unpublished reports and raw data. The follow-up periods averaged five years.

A more recent meta-analysis of ten studies (Cortoni, Hanson, & Coache, 2010) revealed that while female sex offenders have extremely low rates of sexual recidivism (less than 3%), rates of re-arrest for violent crime and general crime were higher—yet still less than their male offender counterparts. While the vast majority of research indicates that sexual recidivism is far more common among male offenders than female offenders, some research has suggested recidivism rates among females may be higher than once thought.

Recent research by Bader, Welsh, and Scalora (2010) revealed that 28% of convicted female child molesters were charged with a subsequent sex crime during an approximate 4.9 year follow-up. Although this sample of female offenders was not compared to a male sample, it nonetheless demonstrates the inconsistencies in reported recidivism rates.

Official arrest records are informative, yet they underestimate the true recidivism rates. For females who sexually offend, the estimation of recidivism is even more underestimated given that female sexual behavior is often minimized by society, treatment providers, and even law enforcement officials (Becker, Hall, & Stinson, 2001; Center for Sex Offender Management, 2007). Bader et al. (2010) illustrated this underestimation in their study of recidivism of female child molesters by examining outcome measures used to determine recidivism. When employing only criminal history records as the outcome measure of recidivism, they found a 17.5% sexual recidivism rate among female offenders. However, when triangulating these data with reported recidivism in child welfare reports, additional recidivism was revealed, increasing the sexual recidivism rate to 28%.

Another study that examined female sex offenders for an average of approximately 19 years reported higher rates of sexual abuse (Vandiver, Braithwaite, & Stafford, IP). In their sample of 471 female sex offenders, 7% were re-arrested for another sex crime after their initial arrest that led to registration as a sex offender. Thus, two studies, one that included multiple measures of abuse and another that followed the offenders for an extended period, found sexual recidivism rates to be relatively moderate. Although more studies are needed on the topic, preliminary research suggests female sex offenders may re-offend at moderate rates.

## CONCLUSION

As noted throughout this textbook, many myths exist regarding sex offenders and sex crimes. For the categories of sex offenders in this chapter, this is likely the result of the unusualness and rarity of the crimes, which often leads media to highlight such unusual cases—giving the impression these categories of offenders occur with much more regularity than they do in comparison to the overall rate of sex crimes.

Research findings are rather consistent, identifying that approximately less than 10% of sex offenders are female.

Furthermore, another myth that exists regarding women who do sexually offend is that they are likely to be teachers. Many news articles and stories have highlighted cases similar to Mary Kay Letourneau. This, however, is only one category of female sex offenders. Others include those who sexually abuse in the context of an abusive relationship. Examples include a boyfriend or husband who forces or coerces the woman to sexually molest a child. Moreover, other women may force another person (child, teenager, or even adult) into prostitution. There are rare reports of a woman raping a woman or man under force or threat of force. Thus, female sex offenders engage in a wide range of behaviors. Research also indicates that women, similar to men (see Chapter 7), have low rates of sexual recidivism, perhaps slightly lower than men's rates of recidivism.

## REVIEW POINTS

- Females make up approximately less than 10% of all reported sex offenders.

- The typologies that have been created show women typically offend in a position of authority/caregiving role or as a co-offender (usually acting with a romantic male partner). Other women who offend typically do so in the context of an incestuous relationship, or for economic gain (forcing someone into prostitution) or, in rare instances, she rapes.

- Explanations for women who sexually abuse include reenactment of abuse, narcissism when sexually abusing one's own child, exposure to previous abuse (extension of battered woman syndrome), desire for intimacy, economic gain, and domestic violence.

- Assessment of female sex offenders typically involves assessing a host of criminal, social, and psychological factors, as no formal assessment tools have been created for female sex offenders.

- Cognitive-behavioral treatments have been developed and tailored to meet the needs of female sex offenders.

- The majority of studies show that sexual recidivism rates of female sex offenders are relatively low—usually less than 5%. More recent studies, though, suggest moderate rates of recidivism.

## REFERENCES

Allen, C. (1991). *Women and men who sexually abuse children: A comparative study*. Brandon, VT: Safer Society Press.

Anderson, R. (2010, April 26, 2010). 'The most dangerous child sex offenders in America' Oprah does McNeil Island. Retrieved January 24, 2016, from http://www.seattleweekly.com/dailyweekly/2010/04/post_5.php

Associated Press. (2005). Letourneau marries Fualaau amid media circus. *Seattle Post-Intel-ligencer.* Retrieved August 1, 2016 , from http://www.seattlepi.com/local/article/Letour-neau-marries-Fualaau-amid-media-circus-1174066.php

Associated Press. (2005, February 9, 2005). Tenn. teacher charged with sexual battery. *USA Today.* Retrieved from http://www.usatoday.com/news/nation/2005–02–09-teach-er-rape_x.htm

Bader, S. M., Welsh, R., & Scalora, M. J. (2010). Recidivism among female child molesters. *Violence and Victims, 25*(3), 349–362.

Becker, J. V., Hall, S., & Stinson, J. D. (2001). Female sexual offenders: Clinical, legal and policy issues. *Journal of Forensic Psychology Practice, 1,* 29–50.

Beech, A. R., Parrett, N., Ward, T., & Fisher, D. (2009). Assessing female sexual offenders' motivations and cognitions: An exploratory study. *Psychology, Crime & Law, 15*(2–3), 201–216.

Blanchette, K., & Brown, S. L. (2006). *The assessment and treatment of women offenders: An integrated perspective.* Chichester, UK: John Wiley & Sons.

Blanchette, K., & Taylor, K. N. (2010). A review of treatment initiatives for female sexual offenders. In T. Gannon & F. Cortoni (Eds.), *Female sexual offenders: Theory, assessment, and treatment* (pp. 119–142). Oxford: John Wiley & Sons.

Bloom, B., Owen, B., & Covington, S. (2003). *Gender-responsive strategies: Research prac-tice, and guiding principles for women offenders.* Washington DC: National Institute of Corrections.

Broadhurst, R., & Loh, N. (2003). The probabilities of sex offender rearrest. *Criminal Behav-iour and Mental Health, 13*(2), 121–139.

Cardona, A. C. (2016). Two more arrests made in human trafficking operation run in South Florida. *Naples Daily News.* Retrieved August 2, 2016 from: http://www.naple-snews.com/story/news/crime/2016/07/01/two-more-arrests-made-in-human-traffick-ing-operation-run-in-south-florida/86631682/

Center for Sex Offender Management. (2000). *Myths and facts about sex offenders.* Wash-ington, DC: U.S. Department of Justice, Office of Justice Programs.

Center for Sex Offender Management. (2007). *Female sex offenders.* Washington DC: GPO.

Correctional Services Canada. (2001). *Women who sexually offend: A protocol for assessment and treatment.* Correctional Services Canada. Ottawa, ON.

Cortoni, F. (2010). The assessment of female sexual offenders. In T. Gannon & F. Cortoni (Eds.), *Female sexual offenders: Theory, assessment, and treatment* (pp. 87–100). Oxford: John Wiley & Sons.

Cortoni, F., & Hanson, R. K. (2005). *A review of the recidivism rates of adult female sexual offenders.* (R-169). Ontario.

Cortoni, F., Hanson, R. K., & Coache, M. E. (2010). The recidivism rates of female sexual offenders are low: A meta-analysis. *Sexual Abuse: A Journal of Research and Treatment, 22*(4), 387–401.

Craig, L. A., Browne, K. D., & Beech, A. R. (2008). *Assessing risk in sex offenders: A practi-tioner's guide.* Chichester, UK: Wiley.

Crawford, E. (2012). A grounded theory analysis of the perpetration of child sexual abuse by female sex offenders. (Unpublished doctoral dissertation). Walden University. Min-neapolis, Minnesota.

Davin, P. A., Hislop, J., & Dunbar, T. (1999). *Female sexual abusers: Three views.* Brandon, Vermont: Safer Society Press.

Denov, M. S. (2004). *Perspectives on female sex offending: A culture of denial.* Burlington, VT: Ashgate Publishing Company.

Eldridge, H., & Saradjian, J. (2000). Replacing the function of abusive behaviors for the offender: Remaking relapse prevention in working with women who sexually abuse children. In D. R. Laws, S. M. Hudson & T. Ward (Eds.), *Remaking relapse prevention with sex offenders: A sourcebook* (pp. 402–426). Thousand Oaks, CA: Sage.

Faller, K. C. (1987). Women who sexually abuse children. *Violence and Victims, 2*(4), 263–276.

Federal Bureau of Investigation. (2016). *Crime in the United States: 2014*. Washington DC: Government Printing Office.

Finkelhor, D., Hotaling, G., Lewis, I. A., & Smith, C. (1990). Sexual abuse in a national survey of adult men and women: Prevalence, characteristics, and risk factors. *Child Abuse and Neglect, 14*(1), 19–28.

Finkelhor, D., Williams, L., & Burns, N. (1988). *Nursery crimes: Sexual abuse in day care*. Newbury Park: Sage Publications.

Foward, S., & Buck, C. (1978). *Betrayal of innocence: Incest and its devastation*. Los Angeles: J. P. Teacher.

Freeman, N. J., & Sandler, J. C. (2008). Female and male sex offenders: A comparison of recidivism patterns and risk factors. *Journal of Interpersonal Violence, 23*(10), 1394–1413.

Gannon, T. A., Rose, M. R., & Ward, T. (2008). A descriptive model of the offense process for female sexual offenders. *Sexual Abuse: A Journal of Research and Treatment, 20*(3), 352–374.

Groth, A. N. (1982). In S. M. Sgroi (Ed.), *The incest offender: Handbook of clinical intervention in child sexual abuse* (pp. 215–239). Lexington, MA: D.C. Heath and Co.

Hardyman, P. L., & Van Voorhis, P. (2004). *Developing gender-specific classification systems for women offenders*. Washington DC: National Institute of Corrections.

Hetherton, J. (1999). The idealization of women: Its role in the minimization of child sexual abuse by females. *Child Abuse and Neglect, 23*(2), 161–174.

Johansson-Love, J., & Fremouw, W. (2009). Female sex offenders: A controlled comparison of offender and victim/crime characteristics. *Journal of Family Violence, 24*, 367–376. doi: 10.1007/s10896–009–9236–5

Knopp, F. H. (1984). *Retraining adult sex offenders: Methods and models*. Orwell, VT: Safer Society Press.

Lawson, C. (1993). Mother-son sexual abuse: Rare or underreported? A critique of the research. *Child Abuse and Neglect, 17*(2), 261–269.

Ling, L. (2010). Female sex offender's first TV interview video. Retrieved January 24, 2016, from http://www.oprah.com/oprahshow/Female-Sex-Offenders-First-TV-Interview-Video

McCarty, L. M. (1981). Investigation of incest: Opportunity to motivate families to seek help. *Child Welfare, 60*(10), 679–689.

McCarty, L. M. (1986). Mother-child incest: Characteristics of the offender. *Child Welfare, 65*(5), 447–458.

Mathews, R., Hunter, J. A., Jr., & Vuz, J. (1997). Juvenile female sexual offenders: Clinical characteristics and treatment issues. *Sexual Abuse: A Journal of Research and Treatment, 9*(3), 187–199.

Mathews, R., Matthews, J. K., & Speltz, K. (1989). *Female sexual offenders: An exploratory study*. VT: Safer Society Press.

Mayer, A. (1992). *Women sex offenders: Treatment and dynamics*. Holmes Beach, FL: Learning Publications, Inc.

Miccio-Fonseca, L. C. (2000). Adult and adolescent female sex offenders: Experiences compared to other female and male sex offenders. *Journal of Psychology and Human Sexuality, 11*(3), 75–88.

Oliver, B. E. (2007). Preventing female-perpetrated sexual abuse. *Trauma, Violence & Abuse, 8*(1), 19–32.

Peterson, K. D., Colebank, K. D., & Motta, L. L. (2001, November). *Female sexual offender recidivism*. Paper presented at the Association for the Treatment of Sexual Abusers.

Petrovich, M., & Templer, D. I. (1984). Heterosexual molestation of children who later became rapists. *Psychological Reports, 54*(3), 810. doi: 10.2466/pr0.1984.54.3.810

Pflugradt, D. M., & Allen, B. P. (2010). An exploratory analysis of executive functioning for female sexual offenders: A comparison of characteristics across offense typologies. *Journal of Child Sexual Abuse, 19*(4), 434–449.

Rowan, E. L., Rowan, J. B., & Langelier, P. (1990). Women who molest children. *Bulletin of the American Academy of Psychiatry and the Law, 18*(1), 79–83.

Salter, A. C. (2003). *Predators: Pedophiles, rapists, and other sex offenders*. New York: Basic Books.

Sandler, J. C., & Freeman, N. J. (2007). Typology of female sex offenders: A test of Vandiver and Kercher. *Sexual Abuse, 19*(2), 73–89. doi: 10.1007/s11194–007–9037–4

Sandler, J. C., & Freeman, N. J. (2009). Female sex offender recidivism: A large-scale empirical analysis. *Sexual Abuse: A Journal of Research and Treatment, 21*(4), 455–473.

Saradjian, J., & Hanks, H. (1996). *Women who sexually abuse children: From research to practice*. New York: John Wiley.

Sarrel, P. M., & Masters, W. H. (1982). Sexual molestation of men by women. *Archives of Sexual Behavior, 11*(2), 117–131.

Syed, F., & Williams, S. (1996). *Case studies of female sex offenders in the Correctional Service of Canada*. Ottawa: Correctional Service of Canada.

Teachey, L. (2000, November 10, 2000). Mom, boyfriend gets 40 years for prostituting girls. *The Houston Chronicle*, p. A40.

Travin, S., Cullen, K., & Protter, B. (1990). Female sex offenders: Severe victims and victimizers. *Journal of Forensic Sciences, 35*(1), 140–150.

Vandiver, D. M. (2003, March). *Female sex offenders: A case study approach*. Paper presented at the Academy of Criminal Justice Sciences, Las Vegas, NV.

Vandiver, D. M. (2006a). Female sex offenders: A comparison of solo offenders and co-offenders. *Violence and Victims, 21*(3), 339–354.

Vandiver, D. M. (2006b). A prospective analysis of juvenile male sex offenders: Characteristics and recidivism rates as adults. *Journal of Interpersonal Violence, 21*(5), 673–688.

Vandiver, D. M. (2010). Assessing gender differences and co-offending patterns of a predominantly "male-oriented" crime: A comparison of a cross-national sample of juvenile boys and girls arrested for a sexual offense. *Violence and Victims, 25*(2), 243–264.

Vandiver, D. M., Braithwaite, J., & Stafford, M. C. (IP). A longitudinal assessment of recidivism rates of female sex offenders: comparing recidivist and non-recidivists. *Sexual Abuse: A Journal of Research and Treatment*.

Vandiver, D. M., Cheeseman, K. A., & Worley, R. (2006). *A qualitative assessment of registered sex offenders: Characteristics and attitudes toward registration*. Paper presented at the Annual Meeting of the Southwestern Association of Criminal Justice, Ft. Worth, TX.

Vandiver, D. M., & Kercher, G. (2004). Offender and victim characteristics of registered female sexual offenders in Texas: A proposed typology of female sexual offenders. *Sexual Abuse: A Journal of Research and Treatment, 16*(2), 121–137.

Vandiver, D. M., & Walker, J. T. (2002). Female sex offenders: An overview and analysis of 40 cases. *Criminal Justice Review, 27*(2), 284–300.

West, S. G., Friedman, S. H., & Kim, K. D. (2011). Women accused of sex offenses: A gender-based comparison. *Behavioral Sciences and the Law, 29*(5), 728–740.

## DEFINITIONS

**Aggressive Homosexual Offenders:** A category of female sex offenders (identified by Vandiver and Kercher) who commit rape against an adult victim.

**Battered Woman Syndrome:** A psychological condition that affects women who have suffered physical and/or verbal abuse from another person, usually a spouse, and resembles symptoms of post-traumatic stress disorder, which includes a state of hyper-vigilance.

**Descriptive Model of Female Sexual Offending:** A model proposed by Gannon that includes cognitive, behavioral, affective (i.e., emotional), and contextual factors that lead to women committing sex crimes. Specifically, it includes three factors that potentially distinguish female sex offenders from male sex offenders: (1) physical, sexual and emotionally abusive childhood; (2) abusive relationships; and (3) co-offender influences.

**Exploration/Exploitation:** A category of female sex offenders (identified by Mathews, Matthews, and Speltz) that involves a female babysitter who molests a child she is babysitting. This category was also identified by Sarrel and Masters as "babysitter abuse."

**Female Sexual Predators:** A category of female sex offenders (identified by Vandiver and Kercher) that includes young women with a lengthy criminal record for various crimes. Their victims are either male or female and typically young.

**Heterosexual Nurturer:** A category of female sex offenders (identified by Vandiver and Kercher) that involves women in a caretaking role or position of authority (e.g., teacher, mentor, etc.) who sexually abuse a young male, typically a teenager, under the guise of a typical romantic relationship.

**Homosexual Criminals:** A category of female sex offenders (identified by Vandiver and Kercher) that involves primarily hands-off offenses, such as prostitution or posing for nude pictures/videos, for a profit.

**Male-Coerced Female Sex Offender:** A category of female sex offenders (identified by Mathews, Matthews, and Speltz) that involves a woman who sexually abuses, as encouraged by a man with whom she is romantically involved, in an attempt to preserve her relationship with that man.

**Narcissism:** A personality trait that involves an overwhelming sense of self-love, grandiose perceptions of one's self, and a sense of entitlement.

**Non-Criminal Homosexual Offenders:** A category of female sex offenders (identified by Vandiver and Kercher) that involves women who sexually abuse a female victim, most likely with a co-offending romantic male partner. She has none/few prior arrests for any type of offense.

**Predisposed Sex Offender:** A category of female sex offenders (identified by Mathews, Matthews, and Speltz) that involves incest, and offenders have a history of childhood sexual abuse.

**Social Junk:** A term coined by Steven Spitzer and influenced by Marxist philosophy. It refers to those who make up a segment of society who are not in a position in society to acquire adequate resources for themselves, often falling between the cracks of social service agencies.

**Teacher/Lover:** A category of female sex offenders (identified by Mathews, Matthews, and Speltz) that involves a female teacher who "falls in love" with an adolescent male student.

**UCR (Uniform Crime Reports):** An annual report of crimes and arrests that have occurred in the U.S., published by the Federal Bureau of Investigation.

**Young Adult Child Exploiters:** A category of female sex offenders (identified by Vandiver and Kercher) that is comparable to the predisposed offender (identified by Mathews, Matthews, and Speltz), which includes incest offenders.

## CHAPTER 8

# Institutional Abuse: Child Molesters and Rapists

## CHAPTER OBJECTIVES

- Define and identify the characteristics of institutional abuse.
- Describe the characteristics and prevalence of clergy, educators, child-care providers, athletic-organization employees, and civic-organization employees/volunteers who molest children.
- Describe the characteristics and prevalence of law enforcement officers who rape.
- Identify types and characteristics of organizations that have recently responded to fostering rape-prone attitudes (athletic organizations, higher-education institutions, prisons, and military).

Those who are in positions to provide key services to children have recently been thrust into the public spotlight by cases of clergy abuse, as well as abuse by those who serve in the capacity of caretaker or in mentorship roles. Others who are in the public eye, such as sports figures, have also found themselves in the media spotlight following rape allegations.

While it may be assumed that those who sexually offend are transient or lack the skill set to be successful in their professional lives, many sex offenders have successful careers and, in some cases, are in positions of authority. Child molestation occurs in a variety of settings and institutions, such as schools, childcare settings, athletic organizations, and civic organizations (e.g., Boy Scouts of America, Big Brothers Big Sisters, and Scouts Canada). Many of these cases surfaced in the 1980s and were considered a social problem (K. Daly, 2014). In this chapter, several groups who do not meet the stereotypical portrayal of a sex offender are considered. This includes clergy, educators, childcare providers, and leaders in athletic and civic organizations. Also, police officers and athletes have been accused of committing rape, and thus, are explored here. In this chapter, incidents of child molestation and rape among these groups are discussed.

We have discussed in Chapter 3 that *sexual violence* is often utilized as a way for an offender to exert power over a victim. In fact, extensive research, both on offenders and victims, suggests that issues of power and anger (not sexual arousal) are important for understanding sex offenders' behavior, particularly rapists. While research using both clinical and non-clinical samples has supported the notion of rape as an expression of power, the road less traveled examines offenders in *professions* of power who commit these crimes. In recent years, professionals who use their work or authority as a guise for targeting and sexually abusing people (particularly women and children) have come into public focus (Sullivan & Beech, 2002). In this chapter, we discuss sexual abuse as a tool used by authority figures.

A common theme in this chapter is that many organizations are ill-equipped to respond to sex crimes. Most lack proper employee training and formal policies about how to respond. This chapter, therefore, focuses on organizational systems and how claims of child molestation and rape have been handled. This includes a discussion of sex crimes that have occurred in an institutional setting and the responses to those sex crimes.

## INSTITUTIONAL ABUSE CHARACTERISTICS

It should be noted that ***institutional abuse*** is estimated to account for only about 3% of all referrals of child sexual abuse. This includes all sex abuse of children by abusers who come in contact with children in some institutional setting. This can include a formal or informal organization, such as a school, Boy Scouts of America, or a local community group that is volunteer based. The offender can be a teacher, a coach, or even a volunteer. Offenders who commit institutional abuse, however, often operate with considerable sophistication in grooming victims and bystanders (Sullivan & Beech, 2002).

Three processes have been identified as critical to the commission of institutional sexual abuse: (1) gaining access to victims, (2) initiating and maintaining the abuse, and (3) concealing the abuse (Colton, Roberts, & Vanstone, 2010). Although these processes occur with child molestation outside of institutional settings, researchers have examined how these processes occur in institutional settings through the examination of eight men who committed institutional abuse with 35 victims. With regard to gaining access to victims, there is anecdotal support for the notion that offenders choose employment opportunities that provide them with access to children. Furthermore, if their job does not provide them with access to children, they will adapt to create such opportunities (Leclerc, Proulx, & McKibben, 2005). This includes taking home-tutoring duties. The institutional setting and context of the job are relied upon to prey on victims (Brannan, Jones, & Murch, 1993). For example, one teacher had contact with his victim when the victim was referred to him by a co-worker (Colton et al., 2010). The offender had become known as someone who could handle troubled youth.

Manipulation is a critical aspect to gaining access to potential victims. The following description shows how a volunteer manipulated those around him to gain access to a victim:

> I manipulated the system, changed the timetables and made sure that [the victim] was on my roster, so we saw a lot of each other.... I manipulated the system very cleverly and made sure that it was well covered up.... I made some very calculated moves.
>
> (Colton et al., 2010, p. 353)

Child molesters often choose victims who are vulnerable, including those who lack a support system or have emotional problems (Salter, 2003). In the following scenario, an abuser describes targeting a particular victim:

> I targeted boys who were loners or less exuberant or less likely to say anything, or those single parents with usually only ... [mom] at home who saw me as a father figure.... I got to know the boy's family and offered to take him home for the weekend to give his ... [mom] a break ... I targeted him at six years old, from when I discovered he was in trouble. He had behavior problems. I was seen as someone who could control him.... If the child was troublesome or a loner, then people were less likely to listen to him.... He was difficult and I preyed on that ... I created a cage for [him]. He'd only talk to me. His ...[mom] would ring me up to ask me to talk to him. I became very pleased with myself that this was an MO that seemed to work.
>
> (Colton et al., 2010, p. 354)

It is clear that the emotional and/or behavioral problems of a child can be used as a way to isolate and victimize him or her. Those who work in an institution become experts in identifying vulnerabilities and using them to target the children (Colton et al., 2010).

The second process is initiating and maintaining the abuse. Child molesters are more likely to use manipulative strategies as opposed to coercion and commit their offenses at their own home or workplace, places that are familiar to them (Leclerc et al., 2005). The offender's manipulative strategies include giving the victim's family the perception that the offender is "helping," using massage, relying on a position of power and authority, providing rewards to the victim, pairing "treats" (taking the child somewhere he/she wants to go) with offers to help the family, and exposing the victim to pornography (Colton et al., 2010). With regard to touch, one offender describes its importance:

> Light, physical contact I would use as well. If I put my arm around them ... I would know straight away, if children backed off ... I wouldn't go near that child again. I would go through a gradual sort of progression.... I would be tactile in various ways outside the clothing, if they didn't object or didn't say anything then I just progressed from that.... I knew it was okay to carry on to an extra stage.... Each child was a potential victim as far as I was concerned.... The [victims] were the children I could get away with it.
>
> (Colton et al., 2010, p. 355).

Thus, this offender perceived all children as potential victims and simply would find ones that could be groomed easily.

The third process is concealing the abuse. Research has found that disclosing abuse within an institutional setting often results in the offender's co-workers not believing the victim (Green, 2001). Building trust among co-workers is critical (Colton et al., 2010). One researcher described an offender who was able to conceal child molestation "by being a good teacher, popular" (Colton et al., 2010, p. 356). The offender noted that everyone, including his own mother, believed he was innocent until he pled guilty.

Combining a good reputation with the closeness to the victim is usually sufficient to dissuade anyone from believing that the person committed a sex crime. For example, one offender noted that he minimized the abuse allegation by stating the victim would always come to him and that her parents knew she was coming over to his house for help with homework. Relying on one's good reputation and the use of implied threats can conceal abuse. One offender who was a home tutor indicated that if the students wanted assistance passing exams, they had to go to him. This is a type of implied threat. If they did not go to him for assistance (and be victimized), they may not pass their exams. He relied on his reputation as an excellent tutor to lure students. Typically, abusers have unsupervised access to children, which allows for victimization to occur and more importantly, for the abuse to be concealed. Furthermore, they are often in a trusted position.

Several researchers (Sullivan & Beech, 2002; Westcott, 1991) have identified four barriers to reporting sexual abuse within an institution:

(1) A lack of policies and procedures that would allow reporting and investigation of sexual allegations.

(2) A view of the problem as limited to an individual person, rather than a larger institutional problem.

(3) The lack of transparency in the institution.

(4) The general "belief system" that surrounds the institution.

Institutional abuse, therefore, is fraught with poor avenues for reporting sexual allegations and a lack of procedures for responding appropriately to such allegations. Specific institutions are now discussed, with attention to the unique problems each faces with regard to reporting and responding to sexual allegations.

## Clergy Who Molest Children

John Geoghan, a Boston priest in the Catholic Church, made headlines in the Boston Globe as an alleged child abuser. This sparked national media attention to the problem of child sexual abuse within the Catholic Church (Terry et al., 2011). Reports of sexual abuse increased substantially as well. The United States Conference of Catholic Bishops (USCCB) developed the Charter for the Protection of Children and Young People in 2002 as a result. The Charter called for a National Review Board to conduct a study regarding the nature and scope of the problem. The Charter and the National Review Board commissioned researchers at John Jay College of Criminal Justice to conduct a study. Two studies, the *Nature and Scope of Sexual Abuse of Minors by Catholic Priests and Deacons: 1950–2002* (2004) and *The Causes and Context of Sexual Abuse of Minors by the Catholic Priests in the United States: 1950–2010* (2011) were conducted and produced the most comprehensive report to date regarding details of sexual abuse of children within the Catholic Church (Terry et al., 2011).

The report addressed a pressing question: how many priests and how many victims existed in the Catholic Church? Based on three surveys administered to a wide range of priests, it was found that 4,392 of 109,694 priests who served for at least some time between 1950 and 2002 had allegations of some sex crime against them (Terry et al., 2011). By 2003, 10,667 reports were known to the dioceses. Thus, approximately 4% of priests were accused of sex crimes. Very few allegations occurred from 1950 through the mid-1970s. The majority of the allegations were made in the late 1970s and early 1980s, and they sharply declined thereafter.

The offending priests were as young as 25 and as old as 90 at the time of the first sex crime. Most (69%) were diocesan priests serving as a pastor or associate pastor at the time. Fifty-six percent of the priests had only one victim. Interestingly, however, 4% of the offending priests were responsible for 26% of the victims who had been identified by 2002. The findings suggest the possibility of a few "'rotten apples,' the colloquial term for a deviant individual who may elude even the most sophisticated of the exclusionary criteria for acceptance into the ministry" (Terry et al., 2011, p. 16).

Also noteworthy, less than 5% of the priests accused of a sex crime against a child engaged in behavior consistent with pedophilia. As noted in Chapter 4, many of those who molest children do not meet the criteria of a pedophile as defined by the DSM-5. The priests who were abusing children did not differ from priests who had not abused children on intelligence tests or psychological tests, yet they did show intimacy deficits and often lacked close personal relationships before and during seminary (Terry et al., 2011).

Most of the victims were male. This is not comparable to U.S. sex-crime data, which show the majority of victims are female. Interestingly, previous research has shown that within institutions, the majority of victims are male. The majority of the incidents (41%) occurred at the priest's home (Puro, Goldman, & Smith, 1997).

The results of the study identified several causes of the sex crimes, which were categorized as:

1. *General cultural factors*: including the impact of social changes in the 1960s and 1970s on individual priests' attitudes and behaviors and on organizational life, including social stratification, emphasis on individualism, and social movements.

2. *Church-specific factors*: including the aftermath of Vatican II, changes in priestly formation, the impact of resignations from ministry, and changes in diocesan structures and leadership.

3. *Environmental factors*: including changes in the patterns of parish activities, youth ministry, and changes in living situations and responsibilities of parish priests.

4. *Psychological factors*: including psychological disorders, sexuality, past behavior, developmental issues, and vulnerabilities of individual priests.

5. *Structural and legal factors*: including changes in the understanding of the legal status of certain behavior in society (Terry et al., 2011, p. 7).

As with sexual abuse in general, sex crimes within the Catholic Church were the result of a multitude of complex factors, rather than a single underlying problem. Thus, they cannot be blamed on the demands of celibacy alone or the presence of pedophilia or pedophilic tendencies (Terry et al., 2011).

The majority of the allegations of sexual abuse within the church resulted in having the priests participate in some type of treatment program, which included sex-offender-specific treatment, spiritual counseling, psychotherapy, or general treatment. When a priest had more than one allegation against him, it was more likely that he would participate in a treatment program. Legal officials were rarely involved in these cases. Only 14% of the offending priests were referred to authorities, and many of those cases involved expired statutes of limitation. Only 3% of priests were convicted, and 2% received a prison sentence (Terry et al., 2011).

It is also important to emphasize that child molestation in the church is not limited to the Catholic Church, nor is it limited to the U.S. Although official studies have been carried out regarding child molestation in the Catholic Church (Terry et al., 2011), such studies are virtually non-existent in other religions. Many reported cases, however, do exist for a wide range of churches. In the excerpt below, for example, a victim of child molesting notes how the Pentecostal Church failed to respond appropriately to molestation allegations committed by a youth pastor:

> The Royal Commission into the Institutional Responses to Child Sexual Abuse has completed hearings into the way Pentecostal churches managed complaints of child sexual abuse in Victoria, New South Wales and Queensland. On the final day of evidence at the Sydney hearing, Peter O'Brien, the lawyer representing a man who was abused by the youth pastor read a statement from his client, known as ALA, that said the past 10 years had been a "living hell". "They failed to detect the abuse. They failed to prevent the abuse. They failed to support us through the criminal trial process," ALA said. "It appears to me they were more concerned about the reputation and financial position of the ACC (Australian Christian Churches) above all else."
>
> (Chettle, 2014, n.p.)

Again, this example shows the lack of an adequate formal response to sex crimes against children. The Australian Christian Churches, however, pledged to pay advisors to develop child-protection policies (Chettle, 2014).

## Educators and Child Molestation

In regard to sex crimes against children that are committed by school employees, a recent report noted this is an understudied topic and there is limited research (Shakeshaft, 2004). In a summary of the topic, however, one researcher relied upon a study by the American Association of University Women, which reported that approximately 7% of eighth- to eleventh-grade students experienced unwanted sexual contact (Shakeshaft, 2004). Of those, 21% involved unwanted sexual contact from educators. Another study noted that 14% of surveyed high school students reported having sex with a teacher (Wishnietsky, 1991). Also noteworthy, educator sexual misconduct is not limited to the U.S.—it is a global problem. For example, one study in Israel reported that 8% of secondary school students suffered sexual victimization by educational staff (Khoury-Kassabri, 2006). Likewise, the problem was recognized in Canada when the Ontario College of Teachers defined educator abuse and established a prevention plan (Ontario College of Teachers, 2002). Research has also been conducted in the Netherlands on teacher sexual misconduct, which shows that teacher-student sexual abuse does not always occur in seclusion (Timmerman, 2003).

Shakeshaft (2004) coined the term *educator misconduct*, which involves someone in a school, such as a teacher or coach, sharing pornography, having conversations with sexual talk, masturbation in the presence of a student, or other sexual behavior. The author noted that some of this behavior is illegal and some is not. All of the behavior, however, is considered inappropriate. Teachers who had jobs that involved time alone with students (e.g., coaches, tutors, etc.) were more likely to engage in educator misconduct than those who did not have such jobs.

Sexual crimes against students can also involve persons in management positions, such as a principal or even a school district board member. An example involving a school district board member in Virginia is given below:

> A former Stafford School Board member agreed to a deal Tuesday in which he was convicted of five charges involving child molestation … In exchange for the pleas … [the] prosecutor … dropped 106 other charges and agreed to seek no more than 4 years in prison when [the defendant] is sentenced … The allegations first surfaced in 1997, when [the defendant], who had a top secret clearance as an employee of the Defense Intelligence Agency, was required to take a polygraph so he could perform work for the Central Intelligence Agency. During that polygraph, [the defendant] admitted having sexual desires for children … [Later, the defendant] again admitted to a lifelong sexual interest in children. He told investigators that he likes children between 4 and 10 and prefers girls, though some of his victims were boys. He detailed in taped interviews and written statements how he would set up circumstances for his sexual gratification in ways in which the children would not recognize what was going on. This included watching them naked in bathtubs and improperly touching them when drying them off. [The defendant's] statements were turned over to the

Stafford Sheriff's Office, which identified four victims who are all now adults.... [the defendant] served on the Stafford School Board for eight years, serving one term as the Garrisonville District representative and one as the Hartwood District representative, and he was the chairman in 2005. His other local community involvement included the Boy Scouts and St. William of York Catholic Church.

(Epps, 2014, n.p.)

None of the victims in this example reported the incident to police. That the defendant also was involved in Boy Scouts and his church illustrates how sex offenders often place themselves in a position of authority and in a position with access to children.

Research has found that other adults often do not report suspected sex crimes, given the serious nature of such accusations (Shakeshaft, 2013). Thus, other adults contribute to the problem by not reporting their suspicions. In an attempt to prevent educator misconduct, Shakeshaft (2013) identifies warning signs for two types of educators that engage in **sexual misconduct**. First, the **fixated abuser** makes up approximately one-third of educator perpetrators. This type of perpetrator is typically a male elementary- or early middle-school teacher who is perceived as an excellent teacher by his peers, and by students, parents and administrators, and has received many teaching awards. He typically victimizes a male student he has groomed. The student's parents have also been groomed by offering extra attention by tutoring and taking the student to special events, such as camping or fishing.

The second type of educator perpetrator identified by Shakeshaft (2013) is the **opportunistic offender**, who make up approximately two-thirds of educator perpetrators. Shakeshaft describes them as regressed because they are not exclusively attracted to children. The teacher has boundary and judgment problems. Such behaviors are relatively easy to identify. The teacher will often chat with students and often go to the same kinds of places the students go in an attempt to fit in with the students and be perceived as "hip" or "cool." The teacher typically knows more about the personal lives of the students than is appropriate. The opportunistic offender can also be a female teacher who victimizes a student under the guise of romantic pursuit. As noted in Chapter 7, other researchers who developed typologies of female sex offenders identified the teacher/lover (Mathews, Matthews, & Speltz, 1989) and heterosexual female nurturer (Vandiver & Kercher, 2004). The student typically has the perception that he/she is in love and dating the teacher.

Grooming of victims by educators typically involves finding vulnerable students (e.g., those estranged from their parents), followed by praising the student, offering additional help, mentoring, and finding opportunities for overnight outings (Knoll, 2010; Robins, 2000). Throughout the process, the teacher increases the level of physical touching until they progress into sex. The teacher may also groom the parents. Parents are typically appreciative of the extra help the teacher is providing. One researcher (Robins, 2000, p. 376), combining several sources of information ("Districts should appoint teacher-led teams to train staff about professional boundaries," 2006; Shakeshaft, 2004; Sutton, 2004), created a list of warning signs of educator sexual misconduct:

- Obvious or inappropriate preferential treatment of a student.
- Excessive time spent alone with a student.
- Excessive time spent with student outside of class.
- Repeated time spent in private spaces with a student.
- Driving a student to or from school.
- Befriending parents and making visits to their home.
- Acting as a particular student's "confidant."
- Giving small gifts, cards, letters to a student.
- Inappropriate calls or emails to a student.
- Overly affectionate behavior with a student.
- Flirtatious behavior or off-color remarks around a student.
- Other students suspect, make jokes, or references.

A case study of one educator who has many of the noted warning signs is presented below:

The summer before [the victim] started high school, John met Mr. Ricci. John was an active member in the school sports club when Mr. Ricci requested a student to sit on the school council; John volunteered. At the same time, Mr. Ricci told John's mother that on occasion John could stay at his house to work on student council business and that he could be paid. Mr. Ricci convinced John's mother that such an arrangement would help John cope with his father's illness. John's mother agreed to this ... Several times, Mr. Ricci called to say John had fallen asleep on the couch and suggested John just stay overnight. John's grades began to fall and he had no explanation for his mother.... Mr. Ricci took John on a trip to New York City. For days after the trip, John['s] behavior markedly changed. He was withdrawn, sarcastic, and isolated himself.... John finally told his mother that Mr. Ricci had taken him to a gay bar and that night he awoke to being orally sodomized by the teacher. The mother reported the abuse to police. An investigative interview revealed that the teacher had been sexually abusing John between the ages of 14 and 17 at the teacher's home. In addition, Mr. Ricci would use explicit sexual talk, show pornographic videos, provide alcohol, invite men over for sex parties, tell John he was gay, buy explicit sexual toys, and threaten him with grave consequences should the activity be disclosed.

(Burgess, Welner, & Willis, 2010, pp. 391–392)

Responses to educator sexual misconduct have varied. In one study of 225 cases of educator sexual misconduct, none were reported to legal officials (Shakeshaft & Cohan, 1995). Only 15% were terminated, while 20% were formally reprimanded or suspended. One percent lost their license to teach. Disciplinary action against teachers for sex crimes against children is usually lengthy (Knoll, 2010). Typical background checks of teachers usually only detect felonies, and many of these cases do not meet the criteria for a felony offense. Offending teachers typically retain their teaching license as they appeal any negative decisions. Teachers are then allowed to move to another state and use their license to get a new teaching position. It has been noted that school districts avoid problems for themselves by agreeing to cease any formal action if the teacher moves and promises not to initiate any civil charges against the school district, a practice known as *"passing the trash"* (Knoll, 2010; Moskowitz, 2001).

There have been efforts to outline prevention strategies. Below is a list of prevention strategies that have been identified by one researcher (Knoll, 2010, p. 382) by combining several sources (Fauske, Mullen, & Sutton, 2006; Shakeshaft, 2004; Sutton, 2004):

- District and school-level policies prohibiting educator sexual misconduct.
- Standardized hiring practices.
- Standardized screening methods and criminal background checks.
- Standardized investigative practices in response to allegations.
- Development of a centralized reporting agency and registry.
- Report all allegations to law enforcement and child protective services.
- Regular training on educator sexual misconduct and prevention.
- Enact state statutes on educator sexual misconduct and prevention.

## Childcare Providers and Child Molesting

Sexual abuse in daycare became well known in the 1980s when the McMartin Preschool case was covered extensively by the media. It was one of the longest and most well-known cases of sex crimes against children. The trial lasted 28 months, and was one of the most expensive trials in U.S. history. The accusation occurred in 1983 when a mother of a two-and-a-half-year-old boy reported that Raymond Buckey at the McMartin's pre-school in Manhattan Beach, California abused her son. She indicated her son had a red anus, which she believed was caused by sodomy. There were allegations that bizarre satanic rituals were occurring.

Mr. Buckey was the only male teacher at the school at the time. When the investigations began, the police sent out letters to 200 parents. Some parents, subsequently, began to question their children and the children reported being touched inappropriately, having pictures taken of them, and being forced to engage in sex. The stories also involved mutilation of animals and hidden underground passageways, which were never found. The children also implicated Peggy Ann Buckey and other teachers (Frontline, n.d.).

In 1984, the police arrested Ray Buckey, Peggy Ann Buckey, Virginia McMartin, and three other teachers. The charges against Virginia McMartin, Peggy Ann Buckey, and the other teachers were dropped, but not until 1986. Ray Buckey and his mother stood trial, which began in April 1987. The trial ended in April 1989 with acquittals and deadlock on the remaining charges. Ray Buckey was tried again on the deadlock charges, which resulted in another deadlock. The prosecutors did not retry him. During this time, Ray Buckey had spent five years in jail, while Peggy Ann Buckey had spent two years in jail (Frontline, n.d.).

Therapists who were experts in sexual-abuse diagnosis interviewed children. The videotapes of the interviews were shown during the trial. Years later, jurors were interviewed, and they said the videotapes led to their deadlock and acquittal decisions. They believed some of the children had been sexually abused, but the interviews were too suggestive (Frontline, n.d.).

This case, along with several subsequent cases, highlighted the problem of investigating sex crimes against children. Such cases are difficult and distinguishing guilt from false allegations is critical. These difficulties are summarized in Chapter 9, which focuses on sex-crime investigations. As of now, official statistics regarding the number of child molestations that occur within daycare settings are not available. It can be speculated that the numbers are low, given the lack of research and government reports.

Few studies have focused specifically on childcare settings. One study by Finkelhor, Williams, and Burns (1988), however, examined sexual abuse claims in 270 daycare centers. From a two-year period, 1983 to 1985, 1,639 victims of sexual abuse were reported; thus, 5.5 out of every 10,000 children were sexually abused. Sexual abuse incidents were higher when there was a low presence of staff. Also, sexual-abuse incidents were higher in informal care settings compared to formal care settings (Margolin, 1991). Another study found that of a sample of 48 children abused in a daycare setting, three-fourths were from a daycare center as opposed to the other one-fourth who came from daycare homes (Faller, 1988).

With regard to the perpetrator characteristics, Faller (1988) found that on average, there were 2.8 offenders per victim. Approximately half included both a male and female perpetrator. Forty-eight percent of the children were abused by a male, while the remaining 2% were abused by a female.

This study also involved the development of a daycare-abuse typology (Faller, 1988). Three categories were identified. The first category, *multi-perpetrator abuse*, included the highest number of cases. An average of 4.7 offenders were involved in each sexual abuse, and at least one of them was male. In some instances, strangers were allowed access to the children to commit sexual abuse. On occasion, the children were taken somewhere to be abused. In all of the cases, all of the staff were involved in the abuse. Typically, multiple children were victimized. In the second category, *one-person involved abuse*, the offender abused the individual by him/herself without the knowledge or consent of the other staff. All of the offenders were male volunteers who were in high-school or college. They all were employees at the daycare center. The third category, *daycare home abuse*, involved an average of 1.3 offenders per victim. The offenders were typically husbands, boyfriends, sons, or friends of the daycare home provider. They typically had access to the children due to their relationship with the daycare provider. Rarely did the abuse involve the daycare home provider. Typically, only one child was victimized in the daycare home, and the victims were more often female than male.

## Athletic Organizations and Child Molesting

Recent headlines have drawn attention to the problem of sexual abuse in athletic organizations when felony charges of sex crimes against a minor were filed against Pennsylvania State University football coach Jerry Sandusky. In one report, it was noted that the authorities handed down 40 criminal counts regarding sex crimes. Twenty-one of those included felonies. It was alleged at the time of the report that Jerry Sandusky sexually victimized eight boys over an eight-year period. The charges were the result of a two-year grand jury investigation. A former graduate assistant reported to the grand jury he saw Sandusky having anal intercourse with a child (Wieberg & Carey, 2012). Sandusky was subsequently convicted and sentenced to 30 to 60 years in prison.

Researchers have examined the prevalence of sex crimes among athletic organizations. For example, in a survey of 1,200 Canadian Olympians, it was found that 8.6% reported forced sexual intercourse with some authority figure within their sport. Approximately 2% of the victims were under the age of 16 when this occurred (Kirby & Greaves, 1996).

A review of media reports has shown that sex crimes occur in a wide range of sports, such as gymnastics, hockey, soccer, football, basketball, track and field, and baseball (Terry et al., 2011). It has been found that the abuser is most likely a coach (Brackenridge, 1997). Other abusers, however, include organization officials, sports medicine professionals, and sports psychologists (Bringer, Brackenridge, & Johnston, 2001). Those who commit sex crimes within an athletic organization typically have between 10 and 12 victims (Terry et al., 2011).

Grooming behavior typically involves socializing with the victim's family (Stirling & Kerr, 2009). This was apparent in Jerry Sandusky's behavior with his alleged victims. For example, it was reported that he gave his victims gifts and promised a "walk-on" for one of the victims (Ganim, 2011). Another common grooming technique is to ask the child to play games with the offender or teach the child a sport (Gallagher, 2000).

Many obstacles exist in discovering and bringing to light sex crimes within a sports organization. Much of the social science research on sex crimes has not been on male victims (Hartill, 2008). Male victims often do not initially disclose the sex crime (Gallagher, 2000). Many sports organizations often reinforce a patriarchal structure with a dominant heterosexual-male culture (Hargreaves, 1986). Also, they are often comprised of men who subscribe to this patriarchal structure (Burstyn, 1999). The environment is not conducive to reporting unwanted sexual advances and victimization. The culture also involves ensuring protection of children, despite evidence to the contrary (Hartill, 2008). The problem of disclosure is compounded when the offender is held in high esteem in the community (Gallagher, 2000). Those in positions of authority in sports organizations, such as staff and managers, are not likely to follow up on claims of sex crimes, perhaps to protect the organization and due to the lack of procedures in place for handling such allegations (Sullivan & Beech, 2002). Thus, organizations become a sort of safe haven for offenders to sexually victimize children without fear of reprisal.

Sex crimes in athletic organizations also occur outside the U.S., and various governments have responded by instituting formal guidelines and practices for prevention and response. For example, in Canada, a documentary reported several female rowers who were sexually assaulted by their coach when they were children (Canadian Broadcasting Corporation Television, 1993). Later, the Canadian Strategy for Ethical Conduct in Sport (2002) specifically prohibited harassment and abuse of any kind. In the U.S., the Little League requires background checks of the adults who are affiliated with the organization to protect children from sex crimes (Little League, 2008).

In Australia, the Australian Sports Commission also provides ethical guidelines to prevent sex crimes against children (see generally: www.ausport.gov.au/ethics/childprotect). In the U.K., the Child Protection Sport Unit has been developed and funded by two organizations, Sport England and the National Society for the Prevention of Cruelty to Children (NSPCC). The organization was led by the efforts of Celia Brackenridge, who was an advocate for preventing and recognizing sex crimes in sports organizations (Hartill, 2008). In the U.K., sex crimes in sports organizations came to the forefront when Paul Hickson, an Olympic swimming coach, was convicted for the rape of teenaged female athletes on his team.

## Civic Organizations and Child Molestation

Sex crimes in civic organizations have also been brought to the attention of many through media and other accounts. For example, a series of news articles in the *Washington Times*, along with a book by Patrick Boyle, resulted in greater public awareness of sex crimes in the Boy Scouts of America (Terry et al., 2011). Information from Boy Scouts of America records indicated 416 employees were accused of sex crimes from 1971 to 1989 (Boyle, 1994). Also, 1,151 cases of sexual abuse were reported during this period. The majority of the abuse, according to Boyle, occurred during camping trips. The response by the Boy Scouts of America was that sex crimes in its organization were not a major crisis. Over 50 lawsuits were filed in response to sex-crime allegations, and the organization has reportedly made settlements between $12,000 and $1.5 million. Through one civil trial, Boy Scouts of America paid $18.5 million to a former scout. After an assistant scoutmaster admitted to sexually victimizing several scouts, Boy Scouts of America continued allowing the assistant scoutmaster to work with young scouts.

In response to the sex-crime allegations, Boy Scouts of America conducted an extensive training program to raise awareness of scouts and scoutmasters. New requirements included having volunteers pass a background check and a minimum of two adults present at every event. Children were not to be left alone with only one adult (Boyle, 1994).

Big Brothers Big Sisters has also been scrutinized for sex crimes in their organization (Terry et al., 2011). This organization was established to provide mentors to economically disadvantaged youth. As recently as 2011, there were no data on sexual abuse occurring within this organization. However, Terry and Tallon (2004) searched major newspapers to establish the prevalence of sex crimes affecting this organization. There were only six published incidents between 1973 and 2001, and in 2002, the president of Big Brothers Big Sisters indicated they received fewer than 10 accusations of sex crimes per year. It was also noted 220,000 children were matched with mentors. One of the allegations of sexual victimization led to a lawsuit, and it was ruled in *Doe v. Big Brothers Big Sisters of America* (2005) that the organization was not liable for the abuse that occurred, given that it had strict hiring and supervision procedures.

Other civic organizations have also been affected by sex crimes. Below, the sexual abuse committed by a scout leader in Scouts Canada is described:

> Scott Stanley always surrounded himself with young teenaged boys because he felt "inadequate" with people his own age. He positioned himself as a City of Ottawa lifeguard and a Scouts Canada leader. And for a year and a half ending in 2013, he groomed and sexually exploited four boys in his Scout troop. They were aged 12 to 15. He preyed on the boys even after Scouts Canada had warned him 22 times to never be alone with any of the boys. On Wednesday, Stanley, 31, was condemned to five years in prison on convictions for sexual exploitation, invitation to sexual interference, and Internet child luring. [The judge] took into account Stanley's presentence custody, so he will actually serve three years and 281 days. In ... sentencing, the judge credited him for immediately pleading guilty, and sparing his young victims from testifying in court. The judge also accepted his remorse as genuine, and she noted his desire to remain in therapy. Though the boys didn't file victim-impact statements, some of their parents did. One father said the boys would be emotionally scarred for life. [The judge] noted: "Clearly, their parents are devastated. They had entrusted their children to your care and supervision and you violated that trust." The judge also said the victims' development might be halted because of the sex crimes against them. Once he's released from prison, Stanley will be forbidden

to be anywhere near children under 16 and must stay two kilometres away from his victims. In September, Stanley stood up in the prisoner's dock and read a brief statement, calling his scheme to molest vulnerable boys as "shameful and monstrous." "Who I am hates who I was and what I've done," Stanley said. He said he has taken full responsibility and acknowledged that "my behaviour was not that of a proper and responsible adult toward my victims.["] "I betrayed their trust … I became a monster."

(Dimmock, 2014, n.p.)

This example highlights how this child molester used his position to gain access to children. It also shows that many civic organizations likely do not have adequate formal procedures to handle allegations of sex crimes against children.

## Law Enforcement Officials Who Rape

Police deviance has been a subject of great concern over the past 40 years. The research on police deviance has covered a wide range of topics, including issues of corruption and graft, excessive force and brutality, and the tragedy of police suicide. However, comprehensive research on police sexual violence has not been fully explored.

It is important to note that we distinguish between sexual *misconduct* and sexual *violence* in this section. Whereas the former refers to sex acts that are not typically classified as sex crimes (e.g., flirting while on duty, consensual sex while on duty, or conducting a traffic stop in order to "get a closer look"), the latter refers to serious sex crimes (e.g., rape, offenses against juveniles, and sexual shakedowns). In a study of police sexual deviance conducted by Maher (2003), sexually violent crimes accounted for only 3% of all sexually deviant acts committed by police officers. It is also important to remember, however, the reality of the hidden nature of sex offending. Not all sexual victimizations are reported to the police. Also troubling is the issue of victims attempting to seek redress from the same group against whom allegations are launched. Needless to say, as with other forms of sex crimes, police sexual violence is very likely underreported with offenders rarely coming to justice.

This is an important population of sex offenders to study, however, due to the likelihood of police sexual violence being a ***pattern-prone offense,*** which refers to offenders who commit the same offense successively (Stinson, Liederbach, Brewer, & Mathna, 2014). For example, in 2008, police sergeant Jeffrey Pelo was tried and convicted of raping four women in Bloomington, Illinois—a medium-sized Midwestern town. Authorities discovered that Pelo had been obsessively tracking women, sneaking into their homes, and sexually assaulting them since 2003. This example, presented in more detail in Focus Box 8.1, showcases how police sexual violence is a public-safety issue, committed by officers who are likely recidivists.

---

*Focus Box 8.1    Timeline of Jeff Pelo's Crimes*

April 2003: Jeff Pelo raped his first victim, 25-year-old Kristi Mills, who awoke to a masked intruder standing in her doorway. Pelo told the victim he was there to burglarize her home, and that he didn't want to hurt her. After binding her with zip ties and duct tape, he slipped a pillowcase over her head and sexually assaulted her for 45 minutes. Pelo then forced the victim to take a long bath and wash herself thoroughly, while walking through her apartment and carefully cleaning up after himself.

January 2005: Pelo raped his fourth victim, Sarah Gliege. As a result of the assault, Gliege lost the child she was carrying at the time.

June 2006: Pelo was arrested after a woman reported a prowler outside her home. Pelo had been stalking this victim since 2005.

February 2007: Pelo unexpectedly submitted his resignation from the Bloomington Police Department.

June 2008: Pelo was convicted of 25 counts of aggravated criminal sexual assault, three counts of home invasion, two counts of residential burglary, two counts of aggravated unlawful restraint, and single counts of intimidation, attempted residential burglary and stalking.

August 2008: Pelo was sentenced to 440 years in prison.

May 2011: Pelo's sentence was reduced to 375 years after an appellate court ruled that Pelo's sentence needed to be recalculated because the penalties added onto Pelo's sexual assault counts were unconstitutional.

Source: (Avila, Lynn & Pearle, 2008)

---

Research has indicated that police sexual violence usually occurs as the result of opportunity, authority, power, and isolation that are all inherent features of policing (Sapp, 1997). Police officers select victims who are weak or vulnerable. This includes victims who are also criminals (such as prostitutes), as well as young and attractive persons (Kappeler, Sluder, & Alpert, 1994). Research has also supported the existence of the recidivist police sexual-violence offender (McGurrin & Kappeler, 2002) and has reported numerous officers had previously been convicted of sex crimes (Jarriel, 1997). More recent research by Rabe-Hemp and Braithwaite (2012) showed that 41% of police sexual violence cases are committed by recidivist officers who averaged four victims each over a three-year span of offending. These results collectively show that cases, such as the Pelo case, are not random aberrations, but are part of a consistent pattern of sex offending for a small number of police officers.

In another case of police rape, the victim called 911 to report a brick thrown through her window. The police officer who responded was convicted of raping the woman. A description of the case is presented below:

Within minutes, two police officers responded. One took her 15-year-old brother outside to speak to him. The other cop, Police Officer Ladmarald Cates, gave her boyfriend $10 and told him to go the store and get some water ... Her boyfriend ...

set off with no promise of returning soon. The cop she had summoned to protect her instead chose this moment to grab the back of her head by her hair and sodomize her. Then he raped her. Her revulsion in the aftermath was so visceral that she vomited as she ran outside.... Cates appeared and grabbed her by the waist, spinning her around. Her swinging feet may or may not have struck the partner. She was handcuffed and taken in, told at the stationhouse that she was being charged with assaulting a police officer. She became more coherent but no less outraged and vocal as she continued cry out from a holding cell that she had been raped. She also continued to vomit. The other cops dismissed her as a liar. After 12 hours, she was interviewed by internal affairs and taken to a hospital, where a rape kit was used to collect evidence. She was then taken to the county jail and held for four days before being released without actually being charged. She took her story to the Milwaukee District Attorney's office.... On January 11, the jury convicted Cates of violating the victim's civil rights by raping her.

(M. Daly, 2014)

This case also shows how difficult it is to hold offenders who are in a position of authority accountable. This is especially true when the offender is a police officer, a person with considerable authority and assumed to be a law-abiding person.

Responses and remedies to cases of police sexual violence are often thorny and contentious. In addition to inflicting physical and emotional harm on the citizens they victimize, police sexual-violence offenders also jeopardize the reputation of fellow police officers, their police agency, and the broader community. Relying on local police departments may not be a comprehensive or realistic solution to police sexual violence due to low rates of investigation and organizational punishment. Exacerbating the difficulty of charging police with sex crimes, these cases are typically one of the hardest types of case to prove in criminal court due to the private nature of the events and the "he said-she said" testimony (Du Mont & Myhr, 2000; Spohn, Beichner, & Davis-Frenzel, 2001). Further, because cases against police officers are usually difficult to win, prosecutors contend that it is best to pursue only the cases with the greatest chance of conviction, which are typically the most egregious.

The lack of criminal justice responses to police sexual violence has led victims to seek redress through civil remedies, usually in the form of lawsuits against individual police departments. Determining liability for police-perpetrated sex crimes usually rests on the offender's prior history of sexual violence, as well as disciplinary record. Unfortunately, the threat of lawsuits may be a deterrent against reporting by police administrators who become knowledgeable of sex crimes that occur in their agencies (Puro et al., 1997). Even more problematic is the threat of *officer shuffle*, which involves the transfer of officers across jurisdictions when allegations of police sexual violence and other forms of misconduct are brought to light. "Passing the buck" on this form of sexual violence allows the crime to flourish, as accused officers are able to maintain their certification, affording them opportunities for repeat offending.

# RAPE WITHIN INSTITUTIONS

Unlike the previous topics, which involve child molesters and rapists relying on their positions of authority, this section discusses other institutions that have been accused of creating an atmosphere in which persons who are not necessarily in any position of authority commit rape. Examples include, athletes, university students, inmates, and the military. For these organizations and institutions, administrators bear the responsibility of preventing rape and creating policies and procedures to effectively respond to rape allegations.

## Professional and University Athletic Organizations

Recently several high-profile cases, one involving Kobe Bryant and another involving several Duke lacrosse team members, directed attention to athletes who commit rape. Both of these cases, however, did not result in convictions due to lack of evidence. Kobe Bryant was accused of raping a 19-year-old hotel employee. He admitted to having sex with the woman, but claimed it was consensual. Subsequently, the judge dropped the criminal charges after the accuser refused to testify as a witness. A civil suit was also filed and settled for an undisclosed amount of money (Shapiro & Stevens, 2004).

The Duke lacrosse scandal began when strippers were requested at a party held off-campus at a home where the captains of the team resided. One of the strippers made rape allegations, which led to the arrest of two of the Duke lacrosse team members. The prosecutor in the case was disbarred for making false allegations during a criminal proceeding. Charges were dropped against the defendants for lack of evidence (Cohan, 2014).

The research on athletes who have committed sex crimes is embedded in the broader topic of athletes who have committed diverse crimes, including murder, assault and battery, weapons charges, and illegal substance abuse (Otto, 2009). Thus, athletes commit not only rape, but also other crimes. With regard to athletes' propensity to commit sex crimes, researchers have found in a comparison of athletes and non-athletes that the athletes have higher rates of reported sex crimes (Chandler, Johnson, & Carroll, 1999; Crossett, Ptacek, McDonald, & Benedict, 1996). Fifteen percent of the athletes reported fondling someone against his/her will, compared to only 5% of non-athletes. Seven percent of athletes reported forcing someone to have sex, compared to 2% of non-athletes. Also, in a study of professional and collegiate athlete convictions from 1991 to 2008, Otto (2009) found 86 athletes were charged with 144 crimes. Fifty-nine percent of the charges involved a sex crime or rape. Twenty-five percent of those who were charged with a sex crime had a reduced charge, whereas 89% of those charged with rape also had a reduced charge. Approximately one-third of those charged with a sex crime or rape received a prison sentence. This corroborates other research that has found that sex-crime allegations against an athlete were more likely than those against non-athletes to result in an arrest and indictment, but less likely to result in a conviction (Benedict & Klein, 1997).

Researchers also have found that approximately one in five National Football League (NFL) players had been charged with a serious crime. Fourteen percent of those crimes were sexual assaults. Very few of those charges, however, led to a conviction (Benedict & Klein, 1997). According to these studies (Benedict & Klein, 1997; Otto, 2009), sex crimes make up a noteworthy portion of crimes committed by athletes. Sports sociologists have proposed that sports are a microcosm of society. That is, athletes' behavior is a reflection of society in general (Coakley, 2007).

Researchers have focused attention on the rape culture that can occur within sports. For example, one researcher noted a recipe for sexual assault:

> Assemble a group of young men. Promise them glory for violently dominating other groups of young men. Bond the group with aggressive joking about the sexual domination of women. Add public adulation that permeates the group with the scent of entitlement. Provide mentors who thrived as young men in the same system. Allow to simmer.
>
> (Wade, Sweeney, Derr, Messner, & Burke, 2014, p. 22)

It is important to note, however, that most athletes do not rape (Wade et al., 2014). Many higher education institutions have implemented programs, such as "Male Athletes against Rape," which involves peer education and encourages bystanders to respond to factors that can lead to rape. Such programs focus on disrupting layers of protective silence that surround high status male groups (e.g., college athletes), which serve to facilitate a rape culture (Wade et al., 2014). The bystander approach encourages students who witness situations, such as a group of men assisting a drunk woman to an isolated location, to intervene and prevent this from occurring (Moynihan, Banyard, Arnold, Eckstein, & Stapleton, 2010). It is clear that a culture of "silence" can perpetuate sexual assaults, as in the case of Jerry Sandusky where many bystanders simply did nothing when they witnessed sexual behaviors. Routine values and a culture of silence in higher education institutions can lead to rape incidents (Wade et al., 2014). This can occur within athletic organizations as well as more broadly in institutions of higher education (Wade et al., 2014).

## Higher Education Institutions

The role that universities have in rape accusations committed by university athletes has been under increased scrutiny recently, especially with regard to the university downplaying or ignoring the rape accusations (Crossett et al., 1996). Situational factors, along with institutional accountability toward rape accusations, are of critical importance to these rape accusations (Wade et al., 2014).

Recently, several cases of rape on college campuses have made headlines, warranting attention to the lack of policies, procedures, and actions taken on several college campuses. These include the University of Chicago, University of Colorado, Florida State, Vanderbilt, Notre Dame, and Harvard (Newman & Sander, 2014; Wade et al., 2014). Institutions of higher education have been under increased "scrutiny as settings that not only fail to deter, but possibly foster rape" (Wade et al., 2014, p. 17). Additionally, the U.S. Congress passed the **Student Right-to-Know and Campus Security Act** in 1990, which requires higher education institutions to release information regarding crime rates on campus. This was based, at least partly, on the increased attention on sexual victimization of women (Fisher, Cullen, & Turner, 2000). In 1992, the **Campus Sexual Assault Victims' Bill of Rights** was passed, requiring higher education institutions to release awareness and prevention policies with regard to sexual victimization and ensure basic rights of sexual-assault victims. In 1998, the Act was amended to **Jeanne Clery Disclosure of Campus Security Policy and Campus Crime Statistics Act**, which included additional reporting obligations, including a daily crime log available to the public. In 2013, the **Campus Sexual Violence Elimination Act** (SaVE Act) was passed in response to **Title IX** violation complaints at Swarthmore College. The Act requires clearer and more publicized policies, students' rights education efforts, and bystander education.

Women are at their highest risk of being raped in their late teens to early 20s (Fisher, Daigle, & Cullen, 2010). Researchers have concluded that college women are more at risk to sexual victimizations than women of the same age who do not attend college (Fisher et al., 2000). Several external factors potentially lead to this phenomenon, such as co-ed housing with unfamiliar persons (Fisher et al., 2000), availability and frequent use of alcohol, and attending parties (Sampson, 2002). A combination of these factors leads to many potential victims and offenders. The relationship between drinking and rape has been well-researched and reveals a high correlation between the two. To clarify, alcohol in and of itself does not cause rape, yet drinking heavily leads to vulnerable potential victims and may disinhibit potential offenders, leading to rape incidents (Wade et al., 2014).

Other factors identified by researchers include psychological factors, the context that facilitates rape, and the presence of a rape culture (Wade et al., 2014). A few men on college campuses are seemingly predisposed to commit sexual assault. Research has shown 6% of college men have admitted to committing sexual assault (Lisak & Miller, 2002). Two-thirds of those admitted to serial rapes with an average of six rapes committed. With regard to context, one researcher noted that rape-prone environments include parties with loud music, dancing, drinking, few places to sit, and flirting (Sanday, 2003). With regard to culture, belief in rape myths, such as date rape isn't really rape, contributes to a rape-prone culture (Wade et al., 2014).

The National College Women Sexual Victimization study (NCWSV) conducted in 1997 assessed the prevalence of sexual victimization at two- and four-year colleges and universities. It reported 2.8% of the female students had experienced either an attempted rape or completed rape. Thus, 28 per 1,000 female students experienced an attempted rape or a rape. Furthermore, 23% of the women were the victims of more than one rape (Fisher et al., 2000). In a subsequent study, based on an examination of over 10,000 cases of rape and other sexual assaults from 2000 to 2011 that were reported by medical providers in Massachusetts (Peters, 2012), 4% occurred on a college campus. These included rapes, other sexual acts, and attempted rape. Thus, rape and other sexual-assault cases on college campuses make up only a small portion of all rape cases.

The majority of the sexual victimization incidents, 97%, involved female victims. Eighty-two percent of the victims were White (Peters, 2012). Ninety-nine percent involved male offenders (Peters, 2012). Alcohol use by the victim is also common. For example, one study reported that almost three-fourths of students who were raped were intoxicated at the time (Mohler-Kuo, Dowdall, Koss, & Wechsler, 2004). Seventy percent of the sexual attacks involved victims and offenders who were acquaintances or friends. Similarly, the NCWSV study also found that approximately 90% of the victims and offenders knew each other (Fisher et al., 2000). Most took place over the weekend, with 71% occurring between 12 p.m. and 4 a.m. (Peters, 2012). Similarly, approximately half of the sexual victimizations in the NCWSV study also occurred after midnight. Eighty-one percent of the victimizations occurred in a dormitory (Peters, 2012). Approximately half (46%) chose not to report the incident to law enforcement (Peters, 2012). Even fewer, only 5%, reported the incident to law enforcement in the NCWSV study (Fisher et al., 2000). Reasons given included that the victim had the perception that the incident was not harmful enough to report. Others reported barriers to reporting, such as not wanting family (or other people) to know about the incident, lack of proof, fear of reprisal, fear of hostility from police, and fear of not being believed (Fisher et al., 2000).

Students often find reporting to the police daunting, and cases involving he said-she said are not prosecuted. Thus, students often turn to civil courts. Title IX, which is a federal law, requires that universities investigate and resolve claims of sexual misconduct. This includes rape allegations. It also provides an avenue for rape victims who are students to file complaints when their rape complaints are not handled appropriately (Newman & Sander, 2014).

Allegations of rape on college campuses have increased substantially over recent years. For example, in fiscal year 2009, only 11 Title IX complaints involving sexual violence occurred. However, in 2013, 30 complaints were filed. During the first six months of 2014, 33 were filed. The government has responded to the increase. A White House task force established a website, NotAlone.gov, which assists students to file Title IX complaints. Universities are responding by hiring Title IX coordinators who are relying on legal and risk-management consultants to translate legal obligations into practical actions (Newman & Sander, 2014).

Title IX complaints, however, are often dismissed or administratively closed by the Office for Civil Rights. An academic news source, *The Chronicle of Higher Education*, conducted an analysis of Title IX complaints filed from 2003 to 2013. This included 801 complaints. Only 2% of those cases resulted in the Office of Civil

Rights declaring the institution was not in compliance with Title IX and the institution agreeing to change their policies and procedures. Another 6% resulted in the university agreeing to change their policies and procedures, despite the Office of Civil Rights not indicating (yet) that the institution was out of compliance. An additional 4% of the claims were referred to another agency. The remaining 88% resulted in closed or dismissed cases. Thus, these cases are largely unsuccessful with regard to universities changing their policies and procedures for handling Title IX allegations (Newman & Sander, 2014).

## Prisons

Rape in prison has also been brought to the attention of the public recently. In 2003, the U.S. Congress passed the ***Prison Rape Elimination Act***, which focuses on the identification, prevention, prosecution, and response to prison sexual violence. Prior to this, it was noted in a U.S. Supreme Court case, *Farmer v. Brennan* (1994), that rape and sexual abuse are "not part of the penalty that criminal offenders pay for their offenses against society." Rape in prisons is problematic in that the facility is operated by the state or the federal government (Wolff, Shi, Blitz, & Siegel, 2007). The prison has the responsibility to keep the inmates safe and not exposed to preventable harm.

The true estimates of prison rape are difficult to attain (Jenness, Maxson, Summer, & Matsuda, 2010). Rape is one of the most underreported crimes (Rennison, 2001). Add the barriers that exist in reporting rape in prison, and the problem of underreporting is compounded (Jenness et al., 2010). Victims may not report through anonymous self-report surveys or in face-to-face interviews (Neal & Clements, 2010). Also, official reports fail to capture unreported offenses.

Estimates of prison rape in the existing research range from less than 1% to 21% (Neal & Clements, 2010). A realistic estimate of prison rape is one out of ten inmates experience rape victimization (Struckman-Johnson, Struckman-Johnson, Rucker, Bumby, & Donaldson, 1996). One factor that has been identified as unique to prison rape is the resulting physical injury that occurs (beyond that caused by the rape itself). Researchers have found that more than half of all rapes in prison involve other physical injuries, such as bruises, cuts, scratches, physical injury to the anus and throat (Wolff et al., 2007). Medical attention was required for almost one-third of rape victims.

Some inmates are more at risk of being sexually victimized than others. These include inmates who are White (Hensley, Tewskbury, & Castle, 2003), young (Wolff et al., 2007), middle- or upper-class, first-time inmates (Man & Cronan, 2001), or perceived as weak (Chonco, 1989). Also if they have feminine characteristics, small stature (Man & Cronan, 2001), or have a homosexual or bisexual orientation (Struckman-Johnson et al., 1996), they are more at risk for sexual victimization. Inmates who have a history of depression, anxiety, posttraumatic stress disorder (PTSD), schizophrenia, and bipolar disorder are also at risk for sexual victimization (Wolff et al., 2007). Similar to rape in other institutions, environmental factors also play a role in prison rapes. Factors that have been identified include prisons with barrack housing, inadequate security, and overcrowding (Struckman-Johnson et al., 1996). Also, rape supportive attitudes, such as "rape is just part of the prison culture," contribute to prison rape (Man & Cronan, 2001). Although the discussion here has been on inmate-on-inmate prison rape, staff-on-inmate rape also exists (Man & Cronan, 2001). Again, true estimates of this are difficult to fully assess.

## Military

Despite recent media attention to a few high-profile cases of rape allegations among military personnel, the most recent reports indicate rape occurs to approximately 5% of active-duty military women and 1% of active-duty military men. In 2014, 6,236 reports of rape occurred, compared to 5,539 that occurred in 2013. Thus, there is an increase in the reported number of rapes. It has been estimated that 1 in 4 rapes is currently reported, compared to 1 in 8 just two years ago (Kime, 2014).

Common to many of the organizations discussed in this chapter is the difficulty in believing that someone in a position of authority (often a revered position, with honor and dedication) can commit rape. This is true of the military. Lieutenant General Crag Franklin overturned Lieutenant Colonel James Wilkerson's court-martial rape conviction. It was noted that a man who adored his wife and son, a man who was promoted to full colonel, could not be a sexual predator (Wade et al., 2014). It is unique to the military is unique in that one's superior is allowed to determine guilt or innocence. As noted by one researcher, "Nowhere in America do we allow a boss to decide if an employee was sexually assaulted or not, except in the U.S. military" (Wade et al., 2014, p. 24).

Current efforts in the U.S. Senate include a push to remove the authority of just a few commanding officers who decide whether a case can proceed to a court-martial, which is the equivalent to trying a case (Kime, 2014). Defense Secretary Chuck Hegal recently released a list of imminent changes that could occur with regard to sexual assaults in the military. These include sexual-assault programs, such as efforts to increase communication of the importance of prevention and response to allegations. Efforts to reduce retaliation against those making an allegation as well as witnesses have been made. Sixty-two percent of those who have reported sexual assault in the military have experienced retaliation—a number that has remained stable over the past two years (Kime, 2014).

## CONCLUSION

In this chapter, we build on Chapters 3 and 4, which examined child molesting and rape. This chapter extends these topics into various organizations and institutions where rape and child molesting have occurred. Overall, known cases of child molesting and rape occur at relatively low rates. Common among many of these incidents, however, is the lack of response to allegations of child molesting and rape, allowing them to go unnoticed for long periods of time. Many organizations and institutions have responded by developing specific policies, procedures, educational efforts, and in some cases, laws that assist victims to report sexual-assault incidents. It is likely in the future that these responses will continue to be developed to protect victims from sexual assault.

## REVIEW POINTS

- Reported cases of institutional sexual abuse account for only 3% of child sexual-abuse allegations.

- Four percent of Catholic priests were accused of sex crimes. Less than 5% of those met the criteria for pedophilia.

- The number of child-molestation cases occurring at childcare centers is unknown, but estimated to be relatively low.

- Sexual abuse within athletic organizations has been reported to occur among approximately 9% of athletes in one study.

- Child molestation within civic organizations is estimated to be low. One study reports fewer than ten sexual accusations occur per year. Many civic organizations have responded by requiring a background check and having two adults present with children.

- A few cases of rape by law enforcement officers have been reported. Although these occur rarely, it has been found those who do rape are often serial rapists, having many victims.

- Rape cases involving athlete offenders often result in an arrest, but rarely result in a conviction.

- Several laws have been enacted to protect university students in allegations of rape. Six percent of college men have admitted to committing sexual assault.

- Estimates indicate one out of ten inmates is sexually victimized.

- Estimates indicate 5% of active-duty military women are raped.

- Sexual abusers can be members of society who are considered to be in a care-taking and/or mentoring-type position. The evidence, however, does not suggest sexual abuse is rampant within athletics and other civic organizations.

## REFERENCES

Avila, J., Lynn, A., & Pearle, L. (2008). Police sergeant doubled as serial rapist. Retrieved January 1, 2016 from http://abcnews.go.com/TheLaw/story?id=6467266&page=1.

Benedict, J., & Klein, A. (1997). Arrest and conviction rates for athletes accused of sexual assault. *Sociology of Sport Journal, 14*(1), 86–94.

Boyle, P. (1994). *Scout's honor: Sexual abuse in America's most trusted institution*. Rocklin, CA: Prima Publishing.

Brackenridge, C. (1997). 'He owned me basically ...' Women's experience of sexual abuse in sport. *International Review for the Sociology of Sport, 32*, 115–130.

Brannan, C., Jones, R., & Murch, J. (1993). *Castle Hill report*. Shrewsbury, England: Shropshire County Council.

Bringer, J. D., Brackenridge, C. H., & Johnston, L. H. (2001). The name of the game: A review of sexual exploitation of females in sports. *Current Women's Health Reports, 1*(3), 225–232.

Burgess, A. W., Welner, M., & Willis, D. G. (2010). Educator sexual abuse: Two case reports. *Journal of Child Sexual Abuse, 19*(4), 387–402.

Burstyn, V. (1999). *The rites of men: Manhood, culture and the politics of sport*. London, UK: University of Toronto Press.

Canadian Broadcasting Corporation Television. (1993). *Crossing the line: Sexual harassment in sport*. The Fifth Estate: November 2.

Canadian Strategy for Ethical Conduct in Sport. (2002). Quebec, Canada: Sport Canada.

Chandler, S. B., Johnson, D. J., & Carroll, P. S. (1999). Abusive behaviors of college athletes. *College Student Journal, 33*(4), 638–645.

Chettle, N. (2014). Child sex abuse inquiry: Youth pastor victim says church more concerned with reputation than him. *News*. Retrieved November 5, 2014, 2014, from http://www.abc.net.au/news/2014–10–17/church-abuse-victim-says-last-decade-a-living-hell/5822918

Chonco, N. R. (1989). Sexual assaults among male inmates: A descriptive study. *The Prison Journal, 69*(1), 72–82.

Coakley, J. (2007). *Sports in society: Issues & controversies, 9th ed*. New York: McGraw Hill.

Cohan, W. D. (2014). *The price of silence: The Duke lacrosse scandal, the power of the elite, and the corruption of our great universities*. New York: Scribner.

Colton, M., Roberts, S., & Vanstone, M. (2010). Sexual abuse by men who work with children. *Journal of Child Sexual Abuse, 19*(3), 345–364.

Crossett, T. W., Ptacek, J., McDonald, M. A., & Benedict, J. R. (1996). Male student athletes and violence against women. *Violence Against Women, 2*(2), 163–179.

Daly, K. (2014). Conceptualising responses to institutional abuse of children. *Current Issues in Crime and Justice, 26*(1), 5–29.

Daly, M. (2014, January 29, 2014). She dialed 911. The cop who came to help raped her. *The Daily Beast*. Retrieved November 5, 2014, from http://www.thedailybeast.com/articles/2012/01/29/she-dialed-911-the-cop-who-came-to-help-raped-her.html

Dimmock, G. (2014, October 30, 2014). Former Ottawa Scout leader Scott Stanley gets 5 years for sexually abusing boys. Retrieved November 4, 2014, from http://ottawacitizen.com/news/local-news/ottawa-scout-leader-scott-stanley-gets-5-years-for-sexually-abusing-boys

Districts should appoint teacher-led teams to train staff about professional boundaries. (2006). *Educator's guide to controlling sexual harassment, 14*(2), 2, 5.

Du Mont, J., & Myhr, T. L. (2000). So few convictions: The role of client-related characteristics in the legal processing of sexual assaults. *Violence Against Women, 6*(10), 1109–1136.

Epps, K. (2014). Former Stafford School Board member takes plea deal in child-molestation case. Retrieved November 5, 2014, from http://news.fredericksburg.com/newsdesk/2014/11/04/former-stafford-school-board-member-takes-plea-deal-in-child-molestation-case/

Faller, K. C. (1988). The spectrum of sexual abuse in daycare: An exploratory study. *Journal of Family Violence, 3*(4), 283–298.

Fauske, J., Mullen, C., & Sutton, L. (2006). *Educator sexual misconduct in schools: Implications for leadership preparation*. Paper presented at the University Council for Educational Administration Conference Proceedings for Convention, San Antonio, Texas.

Finkelhor, D., Williams, L., & Burns, N. (1988). *Nursery crimes: Sexual abuse in day care.* Newbury Park: Sage Publications.

Fisher, B. S., Cullen, F. T., & Turner, M. G. (2000). *The sexual victimization of college women.* Washington DC: Government Printing Office.

Fisher, B. S., Daigle, L. E., & Cullen, F. T. (2010). *Unsafe in the ivory tower: The sexual victimization of college women.* Thousand Oaks, CA: Sage Publications, Inc.

Frontline. (n.d.). Innocence lost: The plea. Retrieved November 8, 2014, from http://www.pbs.org/wgbh/pages/frontline/shows/innocence/etc/other.html

Gallagher, B. (2000). The extent and nature of known cases of institutional child sexual abuse. *British Journal of Social Work, 30*(6), 795–817.

Ganim, S. (2011, November 5, 2011). The complete details of charges: Allegations against Penn State legend Jerry Sandusky involve eight boys as young as 10 said to have showered and traveled with the coach. *The Patriot-News.* Retrieved January 15, 2016 from http://www.pennlive.com/midstate/index.ssf/2011/11/readers_digest_indictment.html

Green, L. (2001). Analysing the sexual abuse of children by workers in residential care homes: Characteristics, dynamics and contributory factors. *Journal of Sexual Aggression, 7*(2), 5–24.

Hargreaves, J. A. (1986). Where's the virtue? Where's the grace?: A discussion of the social production of gender relations in and through sport. *Theory, Culture, & Society, 3*(1), 109–121.

Hartill, M. (2008). The sexual abuse of boys in organized male sports. *Men and Masculinities, 12*(2), 225–249.

Hensley, C., Tewskbury, R., & Castle, T. (2003). Characteristics of prison sexual assault targets in male Oklahoma correctional facilities. *Journal of Interpersonal Violence, 18*(6), 595–606.

Jarriel, T. (1997). ABC News 20/20. New York: ABC.

Jenness, V., Maxson, C. L., Summer, J. M., & Matsuda, K. N. (2010). Accomplishing the difficult but not impossible: Collecting self-report data on inmate-on-inmate sexual assault in prison. *Criminal Justice Policy Review, 21*(1), 3–30.

Kappeler, V., Sluder, R., & Alpert, G. (1994). Forces of deviance. *Understanding the Dark Side of Policing,* 52–54.

Khoury-Kassabri, M. (2006). Student victimization by educational staff in Israel. *Child Abuse & Neglect, 30*(6), 691–707.

Kime, P. (2014, December 5, 2014). Incidents of rape in military much higher than previously reported. Retrieved December 6, 2014, from http://www.militarytimes.com/story/military/pentagon/2014/12/04/pentagon-rand-sexual-assault-reports/19883155/

Kirby, S., & Greaves, L. (1996). *Foul play: Sexual harassment in sport.* Paper presented at the Pre-Olympic Scientific Congress, Dallas, Texas.

Knoll, J. (2010). Teacher sexual misconduct: Grooming patterns and female offenders. *Journal of Child Sexual Abuse, 19*(4), 371–386. doi: 10.1080/10538712.2010.495047

Leclerc, B., Proulx, J., & McKibben, A. (2005). Modus operandi of sexual offenders working or doing voluntary work with children and adolescents. *Journal of Sexual Aggression, 11*(2), 187–195.

Lisak, D., & Miller, P. M. (2002). Repeat rape and multiple offending among undetected rapists. *Violence and Victims, 17*(1), 73–84.

Little League. (2008). Checking backgrounds: Are you doing enough? *ASAP news, 15*(1), 1–8.

Maher, T. M. (2003). Police sexual misconduct: Officers' perceptions of its extent and causality. *Criminal Justice Review, 28*(2), 355–381.

Man, C. D., & Cronan, J. P. (2001). Forecasting sexual abuse in prison: The prison subculture as a backdrop for "deliberate indifference." *The Journal of Criminal Law and Criminology, 92*(1), 127–185.

Margolin, L. (1991). Child sexual abuse by nonrelated caregivers. *Child Abuse & Neglect, 15*(3), 213–221.

Mathews, R., Matthews, J. K., & Speltz, K. (1989). *Female sexual offenders: An exploratory study*. VT: Safer Society Press.

McGurrin, D., & Kappeler, V. E. (2002). Media accounts of police sexual violence: Rotten apples or state supported violence? In K. M. Lersch (Ed.), *Policing and Misconduct* (pp. 121–142). Upper Saddle, NJ: Prentice-Hall.

Mohler-Kuo, M., Dowdall, G., Koss, M. P., & Wechsler, H. (2004). Correlates of rape while intoxicated in a national sample of college women. *Journal of Studies on Alcohol and Drugs, 65*(1), 37–45.

Moskowitz, A. (2001). Assessing suicidality in adults: Integrating childhood trauma as a major risk factor. *Professional Psychology: Research & Practice, 32*(4), 367–372.

Moynihan, M. M., Banyard, V. L., Arnold, J. S., Eckstein, R. P., & Stapleton, J. G. (2010). Engaging intercollegiate athletes in preventing and intervening in sexual and intimate partner violence. *Journal of American College Health, 59*(3), 197–204.

Neal, T. M. S., & Clements, C. B. (2010). Prison rape and psychological sequelae: A call for research. *Psychology, Public Policy, and Law, 16*(3), 284–299.

Newman, J., & Sander, L. (2014, April 30, 2014). Promise unfulfilled? *The Chronicle of Higher Education*. Retrieved August 2, 2016 from http://chronicle.com/article/Promise-Unfulfilled-/146299/

Ontario College of Teachers. (2002). Professional advisory: Professional misconduct related to sexual abuse and sexual misconduct. Retrieved November 1, 2014, from http://www.oct.ca/publications/pdf/advisory100802_e.pdf

Otto, K. E. (2009). Criminal athletes: An analysis of charges, reduced charges and sentences. *Journal of Legal Aspects of Sport, 19*(1), 67–102.

Peters, B. (2012). *Analysis of college campus rape and sexual assault reports, 2000–2011*. Boston, MA: Massachusetts Executive Office of Public Safety and Security.

Puro, S., Goldman, R., & Smith, W. C. (1997). Police decertification: Changing patterns among the states, 1985–1995. *An International Journal of Police Strategies & Management, 20*(3), 481–496.

Rabe-Hemp, C., & Braithwaite, J. (2012). An exploration of recidivism and the officer shuffle in police sexual violence. *Police Quarterly, 19*(2), 127–147.

Rennison, C. M. (2001). *Criminal victimization 2000; changes 1993–2001 (NCJ-187007)*. Washington DC: U.S. Department of Justice.

Robins, S. L. (2000). *Protecting our students*. Ontario, Canada: Ministry of the Attorney General.

Salter, A. C. (2003). *Predators: Pedophiles, rapists, and other sex offenders*. New York: Basic Books.

Sampson, R. J. (2002). *Acquaintance rape of college students*. Washington DC: U.S. Department of Justice, Office of Community Oriented Policing Services.

Sanday, P. R. (2003). Rape-free versus rape-prone: How culture makes a difference. In C. B. Travis (Ed.), *Evolution, gender, and rape* (pp. 337–362). Cambridge, MA: MIT Press.

Sapp, A. D. (1997). Police officer sexual misconduct: A field research study. In P. Cromwell & R. Dunham (Eds.), *Crime and justice in America: Present realities and future prospects* (pp. 139–151). Upper Saddle River, NJ: Prentice-Hall.

Shakeshaft, C. (2004). *Educator sexual misconduct: A synthesis of existing literature*. Huntington, NY: Hofstra University and Interactive, Inc.

Shakeshaft, C. (2013). Know the warning signs of educator sexual misconduct. *Kappan, 94*(5), 8–13.

Shakeshaft, C., & Cohan, A. (1995). Sexual abuse of students by school personnel. *Phi Delta Kappan, 76*(7), 513–520.

Shapiro, J. S., & Stevens, J. (2004). *Kobe Bryant: The game of his life*. New York: Revolution Books, LLC.

Spohn, C., Beichner, D., & Davis-Frenzel, E. (2001). Prosecutorial justification for sexual assault case rejection: Guarding the "Gateway to Justice." *Social Problems, 48*(2), 206–235.

Stinson, P. M., Liederbach, J., Brewer, S. L., & Mathna, B. E. (2014). Police sexual misconduct: A national scale study of arrested officers. *Criminal Justice Policy Review, 0887403414526231*.

Stirling, A. E., & Kerr, G. A. (2009). Abused athletes' perceptions of the coach-athlete relationship. *Sports in Society, 12*(2), 330–335.

Struckman-Johnson, C., Struckman-Johnson, D., Rucker, L., Bumby, K., & Donaldson, S. (1996). Sexual coercion reported by men and women in prison. *Journal of Sex Research, 33*(1), 67–76.

Sullivan, J., & Beech, A. (2002). Professional perpetrators: Sex offenders who use their employment to target and sexually abuse the children with whom they work. *Child Abuse and Review, 11*(3), 153–167.

Sutton, L. (2004). Preventing educator sexual misconduct. *School Business Affairs*, 9–10.

Terry, K. J., Smith, M. L., Schuth, K., Kelly, J. R., Vollman, B., & Massey, C. (2011). *The causes and context of sexual abuse of minors by Catholic priests in the United States, 1950–2010.* (978-1-16-137-201-7). Washington, DC: United States Conference of Catholic Bishops.

Terry, K. J., & Tallon, J. (2004). The nature and scope of sexual abuse of minors by Catholic priests and deacons in the United States, 1950–2002. Washington DC; United States Conference of Bishops: John Jay College.

Timmerman, G. (2003). Sexual harassment of adolescents perpetrated by teachers and peers: An exploration of the dynamics of power, culture, and gender in secondary schools. *Sex Roles, 48*(5/6), 231–244.

Vandiver, D. M., & Kercher, G. (2004). Offender and victim characteristics of registered female sexual offenders in Texas: A proposed typology of female sexual offenders. *Sexual Abuse: A Journal of Research and Treatment, 16*(2), 121–137.

Wade, L., Sweeney, B., Derr, A. S., Messner, M. A., & Burke, C. (2014). Ruling out rape. *Contexts, 13*(2), 16–25.

Westcott, H. (1991). *Institutional abuse of children—from research to policy: A review.* London, UK: National Society for the Prevention of Cruelty to Children (NSPCC).

Wieberg, S., & Carey, J. (2012). Penn State abuse scandal chilling in details. *USA TODAY.* Retrieved August 2, 2016 from http://usatoday30.usatoday.com/sports/college/football/bigten/story/2011-11-06/penn-state-abuse-scandal-chilling/51100830/1

Wishnietsky, D. H. (1991). Reported and unreported teacher-student sexual harassment. *Journal of Education Research, 84*(3), 164–169.

Wolff, N., Shi, J., Blitz, C. L., & Siegel, J. (2007). Understanding sexual victimization inside prisons: Factors that predict. *Criminology and Public Policy, 6*(3), 535–564.

## Court Cases

*Doe v. Big Brothers Big Sisters of America*, No 1-04-1985 Ill. App. 3d LEXIS 803 (2005)
*Farmer v. Brennan* (92–7247), 511 U.S. 825 (1994)

# DEFINITIONS

**Campus Sexual Assault Victims' Bill of Rights:** A federal law passed in 1992, requiring higher education institutions to release awareness and prevention policies with regard to sexual victimization and ensure basic rights of sexual-assault victims.

**Campus Sexual Violence Elimination Act (SaVE Act):** A federal law that was passed in 2013 in response to Title IX violation complaints at Swarthmore College. The Act requires clearer and more publicized policies, students' rights education efforts, and bystander education.

**Educator Misconduct:** A term developed by Shakeshaft that describes inappropriate behavior that involves a school employee, such as a teacher or coach, sharing pornography, conversations with sexual talk, or masturbation.

**Fixated Abuser:** One of two categories of educator misconduct (identified by Shakeshaft) that involves a male or female educator who grooms a student and sexually abuses him/her. The most common fixated abuser involves a male teacher and a male student/victim.

**Institutional Abuse:** A term developed by Gallagher that describes the sexual abuse of children by adults who have contact with them within some institution (e.g., organized sports, community center, school).

**Jeanne Clery Disclosure of Campus Security Policy and Campus Crime Statistics Act:** A federal law passed in 1998, which amended Campus Sexual Assault Victims' Bill of Rights. It included additional reporting obligations, including a daily crime log available to the public.

**Opportunistic Offender:** A term developed by Shakeshaft that describes a large portion of educators who molest children. They are the most common type of child molester and are typically regressed offenders with poor boundaries and judgment.

**Passing the Trash:** An informal practice of handling teachers' sexual misconduct by asking the teacher to move out of the district in lieu of facing any charges from his/her behavior.

**Pattern-Prone Offense:** When offenders are likely to offend multiple times.

**Prison Rape Elimination Act:** A federal law passed in 2003 that focuses on the identification, prevention, prosecution, and response to prison sexual violence.

**Sexual Misconduct:** Sex acts that are not typically classified as sex crimes (e.g., police flirting while on duty, consensual sex while on duty, or conducting a traffic stop in order to "get a closer look").

**Sexual Violence:** Serious sex crimes that are classified as sex crimes (e.g., rape, offenses against juveniles, and sexual shakedowns).

**Student Right-to-Know and Campus Security Act:** A federal law passed in 1990 that requires higher education institutions to release information regarding crime rates on campus.

**Title IX:** A federal law that requires that universities investigate and resolve claims of sexual misconduct.

## CHAPTER 9

# Investigations of Sex Crimes and Sex Offenders

## CHAPTER OBJECTIVES

- Define and identify key concepts related to crime-scene profiling and crime-scene basics.
- Describe the criteria associated with responding to sex crimes.
- Describe the characteristics of sex crimes with unique investigational characteristics.
- Identify three broad categories of types of investigative failures.

## SEX-CRIMES INVESTIGATIONS

The goals of any police investigation, including a sex-crime investigation, include finding out what happened (or if anything happened) and finding out who did what (Milne & Bull, 1999). Law enforcement officers do this through an active investigation, which includes assessing evidence from the crime scene and interviewing witnesses, suspects, and victims. Furthermore, the goal of any police interview is to obtain accurate, complete, and relevant accounts from the interviewee (McGurk, Carr, & McGurk, 1993).

In this chapter, we present information regarding sex-crimes investigations, including various types of profile techniques and crime-scene characteristics that law enforcement officers rely upon during their investigations. We also present critical aspects of responding to crimes with a sexual motivation, including key information for 911 operators and police officers who often encounter vulnerable victims and suspects. For sexual assaults, an essential investigational tool is the medical examination, which involves a specialized nurse. This chapter, therefore, is intended to cover some key components and duties of police officers and other officials who are involved in the investigation of a sexually motivated crime. It is not intended to be a "how-to" manual for those who are part of a sex-crime investigation, but rather the intention is to highlight some of the processes and various official persons who are involved in sex-crime investigations, to provide a broader perspective of the sum of intricacies involved in such matters.

Sex crimes pose unique investigational challenges. For example, when someone commits an alcohol- or drug-facilitated rape, consent of the victim may be difficult to discern. Other scenarios exist that present other challenges, and a few of those are discussed in this chapter, including distinguishing accidental deaths (from *autoerotic asphyxiation*) from suicides, and false rape allegations. Each of these sex crimes is discussed in terms of what they are and how they should be handled through an investigation.

Finally, given some of the recent media attention on false convictions that have occurred in the recent past, an overview of commonly identified investigative mistakes is presented, with attention given to sex crimes. Information is provided about how these common investigative failures can be avoided.

## Profiling and Crime-Scene Basics

Much information can be gained from a sex-crime scene. For example, critical to deconstructing a crime scene are any clues to the offender's ***modus operandi*** (MO). MO refers to an offender's unique behavioral pattern during the commission of the offense. An offender's MO can change depending on several factors, such as a deteriorating mental state, use of drugs and/or alcohol, changes in habits/lifestyle, and learning how to commit the crime more effectively (Bartol & Bartol, 2012; Turvey, 2011). Many offenders do learn how to commit their crimes in a more sophisticated manner. For example, many offenders read media accounts of their crimes (Bartol & Bartol, 2012). This can provide information about the police investigation and cause the offender to change his or her MO (Bartol & Bartol, 2012). For those who molest children, relying on information from the victim's caregiver may also provide information that causes the offender to alter his or her MO for future crimes.

In the 1980s, much information was gained about crime-scene profiling by the FBI's Behavioral Science Unit (BSU). They interviewed sexual murderers, who were incarcerated, to gather information about common motives and behavior patterns (Ressler, Burgess, & Douglas, 1988). This was extended to serial rapists in the late 1980s (Hazelwood & Burgess, 1987). As a result of these interviews and studies, crime scenes were classified as organized, disorganized, or mixed.

*Organized crime scenes* are indicative of premeditation—an offender planning the sex crime ahead of time. Premeditation is typically present. The offender does not choose a random victim, but carefully selects the victim. The offender typically maintains control throughout the commission of the sex crime. A ***disorganized crime scene***, on the other hand, appears chaotic and messy. The offender is usually motivated by rage or some other heightened emotional state. Premeditation does not exist in these types of crimes. The victim is usually decided upon by chance— being in the wrong place at the wrong time. More characteristics of the organized offense and disorganized offense are presented in Table 9.1. A ***mixed crime scene*** includes elements of both. An example includes a sex crime that was premeditated,

**TABLE 9.1**   *Characteristics of Organized and Disorganized Sexual Homicide Offenders' Crime Scene*

| ORGANIZED OFFENDER | DISORGANIZED OFFENDER |
| --- | --- |
| • Plans the offense | • Offense is spontaneous |
| • Targets a stranger victim | • Victim/location known |
| • Personalizes the victim | • Depersonalizes the victim |
| • Has controlled conversations with victim | • Has no/little conversation with victim |
| • Crime scene reflects control | • Crime scene is random/sloppy |
| • Demands the victim is submissive | • Sudden violence to victim |
| • Uses restraints of the victim | • Minimal use of restraints |
| • Engages in aggressive acts before victim's death | • Sexual acts occur after victim's death |
| | • Victim's body is left in view where the offense occurred |
| | • Weapon/evidence is typically present |

Source: (Ressler et al., 1988)

but the plan falls apart while it is being carried out. For example, an offender may encounter a victim who fights back. Emotions quickly set in, and the offense occurs in a chaotic fashion (Bartol & Bartol, 2012).

Another earmark of the criminal profile is the **signature** of the offender (Bartol & Bartol, 2012). This is anything that the offender does that goes beyond what is necessary to carry out the crime. The signature reveals the offender's unique cognitive processes associated with the sex crime. It is relatively consistent when the offender carries out the same crime repeatedly. It is believed to be more consistent than the MO, which changes as the offender learns how to carry out the crime more effectively. It has been argued that profiling crime scenes of serial violent offenders is easier when the offender exhibits psychopathology. This includes sadistic torture, cutting the body after death, or other mutilations (Pinizzotto, 1984).

Another example of a signature is taking something from the crime scene, such as jewelry, a driver's license, or underwear. It is usually a meaningful item that the offender uses to remember the incident. This is known as a **trophy**. In the case of sexual homicide, it can include a body part. Serial killer Jeffrey Dahmer took body parts and kept them in glass jars with formaldehyde.

Another concept related to sexual homicide is **undoing**, which refers to the offender psychologically trying to "undo" the murder. The offender may try to clean up the body and place it in a natural position, such as sleeping in a bed (Bartol & Bartol, 2012). Undoing may be a signature, if it is done repeatedly (at more than one crime scene) (Schröer & Püschel, 2006).

*Staging* refers to altering the crime scene after the crime has occurred but before law enforcement arrives (Bartol & Bartol, 2012). It is usually done to make the crime look like it was committed by someone other than the offender. It can also be done to protect the victim or victim's family from public embarrassment. An example of the latter occurs when the victims died as the result of their own behavior, such as autoerotic asphyxiation, which is discussed later in this chapter.

In the case of serial sex crimes, the offenses often occur within a limited geographical area, which can reveal patterns of offender behavior. *Geographical profiling* involves analyzing the spatial distribution of a set of offenses committed by a single offender. *Geographical mapping* analyzes the spatial patterns of a series of crimes committed over a period of time by all offenders of known offenses. Thus, geographical profiling focuses on an individual offender, whereas geographical mapping focuses on a geographical area where crimes have been committed (Bartol & Bartol, 2012).

The media often refer to the occurrence of a "random" crime. However, the manner in which a sex offender hunts for his victims and the locations where he chooses to offend are not random. The crime locations of a serial rapist can, in effect, be treated as spatial clues and their geographic pattern used to focus a police investigation. Analyzing these patterns is known as geographic profiling. Developed by criminologist and former police officer Kim Rossmo, geographic profiling involves the use of specialized software to generate color probability maps showing the most likely areas of offender residence (Rossmo, 2000). The software is based on a criminal-hunting algorithm called CGT (*Criminal Geographic Targeting*).

The main function of geographic profiling is to prioritize suspects and areas according to where they are situated on the geo-profile's probability surface (the different probabilities are usually shown in different colors, with dark red areas having the highest likelihood, and gray the lowest). The technique may be used in conjunction with a psychological profile, the two techniques outlining the "who" and "where" of the offender. Neither method can solve a crime on its own, but they can help police prioritize the thousands of suspects and tips that often emerge during a major crime investigation. Geographic profiling is related to but different from crime mapping. Geographic profiling is concerned only with the crimes of an individual serial offender, while the latter involves the analysis of locations of all reported crimes committed by all the offenders in a given area over a certain time period (Harries, 1999).

Understanding how criminals hunt—their search for and attack of a victim—is an important element of geographic profiling. The criminal-search typology includes hunters, poachers, trollers, and trappers (Rossmo, 2009a). *Hunters* purposely set out to look for victims. They tend to stay within a relatively stable geographical area near their home and usually search through familiar places where suitable targets might be found. *Poachers* (also known as commuters) are more transient as they travel some distance from their home to search for victims. ***Trollers*** are opportunistic offenders who encounter victims while engaged in routine noncriminal activities. ***Trappers*** entice their victims to a location they control by taking in boarders, entertaining victims, placing ads in newspapers or on the Internet, or offering employment.

## Emergency (911) Operators and First Responders

Emergency (911) operators are critical to the process of sex-crime investigation—as they are typically the first person to have contact with a victim or witness. The information the 911 operator obtains from the victim or witness can be relevant to the investigation. The interaction between the victim or a witness and the 911 operator becomes a starting point for the investigation. 911 operators, when receiving a call regarding a potential sex crime, should tell the victim:

- Not to wash any clothing.

- Not to shower.

- Not to destroy any clothing.

- Keep any evidence (anything the offender had contact with) (Tittle, 2006).

This may be difficult for victims, as they will want to remove their clothing and shower. The operator should tell the victim that a police officer is on the way and attempt to keep the victim calm (Tittle, 2006). They should ask whether the victim is seriously injured and in need of medical attention (Jetmore, 2006). If so, an ambulance should be dispatched. The victim should also be instructed to go to a safe location until a police officer arrives (Jetmore, 2006).

For the police officers who are the first to arrive to a sex-crimes allegation, several activities should occur:

- Reconstruct what happened and establish that a crime occurred.

- Identify, document and collect evidence of what occurred.

- Link the victim and the suspect to the scene of the crime.

- Identify and locate any witnesses.

- Identify and apprehend the person(s) who committed the crime (Jetmore, 2006, n.p.).

Sex crimes pose an additional challenge as they may have occurred at a variety of locations and may have occurred many hours/days/weeks prior to the report. In those cases, corroborating evidence should be identified. Sex crimes can involve a vulnerable victim, which requires additional guidelines to be followed for obtaining information. This is discussed in the next section.

## Interviewing Vulnerable Victims

Child victims can pose unique challenges to a sex-crime investigation, as they may not have the verbal skills to convey what happened to them. As noted in Chapter 8, several allegations of sexual abuse in daycare settings were made in the 1980s. In Focus Box 9.1, some of those cases are presented. Most noteworthy, these cases were overshadowed by poor interviewing techniques and, subsequently, an inability to determine actual guilt or innocence. This brought attention to the lack of guidelines that existed when interviewing *vulnerable victims*, which include children, elderly adults, and those with special needs. More specifically, interviewing children when sexual allegations were made was difficult because of their suggestibility and the need to balance the victims' and the alleged offenders' legal rights. Since these cases, many improvements have been made in establishing guidelines for interviewing children and other vulnerable victims.

---

*Focus Box 9.1    An Overview of Daycare Abuse Cases*

*The McMartin Pre-School Case (1986):* In Manhattan Beach, California, a criminal case was made against Ray Buckey and his mother for sexually abusing children in a satanic ritual. Neither resulted in a guilty verdict, as evidence was lacking.

*Fells Acres Day School (1986–1987):* In Malden, Massachusetts, allegations of sexual abuse were made by one child against Gerald Amirault, the owner's son. Later, several other children made allegations against Violet, Gerald, and Cheryl Amirault. Violet had been running the daycare for two decades. Her son, Gerald, also worked at the school as a bus driver and handyman. Violet's daughter, Cheryl, also worked at the school. At trial, the children were allowed to provide testimony in the courtroom; they were placed where the jury could see them but the defendants could not. All defendants were found guilty and sentenced to lengthy prison sentences. After serving eight years in prison, a new trial was granted because of the children's testimony allowed during the trial for Cheryl and Violet, which violated the defendants' right to face their accusers. Gerald's appeal was denied. Two years later, the judge reinstated the conviction and vacated the order for a new trial. In 1997 a rehearing was ordered again; however, Violet died of cancer. The rehearing for Cheryl never occurred. Cheryl agreed to not discuss the case with others and not to profit from it in exchange for the judge agreeing she would not return to prison to complete her sentence.

Source: (Possley, n.d.)

*Wee Care Nursery School (1988):* In Maplewood, New Jersey, Kelly Michaels was convicted of 115 counts of sexual abuse against 20 children. She denied all accusations, waived her Miranda rights, and passed a polygraph. The investigation continued. During the trial, the judge questioned the children in his chambers on closed-circuit television. He played ball with them, held them on his lap, and whispered in their ears. Kelly was convicted and received a 47-year sentence. She served five years before

---

she successfully appealed the case because of the way the children were questioned by the judge. Kelly was released, and the prosecutor dropped all of the charges.

Source: (Frontline, 1998)

In 1999, important legislation provided for special measures to be taken when handling child testimony and testimony from other vulnerable witnesses (Bull, 2010). This was the 1999 *Youth Justice and Criminal Evidence Act* passed in England and Wales, which included the following measures:

- The use of screens that prevent the witness from seeing the defendant.

- A live television link between the court and the witness.

- Use of a video-recorded investigation interview conducted by the police when the evidence was collected in accordance with best evidence standards.

- Access to an intermediary (i.e., trained advocate) at court or during the police interview.

- Access to aids in communication (e.g., communication board, which is a board that includes pictures and/or symbols to assist in communication) (Bull, 2010).

Critical to conducting an appropriate interview was the development of guidelines that were based on the results of many psychological studies (Bull, 2010). Experts in the field and researchers suggest employing the ***phased approach***, especially when working with vulnerable victims. This has four phases, with each phase occurring only after the previous phase is complete: (1) establish good rapport, (2) obtain as much free narrative as possible, (3) ask questions of the right type and in the right order, and (4) have meaningful closure (Bull, 2010).

The first phase, establishing good rapport, involves discussing topics that are of interest to the witness and are considered neutral. This phase should also include establishing good communication with the witness, making him or her comfortable. It is critical during this stage to reassure the witness that it is acceptable to answer questions with a "don't understand" or "don't know" or "can't remember" response, when that is the case. This is especially critical if the child has low IQ or a learning disability, as these children may give inaccurate information otherwise (Bull, 2010).

The second phase, obtaining as much free narrative as possible, involves asking the witness to provide as much information about the incident as they remember. This should not involve interruptions from the interviewer, who should make statements, such as "tell me more about that." Some vulnerable witnesses such as elderly adults or children with a low IQ, will provide less information than others. Thus, for some individuals, the questioning phase becomes critical (Bull, 2010).

The third, questioning, phase should begin with ***open questions***, which are questions that are based on information that the witness provided in the narrative stage (Bull, 2010). For example, if a witness states during the narrative that a woman appeared in the window of a nearby apartment after the incident, the interviewer can ask, "what did the woman look like?" After open questions have been asked, ***specific questions*** are asked. These questions typically seek additional information or clarify information already provided and assist the witness to understand what is relevant. This typically involves asking what, who, where, and when-type questions. Below are examples of these:

- What was the man wearing when he entered your room?
- Who were you with at the playground?
- Where were you the first time you saw the scary man?
- When did you call for help?

After specific questions are asked, and only then, should ***forced-choice questions*** be asked. These include questions, such as:

- Did the offender cut your necklace off before or after the assault?

Research has shown that vulnerable interviewees may be yes-prone or no-prone, that is always answering yes (or no) regardless of the correct answer (Matikka & Vesala, 1997). Such questions should be asked in an either-or format (Bull, 2010):

- Did he touch you under your clothes or on top of your clothes?

Rather than

- Did he touch you under your clothes?

Either-or questions are more likely than yes-no questions to yield an accurate response (Heal & Sigelman, 1995).

This phase of the interview is critical, as research has shown that the first two stages of interviewing (establishing a rapport and obtaining a free narrative) are conducted relatively well and adhere to these established guidelines. Few interviews that were assessed systematically, however, adhered to criteria established in the third phase: open questions followed by specific questions, and only afterwards using forced-questions (Davies, Wilson, Mitchell, & Milsom, 1995; Warren, Woodall, Hunt, & Perry, 1996). Research has found that interviewers who encouraged free narrative, followed by open questions, obtained interviews that appeared to reflect actual events (Craig, Scheibe, Raskin, Kircher, & Dodd, 1999; Wood & Garven, 2000).

The style of the interviewer also appears to have an effect on the interview quality (Bull, 2010). Research has found that a supportive style is superior to a businesslike or authoritative manner (Paterson, Bull, & Vrij, 2002). A supportive style involves an informal demeanor, smiling, eye contact, and introducing self with a first name. Those who used a supportive style yielded more correct free-recall, recall to open questions, recall to reflection questions (repeating back to the interviewee what he or she said), and recall to final prompt for "more information."

The fourth phase, the closure phase, should:

> [1] summarize the important information provided by the witness as much as possible in the witness' own words, having told the witness to intervene if any summarizing is incorrect, [2] answer any questions the witness has, [3] thank the witness and try to assist the witness leave the interview in as positive frame of mind as possible (e.g., by returning to the neutral topics discussed in the rapport phase) and [4] provide the witness with the interviewer's contact details (e.g. in case the witness decides to provide more information).
>
> (Bull, 2010, p. 9)

In the U.S., researchers have found that training on how to conduct interviews with vulnerable witnesses is "very basic or non-existent" (Bull, 2010, p. 10). Sternberg, Lamb, Esplin, and Baradaran (1999) developed a scripted protocol, based on research findings. This was followed by several other studies in several countries (e.g., Orbach et al., 2000; Sternberg, Lamb, Orbach, Esplin, & Mitchell, 2001), which support the use of a specific protocol, including the following:

- More use of open questions.

- Less use of forced-choice questions.

- Fewer suggestive questions (i.e., those that imply a specific answer).

- More narrative prior to forced-choice questions (Bull, 2010).

Research has also found that the pace of the interview should be much slower for vulnerable witnesses (Milne & Bull, 1999). This includes the interviewer slowing down their speech rate, allowing extra time for witnesses to respond to the questions, providing time for the witness to prepare a response, being patient with slow responses, avoiding rapid-fire questions once the interviewee has responded, and avoiding interruption (Milne & Bull, 1999). Also, it is critical to not underestimate the ability of vulnerable witnesses to provide accurate information, as research has shown that when proper protocol has been followed, vulnerable witnesses are capable of producing accurate information (Agnew & Powell, 2004).

## Medical Examinations of Sexual-Assault Victims

Part of collecting evidence during a sexual-assault investigation involves a medical examination of the victim. A registered nurse (RN) who has additional education and clinical experience in forensic examinations of sexual-assault victims typically conducts these examinations (Littel, 2001). As of 1997, fewer than 100 *Sexual Assault Nurse Examiner* (SANE) programs existed. These programs were developed from a need among nurses to have specialized knowledge and training when conducting forensic examinations. The Office of Victims of Crime (OVC) has provided substantial support to increase the number of SANE programs. Their support led to the development of a practical guide to SANE programs. Today there are more than 700 SANE programs in the U.S., Canada, and Australia (International Association of Nurses, 2015). SANE programs provide valuable knowledge to those who administer forensic examinations to sexual-assault victims. The goals include providing victims with prompt, compassionate care while collecting comprehensive forensic evidence.

Sexual assault victims have obviously been traumatized during the assaults, and, in many instances, victims are re-traumatized during the investigation (Littel, 2001). This is especially true for an invasive medical examination. Many experts in the field have recognized that collecting medical evidence from a victim shortly after the assault encompasses many problems. For example, victims have had to wait for long periods of time to be examined. It is not uncommon for victims to wait four to ten hours. Victims are often denied food, water, and bathroom access while they are waiting for their examinations—as this may destroy evidence. Sexual-assault victims are often seen at local hospitals in the emergency room.

Most SANE programs rely on a group of SANEs who are available any time of day or night. Most respond to a sexual assault report within a short period of time (usually within 30 to 60 minutes). After serious injuries are treated and no immediate medical concerns exist, the SANE begins to assess, treat and collect evidence, which includes the following:

- Obtain information about the victim's pertinent health history and the crime.

- Assess psychological functioning sufficiently to determine whether the victim is suicidal and is oriented to person, place, and time.

- Perform a physical examination to inspect and evaluate the body of the victim (not a routine physical examination).

- Collect and preserve all evidence and document findings.

- Treat and/or refer the victim for medical treatment (a SANE may treat minor injuries, such as minor cuts and abrasions, but further evaluation and care of serious trauma is referred to a designated medical facility or physician).

- Provide the victim with prophylactic medication for the prevention of sexually transmitted diseases (STDs) and other care needed as a result of the crime.

- Provide the victim with referrals for medical and psychological care and support (Littel, 2001, p. 3).

During the collection of evidence, many jurisdictions have sexual-assault victim advocates present to provide support to the victim and ensure victims receive necessary crisis support (Littel, 2001). These services will vary from community to community.

Those who examine the victim may lack experience and training, causing additional stress to the victim (Littel, 2001). Many physicians avoid sexual assault examinations, as they do not want to testify in court. The staff and doctors at emergency departments often view sexual-assault victims as less of a priority than those with life-threatening injuries (Ledray & Simmelink, 1999). They may also not have an understanding of victimization; this could include holding stereotypes or false assumptions, such as the victim may have done something to instigate the sexual assault (Littel, 2001). This can subsequently affect their willingness to collect and document all forensic evidence, especially in non-stranger sexual assaults. SANE programs attempt to address problems experienced by sexual-assault victims (Littel, 2001).

SANE programs provide many benefits to processing sexual-assault cases and responding to sexual-assault victims (Littel, 2001). As one detective in Alexandria, Virginia noted, SANE programs "have taken response to sexual assault victims at the emergency department out of the dark ages" (Littel, 2001, p. 7). SANE programs provide more thorough forensic evidence and more extensive documentation that adds to the information detectives collect. Local and state prosecutors are typically supportive of SANE programs, as they impact the outcome in sexual-assault cases (Littel, 2001).

The efficacy of SANE programs has not been fully assessed. A few studies have been conducted on limited samples of SANE programs. For example, in an assessment of 71 residency program directors in emergency medicine, 52% were not aware of how their sexual-assault examination requirements were established. Thus, increased awareness of SANE requirements is needed (Sande et al., 2013).

## Interviewing Suspects

Part of a police officer's job includes questioning suspected rapists, child molesters, child pornographers, and others who have committed a wide range of sex crimes. Interviewing such offenders is not an easy task. The officer must be able to ask questions with a certain degree of sensitivity (Burns, 1993). Asking questions of suspects is a critical component of the investigation. Police officers encounter many obstacles in obtaining information from a sex-crime suspect. For example, research has found that police officers are often stressed when they interview child sex offenders (Soukara, Bull, & Vrij, 2002).

Research also shows that officers fail to show empathy towards such offenders until a confession has been obtained (Soukara et al., 2002). Police officers also have mental obstacles to overcome when they are confronted with a suspect to interview. For example, they often minimize the offense allegedly committed (Ward, Hudson, Johnston, & Marshall, 1997). Although **_cognitive distortions_**, such as false justifications for sexual abuse, are typically associated with the abuser, police officers can also have cognitive distortions regarding the characteristics and severity of the offense.

Given the severe negative perceptions often associated with sex offenders, police officers will often deny their involvement in the investigation process to close friends and family members (Thomas, 2000). Police officers, like those in the community, typically hold negative attitudes towards sex offenders—sometimes, even more so than towards murderers (Holmberg & Christianson, 2002). Research has, in fact, shown that sex offenders, compared to murderers, were more likely to report negative interviewer behaviors (Holmberg & Christianson, 2002).

The style that police officers adopt during suspect interviews falls into two categories: dominant or humane. ***Dominant interviews*** are associated with impatience, hostility, aggressiveness, and condemnation. ***Humane interviews*** are associated with friendliness, empathy, cooperation and a personal approach. Police officers are more likely to obtain an admission of guilt if they use a humane approach (Holmberg & Christianson, 2002; Kebbell, Hurren, & Roberts, 2006). However, in a study that examined the use of empathy alone, no differences were found in the amount of ***investigation relevant information*** (IRI) obtained, which refers to information that is helpful in determining information about the crime. Quality interviews, in general, will yield IRI, which includes the following key pieces of information: (1) what happened, (2) how the crime was committed, (3) who was involved, (4) when and where the offense occurred, and (5) any objects used to assist in committing the offense.

Research has found, however, that the amount of IRI obtained is significantly improved when ***appropriate (or productive) questions*** are asked by the interviewer as opposed to ***inappropriate questions***. Appropriate questions include open questions (e.g., "Can you describe the room to me?"), probing questions (e.g., "What happened next?"), encouragements/acknowledgements (e.g., "Ok, I see"). Inappropriate questions include echo questions (e.g., Suspect says, "I may have …"; Interviewer says, "You may have …"), closed-questions (e.g., "Did you leave your house last night?"), leading questions (e.g., "Then you went to the living room, right?"), forced-choice questions (e.g., "The phone is in your name or your wife's?"), multiple questions (e.g., "Did you leave before nine o'clock? Where did you go?"), and making opinion-based statements (e.g., "You are just trying to protect yourself") (Oxburgh, Ost, & Cherryman, 2012).

Thus, appropriate questions are more useful to the investigation of sex crimes. Research has shown that police officers typically ask, on average, three inappropriate questions for every one appropriate question, showing a need for additional training with regard to interviewing suspects (Oxburgh et al., 2012).

Two methods of interviewing suspects have also been identified. First, the ***accusatorial method***, primarily used in the U.S., is confrontational and assumes guilt. This method typically establishes control, uses psychological manipulation (e.g., custody and isolation, confrontation, followed by offering sympathy and face-saving excuses), uses closed-ended, confirmatory questions, and focuses on anxiety cues to determine deception (based on the suspect's verbal and non-verbal cues). The primary goal is confession (Meissner, Redlich, Bhatt, & Brandon, 2012).

The second method, *information-gathering,* relies on establishing rapport, using direct, positive confrontation, using open-ended, exploratory questions, and focusing on cognitive clues to deception. The use of cognitive clues is deeply embedded in empirical research that shows individuals will remember an event more accurately after they have been asked to remember the emotions, perceptions and sequence of events in the situation of interest. The primary goal of the information-gathering method is to elicit information. This method is associated with Great Britain. The suspects are given the opportunity to explain the circumstances. Only then are they questioned and asked about any inconsistent or contradictory information. The goal is to establish facts as opposed to obtaining a confession (as in the accusatorial method) (Meissner et al., 2012).

A specific technique, usually associated with the information-gathering method of investigation, is to have the suspect tell the series of events in reverse order. For example, the suspect is asked what happened prior to discovering the crime, and what happened directly before that, and so on. Research has shown that this technique often distinguishes those who are deceptive from truth-tellers (Vrij et al., 2008).

A recent meta-analysis that compared accusatorial and information-gathering interviewing found that the information-gathering style interview is more likely than accusatorial interviews to elicit true confessions and reduce false confessions. These results, however, were based on a small number of studies. More research is needed to determine the outcome of both methods of interviewing a suspect (Meissner et al., 2012).

## SEX CRIMES WITH UNIQUE INVESTIGATIONAL OBSTACLES

Sex crimes can create unique problems for the investigator, given the context of the offense. For example, offenders may be the parents of the victim; the intent may be vengeful (e.g., to expose the victim to a sexually transmitted disease). Also, the victim may be unable to cooperate or understand what happened to him or her (e.g., a vulnerable victim).

In this section, a few additional sexual offenses that present unique investigational obstacles are examined. For example, sexualized homicides involve not only a sex crime, but murder as well. *Alcohol- and drug-facilitated rapes* occur after the victim has been exposed to alcohol or drugs, making consent more ambiguous. Autoerotic asphyxiation deaths are often mistaken for suicides, as opposed to accidental deaths. As you read through this section, you will become aware of the difficulties each of these offenses may cause in terms of investigational demands.

## Sexual Homicide

*Sexual homicide* involves killing someone who is also sexually assaulted at some point before, during, or after killing him or her. The true extent of these types of crimes, considered to be one of the most serious offenses one can commit, is difficult to measure. The FBI does not report statistics on this combination of offenses. Also, statewide or national databases do not exist. Estimates indicate that less than 1% of homicides involve a sexual offense. Much of the research is based on case studies and very small sample sizes. The first study was reported by Dr. Richard von Krafft-Ebing in 1886. Since then, rare case studies have been combined in individual studies to assess similarities and differences among these types of cases (Meloy, 2000).

Sexual homicide offenders are, most often, men who first kill prior to the age of 30. Their victims are typically either strangers or casual acquaintances. They are typically female and the same race as the offender. Some sexual homicide offenders have intimate partners and go outside that relationship to select their victims. They may "practice" behaviors, such as sadism, on their consenting partners before engaging in those behaviors with their victims (Meloy, 2000).

## *A Critical Consideration: Fantasy*

Fantasy is described as a critical factor among sexual homicide offenders—as it can be quite telling as to the motivation for committing a sexual homicide. Fantasy is defined as "an elaborated set of cognitions (thoughts) characterized by preoccupation (or rehearsal), anchored in emotion, and originating in daydreams" (Prentky et al., 1989, p. 889). Violent fantasies, involving rape and/or murder, are more likely to occur among sexual homicide offenders than those who have not committed such an offense (Prentky et al., 1989). In fact, 85% of one sample of serial sexual murderers admitted to such fantasies. Fantasies usually include five components: demographic, relational, paraphilic, situational, and self-perception. The following example exemplifies these five components:

> For example, the perpetrator may imagine that a 15-year-old female (demographic) becomes his sex slave (relational), and he is able to … rape her at his whim (paraphilic) in his isolated mountain cabin (situational), thus enhancing his sense of omnipotence and gratifying himself sadistically (self-perception).
>
> (Meloy, 2000, p. 8)

The offender's fantasy is quite telling as to his motivation for committing an offense—as he has rehearsed the scenario mentally, many times previously. The more one can identify the offender's fantasy, the more complete a psychological profile can become (Geberth, 2014).

Fantasies become functional. They serve to: (1) sustain pleasure when coupled with masturbation, (2) reduce behavioral inhibition, (3) increase grandiosity, potentially compensating for inadequacies, (4) stimulate omnipotence, and (5) allow the perpetrator to practice his paraphilia (Hazelwood as cited in Meloy, 2000; Mac-Culloch, Snowden, Wood, & Mills, 1983; Meloy, 2000). While fantasies serve as a motivation, they do not address the reasons why the perpetrators commit such heinous offenses.

### *Theoretical Explanations of Sexual Homicide*

As noted in Chapter 2, common questions asked are: Why does a person engage in this type of abhorrent behavior? Are they mentally ill? Explanations of why a person becomes a sexual murderer overlap with many of the proposed theories of why a person commits crime in general, while salient factors have also been identified. Researchers have identified seven factors in a motivational model that attempt to explain the development of a sexual homicide offender:

1. **Ineffective social environment:** Sexual homicide offenders often have parents who are not nurturing or protective. Their parents often provide inconsistent punishment. The offender does not bond with his parents. Psychopathy often develops.
2. **Formative traumatic events:** Physical or sexual assault is commonly experienced among sexual homicide offenders. Offenders may pair sexual arousal with violence.
3. **Patterned responses—personality:** Personality traits that develop during childhood include (but are not limited to): entitlement, grandiosity, callousness, disregard for others, and lack of remorse.
4. **Patterned responses—cognitions:** The development of fixed, negative, and repetitive thoughts occurs among sexual homicide offenders.
5. **Patterned responses—arousal:** Some sexual homicide offenders develop hyperarousal (over-arousal) from exposure to early trauma, while others develop hypoarousal (under-arousal), which is a precursor to the development of psychopathy.
6. **Antisocial acts:** Sexual homicide offenders often engage in deviant and criminal acts, likely a displacement of anger towards their parents. This is usually displaced on other children, animals, and property.
7. **Feedback filter (learning):** Sexual homicide offenders often learn from their mistakes and improve on their victimization of others. They often try to match their reality with their fantasy (Burgess, Hartman, Ressler, Douglas, & McCormack, 1986; Meloy, 2000; Ressler et al., 1988).

These are factors that have been developed to explain the motivation of sexual homicide offenders. It should be noted that not all offenders are the same, often varying in the development of these factors. Thus, in the next section, a typology of sexual homicide offenders is discussed.

## *Typology*

Based on research published on sexual homicide, one researcher identified two categories of offenders: *compulsive sexual murderers* and *catathymic sexual murderers*, each with distinct characteristics.

The compulsive sexual murderer is the least common type of sexual homicide offender. They typically leave an organized crime scene (see Table 9.1). That is, the crime scene indicates a certain degree of control was exerted over the victim, planning of the crime occurred, and little evidence is left behind. The sexual offense usually takes place prior to the victim's death. The offender's behavior is associated with an obsessive-compulsive pattern (Meloy, 2000).

The compulsive sexual murderer typically meets the diagnosis criteria of sexual sadism, deriving pleasure from inflicting harm on his victim. Either antisocial personality disorder or narcissistic personality disorder is usually present. Narcissism is usually present by exhibiting a sense of entitlement, grandiosity, and/or emotional detachment. Severe psychopathy is also common and often exhibited through their cruelty to others and predatory behavior. They are typically detached to other people. The autonomic nervous system, which controls such automatic responses as fight-or-flight and ability to relax, is typically underactive. This means that their responses to environmental stimuli (e.g., sudden, loud noises) are often dulled or non-existent. Early trauma is usually absent from their childhood histories (Meloy, 2000).

The catathymic sexual murderer—the most common of the two categories of sexual homicide offenders—typically leaves behind a disorganized crime scene (see Table 9.1), demonstrating a lack of planning of the homicide. The offender typically exhibits a mood disorder and a personality disorder. Their level of psychopathy diverges from the compulsive sexual murderer, in that mild to moderate psychopathy exists. They are often hyperactive and have a history of early childhood trauma (Meloy, 2000).

## Alcohol- and Drug-Facilitated Rapes

Alcohol- and drug-facilitated rapes occur when victims have either voluntarily or involuntarily consumed a legal or illegal substance, rendering them unable to give consent to have sexual intercourse. The victims and offenders can be strangers or acquaintances, just as with other rapes; however, these offenses often occur during a dating situation. They present unique challenges to an investigator. For example, victims will often delay reporting for a variety of reasons—one being that they voluntarily consumed alcohol or illegal drugs. Also, victims may not want to report for fear of identifying friends who also engaged in illegal drug use. They may fear retaliation from the offender, may not want others to know they were raped, or may believe there is insufficient evidence that they were raped.

Another investigational challenge is presented because victims are not sure of what happened. They may not recall, or even have been conscious during the rape.

The victim, therefore, may not remember the event at all. It is also rare that force or coercion occurred (Chancellor, 2012).

Alcohol- and drug-facilitated rapes typically occur through one of two strategies. The *proactive approach* involves intentionally getting a victim drunk or giving her a drug without her knowledge. The victim is usually, then, taken to another location for sexual intercourse. The *opportunistic approach* involves taking advantage of someone who already has been exposed to alcohol or drugs (Chancellor, 2012).

Four important components need to be assessed during an alcohol- and drug-facilitated investigation: (1) actual credibility, (2) ability to perceive at the time of the incident, (3) ability to remember what occurred, and (4) existence of corroborative evidence. First, actual credibility can be established by identifying corroborating evidence, such as forensic evidence and witness testimony. It should be noted that victims do not always cooperate, as they may feel responsible for the rape occurring. The victim may withhold certain information, which could be perceived as a false rape allegation (Chancellor, 2012; Scalzo & National District Attorneys Association, 2007).

Second, as indicated above, the victim may not be able to perceive what was happening at the time of the incident, as the victim may have been unconscious or heavily under the influence of alcohol and/or drugs (Chancellor, 2012; Scalzo & National District Attorneys Association, 2007). An investigator should be aware that the victim may not be able to corroborate what happened, and instead rely on forensic and eyewitness accounts.

Third, the ability of the victim to remember the events may also be diminished—again, requiring the investigator to rely on alternative sources of information. Any details the victim can recall, however, can be helpful in building a case (Chancellor, 2012). Finally, as indicated above, the use of corroborative evidence is critical, especially when the victim was unconscious and cannot recall details of the incident (Chancellor, 2012).

The role of alcohol in rape has been well documented—as many as 50% of sexual assaults involve alcohol to some degree (Chancellor, 2012). Alcohol affects cognitive abilities by lowering one's inhibitions and decreasing one's ability to make logical judgments, and, therefore, can lead to risk-taking situations, including rape. It also affects motor control.

Below is an example of a typical report of an alcohol-facilitated rape where an offender went to a victim's home to "talk." The victim and offender had not had a previous sexual relationship and were simply co-workers.

> We were both off that day, and James, a guy I know from work, came over to my house for lunch.... I think he was looking for someone to talk to about his wife, because I know they were having problems ... he asked for a drink so I gave him a small glass and set a bottle of gin on the table and got ... orange juice out of the refrigerator. We talked for a while longer ... he was telling me about his wife and family and some of their personal issues. I only had two weak drinks and was actually starting on my third when I decided it didn't taste very good and actually poured

most of it down the sink while he was using the restroom ... I started to feel a little sick and was sitting on the toilet ... trying to avoid throwing up.... James walked into the bathroom and took my hand and tried to make me stand up. I was telling him to stop ... I finally was brought to my feet, but my panties and shorts were still around my ankles ...

(Chancellor, 2012, p. 297)

The offender forced her into the bedroom and had sexual intercourse with her against her wishes. She threw up several times during the assault. The suspect corroborated almost every aspect of the incident, with the exception that it was consensual and that the victim was actually the aggressor. This case shows that the offender often gets the victim to voluntarily consume alcohol and then takes advantage of her by forcing sex upon her (Chancellor, 2012).

Drug-facilitated rapes have much in common with alcohol-facilitated rapes. There are differences, however, which make the rape even more difficult to investigate. For example, victims of drug-facilitated rapes are almost always unconscious during the assault. Although someone may take advantage of a victim who is unconscious, most drug-facilitated rapes are planned well in advance. Drug-facilitated rapes are often characterized by the following:

- Force does not occur.
- Victim is not fearful.
- Victim does not resist.
- Offender is sexually gratified by control over the victim.
- Victim may engage in illegal drug use (knowingly).
- Torture typically is not present.
- Almost always a planned event.
- Efforts are made by offenders to hide their action (Littel, 2001).

Four components of a drug-facilitated rape exist: (1) means: offender's access to drugs and knowledge of their effects; (2) opportunity: ability to successfully carry out the rape without detection; (3) plan: having a plan to not only carry out the rape, but to avoid detection; (4) setting: location that allows the victim to be controlled. These four components are known as the MOPS, an acronym referring to the MO of drug-facilitated rapes (LeBeau, Mozayani, & Assault, 2001).

With regard to investigating drug-facilitated rapes, investigation strategies must be adjusted to take into consideration that information normally obtained from the victim may not be available. Also, offender behavior may not be as relevant. It can be assumed there was a lack of consent and evidence indicating victim resistance will likely not exist (Chancellor, 2012). It should also be noted that victims sometimes remember events in short spurts, "flashbulb memories," and these can be useful for investigations (LeBeau et al., 2001). Also, a victim should be questioned about the timing of the effects of the drugs, as some drugs, such as GHB (gamma-hydroxybutyric acid) or Rohypnol, do not take effect immediately. Other drugs that are used include, but are not limited to Xanax, Ecstasy, Klonopin, and street drugs (marijuana, cocaine, opiates, etc.).

With regard to a medical examination, which is usually conducted within 72 hours of the assault, examinations after alcohol- and drug-facilitated rapes can take place up to 96 hours after the assault. The investigator should request additional analyses of the urine, to test for drugs. The investigation may involve several locations, as the event may have involved more than one location (Chancellor, 2012).

## Autoerotic Asphyxiation and Accidental Deaths

Research has found that many sex offenders have paraphilias and a large proportion of them have multiple paraphilias (Abel, Becker, Cunningham-Rathner, Mittelman, & Rouleau, 1988). More specifically, most had some experience with as many as ten different paraphilias. Identifying paraphilias may be helpful to identify the MO of the offender and link crimes that may be related. Also, awareness of paraphilias may be helpful to distinguish cases originally thought to be suicides from accidental deaths caused by autoerotic asphyxiation.

Autoerotic asphyxiation refers to restricting oxygen while sexually aroused for the purpose of enhancingtion orgasm intensity (Bartol & Bartol, 2012). This is often accomplished by masturbating while engaging in near strangulation or suffocation. Unfortunately, much of what is known about autoerotic asphyxiation comes from accidental deaths. Typical autoerotic asphyxiation involves some sort of ligature (dog collar, belt, bungee cord, etc.) around the neck, with a release mechanism. However, the lack of oxygen to the brain will lead to passing out if the release mechanism is not released in time. This leads to accidental death.

Atypical asphyxiation involves some other method, such as a plastic bag over the head. When an accidental death occurs, the family may try to stage the offense to look like a suicide attempt by clothing the individual and removing sexual material, such as pornographic magazines. An estimated 250 to 1,200 accidental deaths occur each year as the result of autoerotic asphyxiation (Cowell, 2009).

## False Rape Allegations

False rape allegations are a highly debated issue with researchers indicating that "false rape allegations are rare" and criminal justice practitioners indicating that they occur often (Saunders, 2012). For example, one study reports an estimated 3% of rape allegations are false allegations. Yet, police officers indicate that about half of rape cases are false (Kelly, Lovett, & Regan, 2005). Three decades of research on the issue indicate low levels of false rape allegations—that is, the overwhelming majority of rape claims are in fact true (Saunders, 2012).

In a critical examination of the divide between front-line practitioners (i.e., police officers) who claim high rates of false rape allegations and academic researchers who claim low rates of false rape allegations, the answer may be in the definition of "false rape allegation." If the researchers' definition of false rape allegations is different from that of police officers, they may be talking about two different events. The definition of a false rape allegation seems straightforward to most: an allegation of rape that is false—that is, the rape the victim alleged occurred, did not occur (Lisak, Gardinier, Nicksa, & Cote, 2010; Rumney, 2006). While the definition itself is not highly debated in the literature, the evidence required to assume a false rape allegation does differ (Saunders, 2012).

One researcher made the distinction between the *false rape complaint* and the *false rape account*. A false complaint is "an allegation that is fabricated in its entirety" (Saunders, 2012, p. 6). Thus, nothing about the rape allegation is true. The author provides an example where a university student claims a man whom she did not know raped her while she was out with friends. Witness statements and CCTV footage showed that she was not present at the alleged location before, during, or after the alleged rape and she was not with the friends she claimed to be with that night. Thus, every detail of the event was fabricated. Motivations for a false complaint are plentiful: an attempt to conceal infidelity, a minor concealing consensual sex, consensual sex that is later regretted, breakdown of a relationship, or an attempt to manipulate or provoke sympathy (Kelly et al., 2005; Saunders, 2012; Turvey, 2011). Another researcher identified five overlapping categories of motivation: avoiding trouble/providing an alibi, anger/revenge, attention seeking, mental illness, and guilt/remorse (O'Neal, Spohn, Tellis, & White, 2014).

A false account, on the other hand, is an allegation of rape where a rape occurred, yet the victim provides inaccurate statements about the rape (Saunders, 2012). Such inaccurate statements can lead a police officer to doubt the rape itself (Saunders, 2012). An example of this is where a victim claims the rape occurred the previous day, when, in fact, it had occurred the week before. Research has shown that rape victims may not reveal certain details of the offense—as the victims believe the information may not be believed or the victim will be blamed (Kelly, 2010). This, however, leads the police officer to believe the victim is lying. Other information, such as how much alcohol the victim consumed, is often concealed as well.

It has been proposed that false accounts are often confused for false complaints—that is, when a victim withholds or misrepresents certain facts about the rape, the rape is (wrongly) alleged to not have occurred at all (Saunders, 2012). Thus, definitions of false allegations of rape should be probed. That the rape occurred, but not the way the victim reports, should be considered.

For the purpose of identifying factors that distinguish false rape allegations from true rape allegations, a study in the U.S. was conducted that compared the two types of allegations. It was found that the following factors were more likely to be associated with false rape allegations: White victim, unemployed victim, victim not under the influence of alcohol, victim alleges the assault occurred outdoors, victim reports a "surprise approach" (i.e., offender sneaked up and grabbed victim), victim reports she did not resist, victim reports that the offender spoke very little or not at all during the incident, victim reports the incident herself to the police, and victim took longer than 24 hours to report the incident (Hunt & Bull, 2012).

Also, the following factors were found to be more likely to occur with genuine rape allegations: victim reports a theft occurred in addition to the rape, more likely to report violence and have injuries, more sexual acts occurred during the rape incident, victim reports verbal resistance, victim reports the offender took one or more precautions (such as binding, gagging, blindfolding), offender spoke more during the offense, someone other than the victim reports the rape to the police, and the rape was reported within 24 hours of it occurring (Hunt & Bull, 2012).

The reader should be cautioned that this study was based on a small sample and the presence or absence of specified factors does not correlate perfectly with genuine or false rape allegations. This information is intended to be a starting point for distinguishing between genuine and false rape allegations. Substantially more research is needed to fully assess the truthfulness of a rape allegation (Hunt & Bull, 2012).

## COMMON INVESTIGATIONAL FAILURES

Researchers have identified several common investigative failures over the past several decades through the careful analysis of past cases. Rossmo has identified those investigative failures in his book, "Criminal Investigative Failures" (Rossmo, 2009b). Investigative failures are organized into three broad categories: (1) cognitive biases, (2) organizational traps, and (3) errors in probability. Each of these is discussed here. Although these are found to occur among a wide range of criminal activities, it can be argued that sex crimes are highly susceptible to such investigative failures.

### Cognitive Biases

Cognitive biases include problems that occur as a result of inaccurate perception, inaccurate intuition, and/or *tunnel vision*. With regard to perception, Rossmo notes "perception is based on both awareness and understanding, we often perceive what we expect to perceive" (Rossmo, 2009b, p. 9). Humans are limited by their working memory, which has been shown in research studies to only hold five to nine items in our conscious memory (Rossmo, 2009b). Thus, while we are bombarded with multiple stimuli at any one time during any one incident, what we remember is quite limited. With regard to sex crimes, it is not uncommon for a victim's perception to vary a great deal from that of the alleged offender and even from the witnesses' accounts, if they exist. For example, an offender may perceive the victim was willing to engage in sex, while the victim believed it was rape.

Another cognitive bias involves intuition, or rather one's "gut instinct." Intuition relies on one's perception (usually derived through an automatic process) and reason (usually derived through a deliberate process). Intuition is prone to error, as it is influenced by emotion. Police officers often make intuitive decisions under chaotic conditions and do so quickly. Such intuition is susceptible to error. Only under a slow methodical analysis of reliable information are decisions less prone to error. Humans are prone to taking cognitive shortcuts, especially when presented with incomplete information. This often leads to error (Rossmo, 2009b).

Another cognitive bias that can occur, especially in a criminal investigation, is tunnel vision. This occurs "when there is a narrow focus on a limited range of alternatives" (Rossmo, 2009b, p. 13). With regard to the type of work to which police officers are exposed, they can quickly eliminate the actual offender and/or quickly narrow their focus on an innocent person (Cory, 2001). Tunnel vision can also affect a victim's account as well. The victim may remember the gun that was pointed at her, in great detail, but not be able to identify the race of the offender.

These cognitive biases (inaccurate perception, inaccurate intuition, and tunnel vision) can lead to problems in evaluating evidence, such as ignoring context and misjudging a situation. For example, a police officer can mistakenly shoot someone jogging after a robbery is reported. The police officer fails to recognize the context—the person was in jogging clothing on a jogging trail and not involved in the robbery.

*Confirmation bias* can also occur, which involves paying attention only to information that corroborates one's theory and ignoring any information that discredits the theory. Additionally, research shows that individuals are more influenced by vivid information, as opposed to data and statistics (Heuer, 1999). Thus, eyewitness description (which can be inaccurate) carries a lot of weight. Police officers can also fail to account for a lack of evidence. For example, a missing bottle of the victim's favorite perfume, given by an ex-boyfriend, can easily be overlooked (Rossmo, 2009b).

## Organizational Traps

In addition to an individual's susceptibility to error, several organizational traps exist: (1) groupthink, (2) rumor, and (3) ego. Each of these traps contributes to criminal investigative failures in unique ways.

*Groupthink* involves the unwillingness of a person to question a "dominant" theory or idea among a cohesive group of individuals, such as police officers. The result can be disastrous: failing to critically assess ideas and wrongly discarding alternative ideas or theories. Thus, in an investigation, the dominant theory could be that a rape did not occur; the victim is making up the incident. Subsequently, others jump on board, refusing to challenge the status quo (Rossmo, 2009b).

Rumors, also, can negatively affect a case. These are termed *red herrings*, which refer to tips that misdirect a case. It is particularly problematic in high-profile cases where tip-lines are established for anyone to contact. In such cases certain components, often dramatic in nature, are exaggerated in importance. Information, however, that could be quite valuable is often lost in the process (Rossmo, 2009b).

Correctly identifying offenders often involves being able to question assumptions. Personal ego and organizational ego can negatively affect the outcome of a case. In the following excerpt Rossmo (2009b) provides an example of this:

> Supervisory Special Agent John Douglas of the FBI's Behavioral Science Unit prepared a psychological profile for the sexual killer of nine-year-old Christine Jessop from Queensville, Ontario … When police later arrested Guy Paul Morin, who closely matched the profile, Douglas touted the case as a success story … DNA testing of semen stains on Jessop's underwear later exonerated Morin.
>
> (Rossmo, 2009b, pp. 27–28)

In this case, personal ego and organizational ego (the "power" of the FBI and its employees) led to the assumption that the FBI profile was accurate, when, in actuality, it led to the arrest of an innocent individual.

## Errors in Probabilities

Probabilities, the likelihood that something will happen/has happened or won't happen/didn't happen, are critical to investigation of all crimes, including sex crimes. Critical to probabilities are coincidences and how often they can occur during the investigation of a crime, as noted by Rossmo in the following quote:

> Mark Kennedy, a St. Louis sex crimes detective pursuing a serial rapist responsible for numerous crimes in several jurisdictions over many years, once commented to me—half seriously—that he could have convicted three people if it were not for DNA. What he meant was the task force had looked at so many suspects that some of them, by sheer chance, circumstantially appeared guilty—until they were cleared by DNA testing. A few people will just be in the wrong place at the wrong time.
>
> (Rossmo, 2009b, p. 37)

Thus, investigators are exposed to numerous coincidences that can, inevitably, lead to arresting an innocent person. Police officers must rely on all tools available to them, including DNA, to identify the guilty person.

Although DNA is often used as the ultimate resource for determining guilt, it is important to note that it is a science that is also susceptible to human error. Humans are responsible for collecting material with DNA, a process that is subject to error. In 2003, at the height of relying on DNA in criminal cases, the New York Times reported that a lab oratory in Houston had a leaky roof, contaminating many DNA samples. This was only the beginning of problems with the lab oratory. It was reported that the lab oratory, in general, utilized poor methods for processing samples. Calibration and maintenance of equipment was considered to be poor. A lack of safeguards existed for contaminating samples. Poor record keeping was also found. Below is just one of the cases where DNA evidence was linked to the wrong suspect:

> Mr. Sutton, who is serving a 25-year sentence, was convicted of raping a woman in October 1998 after she was taken from her apartment complex here by two men and later left in a field. Several days later, he and a companion were arrested, although only Mr. Sutton was charged.
>
> During his trial, a police crime laboratory employee offered evidence to suggest that a DNA sample recovered by investigators was a precise match for Mr. Sutton's. Other DNA experts disagreed.
>
> (Madigan, 2003, n.p.)

Mr. Sutton was exonerated in 2003, having been arrested in 1999, after serving several years in prison (Flynn, 2015).

The problems with DNA testing have not disappeared over the years, despite improvements in DNA testing. As recently as 2015, it was noted that the way DNA was examined when several people were present involved questionable protocol: "In a statement ... Travis County District Attorney ... said her office ... discovered an issue with the database it uses to calculate DNA statistics" (Osborn, 2015, p. A1). It was noted that the state was using an outdated protocol. Prosecutors, inevitably, overstated the reliability of linking the DNA sample to the suspect. Often this involved stating in court that a specific suspect is accurately linked to the material found at a crime scene (i.e., semen from a rape examination), within "a fraction of a fraction of a percent" (Osborn, 2015, p. A4).

In summary, investigative failures often boil down to one commonality: human error. Humans are limited by their ability to process only limited information at one time. Crime scenes involving sex crimes are often complex, in that the victim, offender, and witnesses bring their own biases and distortions to the table. Organizational structures also lead to the potential errors, especially given that they are comprised of humans who often make errors.

## CONCLUSION

Investigating sex crimes often involves following guidelines that have been developed as a result of identifying mistakes from past investigations. Much can be gained from examining a crime scene about the offender. In some instances, in particular when the victim is young or does not remember the sex crime occurring due to alcohol or drugs, the investigators must rely on alternative sources of information. Many of those who investigate sex crimes have received specialist training, as working with sex crimes can be psychologically draining. Those who are first-responders and those who interview suspects must be aware of the mistakes that can occur during an investigation, potentially damaging the case. Given that people are involved in the process, human error may occur. Special care must therefore be taken to eliminate or at least minimize mistakes.

## REVIEW POINTS

- Profiling a sex crime involves identifying a *modus operandi*, determining whether a crime scene is organized or disorganized, identifying any signature, and potentially conducting a geographical profile.

- Emergency 911 operators and first responders to a sex crime must take great care to preserve and identify any potential evidence.

- Interviewing vulnerable victims involves taking additional precautions, such as allowing a trained advocate to be present and asking questions in a phased approach.

- A medical examination is usually required, which should be conducted by a specially trained nurse, usually through a Sexual Assault Nurse Examiner program.

- Interviewing a sex-crime suspect should be done using a humane interview approach, asking appropriate questions, and an information-gathering approach.

- Several types of sex crimes involve unique investigational obstacles. These include sexual homicide, alcohol- and drug-facilitated rapes, deaths caused from autoerotic asphyxiation, and false rape allegations.

- Sexual homicides are rare occurrences, usually fueled by fantasy, and are believed to be committed by either compulsive sexual murders or catathymic sexual murders.

- Alcohol- and drug-facilitated rapes present unique investigational challenges, as the victim often does not remember the incident.

- Many who die accidentally from autoerotic asphyxiation are posed as suicides by those who find the victim.

- Criminal justice practitioners and researchers disagree on the extent of false rape allegations. This may be due to applying different definitions of false rape allegations.

- There are three broad categories of common investigational mistakes that can affect a sex crime investigation: cognitive biases, organizational traps, and errors in probabilities.

## REFERENCES

Abel, G., Becker, J. V., Cunningham-Rathner, J., Mittelman, M., & Rouleau, J. L. (1988). Multiple paraphilic diagnoses among sex offenders. *Journal of the American Academy of Psychiatry and the Law, 16*(2), 153–168.

Agnew, S., & Powell, M. (2004). The effect of intellectual disability on children's recall of an event across different question types. *Law and Human Behavior, 28*(3).

Bartol, C. R., & Bartol, A. M. (2012). *Forensic psychology and criminal behavior.* Thousand Oaks, CA: Sage.

Bull, R. (2010). The investigative interviewing of children and other vulnerable witnesses. Psychological research and working/professional practice. *Legal and Criminological Psychology, 15*(1), 5–23.

Burgess, A. W., Hartman, C., Ressler, R., Douglas, J., & McCormack, A. (1986). Sexual homicide: A motivational model. *Journal of Interpersonal Violence, 1*(3), 251–272.

Burns, I. M. (1993). Foreword to McGurk, B., Carr, M. J., & McGurk, D., *Investigative interviewing courses for police officers: An evaluation.* London: Home Office.

Chancellor, A. S. (2012). *Investigating sexual assault cases.* Chicago, IL: Jones & Bartlett Publishers.

Cory, P. (2001). *The injury regarding Thomas Sophonow.* Winnipeg: Government of Manitoba.

Cowell, D. D. (2009). Autoerotic asphyxiation: Secret pleasure—Lethal outcome? *Pediatrics, 124*(5), 1319–1324.

Craig, R., Scheibe, R., Raskin, D., Kircher, R., & Dodd, D. (1999). Interviewer questions and content analysis of children's statements of of sexual abuse. *Applied Developmental Science, 3*(2), 77–85.

Davies, G., Wilson, C., Mitchell, R., & Milsom, J. (1995). *Videotaping children's evidence: An evaluation.* London, UK: Home Office.

Flynn, M. (2015). Advances in DNA testing could put thousands of Texas cases in legal limbo. *Houston Press.* Retrieved October 23, 2015 from http://www.houstonpress.com/news/advances-in-dna-testing-could-put-thousands-of-texas-cases-in-legal-limbo-7816089

Frontline, P. (1998). Innocence lost: The plea. Retrieved October 23, 2015, from http://www.pbs.org/wgbh/pages/frontline/shows/innocence/etc/other.html

Geberth, V. J. (2014). *Sex-related homicide and death investigation: Practical and clinical.* New York: CRC Press.

Harries, K. (1999). *Mapping crime: Principle and practice* (NCJ 178919). Washington, DC: National Institute of Justice.

Hazelwood, R., & Burgess, A. W. (1987). An introduction to the serial rapist: Research by the FBI. *FBI Law Enforcement Bulletin, 56*(9), 16–24.

Heal, L., & Sigelman, C. (1995). Response bias in interviews of individuals with limited mental ability. *Journal of Intellectual Disability Research, 39*(4), 331–340.

Heuer, R. J., Jr. (1999). *Psychology of intelligence analysis.* Washington DC: Center for the Study of Intelligence, Central Intelligence Agency.

Holmberg, U., & Christianson, S. Å. (2002). Murderers' and sexual offenders' experiences of police interviews and their inclination to admit or deny crimes. *Behavioral Sciences and the Law, 20*(1–2), 31–45.

Hunt, L., & Bull, R. (2012). Differentiating genuine and false rape allegations: A model to aid rape investigations. *Psychiatry, Psychology and Law, 19*(5), 682–691.

International Association of Nurses. (2015). SANE Program Listing. Retrieved October 23, 2015, from http://www.forensicnurses.org/?page=a5

Jetmore, L. (2006). Investigating rape crimes, part 1: Guidelines for first responders. Retrieved October 24, 2015, from https://www.policeone.com/police-products/investigation/evidence-management/articles/509858-Investigating-Rape-Crimes-Part-1-Guidelines-for-first-responders/

Kebbell, M. R., Hurren, E. J., & Roberts, S. (2006). Mock suspects' decisions to confess: Accuracy of eyewitness evidence is crucial. *Applied Cognitive Psychology, 20*(4), 477–486.

Kelly, L. (2010). The (in)credible words of women: False allegations in European rape research. *Violence Against Women, 16*(2), 1345–1355.

Kelly, L., Lovett, J., & Regan, L. (2005). *A gap or a chasm? Attrition in reported rape cases.* London, UK: Great Britain. Home Office. Research, Development and Statistics Directorate.

LeBeau, M. A., Mozayani, A., & Assault, D. F. S. (2001). *A forensic handbook*. New York: John Wiley & Sons, Ltd.

Ledray, L. E., & Simmelink, K. (1999). Sexual assault: Clinical issues, efficacy of SANE evidence collection, a Minnesota study. *Journal of Emergency Nursing, 23*(1), 75–77.

Lisak, D., Gardinier, L., Nicksa, S. C., & Cote, A. M. (2010). False allegations of sexual assault: An analysis of ten years of reported cases. *Violence Against Women, 16*(2), 1318–1334.

Littel, K. (2001). *Sexual assault nurse examiner (SANE) programs: Improving the community response to sexual assault victims*. Washington, DC: GPO. Retrieved October 23, 2015 from http://www.vawnet.org/Assoc_Files_VAWnet/OVC_SANE0401–186366.pdf.

MacCulloch, M., Snowden, P., Wood, P., & Mills, H. (1983). Sadistic fantasy, sadistic behavior and offending. *British Journal of Criminology, 143*(1), 20–29.

Madigan, N. (2003). Houston's troubled DNA crime lab faces growing scrutiny. *The New York Times*. Retrieved October 23, 2015 from http://www.nytimes.com/2003/02/09/us/houston-s-troubled-dna-crime-lab-faces-growing-scrutiny.html

Matikka, L., & Vesala, H. (1997). Acquiescence in quality of life interviews with adults who have mental retardation. *Mental Retardation, 35*(2), 75–82.

McGurk, B., Carr, J., & McGurk, D. (1993). *Investigative interviewing courses for police officers: An evaluation. Police Research Series: Paper No. 4*. London: Home Office.

Meissner, C. A., Redlich, A. D., Bhatt, S., & Brandon, S. (2012). Interview and interrogation methods and their effects on true and false. *Campbell Systematic Reviews, 13*(1), 1–52.

Meloy, J. R. (2000). The nature and dynamics of sexual homicide: An integrative review. *Aggression & Violent Behavior, 5*(1), 1–22.

Milne, R., & Bull, R. (1999). *Investigative interviewing: Psychology and practice*. Chichester, UK: Wiley.

O'Neal, E. N., Spohn, C., Tellis, K., & White, C. (2014). The truth behind the lies: The complex motivations for false allegations of sexual assault. *Women and Criminal Justice, 24*(4), 324–340.

Orbach, Y., Hershkowitz, I., Lamb, M., Sternberg, K., Esplin, P., & Horowitz, D. (2000). Assessing the value of structured protocols for forensic interviews of alleged abuse victims. *Child Abuse & Neglect, 24*(6), 733–752.

Osborn, C. & Ulloa, J. (2015). Hundreds of local criminal cases to be reviewed. DNA lab issues affect Texas cases. *Austin American-Statesman*. A1, Front Page.

Oxburgh, G., Ost, J., & Cherryman, J. (2012). Police interviews with suspected child sex offenders: Does use of empathy and question type influence the amount of investigation relevant information obtained? *Psychology, Crime & Law, 18*(3), 259–273.

Paterson, B., Bull, R., & Vrij, A. (2002). *The effects of interviewer style on children's event recall*. Paper presented at the 25th Congress of Applied Psychology, Singapore.

Pinizzotto, A. J. (1984). Forensic psychology: Criminal personality profiling. *Journal of Police Science and Administration, 12*(1), 32–40.

Possley, M. (n.d.) The National Registry of Exonerations: Violet Amirault. Retrieved July 18, 2016 from http://www.law.umich.edu/special/exoneration/pages/ casedetail.aspx?caseid=3863

Prentky, R. A., Burgess, A. W., Rokous, F., Lee, A., Hartman, C., Ressler, R., & Douglas, J. (1989). The presumptive role of fantasy in serial sexual homicide. *American Journal of Psychiatry, 146*(7), 887–891.

Ressler, R. K., Burgess, A. W., & Douglas, J. E. (1988). *Sexual homicide: Patterns and motives*. New York: Simon and Schuster.

Rossmo, D. K. (2000). *Geographic profiling*. Boca Raton, FL: CRC Press.

Rossmo, D. K. (2009a). Geographic profiling in serial rape investigations. In R. R. Hazelwood & A. W. Burgess (Eds.), *Practical aspects of rape investigation: A multidisciplinary approach* (4th ed.) (pp. 139–169). Boca Raton, FL: CRC Press.

Rossmo, D. K. (2009b). *Criminal investigative failures*. Boca Raton, FL: CRC Press, Taylor & Frances Group, LLC.

Rumney, P. N. (2006). False allegations of rape. *The Cambridge Law Journal, 65*(01), 128–158.

Sande, M. K., Broderick, K. B., Moreira, M. E., Bender, B., Hopkins, E., & Buchanan, J. A. (2013). Sexual assault training in emergency medicine residences: A survey of program directors. *Western Journal of Emergency Medicine, 14*(5), 461–466.

Saunders, C. L. (2012). The truth, the half-truth, and nothing like the truth: Reconceptualizing false allegations of rape. *British Journal of Criminology, 52*(6), 1152–1171.

Scalzo, T. P., & National District Attorneys Association, a. U. S. o. A. (2007). *Prosecuting alcohol-facilitated sexual assault.* Alexandria, VA: American Prosecutors Research Institute.

Schröer, J., & Püschel, K. (2006). Special aspects of crime scene interpretation and behavioural analysis—the phenomenon of "undoing." In Tsokos, M. *editor. Forensic pathology reviews*, vol. 4. Totowa: Humana Press, pp. 193–202.

Soukara, S., Bull, R., & Vrij, A. (2002). Police detectives' aims regarding their interviews with suspects: Any change at the turn of the millennium? *International Journal of Police Science and Management, 4*(2).

Sternberg, K., Lamb, M., Esplin, P., & Baradaran, L. (1999). Using a scripted protocol to guide investigative interviews: A pilot study. *Applied Developmental Science, 3*(2), 70–76.

Sternberg, K., Lamb, M., Orbach, Y., Esplin, P., & Mitchell, S. (2001). Use of a structured investigative protocol enhances young children's responses to free recall prompts in the course of forensic interviews. *Journal of Applied Psychology, 86*(5), 997–1005.

Thomas, T. (2000). *Sex crime: Sex offending and society.* Chichester: Wiley.

Tittle, T. (2006). *Rape and sexual assault investigation.* Paper presented at the Police training session, Normal, IL.

Turvey, B. E. (2011). *Criminal profiling: An introduction to behavioral evidence analysis.* New York: Academic Press.

Vrij, A., Mann, S. A., Fisher, R. P., Leal, S., Milne, R., & Bull, R. (2008). 2 Increasing cognitive load to facilitate lie detection: The benefit of recalling an event in reverse order. *Law and Human Behavior, 32*(3), 253–265.

Ward, T., Hudson, S. M., Johnston, L. H., & Marshall, W. L. (1997). Cognitive distortions in sexual offenders: An integrative review. *Clinical Psychology Review, 17*(5), 1–29.

Warren, A., Woodall, C., Hunt, J., & Perry, N. (1996). 'It sounds good in theory, but … ': Do investigative interviewers follow guidelines based on memory research? *Child Maltreatment, 1*(3), 231–245.

Wood, J. L., & Garven, S. (2000). How sexual abuse interviewers go astray: Implications for prosecutors, police and child protection services. *Child Maltreatment, 5*(2), 109–118.

## DEFINITIONS

**Accusatorial Method (of Suspect Interviewing):** A style of interviewing suspects that is used primarily in the U.S. It is confrontational and assumes guilt. This method typically establishes control, uses psychological manipulation (e.g., custody and isolation, confrontation, followed by offering sympathy and face-saving excuses), uses closed-ended, confirmatory questions, and focuses on anxiety cues to determine deception (based on the suspect's verbal and non-verbal cues). The primary goal is confession.

**Alcohol- and Drug-Facilitated Rape:** A rape that occurs when a victim has either voluntarily or involuntarily consumed a legal or illegal substance, rendering them unable to give consent to have sexual intercourse.

**Appropriate (or Productive Interview) Questions:** A type of question that is asked during a criminal investigation. It includes open questions (e.g., "Can you describe the room to me?"), probing questions (e.g., "What happened next?"), encouragements/ acknowledgements (e.g., "Ok, I see."). (See inappropriate questions.)

**Autoerotic Asphyxiation:** Restricting oxygen while sexually aroused for the purpose of enhancing orgasm intensity.

**Catathymic Sexual Murderer:** One of two types of sexual murderers. This person typically has a mood disorder, such as a personality disorder. They usually leave a disorganized crime scene behind and are the most common type of sexual murderer. (See Compulsive Sexual Murderer.)

**Cognitive Distortions:** Minimize or deny the dangerousness of the behavior, justify it, and relieve the offender of responsibility. (Examples: children need to be taught about sex; children are very seductive; the child is too young to know what is happening.)

**Compulsive Sexual Murderer:** One of two types of sexual murderers. This person is typically sadistic, has psychopathy, and meets the criteria for antisocial personality disorder or narcissistic personality disorder. This person usually leaves an organized crime scene behind and is the least common type of sexual murderer. (See Catathymic Sexual Murderer.)

**Confirmation Bias:** Paying attention only to information that corroborates one's theory and ignoring any information that discredits the theory.

**Criminal Geographic Targeting (CGT):** Developed by criminologist, Kim Rossmo, and used in conjunction with criminal profiling. It analyzes spatial characteristics of a specified offender's crime patterns. The program creates a topographical map that identifies probabilities that a specific area falls within the offender's territory. Geographical profiling is simply an investigative tool that assists to solve crimes, but does not solve crimes. Rather, it assists to identify locations that can be closely monitored.

**Disorganized Crime Scene:** A chaotic and messy crime scene, indicative of a lack of planning and/or rage associated with the offender. (See Organized Crime Scene and Mixed Crime Scene.)

**Dominant (Suspect) Interview:** A type of suspect interview that is associated with impatience, hostility, aggressiveness, and condemnation. Police officers are less likely to obtain an admission of guilt if they use a humane approach. (See Humane (Suspect) Interview.)

**False Rape Account:** A rape allegation where a rape has actually occurred, yet the victim provides inaccurate statements about the rape.

**False Rape Complaint:** A rape allegation that is fabricated in its entirety. Thus, nothing about the rape allegation is true.

**Forced-Choice Questions:** A type of interview question in which the answer has only limited options. These include such questions as: Did the offender cut your necklace off before or after the assault?

**Geographical Mapping:** Analysis of the spatial patterns of a series of crimes committed over a period of time by all offenders of known offenses. The focus is on a specific geographical area.

**Geographical Profiling:** Analysis of the spatial distribution of a set of offenses committed by a single offender. The focus is on the individual offender.

**Groupthink:** The unwillingness of a person to question a "dominant" theory or idea among a cohesive group of individuals, such as police officers.

**Humane (Suspect) Interview:** A type of suspect interview that is associated with friendliness and empathy and is cooperative and personal. Police officers are more likely to obtain an admission of guilt if they use a humane approach. (See Dominant (Suspect) Interview.)

**Hunters:** A type of criminal who seeks victims as they set out from their home base, in places they are familiar with and believe suitable targets can be found. Hunters tend to stay within a relatively stable geographical area that is near their own home. (See Trollers, Trappers, and Poachers.)

**Inappropriate (Interview) Questions:** Types of questions that are used during an investigation. They include echo questions (e.g., Suspect says, "I may have … "; Interviewer says, "You may have …"), closed-questions (e.g., "Did you leave your house last night?"), leading questions (e.g., "Then you went to the living room, right?"), forced-choice questions (e.g., "The phone is in your name or your wife's?"), multiple questions (e.g., "Did you leave before nine o'clock? Where did you go?"), and making opinion-based statements (e.g., "You are just trying to protect yourself"). (See Appropriate Questions.)

**Information-Gathering:** Relies on establishing rapport, using open-ended, exploratory questions, and focusing on cognitive clues to deception. The use of cognitive clues is deeply embedded in empirical research that shows individuals will remember an event more accurately after they have been asked to remember the emotions, perceptions and sequence of events in the situation of interest. The primary goal of the information-gathering method is to elicit information. This method is associated with Great Britain. The suspects are given the opportunity to provide explanations and explain the circumstances. Only then are they questioned and asked about any inconsistent or contradictory information. The goal is to establish facts as opposed to obtaining a confession (as in the accusatorial method).

**Investigation Relevant Information (IRI):** Information that is helpful in determining information about the crime. Quality interviews, in general, will yield IRI, which includes the following key pieces of information: (1) what happened, (2) how the crime was committed, (3) who was involved, (4) when and where the offense occurred, and (5) any objects used to assist in committing the offense.

**Mixed Crime Scene:** A crime scene that includes elements of both the organized and disorganized crime scene. (See Organized Crime Scene and Disorganized Crime Scene.)

*Modus Operandi (MO)*: An offender's unique behavioral pattern during the commission of the offense.

**Open Questions:** Questions that are based on information that the witness provided in the narrative and are open-ended (e.g.,What did the offender look like?).

**Opportunistic Approach**: A type of approach that occurs during an alcohol- and drug-facilitated rape. It involves taking advantage of someone who already has been exposed to alcohol or drugs.

**Organized Crime Scene:** A crime scene that reveals planning on the part of the offender; the crime scene appears in order. (See Dis organized Crime Scene and Mixed Crime Scene.)

**Phased Approach**: An approach that is suggested to be used when working with vulnerable victims. The phased approach includes four phases: (1) establish good rapport, (2) then obtain as much free narrative as possible, (3) then ask questions of the right type and in the right order, and (4) then have meaningful closure.

**Poachers:** A type of offender who is usually more transient—as they will travel some distance from their residence to search for victims. (See Hunters, Trollers, and Trappers.)

**Proactive Approach:** Involves intentionally getting a victim drunk or to give her a drug without her knowledge. The victim is usually, then, taken to another location for sexual intercourse.

**Red Herrings:** Tips received in a crime investigation, usually a high-profile case, that misdirect a case.

**Sexual Assault Nurse Examiner (SANE):** Nurses who have specialized knowledge and training to conduct forensic examinations of sexual assault victims.

**Sexual Homicide:** Involves killing someone who is also sexually assaulted at some point before, during, or after killing him or her.

**Signature:** Anything that the offender does that goes beyond what is necessary to carry out the crime. It reveals the offender's unique cognitive processes associated with the sex crime. The signature is relatively consistent when the offender carries out the crime repeatedly.

**Specific Questions:** Questions that typically seek additional information or clarify information already provided and assist the witness to understand what is relevant. This usually involves asking what, who, where, and when-type questions.

**Staging:** Altering the crime scene after the crime has occurred but before law enforcement arrives. It is usually done to make the crime look like someone else did it, moving the investigation away from the most obvious person.

**Trappers:** A type of offender who places his/her victims in a position of opportunity by taking on boarders, entertaining victims, placing ads, or assuming an employment position that brings victims to them. (See Hunters, Poachers, and Trollers.)

**Trollers:** Often encounter their victim randomly and do not specifically search out victims. They locate their victims while engaging in some other activity. (See Hunters, Poachers, and Trappers.)

**Trophy:** An item that is taken by the offender from the crime scene, such as jewelry, a driver's license, or underwear. It is usually a meaningful item that the offender uses to remember the incident.

**Tunnel Vision:** When one has a narrow focus on a limited range of alternatives.

**Undoing:** The offender psychologically trying to "undo" the murder. The offender may try to clean up the body and place it in a natural position, such as sleeping in the bed.

**Vulnerable Victims:** A type of victim who may have difficulty communicating events, such as children, elderly adults, and those with special needs.

## CHAPTER 10

# Assessment Tools and Treatment of Sex Offenders

## CHAPTER OBJECTIVES

- Describe the purpose of assessment tools in evaluating sex offenders.
- Identify the key components of the Risk, Need, and Responsivity Model as applied to sex-offender treatment.
- Define and describe non-actuarial assessment tools.
- Define and describe assessment tools that rely on objective measures, yet do not provide cut-off scores for risk levels.
- Define and describe actuarial assessment tools, which involve assessment tools that provide cut-off for levels of risk and are based on empirical findings from systematic research.
- Define *psychopathy* and how it affects sex-offender assessments.
- Identify treatment developments that have been used for sex offenders with an emphasis on cognitive-behavioral treatment, which is the most common type of treatment used currently.

Sex offenders target different types of victims, and they differ with regard to their type and degree of motivation. They also differ with regard to recidivism risk and the types of interventions that will be most effective in reducing that risk. One way to differentiate sex offenders and identify unique risk factors for recidivism is through an assessment process.

Assessments assist in the criminal-justice processing of a sex offender, which typically determines the amount and type of treatment and punishment. As noted in Focus Box 10.1, assessments can make the difference between sentences that involve treatment as opposed to a stand-alone prison sentence. Assessment results can lead to a requirement that the community be notified of an offender's presence (Lanterman, Boyle, & Ragusa-Salerno, 2014). Assessments can be conducted during sentencing and in determining prison and probation conditions. They can also be conducted when the offender is being released from prison in deciding re-entry plans. Additionally, assessments can also be conducted to determine progress and compliance with treatment (Center for Sex Offender Management, 2007).

---

*Focus Box 10.1    Assessment and Sentencing*

In a case in Melbourne, Australia, a judge found that the defendant, based on an assessment of his background, warranted rehabilitation. The defendant was accused of committing a serious sex crime against a teenager. The assessment included several factors from the defendant's childhood. The judge described the abuse that the defendant experienced as the worst sexual abuse he had seen in 30 years as a judge. From the age of three until seven, the defendant experienced sexual abuse by his father, his stepmother, and a child molester. As an infant, he was seen at the hospital for failure to thrive, a condition of developmental stagnation. He was later diagnosed with attention deficit hyperactivity disorder, post-traumatic stress disorder, and depression. His doctor reported that the effects of exposure to childhood trauma would be lifelong. The clinicians who assessed the defendant did note that he had protective factors that could moderate his risk level. Thus, the defendant likely had some factors that would provide him with a source of support. The judge rhetorically asked:

> Do you really think the community would expect me, when the expert opinion so far is that what this man needs is a case manager to try to do something about the large number of problems he has, to jail him, where he is unlikely to receive any of that sort of assistance?

The judge sentenced the defendant to treatment and noted:

> When you combine the issues of your childhood and your mental health issues your moral culpability is considerably lessened.

The judge, in addition to treatment, ordered additional assessments to be conducted, including psychological, neuropsychological, and psychiatric. He was also ordered to register for life as a sex offender. He was placed on probation for 30 months and ordered to conduct 200 hours of community service.

Source: (Butcher, 2014).

---

Assessments are critical to the criminal justice process, but it warrants emphasis that assessments are not used to determine guilt or innocence. There is no assessment tool that unequivocally determines whether a person has committed a sex crime. Rather, assessments are used to provide objective information for judges in determining the most appropriate judicial response to those who have already committed a sex crime (Center for Sex Offender Management, 2007).

Many factors affect whether an offender will commit a future sex crime. Assessments assist in determining what the risk level is with regard to committing a future sex crime. Sexual recidivism rates of sex offenders, overall, are relatively low, typically between 10 to 15% (Hanson & Bussière, 1998), making predictions difficult. No assessment is perfect. They can, however, provide an informed prediction, based on known factors, whether a person is at a low, moderate, or high risk of recidivating. Two false outcomes are possible (Craig, Browne, & Stringer, 2004). First, the outcome of an assessment can place someone in a high level of risk, and the person does not recidivate. This is known as a false positive. Second, someone can be assessed at low risk, but does recidivate, which is a false negative, and a more serious problem. The goal is to correctly predict level of risk and provide the appropriate level of supervision. This principle, applying the appropriate level of response based on a person's level of need, is inherent in the ***Risk, Need, and Responsivity Model (RNR)***.

The RNR Model is often applied to sex-offender treatment (Center for Sex Offender Management, 2007). It is based on the assumption that supervision and treatment are most effective when more resources are geared towards high-risk offenders, and also low-risk offenders are provided with fewer resources. Assessment predictions can assist decision making to appropriately direct and conserve resources, while at the same time increasing public safety (Gottfredson & Moriarty, 2006). Research has shown that providing a low-risk offender with high levels of treatment can actually lead to increased recidivism (Bonta & Andrews, 2007).

Within the RNR Model, ***criminogenic needs*** (i.e., crime-causing factors) are targeted for treatment (Andrews & Bonta, 2006). The RNR Model also recognizes that treatment should take into account individual learning styles, motivation level, and level of functioning (Bonta & Andrews, 2007). Although the RNR Model has been applied to offenders in general, recent research has shown that it has been effectively applied to sex offenders (Hanson, 2006). Assessments enhance the RNR Model, by utilizing resources most effectively (Center for Sex Offender Management, 2007), which includes conducting a thorough assessment to appropriately and effectively target people with the correct amount of treatment (Smid, Kamphuis, Wever, & Van Beek, 2014).

We discuss three broad categories of assessments in this chapter: (1) ***non-actuarial***, which are based solely on a clinician's judgment, (2) assessment tools that rely on objective measures, yet do not provide cut-off scores for risk levels, and (3) ***actuarial***, which involve assessment tools that provide cut-offs for levels of risk and are based on empirical findings from systematic research. Also, static and dynamic factors are critical to the assessments. ***Static factors*** refer to unchangeable or "fixed" factors related to an offender. They include factors that will not change in the future. For example, age at first sexual experience does not change over time—it is, therefore, a static factor. ***Dynamic factors*** can and do change over time. This can include a person's attitude toward treatment, for example, or employment status. Some assessment tools include either static factors or dynamic factors, while others include both. This chapter provides a summary of several types of assessment tools. These are just a few of the more widely used assessments and are not intended to comprise an exhaustive list. Also, to conduct an assessment, specialized training and education are required.

We also discuss the accuracy of various assessments. Each assessment has been tested with a broad range of samples. Assessments go hand-in-hand with treatment.

Thus, we will discuss various types of treatment, with an emphasis on cognitive-behavioral treatment—the most common type of treatment provided to sex offenders today (Moster, Wnuck, & Jeglic, 2008). Treatment is important, given that most sex offenders live in the community (Terry, 2013). Even those who receive prison sentences will eventually be released and returned to the community.

# OVERVIEW OF SEX-OFFENDER ASSESSMENTS

Assessing sex offenders is not new, yet it was not until the 1980s and 1990s that many assessment tools were developed. This section provides a history of the development of sex-offender assessment tools. The goals of the assessments are also provided, with an acknowledgement that this is still a developing area. Also noteworthy, methods for utilizing sex-offender assessments are discussed.

## Development of Assessments

Two generations of sex-offender assessments have been identified in the existing literature. The first generation involved "unstructured professional judgment." This type of assessment yielded more wrong than accurate results (Monahan, 1981). They were based on clinicians interviewing clients and basing their judgment on psychological constructs (Hanson, 2009). Thus, formal risk factors were not identified or relied upon to develop a prediction of risk. They were ineffective and only distinguished the most dangerous from the least dangerous (Mossman, 1994).

The second generation of sex-offender assessments has existed for a long time, although their use increased substantially during the 1990s. They involve relying on empirical-based risk factors that correlate with recidivism, such as criminal history and offender demographics. In 1928, Burgess developed an empirical-based recidivism assessment for parolees. Although not widely used, similar assessments were developed subsequently and heavily relied upon. For example, the Statistical Information on Recidivism Scale (SIR) was adopted by the Correctional Services of Canada to predict recidivism of male sex offenders. (It was later revised to the Statistical Information on Recidivism Scale-Revised 1.) These scales were not viewed as psychological tools, but rather were created to be used by criminal-justice decision makers. Another important assessment, Hare's psychopathy scale (*Psychopathy Checklist-Revised*), assesses psychological constructs as they relate to violence and criminality. In fact, many other assessments include the Hare psychopathy scale. Another psychopathy assessment tool is the *Levenson Self-Report Scale of Psychopathy*.

This second generation of assessments tools reflected a criminal justice model focused on community protection (Vess, 2011). As we will discuss in Chapter 11, the laws regarding sex offenders began to focus on protection of the community. Assessment tools began to identify high-risk sex offenders who required the most stringent treatment, including civil commitment.

## Goals of Assessments

Many of the actuarial risk assessments discussed in this chapter provide a score that relates to a risk level, usually low, moderate, or high. Much information is needed, however, to assess someone (Hanson, 2009). Decision-makers, for example, want not only an estimate of risk, but an estimate of the potential consequences of committing a sex crime and possible mitigating factors (Hanson, 2009). An example of use of assessments is presented below in a summary of a bail hearing of an alleged sex offender accused of molesting a nine-year-old girl:

> The judge was provided a document, called a superform, which generally spells out why police believe there is probable cause to hold someone in jail … As a district court judge, [she] is asked to determine if police have proven that enough probable cause exists for the arrest. She is also asked to decide if bail is warranted. She is expected to consider whether the defendant poses a danger to the community and is likely to commit a violent offense, or if the defendant is likely to interfere with the administration of justice … [The judge] declined to discuss [the defendant's] case specifically, saying it wouldn't be appropriate for her to talk about a case now pending … In general, she said that she considers what information the police have provided in the superform. She also considers the static adult risk assessment, which uses a person's age, gender, and criminal history to predict future behavior. She also may hear from alleged victims or from people who support the accused. "These are difficult decisions. We take them very seriously. We're talking about a person's freedom and also the potential effects on the alleged victims and the effects on the public" [the judge] said. "We do the best we can with the information we have. We don't have the benefit of hindsight or a crystal ball."
>
> (Hefley, 2014, n. p.)

In this case, the accused was released from jail without bail. This, however, is not always the case, as the judge may order a specific bail amount for the defendant to be released. Also, the judge can deny bail altogether, requiring the defendant to remain in jail until trial. The assessments discussed in this chapter are often used for similar purposes portrayed in the above scenario.

One researcher (Hanson, 2009, p. 173) provided a list of what assessments should do:

- Assess risk factors whose nature, origins, and effects can be understood.
- Enable reliable and valid assessment of clinically useful causal factors.
- Provide precise estimates of recidivism risk.
- Allow all relevant factors to be considered.
- Inform the development of treatment targets and risk management strategies.
- Allow the assessment of both long-term and short-term changes in risk.

- Incorporate protective factors as well as risk factors.
- Facilitate engaging the patient/offender in the assessment process.
- Be easy to implement in a broad range of settings.

The assessments that exist today fall short of addressing all of the above goals. Thus, we have much more progress to make.

### Common Risk Factors

Research has identified several risk factors correlated with sexual recidivism among known sex offenders (Hanson, Helmus, & Thornton, 2010). These factors include demographics, prior offense history, and several psychosocial factors. In order from least to most correlated, these factors include: personal distress/mood disorder, psychosis, violence used in the index offense, substance abuse, prior violent offense, low intelligence, a juvenile criminal record, a prior adult criminal record, age, negative/criminal companions, antisocial personality disorder/psychopathy, and deviant sexual interests (Hanson & Bussière, 1998; Hanson & Morton-Bourgon, 2005; Mann, Hanson, & Thornton, 2010). Each of these known correlates is included in the assessment tools discussed in this chapter.

## SEX-OFFENDER ASSESSMENT TOOLS

There are essentially three broad categories of sex-offender assessment tools. First, non-actuarial assessments of sex offenders rely exclusively on clinical judgments. Second, a sort of hybrid type of assessment includes clinical judgment along with some objective measurement. These types of assessments, however, do not provide a cut-off score for risk levels. Third, actuarial assessments include empirically-derived scales that have been validated (Monahan, 1996) and usually provide some sort of cut-off score for various levels of risk. Typically, non-actuarial assessments are combined with other assessment types (Tully, Chou, & Browne, 2013). The following factors are usually included in a non-actuarial assessment of an offender:

- Developmental history.
- Intellectual and cognitive functioning.
- Educational achievement academic performance.
- Employment, recreation, and leisure.
- Physical health.
- Psychological adjustment, mental health, and personality.
- Substance use and abuse.
- Sexual development, attitudes, behaviors, interests, and preferences.

- Family structure and dynamics.
- Interpersonal relationships, peers/associates, and intimate relationships.
- Prior legal involvement and history of delinquent and criminal behavior.
- Response to prior interventions and motivation to change (Center for Sex Offender Management, 2007, p. 3).

Non-actuarial assessments do not provide specific cut-off for risk levels, as the clinician makes that determination.

## Overview of Commonly Used Assessment Tools

A summary of assessment tools is presented in Table 10.1, followed by a brief discussion of each.

**TABLE 10.1** *Summary of Assessment Tools*

| ASSESSMENT TOOL | DEVELOPED BY: | PROVIDES CUT-OFF SCORES | DESCRIPTION OF ITEMS |
|---|---|---|---|
| I. Non-Actuarial Assessments | N/A | No | Relies on clinician judgment. |
| II. Assessment Tools with Objective Measures without Cut-Off Scores | | | |
| Phallometric Tests | Freund (1963) | No | Measures penile reaction to various images. |
| ABEL Assessment for Sexual Interest-3™ (AASI-3) | Abel (1995) | No | Measures sexual interest in children, cognitive distortions, social desirability, sexual victimization, past child sexual abuse by assessing visual reaction time and includes 10 self-report items (i.e., admitted sexual history of behavior, fantasy, alcohol and drug use, etc.). |
| Sexual Violence Risk-20 (SVR-20) | Boer, Hart, Kropp, and Webster (1997) | No | 20 items (yes/no) based on 3 areas: (1) *Psychosocial adjustment:* sexual deviancy, victim of abuse, mental illness, substance use, suicidal/homicidal thoughts, relationships, employment issues, and prior criminal history; |

*(Continued)*

**TABLE 10.1** (Continued)

| ASSESSMENT TOOL | DEVELOPED BY: | PROVIDES CUT-OFF SCORES | DESCRIPTION OF ITEMS |
|---|---|---|---|
| | | | (2) *Sexual offenses:* prior sex offense characteristics, denial of offenses, and attitude in support of sex offenses; <br> (3) *Future plans:* presence/lack of realistic future plans, and attitude towards intervention. |

**III. Actuarial Assessments**

| ASSESSMENT TOOL | DEVELOPED BY: | PROVIDES CUT-OFF SCORES | DESCRIPTION OF ITEMS |
|---|---|---|---|
| Structured Anchored Clinical Judgment (SACJ-Min) | Thornton (1997) | Yes | Conducted in three steps: <br> (1) Determine current conviction history; <br> (2) Assessing aggravating factors (i.e., stranger victim, male victims, never married, convictions for noncontact sex offenses, substance abuse, placement in residential care as a child, deviant sexual arousal and psychopathy); <br> (3) Assessing current behavior (dynamic factors). |
| Rapid Risk Assessment of Sex Offender Recidivism (RRASOR) | Hanson (1997) | Yes | 4 items: prior sex offenses, male victim, unrelated victim, ages between 18–25. |
| Static-99R | Hanson and Thornton in 1999 (and revised subsequently) | Yes | 10 items based on a combination of the SACJ-Min and RRASOR. |
| Static-2002 | Hanson and Thornton (2003) | Yes | 14 items based on five concepts: age at offense, persistence of offending, deviant sexual interest, relationship to victim, and general criminality. |
| Sex Offender Risk Appraisal Guide (SORAG) | Quinsey, Harris, Rice, and Cormier (2006) | Yes | 14 items to measure violent recidivism among sex offenders: lived with biological parents, adjustment problems, alcohol abuse history, marital status, criminal history, victim characteristics, age, mental health history, deviant sexual interest, and psychopathy. |

| ASSESSMENT TOOL | DEVELOPED BY: | PROVIDES CUT-OFF SCORES | DESCRIPTION OF ITEMS |
|---|---|---|---|
| Violence Risk Appraisal Guide (VRAG) | Quinsey et al. (2006) | Yes | 12 items to determine violent recidivism among sex offenders. To be used in conjunction with SORAG when the offender has a sex offense. |
| Risk Matrix 2000/S (RM2000/S) | Thornton (2007) | Yes | 7 concepts measured that predict future sex offenses. Based on the SACJ-Min and empirical factors associated with sexual recidivism. |
| Minnesota Sex Offending Screening Tool (MnSOST) | Minnesota Department of Corrections (2012) | Yes | 9 items to determine sexual recidivism based on criminal history, age, type of release from criminal justice system, completion of sex offender and substance abuse treatment, and male victim. |

## Assessment Tools with Objective Measures, but without Cut-Off Scores

### Phallometric Assessments

The first phallometric assessment, a penile *plethysmograph*, was developed in 1957 by Kurt Freund (Freund, 1963). The purpose was to measure penile engorgement while erotic visual material was presented. Later, several others introduced a phallometric test that measured change in the circumference of the penis (Bancroft, Jones, & Pullan, 1966). By measuring sexual arousal to various stimuli, it was believed that a person's true sexual deviance could be identified, given that his physiological response was involuntary. It can also be used in conjunction with *behavior al-therapy* approaches to modify one's sexual deviance (Marshall & Laws, 2003). A similar apparatus has also been developed for women, called a vaginal plethysmograph (Pras et al., 2003). An example of current-day usage of the plethysmograph is described below:

> Massil Benbouriche, a professor at the University of Montreal's school of criminology, invented the system to assess whether sex offenders are likely to re-offend. The system incorporates … [the] "penile plethysmography," which involves outfitting a patient's penis with a sensor-equipped "ring" and presenting him with visual and auditory stimuli … to assess their state of arousal … Benbouriche took the technique one step further by administering it in a cube-shaped "vault," creating an all-immersive virtual reality experience. Because sex offenders often try to throw the results of penile plethysmographs by averting their eyes from the contents onscreen, Benbouriche's virtual reality system uses "eye-tracking" technology to ensure that the

person inside the booth is keeping his eyes fixed on the images onscreen … many experts on pedophilia believe that sexual attraction to children is a fixed and immutable sexual orientation … it's unlikely that a self-avowed pedophile would be able to control his biological response to the stimuli onscreen …

(Dickson, 2014, n.p.)

Research regarding the penile plethysmograph is contradictory (Laws & Marshall, 2003). Many methodological problems exist in the research that has examined its use. No current standards exist for implementing its use (Marshall & Fernandez, 2000; Marshall & Laws, 2003). Information gained from a plethysmograph is not admissible in court (Dickson, 2014). Also, it is speculated that many pedophiles never act on their sexual arousal (Dickson, 2014). Thus, despite a sexual arousal to children, one may never sexually abuse a child. The plethysmograph, however, is still widely used today despite the existing problems (Laws & Marshall, 2003) and can be used for treatment purposes (Dickson, 2014).

### ABEL Assessment for Sexual Interest-3™ (AASI-3)

The *ABEL Assessment for Sexual Interest-3™ (AASI-3)* assesses not only sexual deviancy, but also a broad range of problems. It was developed by Abel in 1995. This assessment is unique in that it can be used for male and female clients. It has been validated through several research studies. "It is specifically designed to measure a client's sexual interest and to obtain information regarding involvement in a number of abusive or problematic or sexual behaviors" (Abel Screening, n.d.). The assessment is taken on a computer and subsequently sent to Abel Screening where a detailed report is provided.

Critical to the AASI assessment tool is the level of arousal toward a person. Research has shown that an individual will act in a sexual manner towards a person when he or she is sexually aroused by that person (Hanson & Bussière, 1996; Hanson & Bussière, 1998). The assessment involves showing a series of 160 photographs of various people with diverse characteristics (young, old, male, female, etc.). The subject is asked to rate the attractiveness of the person he or she is viewing. This assessment, however, considers the visual reaction time, that is how long the subject examines the photograph. The visual reaction time is used as a measure of who the subject is most attracted to (Tong, 2007). The AASI test is seen as a replacement to the plethysmograph, which as mentioned previously is an instrument that measures genital blood flow (Tong, 2007).

An advantage of this assessment is that it can be used with sex offenders who deny their attraction to children. Below is a description of the problem and how this assessment is useful:

It may be inevitable that some deniers will be ordered into community based treatment. Frequently these individuals are persons released from prison, or who are involved in child protective services cases where there is insufficient case information to generate a charge … This raises the question of how can clinicians break through denial in these clients, so as to enable moving on with the formalized sexual offender specific treatment … [Blasingame] directed a pilot project involving paroled sexual offenders … Two of the original twelve parolees were in complete denial when they presented for the intake interview, and two admitted only that they had been charged for molestation (but made no real admissions). After completion of their Abel Assessments, review of the victim information in their charges was found to be congruent with the sexual interest categories identified by the Abel Assessment. Three of the four admitted to their offenses when confronted with this information and the reminder that there would be a polygraph examination soon. The fourth client was returned to prison for a parole violation … The three had been charged with a total of three victims and while their original admissions after the intake were at one (1) victim/charge, their final admissions totaled nineteen (19) victims with approximately two-hundred and fifty acts committed against those victims, all in the age and gender categories on the Abel Assessment for Sexual Interest.

(Blasingame, 2001, n.p.)

### Sexual Violence Risk-20 (SVR-20)

Mental health professionals use the *Sexual Violence Risk-20* (SVR-20) for the purpose of evaluating an individual's sexual violence risk. The SVR-20 is based on six activities: (1) gather information about the examinee's personal, social, occupational, mental health, illegal, and other relevant behavior; (2) gather information by using a variety of sources and methods, including (but not limited to) record reviews, interviews, and psychological, physiological, and medical techniques; (3) gather information from the offender, relatives and acquaintances, the victim(s), professionals who have interacted with the examinee, and any other sources likely to yield useful information; (4) consider the offender's history and future exposure to risk factors; (5) critically weigh the accuracy, credibility, and applicability of the data that have been gathered; and (6) conduct ongoing risk assessment, with regular re-assessments for many examinees (Boer, Hart, Kropp, & Webster, 1997).

The results of the SVR-20 yield low, moderate, or high-risk levels of offenders. The developers of the risk assessment suggest a final report that addresses the following questions: (a) What is the likelihood that the person will engage in sexual violence if no efforts are made to manage the risk?; (b) What is the probable nature, frequency, and severity of any future sexual violence?; (c) Who are the likely victims of any future sexual violence?; (d) What steps could be taken to manage the person's risk for sexual violence?; and (e) What circumstances might exacerbate the person's risk for sexual violence? (Boer et al., 1997).

## *Actuarial Assessments*

Actuarial models are relied upon more often than clinical judgments alone because actuarial models are based on empirically derived scales that have been validated (Monahan, 1996). They also include a cut-off score for various risk levels. Actuarial models have outperformed clinical judgments by accurately predicting outcomes (i.e., sexual recidivism) in more cases than clinical judgment (Goggin, 1994).

### Structured Anchored Clinical Judgment (SACJ-Min)

The *Structured Anchored Clinical Judgment (SACJ-Min)* model was relied upon for the development of several other risk-assessment scales (Craig et al., 2004). The first two stages make up the SACJ-Min score, and are based on a person's conviction history and aggravating factors (stranger victim, male victim, never married, convictions for non-contact sex offenses, substance abuse, placement in residential care as a child, deviant sexual arousal and psychopathy). There can be a third stage, which includes an assessment of current behavior, including response to a treatment program (Grubin, 1998).

### Rapid Risk Assessment of Sex Offender Recidivism (RRASOR)

Those who have received training and have experience in actuarial risk scales can administer the *Rapid Risk Assessment of Sex Offender Recidivism (RRASOR).* Hanson found that general-offender recidivism scales do not work well in predicting sexual recidivism among sex offenders. Based on a large sample of approximately 2,500 sex offenders four items were highly correlated with sex-offender recidivism and became the RRASOR. The scores range from zero to six, with a higher score indicating high risk. This is one of the most widely used actuarial tools and is effective at accurately predicting sexual recidivism. Given that the items are static and there are only four of them, it is possible to score an offender with only the person's administrative records. The items that make up the RRASOR are also used in the *Static-99R* (Harris, Phenix, Hanson, & Thornton, 2003).

### Static-99R and Static-2002

Those who have completed a Static-99R training session can use the Static-99R. It is the most widely used sex-offender assessment scale in the world (National Institute of Corrections, n.d.). The questions assess the following: age at release, history of living with a romantic partner for at least two years, non-sexual violence committed during the index offense, convictions for non-sexual violence prior to index offense, number of prior sentencing dates, convictions for non-contact sex offenses, unrelated victims, stranger victims, and male victims.

The questions, although quite simple on their face, can be complicated to accurately score. The authors provide an 80-page manual explaining how to score each item. For example, the second item may be difficult to score, if the offender has lived with someone for two years, but it was a same-sex relationship. The authors clarify situations such as this, by noting that same-sex relationships should be counted in this category. Other situations are also clarified, such as the offender being incarcerated for much of his adult life. This is scored as not having lived with a lover for at least two years. Also, if the offender lived with a lover for two years, but with different persons, this item is scored as not living with a lover for two consecutive years. Clarifications are made for each item (Harris et al., 2003).

Each of the items is based on empirical findings showing that it is associated with risk of recidivism. For example, the first item is based on a correlation between offender age and the likelihood of recidivism. The younger the offender is at the time of the risk evaluation, the more likely he is to recidivate. It should be noted that the Static-99R is intended for male adults at least 18 years old (Beck & Harrison, 2008).

Each answer is given a score. The scores are then added for a possible range from 0 to 12. Based on their score, they are considered either a low, low-moderate, moderate-high, or high risk for sexual recidivism (Harris et al., 2003).

The *Static-2002* is based on similar items to the Static-99R and was developed to increase conceptual cohesion and clarification (Hanson & Thornton, 2003). A weighted score is calculated for each of the five sets of questions. Those scores are then totaled to yield one of five possible risk levels: low, low-moderate, moderate, moderate-high and high. This assessment predicts sexual recidivism slightly better than the Static-99R (Phenix, Doren, Helmus, Hanson, & Thornton, 2008), yet both are still widely used today.

### Sex Offender Risk Appraisal Guide (SORAG) and Violence Risk Appraisal Guide (VRAG)

The *Sex Offender Risk Appraisal Guide (SORAG)* and *Violence Risk Appraisal Guide (VRAG)* were developed by Quinsey, Harris, Rice, and Cormier (2006) and based on empirical research. When an offender commits a sexual offense, both should be used. For those without a sex crime, only the VRAG should be used. The purpose of the SORAG is to predict violent recidivism among sex offenders. Violent recidivism includes sexual recidivism. The VRAG includes 12 items and includes many of the items from the SORAG, but also asks about female victims and harm to victims. It also includes a childhood and adolescent component, which assesses childhood problems, including alcohol problems and conduct-disorder symptoms. The test items are scored, totaled, and given a risk level of either low, medium, or high.

### Risk Matrix 2000/S (RM2000/S)

The *Risk Matrix 2000/S (RM2000/S)* was developed by Thornton and is a sexual offense prediction scale. It was developed in conjunction with two other scales: RM2000/C, a prediction scale for non-sex offenses, and RM2000/V, which is a combination of the other two scales, predicting sexual and non-sexual violence. The RM2000/S was developed from an existing scale, the Structured Anchored Clinical Judgment (SACJ). Additional factors from the literature were added to the scale and tested for predictive accuracy on a sample of offenders, which led to the development of the SACJ-Min in 2000. Based on substantive findings in the literature and for the purpose of seeking a parsimonious model, the SACJ was modified to include three variables that were combined to identify four levels of risk. Aggravating factors in the SACJ were included in the model, which includes male victim, stranger victim, non-contact sex crime, and never married. All of these factors have consistently been found to correlate with subsequent sex crimes.

The RM2000/S scale assesses age, number of appearances for (any) crimes, number of appearances for sex crimes, and aggravating factors (male victim, stranger victim, non-contact sex crime, and never married). The scores are totaled according to the guidelines established by the author of the scale and yield low, medium, high, and very high risk levels (Thornton, 2007). This scale was first validated in 2003 (Thornton et al., 2003).

### Minnesota Sex Offender Screening Tool-3.1 (MnSOST-3.1)

The work for the Minnesota Sex Offender Screening Tool (MnSOST) began over two decades ago, and the tool has undergone several revisions since then, resulting in the latest version, *Minnesota Sex Offender Screening Tool-3.1 (MnSOST-3.1)* (Duwe & Freske, 2012). It is also one of the most widely used assessments. It includes nine items: (1) sentences for predatory offenses, (2) number of felony sentences, (3) number of harassment sentences (harassment, stalking, violate protective order, violate no-contact order, violate restraining order), (4) number of disorderly conduct sentences in previous three years, (5) age at release, (6) released without correctional supervision, (7) completion of both sex-offender and substance-abuse treatment, (8) sentences involving male victims, and (9) committed a sex/sex-related charge in public (Minnesota Department of Corrections, 2012). The totaled score results in one of three risk levels (Level 1, 2, and 3).

## Effectiveness of Sex-Offender Assessment Tools

A common method of assessing the effectiveness of predicting sexual recidivism is to test the tool with a sample of sex offenders. The assessment is scored for each person. Subsequently, the level of risk is compared to whether the offender actually recidivated. A statistical test is conducted, and the results are expressed as "area under the curve" (AUC). That number indicates the accuracy of the test in predicting sexual recidivism. For example, if a test places all those who do not actually recidivate in a low-risk category and places all those who do actually recidivate in a high-risk category, the measure is considered perfect. As indicated earlier, no test is perfect. Many of the tests have exceedingly high accuracy, as high as 0.9 AUC, where 1 corresponds to a perfect measure. The lowest AUC is 0, and any test that yields 0.5 or less is considered a failed test, or rather, no better than guessing. Thus, it does not accurately predict enough cases to warrant its use. Table 10.2 contains a summary of the results of a meta-analysis that assessed several sex-offender assessments (Tully et al., 2013). Most of the scales, on average, fall in the "moderate" range of predicting recidivism (Rice & Harris, 2005).

**TABLE 10.2**  *Summary of Actuarial Assessments Tools' Effectiveness*

| ASSESSMENT | NUMBER OF STUDIES CONDUCTED | AUC RANGE | AUC AVERAGE |
|---|---|---|---|
| Static-99[1] | 30 | .57 – .92 | .69 |
| RRASOR[1] | 13 | .42 – .77 | .69 |
| SORAG[1] | 9 | .67 – .77 | .68 |
| RM2000/S[1] | 8 | .58 – .76 | .67 |
| Static-2002[1] | 7 | .67 – .76 | .70 |
| SVR-20[1] | 5 | .59 – .83 | .70 |
| MnSOST-R[1] | 5 | .59 – .71 | .64 |
| SACJ-Min[2] | 1 | .67 | .67 |

Sources:

[1] (Tully, Chou & Browne, 2013)
[2] (Hanson and Thornton, 2000)

# PSYCHOPATHY

*Psychopathy* is a critical factor for many assessment tools. Psychopathy refers to a personality disorder that includes antisocial behavior, lack of empathy towards others and a lack of remorse for harming others. Those with high levels of psychopathy have a higher likelihood of committing crime. Treating someone with a moderate to high level of psychopathy can be difficult and may require a secure setting. Two measures of psychopathy are discussed here: The Hare Psychopathy Checklist Revised (PCL-R) and Levenson Self-Report Scale of Psychopathy.

A clinician administers the Hare Psychopathy Checklist Revised (PCL-R). The clinician conducts a semi-structured interview with the individual and relies on a checklist of 20 items. The clinician provides a score of either 0, 1, or 2 to each item, depending on the interviewee's response. Given that the clinician chooses which score to assign to responses, the clinician should be well trained with appropriate credentials for performing psychological examinations (Hare, 1991).

The first factor measures personality characteristics of psychopathy and includes an interpersonal facet and an affective facet. "Interpersonal" refers to a person's ability to communicate with others. This includes the following components: glibness (i.e., superficial charm), grandiose sense of self-worth, pathological lying, and cunning/manipulative. The second facet, "affect," refers to a person's display of emotional states. This includes lack of remorse or guilt, emotionally shallow, callousness/lack of empathy, and failure to accept responsibility for one's own actions (Hare, 1991).

The second factor measures antisocial behavior and includes the third and fourth facets. The third facet includes lifestyle. The lifestyle facet includes need for stimulation/proneness to boredom, parasitic lifestyle (living off of someone else's work, wealth, etc.), lack of realistic, long-term goals, irresponsibility, and impulsivity. The fourth facet reflects antisocial factors and includes poor behavioral control, early behavioral problems, juvenile delinquency, revocation of conditional release, and criminal versatility (Hare, 1991).

In addition to the four facets, a few other items are also included in the checklist: successive, short-term marital relationships and promiscuous sexual behavior. All of these items are relied upon for a clinician to assess the degree of psychopathy (Hare, 1991).

The Levenson Self-Report Scale of Psychopathy was developed in 1995 by Michael Levenson. The scale includes 26 items in a self-report survey (Levenson, Kiehl, & Fitzpatrick, 1995). For each item, an individual responds to what extent he or she agrees with the item, from agree to disagree, on a five-point scale. Sample items are:

- Success is based on survival of the fittest; I am not concerned about the losers.

- My main purpose in life is getting as many goodies as I can.

- I let others worry about higher values; my main concern is with the bottom line.

- People who are stupid enough to get ripped off usually deserve it.

- When I get frustrated, I often "let off steam" by blowing my top.

The scores are totaled for a final score between one and five on primary and secondary psychopathy, where primary refers to the emotional aspects of psychopathy and secondary refers to antisocial aspects of psychopathy.

An example of a sex offender who exhibited psychopathic traits is described in excerpts from a news article below:

Serial sex offender and convicted killer William Chandler Shrubsall is still too dangerous to be released from prison, the Parole Board of Canada decided … "You are noted to be able to camouflage your deviant behaviours" the parole board wrote …" Mr. Shrubsall used a bat to attack a clerk in a Halifax waterfront store during a robbery … Mr. Shrubsall beat, robbed and sexually assaulted a 21-year-old student in a Tower Road driveway. He repeatedly smashed her face on the asphalt. That woman's injuries were so severe that she required surgery to have her contact lens removed … He was also found guilty of aggravated sexual assault – choking and confining a 26-year-old woman he'd met at a Halifax nightclub in June 1998 …

"You admit to being extremely sensitive to slights, especially slights by females with whom you have a romantic interest," the parole documents said. "You admit to low self-esteem and take criticism as a personal attack … It was noted that you lacked empathy with your primary focus tending to be your own victimization. Of note, you indicated you were willing to forgive your mother and 'didn't know how.' "

(The Chronicle Herald, 2014, n.p.)

The sex offender in this description adheres to many of the criteria of psychopathy: lack of empathy, impulsivity, low self-esteem, and extensive criminal behavior.

## TREATMENT OF SEX OFFENDERS

The treatment of sex offenders has changed over time, as emphasis has been placed on different theories during the past several decades. Here, we will discuss several types of treatment that have existed over time. Currently ***cognitive-behavioral therapy*** is the most common type of treatment (Moster et al., 2008). Here, we discuss developments that led to cognitive-behavioral therapy to provide an understanding of the many elements that comprise it.

### History of Treatment Developments

It should be noted that although sex offenders are different and various theoretical models have been applied to various groups (e.g., rapists vs. child molesters), many of the treatment efforts involve one broad type of treatment. Cognitive-behavioral treatment is a broad type of treatment that does allow for variation among sex-offender clients. For example, ***cognitive distortions*** are found to exist among all types of sex offenders, but the kinds of distortions vary among sex offenders. For rapists, cognitive distortions include rape myths. These include: "no" means "yes," or if a girl dresses a certain way, she must want sex. For child molesters, however, the cognitive distortion may be that the child was acting sexually and must want to have sex. Cognitive-behavioral therapy allows a therapist to focus on cognitive distortions, in general, as well as specific ones as they arise in the context of therapy sessions.

A brief overview of the various assessments and treatment developments is presented in Table 10.3. It should be noted, that all of the developments, with the exception of treatment based on medical procedures (hormonal response and ***castration***), comprise today's cognitive-behavioral therapy. Phallometric tests, specifically, are used primarily for assessment purposes. Each of the remaining treatment developments is discussed below, along with the elements that make up today's cognitive-behavioral treatment approach.

**TABLE 10.3**   *Modern History of Assessment/Treatment Developments Leading to Cognitive-Behavioral Therapy*

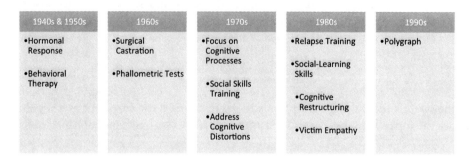

| 1940s & 1950s | 1960s | 1970s | 1980s | 1990s |
|---|---|---|---|---|
| •Hormonal Response | •Surgical Castration | •Focus on Cognitive Processes | •Relapse Training | •Polygraph |
| •Behavioral Therapy | •Phallometric Tests | •Social Skills Training | •Social-Learning Skills | |
| | | •Address Cognitive Distortions | •Cognitive Restructuring | |
| | | | •Victim Empathy | |

Sources: Laws and Marshall, 2003; Marshall and Laws, 2003; Terry, 2013

## Hormonal Response

Responses to sex offenders in the 1940s were based on a medical model (Terry 2013). It was assumed that a disease, rather than the choice made by a person (i.e., free-will), was the root cause of committing a sex crime (Terry, 2013). The first hormonal-response treatment (chemical castration) was used in 1940 when one incarcerated sex offender was given stilboestrol, a type of estrogen (Dunn, 1940). These types of medications are known as anti-androgens, testosterone-reducing medications. It was considered relatively successful, but was not widely implemented due to the negative side effects, which included feminization (Bowden, 1991). Later, other drugs (e.g., cyproterone acetate (CPS) and medroxyprogesterone acetate (MPA)) were used to reduce libido, and are still used today.

Whether chemical castration is effective for sex offenders is difficult to determine. Based on a thorough review of the literature, several researchers acknowledge that such treatment likely reduces sexual desire and sexual behavior (Rice & Harris, 2011). What is not known, however, is whether this treatment reduces recidivism among sex offenders. As noted by these researchers, "good evidence is sorely lacking … much more research is needed before … [chemical castration] has a sufficient scientific basis to be relied upon as a principal component of sex offender treatment" (p. 315).

## Behavioral Therapy

Behaviorist approaches for sex offenders were largely based on Pavlov's conditioning model or Skinner's operant-conditioning model (Marshall & Laws, 2003), as discussed in Chapter 2. It was a popular form of treatment for a variety of psychological maladies from 1920 to 1960 (Marshall & Laws, 2003). An assumption during this time was that sex offenders were acting on their deviant sexual thoughts. An example of a behaviorist treatment for sex offenders would involve pairing an undesirable stimulus (noxious smell, induced vomiting, mild shock, etc.) with the deviant sexual act. This is known as ***aversion therapy***. This type of therapy, however, has not ever been observed to lead to permanent changes in sexual behavior (Quinsey & Earls, 1990; Quinsey & Marshall, 1983).

## Castration

Castration can involve either chemical castration (as discussed earlier) or surgical castration. This type of treatment is based on a biological premise that if a person cannot maintain an erection, he will not be able to commit a sex crime that involves penetration (Mancini, 2014). It is also based on the logic that a reduction in sexual urges will lead to reduced recidivism among known sex offenders (Mancini, 2014). It is based on several assumptions that do not have complete empirical support.

First, it is assumed that only male offenders commit sex crimes. As noted in Chapter 7, women comprise a small, yet noteworthy portion of sex offenders. Second, it is assumed that forcible rape is the most common type of sex crime (Mancini, 2014). Statistics, however, show that other offenses make up a substantial portion of sex crimes (Federal Bureau of Investigation, 2016). These include child-pornography offenses and other types of victimization, including fondling (Terry, 2006). Third, it is assumed that sex crimes are motivated by sexual desire (Mancini, 2014). It has been documented in the literature that many sex offenders offend for reasons other than sexual desire. As noted in Chapter 3, several categories of rapists offend for reasons of power (Prentky, Cohen, & Segnorn, 1985). For such reasons, many organizations formally oppose the use of castration for sex offenders, including the Association for the Treatment of Sexual Abusers and the American Civil Liberties Union.

Surgical and chemical castrations are rare types of treatment. News sources have reported that at least 15 sex offenders in California have undergone surgical castration as a way to avoid civil commitment, which requires incapacitation of sex offenders indefinitely (Sealy, 2014).

Several research studies have indicated that sex offenders who have been castrated recidivate at lower levels than those who refused castration (Heim & Hursch, 1979; Stürup, 1972). It should be noted, however, that being castrated does not eliminate sexual recidivism. One of the study participants sought and obtained testosterone, for example, and subsequently recidivated (Stürup, 1972). This type of research is criticized on methodological grounds, in that those who volunteer to be castrated may have more desire to cease sex offending than those who refuse, thus affecting the results of the study (Rice & Harris, 2005).

## Cognitive Processes

In the 1970s, cognitive processes began to make their way into sex-offender treatment that was once solely based on behaviorism (Marshall & Laws, 2003). An example of this is the modification of sexual fantasies (Abel & Blanchard, 1974). This could involve encouraging people to have sexual fantasies that involve age-appropriate partners and consensual, non-deviant thoughts. Other cognitive processes that emerged included social-skills training and ways to address cognitive distortions (Terry, 2013), a relapse prevention plan, increased social learning skills, which include *cognitive restructuring* (Beck & Weishaar, 1995), and development of victim empathy (Marshall & Laws, 2003). Many of these are used in today's cognitive-behavioral treatment and are discussed below.

## Polygraph

A *polygraph test*, also known as a "lie detector test," does not directly detect lies necessarily, but rather is a physiological measure of blood pressure, respiration patterns, and skin conductance (i.e., perspiration) to determine truthfulness (Rosenfeld, 1995). The ability of a polygraph test to accurately assess truthfulness has been questioned and is debated in the field (Rosky, 2012). Discussions of polygraph use among criminal justice professionals usually involve the possibility of "fooling" the machine (i.e., countermeasures) and also the inability to use the results in court proceedings (Committee to Review the Scientific Evidence on the Polygraph: National Research Council U.S., 2003; English, Jones, Pasini-Hill, Patrick, & Cooley-Towell, 2000).

In 2003, the National Academy of Sciences provided an executive summary of the usefulness of the polygraph exam (Committee to Review the Scientific Evidence on the Polygraph: National Research Council U.S., 2003). They noted there are many limitations of assessing the ability of the polygraph, as many studies are based on "mock" situations and may not apply to real-world situations. For example, a mock situation is contrived, such as asking someone to steal one of three items (paper clip, scissors, or pencil) and then asking them to lie when asked about which item they stole. The response to a contrived situation may not be the same as lying about a real-world situation. The National Academy of Sciences, however, concluded that "polygraph tests can discriminate lying from truth telling at rates well above chance, though well below perfection." They limit this conclusion to those who have not been trained to "fool the machine" (i.e., countermeasures) and to specific-incident polygraph exams. A specific-incident polygraph exam usually involves a mock incident where the person is given a precise recent incident about which to lie (e.g., take one of several items and lie about which item you took).

The effectiveness of a polygraph exam depends on the examiner's experience level, verbal and non-verbal communication style, and style of engagement (Blasingame, 1998; Jensen, Shafer, Roby, & Roby, 2014). Other factors, such as mental disorders, mental retardation, drug and alcohol use, and refusal to cooperate can also affect the results of a polygraph exam (Jensen et al., 2014).

Although there are limits to the use of the polygraph, it can still be a valuable tool for criminal justice professionals working with sex offenders. An example of the usefulness of a polygraph test was seen in the abduction and murder of nine-year-old

Jessica Lunsford in Florida. During the investigation, a person of interest and a registered sex offender, John Evander Couey, confessed *after* he had submitted to a polygraph test (Candiotti & Courson, 2005). Couey stated, "you don't need to tell me the results, I already know what they are, could I have the investigators come back in?" (Hawke, 2005, n.p.). He apologized to the investigators for wasting their time. The results of the polygraph were not reported in the news. This shows how simply having someone submit to a polygraph can gain truthful information.

Furthermore, the process of exposing someone to a polygraph test yields substantial information that would not have been gathered otherwise. Research has found that those exposed to a polygraph test are more likely to disclose information, and more likely to cooperate with treatment (Gannon et al., 2014). The preparation for an exam also produces substantial information from sex offenders. Research has found that as an individual prepares for a polygraph test through answering a series of questions, that person is more likely to disclose information to avoid deceit (Blasingame, 1998).

Polygraph testing is used for assessment, management (English, 2005), and as noted earlier, investigative purposes for sex offenders. One researcher identified five types of polygraph-exam uses with sex offenders:

1. **Initial Sexual Offense Exam ination**: Assess the type and extent of offenses committed. It can be used to resolve discrepancies in information.
2. **Sexual History Examination**: Confirm an offender's report of his/her sexual history, such as any victimizations and sexual experiences.
3. **Compliance Examination:** Used to determine compliance with treatment and/or probation/parole restrictions. It can be administered every four to six months, or more frequently if needed. It can identify and deter high-risk behavior.
4. **Parental Risk Assessment Polygraph Examination:** Used to determine offender's risk to sexually offend against his/her own children.
5. **Specific Issue Examination:** Used to determine information regarding a specific issue or allegation. It can be used with any of the above-mentioned examinations (English, 2005).

Although the results of polygraph examinations are not generally admissible in a court of law, they can still be a valuable tool for criminal justice and treatment providers who work with sex offenders (English, 2005). Sex offenders have honed their skills to deceive others (Salter, 2003). Gaining truthful information from them can prove to be a difficult task, and polygraph examinations can be an effective tool to help with this.

More recently, alternatives to the polygraph test have been suggested. Rather than measuring a physiological response during a structured question-and-answer session, measuring an individual's brain wave channel has been proposed as a superior method (Bashore & Rapp, 1993). Measuring brain waves, however, is not without criticism; it may not be superior to the traditional polygraph test (Rosenfeld, 1995). More research is needed to fully assess these two methods.

## Cognitive-Behavioral Therapy

Cognitive-behavioral therapy is typically a structured, short-term type of treatment (Beck, 1995). It is deeply rooted in behaviorism, cognitive therapy, and a combination of the two (Beck, 1995; González-Prendes & Resco, 2012). This type of therapy is used for a broad range of psychological disorders, including but not limited to, depression, anxiety, post-traumatic stress disorders, and sex crimes. It began to emerge in the late 1960s and is presently the most common type of treatment for sex offenders (Laws & Marshall, 2003).

Cognitive-behavioral therapy has been described by the National Alliance for the Mentally Ill (2012, n.p.) as "a form of treatment that focuses on examining the relationships between thoughts, feelings and behaviors." Individuals are encouraged to explore patterns of thinking that led to self-destructive behavior, including committing sex crimes. The objective is for sex offenders to change their current thought patterns to reduce or eliminate undesirable behavior. The client and therapists actively work together (National Alliance for the Mentally Ill, 2012). The therapist is "problem-focused, and goal-directed in addressing the challenging symptoms" (n.p.). Thus, the therapist and client address specific problems (e.g., commission of sex crimes) and assist the client in selecting specific strategies for countering the thought process that leads to the behavior. Cognitive-behavioral therapy is an active intervention, and the client can expect to do homework outside of sessions with the therapist (National Alliance for the Mentally Ill, 2012).

Cognitive-behavioral therapy is based on three assumptions. First, it is assumed the client can access and be aware of cognitive processes that occur. This may require training and practice, as the client may not be immediately able to access such information. Second, it is assumed that one's reaction to events is highly dependent upon one's thinking. Thus, if someone has had a negative experience with a given event or person in the past, he or she may avoid a similar situation, given the history. Third, it is assumed that the way one thinks and feels about a certain situation, event, or person can be identified. Those thoughts and feelings can then be modified and changed (Dobson & Dobson, 2009).

An example of these assumptions can be found easily in cognitive-behavior treatment for sex offenders. For example, an offender may have the belief that it is acceptable to view children as sexual objects. This can lead to perceiving a certain situation (e.g., children in bathing suits playing at a local swimming pool) as a cue to commit a sex crime. This type of thought may be formed from a person's past experiences with children. This type of thought is a cognitive distortion and can be targeted for change through a myriad of processes. For example, it can involve group therapy, where others confront the person with information to the contrary—children are not sexual objects and should not be targeted for a sex crime.

Cognitive-behavioral therapy programs vary widely in how they treat sex offenders (Terry, 2013). Many commonalities, however, also exist among them. Terry (2013) identified nine goals of cognitive-behavioral programs for sex offenders. These include the following goals that offenders should be able to attain:

1. Recognize their problems and behaviors.
2. Understand the feelings that led to their deviant behavior.
3. Identify and eventually eliminate their cognitive distortions.
4. Accept responsibility for their behavior.
5. Reevaluate their attitudes and behaviors.
6. Acquire pro-social expressions of sexuality.
7. Gain a higher level of social competence.
8. Be able to identify their high-risk situations.
9. Understand the repetitive nature of their behavior and be able to break the sequence of offending.

It is also critical when applying cognitive-behavioral therapy to known sex offenders that not only are the needs of the offender addressed, but the community is protected as well (Moster et al., 2008).

Cognitive-behavioral therapy for sex offenders can involve several areas of focus, including addressing cognitive distortions, learning to manage emotions, increasing interpersonal skills, addressing empathy deficits, reducing **deviant sexual behavior**, and ensuring **relapse prevention**, along with learning self-management skills (Moster et al., 2008). Cognitive distortions are false beliefs that support offending behaviors (Marshall, Anderson, & Fernandez, 1999). The rape myths discussed in Chapter 3 are cognitive distortions. An example of this includes: if a woman is dressed provocatively, she must want to have sex. Research has found that sex offenders often have cognitive distortions that justify or minimize their sex crimes (Blumental, Gudjonsson, & Burns, 1999).

Through a process of cognitive restructuring, the therapist explains the role of the falsely held belief and provides the offender with information regarding how to correct it (Marshall et al., 1999). Subsequently, the offender distinguishes cognitive distortions from reality, paving the way for the offender to no longer have the cognitive distortion (Murphy, 1990). Group therapy also can be utilized during this process. Members of a group can evaluate an offender's false beliefs as he describes the sex crime in detail (Marshall et al., 1999).

Managing emotion is also a critical component of cognitive-behavioral therapy with sex offenders. Psychological well-being is positively related to how well one can cope with negative emotion and events (Endler & Parker, 1990). Offenders are asked to identify emotions that can lead to committing a sex crime. For some offenders, it may not be just negative emotions, but positive ones as well, that can lead to offending. For example, a positive event can lead to a sense of entitlement and subsequently lead to the commission of a sex crime (Howells, Day, & Wright, 2004). A diagram may be drawn of the offense cycle for the offender to identify the chain of events. Offenders are asked to be aware when they experience such emotions and be mindful of these as they occur (Moster et al., 2008).

With regard to interpersonal skills and sex offenders, such areas as intimacy, loneliness, attachment deficits, self-esteem, and relationships have been identified as of critical importance (Marshall et al., 1999; Moster et al., 2008). It has been theorized that interpersonal skills are directly affected by inadequate attachments formed in childhood (Marshall, 1989). Thus, communication skills are necessary to create and maintain intimate relationships with appropriate partners (Correctional Services of Canada, 1995). Topics addressed should include intimacy along with developing and maintaining appropriate relationships (Moster et al., 2008).

Empathy deficits should also be addressed in cognitive-behavioral therapy (Moster et al., 2008). Empathy refers to the ability to recognize another person's perspective by recognizing his or her emotions and having compassion for that person's feelings (Pithers, 1999). It is hypothesized that when sex offenders empathize with their victims, future sex crimes are prevented (Fernandez & Marshall, 2003). Techniques to increase empathy include the use of videos, victim-impact statements, and letter writing (to/from victim and offender) (Moster et al., 2008). Videos can involve documentaries where a victim has detailed his or her struggle with a sex crime. Victim-impact statements are often provided during the criminal justice process and involve victims detailing how the offender's action affected their lives. Occasionally, victims write letters directly to the offender about their experience. The offender can share with group members and discuss their reactions to this letter.

Cognitive-behavioral therapy for sex offenders often involves addressing deviant sexual behavior, which is sexual behavior that involves children and/or violent sexual activities (Dougher, 1996). This is usually measured during the assessment process by using a plethysmograph or the AASI-3. Several techniques are available to reduce deviant sexual behavior. One example involves covert sensitization, which involves introducing a negative stimulus (e.g., noxious smell, electrical impulse, or simply imagining a negative feeling such as nausea) while engaging in the deviant sexual behavior (Dougher, 1996).

A critical component to many cognitive-behavioral programs includes relapse prevention and self management. The goal is to assist sex offenders to maintain behavioral changes through anticipation and use of coping strategies (Center for Sex Offender Management, 2000). Relapse prevention involves development of a plan that identifies triggers and dangerous situations. Strategies are developed to avoid high-risk situations and to cope with them when they occur. For example, a child molester may be asked to babysit a friend's child. This is a high-risk situation for him, as he is sexually attracted to children. He can develop strategies for responses he may have to this type of situation, which may include telling the friend that he is not able to watch the child as he is not good with children or has a prior engagement.

## Treatment Effectiveness

A typical question one may ask about sex offenders and treatment is: can sex offenders be "cured?" In general, those who treat sex offenders do not discuss them in terms of whether they can be "cured"—rather, they are discussed in terms of *management*. Similar to an alcoholic, who is not cured but rather can control his or her urges to consume alcohol, sex offenders are taught to resist the urges to commit a sex crime, and focus is placed on developing and maintaining healthy relationships.

Assessing effectiveness is difficult, given the necessary methodological criteria needed (e.g., lengthy follow-ups and control groups are required). Studies to assess treatment are often constrained by those who drop-out of treatment along with the problem that few sex offenders recidivate. Measuring recidivism is difficult, as many sex crimes go undetected. Despite these constraints, several meta-analyses have been conducted to determine the effectiveness of treatment for sex offenders.

It is no surprise that many may believe that sex offenders cannot be effectively treated—as the research in the 1990s reported just that. One meta-analysis conducted in 1995 (Hall, 1995) reported that those in treatment had higher sexual-recidivism rates than those not treated. Just a few years later, in 1999, another meta-analysis found that those treated were slightly less likely than those not treated to sexually recidivate (Alexander, 1999). Hanson et al. (2002), in a meta-analysis of 43 studies, found those treated recidivated less compared to those not treated. More specifically, 17.5% of those who did not receive treatment sexually recidivated, whereas 11.1% of those treated sexually recidivated. Thus, treatment led to an average of a 6% reduction in sexual recidivism.

More recently, Lösel and Schmucker (2005) in their meta-analysis concluded that "the last decade has shown a strong increase and more positive outcomes in evaluations of sex offender treatment" (p. 119). In their meta-analysis involving 22,181 subjects, the treated offenders sexually recidivated 6% less than those not treated. While this may not seem like much of a difference, it translates into substantially less recidivism. A problem with sexual recidivism research is that so few of the offenders recidivate, often referred to as a low base-rate problem. Given that, one may ask what is the difference between 11.1% and 17.5%? The answer is that it means over a third (37%) fewer individuals in the treatment group committed a further sexual offense compared to the non-treatment group, a significant difference. With regard to sex-offender treatment, cognitive-behavioral programs currently have the best outcome.

## CONCLUSION

Given the heterogeneous nature of sex offenders, there is a need to determine their risk for sexual recidivism. A variety of assessment tools have been developed over the past several decades. One may ask whether there is a need for so many different types of assessment tools. One researcher recently noted that by relying on more than one assessment tool, prediction of risk is incrementally increased (Eher, Schilling, Haubner-Maclean, & Rettenberger, 2011; Hanson & Thornton, 2000). Thus, sex-offender treatment providers often use a variety of assessment tools. Most of the treatment programs for sex offenders today are based on cognitive-behavioral therapy. Although treatment in the past has revealed little impact on sexual recidivism rates, the more recent assessments of cognitive-behavioral treatment for sex offenders reveal lower recidivism rates when compared to sex offenders who have not received such treatment.

## REVIEW POINTS

- Risk factors for sex offenders to sexually recidivate are examined through the use of assessments, which rely on static (unchanging) and dynamic (changing) factors.

- The Risk, Need, and Responsivity Model (RNR) is often applied to sex offenders and suggests applying the appropriate level of criminal justice and treatment response based on the person's level of need. It also focuses on criminogenic needs, crime-causing factors that led to the commission of the sex crime.

- Non-actuarial assessments are based solely on a clinician's judgment and are less predictive of risk than actuarial assessments, which provide cut-off levels of risk and are based on empirical findings from systematic research.

- Common risk factors for assessments include demographics, prior offense history, and several psychosocial factors.

- Commonly used assessment tools for sex offenders include non-actuarial assessments (clinician judgment), assessments that include some objective measurement but do not provide cut-off scores (Phallometric tests, AASI-3, SVR-20), and actuarial assessments (SACJ-Min, RRASOR, Static-99R, Static-2002, SORAG, VRAG, and MnSOST).

- Assessment tools do not perfectly predict recidivism, but most are in the moderate range of predicting recidivism.

- Psychopathy is a personality disorder that includes antisocial behavior, lack of empathy, and lack of remorse for harming others, and can be measured by the Hare Psychopathy Checklist Revised (PCL-R) and the Levenson Self-Report Scale of Psychopathy.

- Many treatment developments (hormonal response, behavioral therapy, surgical castration, phallometric tests, focus on cognitive processes, social-skills training, addressing cognitive distortions, relapse training, social learning skills, victim empathy, and the polygraph) were emphasized prior to today's use of cognitive-behavioral treatment.

- Cognitive-behavioral therapy is the most common type of treatment for sex offenders today and focuses on thoughts, feelings, and behaviors of the offender.

- Sex offenders are not "cured," but rather managed to control their impulses. Those treated with cognitive-behavioral therapy recidivate at a lower rate than those not treated.

# REFERENCES

Abel, G. G., & Blanchard, E. B. (1974). The role of fantasy in the treatment of sexual deviation. *Archives of General Psychiatry, 30*(4), 467–475.

Abel Screening. (n.d.). Abel Screening. Retrieved January 15, 2016 from: http://abelscreening.com/products/evaluation-treatment-planning/aasi-3/

Alexander, M. A. (1999). Sexual offender treatment efficacy revisited. *Sexual Abuse: A Journal of Research and Treatment, 11*(2), 101–116.

Andrews, D. A., & Bonta, J. (2006). *The psychology of criminal conduct, 4th ed.* Newark, NJ: Lexis/Nexis.

Bancroft, J. H. J., Jones, H. G., & Pullan, B. R. (1966). A simple transducer for measuring penile erection, with comments on its use in the treatment of sexual disorders. *Behaviour Research and Therapy, 4*(3), 239–241.

Bashore, T. T., & Rapp, P. E. (1993). Are there alternatives to traditional polygraph procedures. *Psychological Bulletin, 113*(1), 3–22.

Beck, J. (1995). *Cognitive therapy: Basics and beyond.* New York: Guilford.

Beck, A., & Harrison, P. M. (2008). Sexual victimization in state and federal prisons reported by inmates, 2007. *Bureau of Justice Statistics, Special Report,* http://www.bjs.gov/content/pub/pdf/svsfpri07.pdf.

Beck, A. T., & Weishaar, M. E. (1995). Cognitive therapy. In R. J. C. D. Wedding (Ed.), *Current psychotherapies.* Itasca, IL: F. E. Peacock Publishers.

Blasingame, G. D. (1998). Suggested clinical uses of polygraphy in community-based sexual offender treatment programs. *Sexual Abuse: A Journal of Research and Treatment, 10*(1), 37–45.

Blasingame, G. D. (2001). California Coalition on Sexual Offending: Newsletter features; Articles drawn from 'Perspectives' the quarterly newsletter of the CCOSO. Retrieved from http://www.ccoso.org/newsletter/able.html

Blumental, S., Gudjonsson, G., & Burns, J. (1999). Cognitive distortions and blame attribution in sex offenders against adults and children. *Child Abuse and Neglect, 23*(2), 129–143.

Boer, D. S., Hart, P., Kropp, P., & Webster, C. (1997). *Manual for the Sexual Violence Risk-20.* Burnaby, British Columbia: The British Columbia Institute Against Family Violence, co-published with the Mental Health, Law, and Policy Institute at Simon Fraser University.

Bonta, J., & Andrews, D. A. (2007). *Risk-Need-Responsivity Model for offender assessment and treatment (User Report No. 2007–06).* Ottawa, Ontario: Public Safety Canada.

Bowden, P. (1991). Treatment: Use, abuse and consent. *Criminal Behaviour and Mental Health, 1*(2), 130–136.

Butcher, S. (2014, October 28, 2014). Judge finds sex offender needs rehabilitation rather than jail. Retrieved from http://www.theage.com.au/victoria/judge-finds-sex-offender-needs-rehabilitation-rather-than-jail-20141028-11d1d4.html

Candiotti, S., & Courson, P. (2005, March 20, 2005). Suspect in 9-year-old's death booked into Florida jail. Retrieved January 18, 2016 from http://www.cnn.com/2005/US/03/19/missing.girl/

Center for Sex Offender Management. (2000). *Myths and facts about sex offenders.* Washington, DC: U.S. Department of Justice, Office of Justice Programs.

Center for Sex Offender Management. (2007). *The importance of assessment in sex offender management: An overview of key principles and practices.* Washington DC: Government Printing Office.

Committee to Review the Scientific Evidence on the Polygraph: National Research Council U.S. (2003). *The polygraph and lie detection—Evaluation.* Washington DC: The National Academic Press.

Correctional Services of Canada. (1995). *Sex offenders and programs in CSC.* Retrieved January 20, 2016 from: http://www.csc-scc.gc.ca/text/pa/cop-prog/cp-eval-eng.shtml

Craig, L. A., Browne, K. D., & Stringer, I. (2004). Comparing sex offender risk assessment measures on a UK sample. *International Journal of Offender Therapy and Comparative Criminology, 48*(1), 7–27.

Dickson, E. J. (2014, November 4, 2014). 'Virtual reality penis sensors' are being used to monitor sex offenders. Retrieved January 18, 2016 from http://www.dailydot.com/technology/virtual-reality-penis-ring/

Dobson, D., & Dobson, K. S. (2009). *Evidence-based practice of cognitive-behavioral therapy.* London: Guilford Press.

Dougher, M. J. (1996). In S. H. R. Cellini (Ed.), *The sex offender: Corrections, treatment and legal practice* (pp. 15–11–15–18). Kingston, NJ: Civic Research Institute.

Dunn, C. W. (1940). Stilbestrol-induced gynecomastia in the male. *Journal of the American Medical Association, 115*(26), 2263–2264.

Duwe, G., & Freske, P. J. (2012). Using logistic regression modeling to predict sexual recidivism: The Minnesota Sex Offender Screening Tool-3 (MnSOST-3). *Sexual Abuse: A Journal of Research and Treatment,* Advance online publication: DOI 10.1177/1079063211429470.

Eher, R., Schilling, F., Haubner-Maclean, T., & Rettenberger, M. (2011). Dynamic risk assessment in sexual offenders using STABLE-2000 and the STABLE-2007: An investigation of predictive and incremental validity. *Sexual Abuse: A Journal of Research and Treatment, 24*(1), 5–28.

Endler, N. S., & Parker, D. A. (1990). Multidimensional assessment of coping: A critical evaluation. *Journal of Personality and Social Psychology, 58*(5), 844–854.

English, K. (2005). *To tell the truth: The latest in polygraph research.* Paper presented at the Illinois Association for the Treatment of Sexual Abuse, Normal, IL.

English, K., Jones, L., Pasini-Hill, D., Patrick, D., & Cooley-Towell, S. (2000). *The value of polygraph testing in sex offender management.* Washington DC: U.S. Department of Justice, National Institute of Justice.

Federal Bureau of Investigation. (2014). *National Incident-Based Reporting System: 2012.* Washington DC: Government Printing Office. Retrieved January 15, 2016 from https://www.fbi.gov/about-us/cjis/ucr/nibrs/2012/data-tables.

Fernandez, Y. M., & Marshall, W. L. (2003). Victim empathy, social self-esteem, and psychopathy in rapists. *Sexual Abuse: A Journal of Research and Treatment, 15*(1), 11–26.

Freund, K. (1963). A laboratory method for diagnosing predominance of homo- or hetero-erotic interest in the male. *Behaviour Research and Therapy, 1*(1), 85–93.

Gannon, T. A., Wood, J. L., Pina, A., Tyler, N., Barnoux, M. F., & Vasquez, E. A. (2014). An evaluation of mandatory polygraph testing for sexual offenders in the United Kingdom. *Sexual Abuse: A Journal of Research and Treatment, 26*(2), 178–203.

Goggin, C. E. (1994). *Clinical versus actuarial prediction: A meta-analysis.* University of New Brunswick. St. John, New Brunswick, Canada.

González-Prendes, A. A., & Resco, S. M. (2012). Cogntive-behavioral therapy. In S. Ringel & J. Brandell (Eds.), *Trauma: Contemporary directions in theory, practice, and research* (pp. 14–40). Thousand Oaks, CA: Sage Publications, Inc.

Gottfredson, S. D., & Moriarty, L. J. (2006). Clinical versus actuarial judgments in criminal justice decisions: Should one replace the other. *Federal Probation, 15*(2), 15–18.

Grubin, D. (1998). *Sex offending against children: Understanding the risk.* Home Office Research, Development, and Statistics Directorate research findings, Police Research

Series (Paper 99). London, UK: Research, Development, and Statistics Directorate, Policing and Reducing Crime Unit.

Hall, G. C. N. (1995). Sexual offender recidivism revisited: A meta-analysis of recent treatment studies. *Journal of Consulting and Clinical Psychology, 63*(5), 802–809.

Hanson, R. K. (2006). Long-term follow-up studies are difficult: Comment on Langevin et al. (2004). *Canadian Journal of Criminology and Criminal Justice, 48*(1), 103–105.

Hanson, R. K. (2009). The psychological assessment of risk for crime and violence. *Canadian Psychology, 50*(3), 172–182.

Hanson, K., & Bussière, M. T. (1996). *Predictors of sexual offender recidivism: A meta-analysis (1996–04)*. Ottawa: Canada: Department of the Solicitor General of Canada.

Hanson, R. K., & Bussière, M. T. (1998). Predicting relapse: A meta-analysis of sexual offender recidivism studies. *Journal of Consulting and Clinical Psychology, 66*(2), 348–362.

Hanson, R. K., Gordon, A., Harris, A. J. R., Marques, J. K., Murphy, W. D., Quinsey, V. L., & Seto, M. C. (2002). First report of the collaborative outcome data project on the effectiveness of psychological treatment for sex offenders. *Sexual Abuse: A Journal of Research and Treatment, 14*(2), 169–194.

Hanson, R. K., Helmus, L., & Thornton, D. (2010). Predicting recidivism amongst sexual offenders: A multi-site study of Static-2002. *Law and Human Behavior, 34*(3), 198–211. doi:10.1007/s10979–009–9180–1

Hanson, R. K., & Morton-Bourgon, K. E. (2005). The characteristics of persistent sexual offenders: A meta-analysis of recidivism studies. *Journal of Consulting and Clinical Psychology, 73*(6), 1154–1163.

Hanson, R. K., & Thornton, D. (2000). Improving risk assessments for sex offenders: A comparison of three actuarial scales. *Law and Human Behavior, 24*(1), 119–136.

Hanson, R. K., & Thornton, D. (2003). *Notes on the development of Static-2002 (User Report No. 2003–01)*. Ottawa, ON: Department of the Solicitor General of Canada.

Hare, R. (1991). *The Hare psychopathy checklist-revised*. Toronto: Multi-Health Sytsems.

Harris, A., Phenix, A., Hanson, K., & Thornton, D. (2003). *STATIC-99 Coding Rules Revised – 2003*. Retrieved January 18, 2016 from http://www.static99.org/pdfdocs/static-99-coding-rules_e.pdf

Hawke, C. (2005, March 18, 2005). Cops: Man admits killing Fla. girl. Retrieved January 18, 2016 from http://www.cbsnews.com/news/cops-man-admits-killing-fla-girl/

Hefley, D. (2014, June 6, 2014). Man released from jail without bail again a molestation suspect. Retrieved from http://www.heraldnet.com/article/20140606/NEWS01/140609502

Heim, N., & Hursch, C. J. (1979). Castration for sex offenders: Treatment or punishment? A review and critique of recent European literature. *Archives of Sexual Behavior, 8*(3), 281–304.

Howells, K., Day, A., & Wright, S. (2004). Affect, emotions and sex offending. *Psychology, Crime & Law, 10*(2), 179–195.

Jensen, T. M., Shafer, K., Roby, C. Y., & Roby, J. L. (2015). Sexual history disclosure polygraph outcomes do juvenile and adult sex offenders differ? *Journal of Interpersonal Violence, 30*(6), 928–944..

Lanterman, J. L., Boyle, D. J., & Ragusa-Salerno, L. M. (2014). Sex offender risk assessment, sources of variation, and the implications of misuse. *Criminal Justice and Behavior, 41*(7), 822–843.

Laws, D. R., & Marshall, W. L. (2003). A brief history of behavioral and cognitive behavioral approaches to sexual offenders: Part 1. Early developments. *Sexual Abuse: A Journal of Research and Treatment, 15*(2), 75–92.

Levenson, M. Levenson Self-Report Scale of Psychopathy. Retrieved January 20, 2016 from http://personality-testing.info/tests/LSRP.php

Levenson, M., Kiehl, K., & Fitzpatrick, C. (1995). Assessing psychopathic attributes in a non-institutionalized population. *Journal of Personality and Social Psychology, 68*(1), 151–158.

Lösel, F., & Schmucker, M. (2005). The effectiveness of treatment for sexual offenders: A comprehensive meta-analysis. *Journal of Experimental Criminology, 1*(1), 117–146.

Mancini, C. (2014). *Sex crime, offenders, and society: A critical look at sexual offending and policy*. Durham, North Carolina: Carolina Academic Press.

Mann, R., Hanson, R. K., & Thornton, D. (2010). Assessing risk for sexual recidivism: Some proposals on the nature of psychologically meaningful risk factors. *Sexual Abuse: A Journal of Research and Treatment, 22*(2), 191–217.

Marshall, W. (1989). Intimacy, loneliness, and sexual offenders. *Behavior Research and Therapy, 27*(5), 491–503. Retrieved January 20, 2016 from http://www.ncbi.nlm.nih.gov/pubmed/2684132

Marshall, W. L., Anderson, D., & Fernandez, Y. (1999). *Cognitive behavioural treatment for sexual offenders*. Chichester, U.K.: Wiley.

Marshall, W. L., & Fernandez, Y. M. (2000). Phallometric testing with sexual offenders: Limits to its value. *Clinical Psychology Review, 20*(7), 807–822.

Marshall, W. L., & Laws, D. R. (2003). A brief history of behavioral and cognitive behavioral approaches to sexual offender treatment: Part 2. The modern era. *Sexual Abuse: A Journal of Research and Treatment, 15*(2), 93–120.

Minnesota Department of Corrections. (2012). *The Minnesota Sex Offender Screening Tool-3.1 (MNSOST-3.1): An update to the MnSOST-3*. St. Paul, Minnesota: Minnesota Department of Corrections.

Monahan, J. (1981). *Predicting violent behavior: An assessment of clinical techniques*. Beverly Hills, CA: Sage.

Monahan, J. (1996). Violence prediction: The past twenty and the next twenty years. *Criminal Justice and Behavior, 23*(1), 107–120.

Mossman, D. (1994). Assessing predictions of violence: Being accurate about accuracy. *Journal of Consulting and Clinical Psychology, 62*(4), 783–792.

Moster, A., Wnuck, D. W., & Jeglic, E. L. (2008). Cognitive behavioral therapy interventions with sex offenders. *Journal of Correctional Health Care, 14*(2), 109–121.

Murphy, W. D. (1990). Assessment and modification of cognitive distortions in sex offenders. In W. L. Marshall, D. R. Laws, & H. E. Barbaree (Eds.), *Handbook of sexual assault: Issues, theories, and treatment of the offender* (pp. 331–342). New York: Plenum.

National Alliance for the Mentally Ill. (2012, July 2012). Cognitive behavioral therapy? Retrieved January 20, 2016 from http://www.nami.org/Content/NavigationMenu/Inform_Yourself/About_Mental_Illness/About_Treatments_and_Supports/Cognitive_Behavioral_Therapy1.htm

National Institute of Corrections. (n.d.). Offender assessment/screening: Static-99/Static-99R. Retrieved January 20, 2016 from http://nicic.gov/library/027582

Phenix, A., Doren, D., Helmus, L., Hanson, R. K., & Thornton, D. (2008). *Coding rules for Static-2002*. Ottawa, Canada: Public Safety Canada.

Pithers, W. D. (1999). Empathy: Definition, enhancement, and relevance to the treatment of sexual abusers. *Journal of Interpersonal Violence, 14*(3), 257–284.

Pras, E., Wouda, J., Willemse, P. H., Zwart, M., de Vries, E. G., & Schultz, W. C. (2003). Pilot study of vaginal plethysmography in women treated with radiotherapy for gynecological cancer. *Gynecology Oncology, 91*(3), 540–546.

Prentky, R. A., Cohen, M., & Segnorn, T. (1985). Development of a rational taxonomy for the classification of rapists: The Massachusetts treatment center system. *Bulletin of the American Academy of Psychiatry and the Law, 18*(1), 79–83. Retrieved from http://www.ncbi.nlm.nih.gov/pubmed/3995189

Quinsey, V. L., & Earls, C. M. (1990). The modification of sexual preferences. In W. L. Marshall, D. R. Laws, & H. E. Barbaree (Eds.), *Handbook of sexual assault: Issues, theories and treatment of the offender* (pp. 279–295). New York: Plenum.

Quinsey, V. L., Harris, G. T., Rice, M. E., & Cormier, C. A. (2006). *Violent offenders: Appraising and managing risk*, 2nd ed. Washington DC: American Psychological Association.

Quinsey, V. L., & Marshall, W. L. (1983). Procedures for reducing inappropriate sexual arousal: An evaluation review. In J. G. Greer & I. R. Stuart (Eds.), *The sexual aggressor: Current perspectives on treatment* (pp. 267–289). New York: Van Nostrand Reinhold.

Rice, M. E., & Harris, G. T. (2005). Comparing effect sizes in follow-up studies: ROC area, Cohen's d, and r. *Law and Human Behavior, 29*(5), 615–620.

Rice, M. E., & Harris, G. T. (2011). Is androgen deprivation therapy effective in the treatment of sex offenders? *Psychology, Public Policy and Law, 17*(2), 315–332.

Rosenfeld, J. P. (1995). Alternative views of Bashore and Rapp's (1993) alternatives to traditional polygraphy: A critique. *Psychological Bulletin, 117*(1), 59–166.

Rosky, J. W. (2012). The (f)utility of post-conviction polygraph testing. *Sexual Abuse: A Journal of Research and Treatment, 25*(3), 259–281.

Salter, A. C. (2003). *Predators: Pedophiles, rapists, and other sex offenders.* New York: Basic Books.

Sealy, G. (2014, March 2, 2014). Some sex offenders opt for castration. Retrieved January 20, 2016 from http://abcnews.go.com/US/story?id=93947

Smid, W. J., Kamphuis, J. H., Wever, E. C., & Van Beek, D. J. (2014). A comparison of the predictive properties of nine sex offender risk assessment instruments. *Psychological Assessment,* Advance online publication. doi: 10.1037/a0036616.

Stũrup, G. K. (1972). Castration: The total treatment. In H. L. P. Resnick & M. E. Wolfgang (Eds.), *Sexual behaviors: Social, clinical, and legal aspects* (pp. 361–382). Boston: MA: Little, Brown and Company.

Terry, K. J. (2006). *Sexual offenses and offenders: Theory, practice, and policy.* Belmont, CA: Wadsworth.

Terry, K. J. (2013). *Sexual offenses and offenders: Theory, practice and policy.* Belmont, CA: Wadsworth Cengage Learning.

The Chronicle Herald. (2014, November 18, 2014). Sex offender, killer William Shrubsall denied parole again. Retrieved January 20, 2016 from http://www.thechronicleherald.ca/metro/1251813-sex-offender-william-shrubsall-denied-parole-again

Thornton, D. (2007). Scoring guide for risk matrix 2000.9/SVC. Retrieved January 20, 2016 from http://www.birmingham.ac.uk/Documents/college-les/psych/RM2000scoring-instructions.pdf

Thornton, D., Mann, R., Webster, S., Blud, L., Travers, R., Friendship, C., & Erikson, M. (2003). Distinguishing and combining risks for sexual and violent recidivism. In R. A. Prentky, E. S. Janus, & M. C. Seto (Eds.), *Sexually coercive behavior: Understanding and management* (pp. 225–235). New York: New York Academy of Sciences.

Tong, D. (2007). The penile plethysmograph, Abel Assessment for Sexual Interest, and MSI-II: Are they speaking the same language? *The American Journal of Family Therapy, 35*(3), 187–2007.

Tully, R. J., Chou, S., & Browne, K. D. (2013). A systematic review on the effectiveness of sex offender risk assessment tools in predicting sexual recidivism of adult male sex offenders. *Clinical Psychology Review, 33*(2), 287–316.

Vess, J. (2011). Ethical practice in sex offender assessment consideration of actuarial and polygraph methods. *Sexual Abuse: A Journal of Research and Treatment, 23*(3), 381–396.

## DEFINITIONS

**ABEL Assessment for Sexual Interest-3™ (AASI-3):** A sex offender assessment that measures visual reaction time to various pictures for the purpose of determining a person's deviant sexual interests.

**Actuarial Assessments:** A method for determining whether an event (i.e., recidivism) will occur based on known factors. This method relies on statistical analysis of an objective measure.

**Aversion Therapy:** A type of behavioral therapy that involves pairing an undesirable stimulus with an undesirable behavior (deviant sexual act) for the purpose of eliminating the undesirable behavior.

**Behavioral Therapy**: A type of therapy based on Pavlov's conditioning model or Skinner's operant-conditioning model. It focuses on stimuli present and the responses produced.

**Castration:** The physical removal of the testes (physical castration) or providing a medication that reduce testosterone (chemical castration) for the purpose of reducing sexual recidivism.

**Cognitive-Behavioral Therapy:** A type of therapy based on behaviorism and cognitive therapy. It is used for a broad range of psychological disorders, including but not limited to, depression, anxiety, post-traumatic stress disorders, and sex crimes. It is the most common type of therapy used for sex offenders currently.

**Cognitive Distortions:** Minimize or deny the dangerousness of the behavior, justify it, and relieve the offender of responsibility. (Examples: children need to be taught about sex; children are very seductive; the child is too young to know what is happening.)

**Cognitive Restructuring:** A key component of cognitive-behavioral therapy. It involves a therapist explaining the role of a falsely held belief and provides the offender with information regarding how to correct it.

**Criminogenic Needs:** Factors that cause crime, such as young age, sex, antisocial attitudes and behaviors, delinquent peers, etc.

**Deviant Sexual Behavior:** Sexual behavior that involves children and/or violent behaviors.

**Dynamic Factors:** Factors that will change throughout one's life depending on one's situation. These include attitude towards work and employment status.

**Levenson Self-Report Scale of Psychopathy:** A 26-item self-report survey that assesses a person's level of psychopathy.

**Minnesota Sex Offender Screening Tool-3.1 (MnSOST-3.1):** A nine-item actuarial assessment used to predict future sex crimes. It is based on criminal history, age, type of release from criminal justice system, completion of sex-offender and substance abuse treatment, and male victim.

**Non-Actuarial Assessments:** A method for determining whether an event (i.e., recidivism) will occur based on known factors. This method relies exclusively on the judgment of a clinician.

**Plethysmograph:** An instrument developed to measure penile engorgement while erotic visual material was presented.

**Polygraph Test:** (Also known as a lie detector test) is a physiological measure of blood pressure, respiration patterns, and skin conductance (i.e., perspiration) to determine truthfulness.

**Psychopathy:** A personality disorder that includes antisocial behavior, lack of empathy towards others and a lack of remorse for harming others.

**Psychopathy Checklist-Revised:** An assessment developed by Hare involving a semi-structured interview to determine level of psychopathy one has.

**Rapid Risk Assessment of Sex Offender Recidivism (RRASOR):** An actuarial test based on four static questions used to predict future risk for sexual recidivism.

**Relapse Prevention:** A key component of cognitive-behavioral therapy. It involves identifying and preventing high-risk situations that can lead to sex crimes.

**Risk, Need, and Responsivity Model** (RNR): A guiding principle in the criminal justice system that subscribes to applying the appropriate level of response based on the person's level of need.

**Risk Matrix 2000/S (RM2000/S):** An actuarial assessment used to predict future sex crimes. The RM2000/S was developed from an existing scale, the Structured Anchored Clinical Judgment (SACJ), in addition to combining empirical factors in the literature.

**Sex Offender Risk Appraisal Guide (SORAG):** A 14-item actuarial assessment used to measure violent recidivism among sex offenders.

**Sexual Violence Risk-20 (SVR-20):** A non-actuarial assessment tool comprised of 20 yes/no questions used to measure one's risk level for committing future sexual crimes.

**Static Factors:** Factors that will remain stable throughout one's life. These include such factors as age at first sexual experience and whether one has been victimized as a child.

**Static-99R:** A ten-item actuarial assessment of sex offenders based on static factors used for the purpose of predicting sexual recidivism.

**Static-2002:** A revised version of the Static-99 assessment of sex offenders used for the purpose of predicting sexual recidivism.

**Structured Anchored Clinical Judgment (SACJ-Min):** An actuarial risk assessment tool used to predict future sex crimes. It is conducted in three stages: (1) determine current conviction history, (2) assess aggravating factors, and (3) assess current behavior (dynamic factors).

**Violence Risk Appraisal Guide (VRAG):** A 12-item actuarial assessment used to determine violent recidivism among sex offenders. It is to be used in conjunction with SORAG when the offender has committed a sex offense.

## CHAPTER 11

# Registration Laws and Civil Commitment of Sex Offenders

## CHAPTER OBJECTIVES

- Identify sex-crimes prevention strategies.
- Describe the development of U.S. sex-offender registration laws; identify the key components of federal laws regarding sex-offender registration.
- Identify the role of the Office of Sex Offending Sentencing, Monitoring, Apprehending, Registering, and Tracking (SMART).
- Describe Erin's Law.
- Discuss the assumptions and effects of sex-offender registration laws.
- Summarize civil commitment laws for sex offenders.

In the 1990s and through the 2000s, several U.S. high-profile cases that involved abduction, sexual assault, and murder of children or young adults led to a public outcry to take preventive action. State legislatures, and subsequently the federal government, responded with laws that required convicted sex offenders to register with their local law enforcement officials. This was later expanded to require notification of where registered sex offenders live, along with details of their offenses. More restrictive laws followed, and local jurisdictions were given minimum standards to implement and, to a large extent, license to develop additional restrictive guidelines, such as prohibiting sex offenders from living within a certain distance from places where children congregate.

This textbook considers many myths about sex crimes and sex offenders and how they are refuted by existing research. Many false assumptions have fueled recent sex-offender laws. For example, many people assume that identification of sex offenders on a public website will cause people to act more cautiously (e.g., supervise their children more closely) and that this will lead to a decrease in sexual victimizations. These assumptions, along with several others, are closely examined in this chapter.

This chapter provides an overview of sex-crimes prevention strategies associated with sex-offender registration and notification. Sex-offender registration/notification laws in various countries are identified, with emphasis on U.S. laws. This includes discussion of the *Jacob Wetterling Crimes Against Children and Sexually Violent Offender Registration Act (the Wetterling Act)*, the first law that required sex offenders to register with law enforcement officials. Subsequent to this, *Megan's Law* was enacted, requiring sex-offender information to be publicly posted. *The Pam Lynchner Sex Offender Tracking and Identification Act* required a national sex-offender registry. Given differences among states in how they implemented these laws, a federal law was passed, the *Adam Walsh Act*, to create minimum guidelines for sex-offender registration and notification. Each of these laws/acts was enacted in response to high-profile cases, followed by highly emotional public responses. The assumptions underlying these laws are examined.

In addition to enactment of laws about sex-offender registration and notification, the courts have shaped sex-offender policy by allowing sex offenders released from prison to be further detained through a process of civil commitment. The key U.S. Supreme Court case was *Kansas v. Hendricks (1997)*, which will be examined in this chapter, along with the current state of civil commitment policies among the U.S. states.

## SEX-CRIMES PREVENTION STRATEGIES

The primary goal of sex-offender laws is prevention of sex crimes. More specifically, the Association for the Treatment of Sexual Abusers (n.d.) states: "Prevention refers to efforts intended to stop the perpetration of unhealthy, harmful, dangerous, and illegal behavior and acts, as well as victimization and re-victimization by others." Three types of prevention strategies have been identified: primary, secondary, and tertiary.

*Primary prevention strategies* attempt to stop sex crimes before they occur (Townsend, 2008) and involve different components:

- Teaching people about healthy relationships, how to identify potentially abusive situations.
- Teaching people what to do if they suspect that someone is at risk of abusing or being abused.
- Working to change social structures and social norms that allow sex crimes to occur.

In this chapter, *Erin's Law* is discussed to highlight an example of a primary prevention strategy. Although this law is not a national law, it provides insight into how an individual state is responding to sex offenders.

*Secondary prevention strategies* occur after commission of a sex crime and involve an immediate reaction. The focus is on the short-term consequences of the crime. The goal is to reduce victim harm as soon as possible. This can include, for example, separating the victim and the offender, providing immediate counseling to the victim, and locating the offender. Secondary prevention strategies are, therefore, directed toward the victim and the offender (Association for the Treatment of Sexual Abusers, 2000).

*Tertiary prevention strategies* do not attempt to stop sex crimes before they occur, nor do they involve an immediate reaction to a sex crime. Instead, they attempt to manage the impact of such crimes (Association for the Treatment of Sexual Abusers, n.d.). The goal of tertiary strategies is to prevent further harm caused by sex offenders who have been apprehended and convicted. Federal prevention policy has focused most of its attention and funding on tertiary prevention policies. The majority of the sex-offender registration laws discussed in this chapter are tertiary prevention strategies. In this chapter, we will discuss several federal-level laws that are considered tertiary prevention strategies.

**TABLE 11.1**  *Sex-Offender Registration Laws Across the Globe*

| COUNTRY | SEX-OFFENDER REGISTRATION LAW ENACTED | PUBLIC NOTIFICATION SYSTEM | PUBLIC REGISTRY WEBSITE | INTERNATIONAL TRAVEL NOTICE REQUIRED | SCOPE OF REGISTERABLE OFFENSES | DURATION AND FREQUENCY OF REGISTRATION |
|---|---|---|---|---|---|---|
| Argentina | 2013 | None | None | No | Sexual abuse of minors, forcible sexual abuse of any person. | Indefinite duty to update address. |
| Australia | 2004 (national database) | None (at the national level) | No national website | Varies across states/territories. | Varies across states/territories. | Varies across states/territories. |
| Bermuda | 2001 | 2009[1] | None | No | Carnal knowledge, sexual exploitation, indecent acts, sexual assault. | 10 years. Must update name changes or residence changes. |
| Canada | 2004 (national) | None (at the national level) | None (at the national level)[2] | No[3] | Nearly all sexually-related offenses. | Ranges from 10 years to lifetime registration, depending on maximum incarceration term. |

| COUNTRY | SEX-OFFENDER REGISTRATION LAW ENACTED | PUBLIC NOTIFICATION SYSTEM | PUBLIC REGISTRY WEBSITE | INTERNATIONAL TRAVEL NOTICE REQUIRED | SCOPE OF REGISTERABLE OFFENSES | DURATION AND FREQUENCY OF REGISTRATION |
|---|---|---|---|---|---|---|
| France | 2004 | None | None | No | Serious sexual assaults, corruption of a minor under 15, certain other offenses, at the discretion of the court/prosecutor. | 10–20 years (depends on severity of offense). Verification every 6 months or annually. Address change within 15 days. |
| Germany | No national system | None | None | No | N/A | N/A |
| Republic of Ireland | 2001 | None | None | Yes | All (on listed schedule). | 5 years – lifetime (depends on severity of offense). Any changes to registration information must be reported. |
| Jamaica | 2009 | None | None | Yes | Most serious sex offenses. | Indefinite. After 10 years, offender can petition to be removed. Must verify annually and verify name/address changes within 14 days. |
| Jersey | 2011 | None | None | Discretionary | Most serious sex offenses. | Specified by sentencing court. Suggested minimum is 5 years. Address/name changes made within 24 hours. |
| Kenya | 2006 | Anyone with reasonable interest can inquire | None | Yes | Unclear from legislation. Any sex offense can potentially be included. | Lifetime. Address, employment/school, any other changes must be made in advance, where feasible. |
| Maldives | 2009 | Enacted law provides for public website disclosure | Authorized, but not yet established | | Most serious sexual offenses involving children. | Unclear. |

| COUNTRY | SEX-OFFENDER REGISTRA-TION LAW ENACTED | PUBLIC NOTIFICA-TION SYSTEM | PUBLIC REGISTRY WEBSITE | INTERNA-TIONAL TRAVEL NOTICE REQUIRED | SCOPE OF REGISTERABLE OFFENSES | DURATION AND FREQUENCY OF REGISTRATION |
|---|---|---|---|---|---|---|
| Malta | 2012 | None | None | Yes | Most serious sex offenses. | 2 years – lifetime, depends on severity. Must update any information changes within 3 days. |
| Pitcairn Islands | 2010 | None | None | Yes | Most serious sex offenses. | 2 years – lifetime, depends on severity. Must update any information changes within 3 days. |
| South Africa | 2007 | None | None | No | Any sex offense against a child. | 5 years – lifetime, depends on severity. Updating information requirements not developed. |
| South Korea | 2000 | Yes | Yes[4] | No | Any sex offense against a child. | 20 years. Changes in information must be reported within 30 days. Verify information required annually. |
| Taiwan | 2005 | None | None | No | Rape and indecent acts. | 5–7 years, depending on severity. Changed information must be made within 7 days. |
| Trinidad and Tobago | 2000 | None | None | No | Any sex offense. | 5 years – lifetime, depending on severity. Name and address changes must be made within 14 days of any change. |
| United Kingdom | 1997 | Varies | None | Yes | Nearly all sex offenses. | 2 years – lifetime, depending on severity. Any changes must be made within 3 days. |
| United States | 1994 (federal) | Yes | Yes | Yes | Most sex offenses. | 15 years, 25 years, or lifetime, depending on severity. Annual, semi-annual, or quarterly verification required. |

Source: Office of Sex Offender Sentencing, Monitoring, Apprehending, Registering, and Tracking (SMART). (2014). *Global overview of sex offender registration and notification systems*. Washington, DC: GPO.

[1] A risk assessment is required for disclosure of information. It can vary from limited disclosure to specific persons, but can include broad-casting/publishing information about the offender.
[2] Alberta and Manitoba have limited public-registry websites.
[3] Those who are in Canada for more than seven days, but convicted outside of Canada, are required to register.
[4] Offender information is posted for 5 to 10 years, depending on sentence received.

## Sex-Offender Registration/Notification Laws

The U.S. is not the only country to require sex offenders to register and notify the public where they live. Table 11.1 presents information about registration/notification laws in diverse countries. The table shows that the U.S. was the first country to require sex-offender registration. Many other countries followed suit by enacting their own sex-offender registration laws. Also noteworthy, a few countries (Bermuda, Kenya, Maldives, South Korea, parts of the U.K, and the U.S.) require some form of notification about where sex offenders live. In most countries, there would not be postcard mailings notifying people of registered sex offenders living in their neighborhood, as in the U.S. The U.S. is the only country that requires a *public* registry. This means that the information is maintained by a registering authority (usually local law enforcement officials) and the public can access a database (via the Internet). Most countries listed in Table 11.1 do not require registered sex offenders to notify law enforcement officials when traveling to them. The offenses considered registerable and the length of registration vary among countries.

## U.S. Sex-Offender Registration Laws

Registration of sex offenders in the U.S. began with the 1994 Jacob Wetterling Crimes Against Children and Sexually Violent Offender Registration Act. The Wetterling Act required sex offenders to register with the appropriate law enforcement officials, usually local police. The Wetterling Act, however, did not require information to be released to the public. That would come later.

The federal Megan's Law was enacted in 1996 and required that information about sex offenders be released to the public. The Pam Lynchner Sex Offender Tracking and Identification Act was enacted in 1996, requiring a national sex-offender registry (***National Sex Offender Registry*** (NSOR)). Subsequently, in 2006, the Adam Walsh Act, also known as the Sex Offender Registration and Notification Act (SORNA), was enacted. Also, in 2006, the name of the National Sex Offender Registry was changed to the ***Dru Sjodin National Sex Offender Public Registry***. This encompassed a national registry where anyone could seek information about registered sex offenders, regardless of where the offenders lived.

## *Jacob Wetterling Crimes Against Children and Sexually Violent Offender Registration Act*

### Background

Jacob Wetterling was nine in 1989 (Farley, 2008). Jacob, his younger brother, and a friend rode their bikes to rent a movie at a local store. They were riding back on a country road in St. Joseph, Minnesota when a man approached them, brandished a gun, and ordered them off their bikes. The man took Jacob and ordered the others to ride away without looking back. No one saw Jacob after that. Although no direct evidence indicated a sex offender took Jacob, it was speculated that is what occurred. It was not known to local police at the time, but discovered later, that halfway houses in the city housed sex offenders post-release from incarceration (Pennsylvania State Police, n.d.). Jacob's mother, Patty, became an advocate for missing children. She was subsequently appointed to a governor's task force, which led to tougher laws, including the Wetterling Act, which was part of the Federal Violent Crime Control and Law Enforcement Act of 1994. (As this textbook went to press, a convicted sex offender admitted to molesting and killing Jacob, and the killer led law enforcement officials to Jacob's remains.)

### Enactment

The Wetterling Act established guidelines for states to track sex offenders. Each state would track them for ten years after their release into the community. Sex offenders would have their place of residence confirmed once a year for ten years. If sex offenders committed a violent sex crime, their place of residence would be confirmed four times a year for the rest of their lives. Registered sex offenders also were required to update their address when there was a change. Information was released to the public only when there was an interest to do so—for public safety reasons (SMART, n.d.). Thus, information was rarely released to the public. This, however, would change with Megan's Law.

## Megan's Law

### Background

Megan Kanka was seven in 1994 when she was abducted and killed by a neighbor in Hamilton Township, New Jersey. The neighbor, a twice-convicted child molester, lured Megan by asking if she wanted to see a puppy. Megan was raped, killed, and dumped in a nearby park. Her parents, devastated, indicated they would never have left Megan unsupervised in their neighborhood if they had known a sex offender lived nearby. This led to "Megan's Law," requiring public notification of sex offenders (Farley, 2008; Pennsylvania State Police, n.d.).

### Enactment

Although the Wetterling Act had substantial consequences for convicted sex offenders, the federal Megan's Law, enacted in 1996, required that information regarding sex-offenders' registration be made public. The law was an amendment to the Violent Crime Control Act of 1994. Prior to Megan's Law, the focus was to inform law enforcement officials of sex offenders. This law broadened the focus to include community notification.

## Pam Lynchner Sex Offender Tracking and Identification Act of 1996

### Background

Pam Lynchner was a real estate agent in the Houston area. The following describes her harrowing incident that she survived:

One day in 1990 [Pam Lynchner] received a telephone call at home from a man who expressed an interest in looking at a house. Pam asked her husband, Joe, to come along for the showing. Pam stayed in the kitchen, and Joe went to another part of the house. A laborer who worked for the company Pam had hired to clean the house entered the house at the time of the appointment, claiming he had returned to finish the job. Police later theorized that it was he who had called to make the appointment. When Pam turned her back, the laborer—apparently unaware that someone else was in the house—grabbed her from behind, put his hand over her mouth, and attempted to rape her.

Hearing noises, Joe rushed to help his wife. While Joe struggled with the assailant, Pam ran to a neighbor's house for assistance. The suspect was arrested, convicted, and eventually sent to prison for 20 years. The suspect turned out to be a convicted rapist and child molester who had been released from state prison under a mandatory early release policy designed to ease prison overcrowding.

(Albro, 1997, n.p.)

Pam Lynchner's ordeal led to her becoming an activist for victims. This eventually led to the Pam Lynchner Sex Offender Tracking and Identification Act of 1996 (Albro, 1997).

**Enactment**

The Pam Lynchner Sex Offender Tracking and Identification Act of 1996 led to the establishment of the NSOR. It allowed the FBI to require sex offenders who lived in states with only minimal sex-offender registry programs to register on this national registry. It also required the FBI to periodically verify the addresses of the registered sex offenders. As needed, information could be released to the public. The Act also established guidelines for sex offenders to notify the registering authority when they moved to other states.

## Adam Walsh Act (SORNA)

**Background**

In July, 1981, Adam Walsh and his mother went to a department store in Hollywood, Florida. Adam saw a small group of other children playing a video game in the store. His mother left him with the other children and shopped in another part of the store, approximately 75 feet away. When she returned, Adam was gone. A security guard said there had been a small skirmish, and the children were told to leave. It was speculated Adam was taken by Ottis Toole, a serial killer, who confessed, but was never convicted (CNN, 2008; Pennsylvania State Police, n.d.). Toole was associated with another serial killer, Henry Lee Lucas.

Adam Walsh's father, John Walsh, became an advocate for abducted children. He later became the star of the television show "America's Most Wanted." This show highlighted heinous crimes and asked the public to contact police with any information that could lead to capture of the offenders. The show last aired in 2011 and claimed responsibility for the arrest of over 1,000 offenders.

### Enactment

The Adam Walsh Act, also known as the Sex Offender Registration and Notification Act (SORNA), became law on July 27, 2006. It replaced the requirements of the Wetterling Act and its amendments. In addition to creating a new federal felony offense for failing to register as a sex offender, it established minimum guidelines for sex-offender registration.

It is noteworthy that once these minimum guidelines are established, state legislatures and local governments can go further and enact stricter guidelines. For example, if SORNA requires a minimum of ten years of registration for a particular offense, a state can require more than that, such as 15 years or even lifetime registration (McPherson, 2007).

SORNA establishes three tiers of sex offenders, and each tier has specific registration guidelines. Tier III includes the most serious offenders, based on the offense committed. These offenders are required to register for life. They are required to renew their registration every three months. Additionally, any person who was a Tier II sex offender, a less serious tier, and commits a subsequent felony sex offense will become a Tier III sex offender, regardless of the tier level of the subsequent felony sex offense. The sex offenses that qualify a person as Tier III are punishable by at least one year of incarceration. They include:

- Sex acts with another by force or threat.
- A sex act with another who has been rendered unconscious or involuntarily drugged, or who is otherwise incapable of appraising the nature of the conduct or declining to participate.
- Sex acts with a child under age 12.
- Non-parental kidnapping of a minor (McPherson, 2007, p. 2).

Next, Tier II offenses are less serious than Tier III offenses, yet are considered more serious than Tier I offenses. Tier II offenders are required to register for 25 years. Again, anyone who was a Tier I offender and commits a subsequent felony sex offense will become a Tier II sex offender, regardless of the tier level of the subsequent felony sex offense. Tier II sex offenses include:

- Offenses involving the use of minors in prostitution.
- Offenses against minors involving sexual contact.
- Offenses involving the use of a minor in a sexual performance.
- Offenses involving the production or distribution of child pornography (McPherson, 2007).

Next, Tier I sex offenders are considered the least serious. They are required to register for 15 years. They renew their registration once a year. This tier of sex offender is a "catch-all" tier for sex offenders who are not Tier II or Tier III. It includes people who have committed misdemeanor and felony sex offenses that meet the criteria of a sex offense as defined in federal law (see: § 18 U.S.C. 16911 (5)) (McPherson, 2007).

In addition to establishing a tier system, seven key requirements/policies were established for all tier levels: (1) the information required, (2) location of registration, (3) forensic information kept on file, (4) public notification requirements, (5) guidelines for removal from the sex-offender registry, (6) application of retroactivity, and (7) application to juveniles.

With regard to the information required, all registered sex offenders are required to submit, *at least*, the following information to law enforcement officials:

- Name (including nicknames, pseudonyms).
- Social security number (actual and purported).
- Home, work, and school address.
- License plate number.
- Description of any vehicle he/she owns or drives.
- Date of birth (actual and purported).
- Email addresses.
- Pseudonyms used for instant messaging programs.
- Passport numbers.
- Phone numbers (cell phones and land lines) (McPherson, 2007).

Additionally, when sex offenders travel for more than seven days, they are required to notify their local law enforcement officials for the purpose of notifying officials in the destined location (McPherson, 2007).

With regard to the location, registered sex offenders are required to register where they live, work, and attend school. For their initial registration, they are required to register where they were convicted prior to release from prison, if they served a prison sentence. Typically, sex offenders begin registering when they are released from prison or after they are sentenced to probation. They are required to register within three days when not serving a prison sentence. If they did serve a prison sentence, they are required to register upon release (McPherson, 2007).

Forensic information sex offenders are required to submit to law enforcement officials includes DNA, fingerprints, and palm prints. Additionally, officials will maintain a copy of the violated law that led to the registration, and the offender's criminal history (McPherson, 2007).

The information sex offenders are required to submit to law enforcement officials is released to the public—with a few exceptions. For example, the victim's identity, offender's social security number, passport/immigration documents, and arrests other than the one that led to the registration requirement are not released to the public. Law enforcement officials may also opt to exclude the offender's employer and/or school.

There is a process for a sex offender requesting to be exempt from the registration requirements. This request can be made, however, only after the sex offender has been registered for an extensive period of time. For example, Tier III offenders, which include the most serious sex offenders, must wait 25 years. Tier I offenders must wait 10 years (McPherson, 2007). Offenders can make the request that their registered time be reduced only after maintaining a clean record (U.S. Department of Justice, 2008).

SORNA specifically allows for retroactive application of the law for some sex offenders. For example, offenders who are in prison or criminal justice supervision (i.e., probation or parole) for the registerable offense or for another crime are required to register under SORNA. Also, those who were already subject to a former registration requirement (i.e., the Wetterling Act), and those who are re-arrested for another crime (any crime) are required to register. These offenders are required to register in accordance with SORNA within three months to one year, depending on their tier level (Tier III: three months; Tier II: six months; and Tier I: one year) (McPherson, 2007).

Juveniles are not exempt from SORNA's registration requirements. Juveniles adjudicated in juvenile court and who are at least 14 years old and commit an offense that is similar to, or more serious than, the federal aggravated sexual-assault statute are also required to register. This includes any type of forcible rape or any crime that involves sexual penetration of a victim who is younger than 12. A *"Romeo and Juliet" clause* also exists, which allows for exemption of registration for those who have engaged in consensual sex with a victim at least 13 years old and involves an offender who is no more than four years older than the victim (McPherson, 2007).

In 2000, the *Campus Sex Crimes Prevention Act* (CSPCA) supplemented the Wetterling Act's standards. This required that institutions of higher education maintain and disseminate information about known registered sex offenders (U.S. Department of Education, 2002). Most universities/colleges report known sex offenders who work at or attend their institutions on a website.

In summary, SORNA represents an attempt to "level the playing field" by establishing minimum guidelines that all states are required to enact. Although it was passed with overwhelming support, it is still considered controversial by some. For example, here are titles of a few publications written about SORNA:

- The Adam Walsh Act: The scarlet letter of the twenty-first century (Farley, 2008).

- Quickly assuaging public fear: How the well-intended Adam Walsh Act led to unintended consequences (Enniss, 2008).

- Adam Walsh Act and the failed promise of administrative federalism (Logan, 2009).

- Adam Walsh Child Protection and Safety Act of 2006: Is there a better way to tailor the sentences for juvenile offenders? (Bowater, 2007)

- Throwing away the key: Has the Adam Walsh Act lowered the threshold for sexually violent predator commitment too far? (Lave, 2011)

- Children sex offenders: How the Adam Walsh Child Protection and Safety Act hurts the same children it is trying to protect (Young, 2008).

Perhaps the most debated aspects of SORNA are its retroactive application of the law and inclusion of juveniles, who are often seen as more amenable to treatment and exempt from many of the punishments of the adult criminal court system.

## Office of Sex Offending Sentencing, Monitoring, Apprehending, Registering, and Tracking (SMART)

SORNA also established the *Office of Sex Offending Sentencing, Monitoring, Apprehending, Registering, and Tracking* (SMART) to assist states with implementation of SORNA's requirements. It also tracks important legal developments regarding SORNA. At the end of 2015, only 17 states had fully implemented SORNA's requirements: Alabama, Colorado, Delaware, Florida, Kansas, Louisiana, Maryland, Michigan, Mississippi, Missouri, Nevada, Ohio, Pennsylvania, South Carolina, South Dakota, Tennessee, and Wyoming. (For an updated list, refer to: www.smart.gov). States that do not comply risk losing a portion of their federal funding. Officials from several states (Arizona, Arkansas, California, Texas, and Nebraska) have indicated it is too expensive to implement and have refused (Prison Legal News, 2015). Texas, for example, indicated it would cost $38 million to implement, but risk losing only $2.2 million of federal funding.

## National Sex Offender Public Registry

### Background

Dru Sjodin, a college student at the University of North Dakota in Grand Forks, went missing in 2003. She was on her way home from work. The investigation led to the arrest of Alfonso Rodriguez, Jr., who was a registered sex offender in Minnesota and had recently been released from a 23-year prison sentence. Five months after the arrest, Dru Sjodin's body was found. Rodriguez was sentenced to death for the crime; he had crossed state lines to commit it, making it an aggravated homicide. This case put a spotlight on identifying information on registered sex offenders, regardless of their resident state (SMART, n.d.).

### Enactment

SORNA included Dru Sjodin's law. It changed the name of the National Sex Offender Public Registry to the Dru Sjodin National Sex Offender Public Registry. This website (https://www.nsopw.gov) provides information about registered sex offenders across all states.

## State-Level Laws: Erin's Law

Erin's Law, unlike the federal laws covered thus far, is a state law. Also, unlike the laws discussed thus far, it is a primary prevention effort, meaning it is aimed at preventing sex crimes from occurring in the first place rather than responding after they have already occurred. It was championed by author, activist, and childhood sex-assault survivor, Erin Merryn. She introduced the legislation in her home state of Illinois. Merryn was a victim of child rape by an uncle from ages 6 to 8 years, as well as incest by an older cousin from ages 11 to 13. Erin's Law (IL PA 096–1524) was drafted and introduced in the Illinois Senate in early 2010 to amend the school code within the education law of Illinois.

There are two main components of the law: (1) creation of a task force to gather information about evidence-based sex-abuse prevention programs, and (2) implementation of sex-abuse prevention programs in Illinois public schools based on task-force findings. The law requires all public schools to adopt a prevention-oriented child sex-abuse program that teaches children, pre-Kindergarten through twelfth grade, age-appropriate techniques to recognize sex abuse, as well as educate school personnel and parents on child sex abuse, including warning signs and referral and resource information to support child victims.

After the successful passage of Erin's Law in Illinois, Merryn continued her advocacy efforts in other states. Many states have since passed Erin's Law, requiring schools to adopt sex-abuse prevention programs. By the end of 2015, 26 states had passed Erin's Law (see erinslaw.org for updated list). It is too early to ascertain the long-term impacts of the law, given that primary prevention efforts are predicated on changing social structures and social norms that allow sex crimes to occur. However, many policy analysts argue that a combination of primary, secondary, and tertiary prevention strategies is necessary to holistically combat sex crimes in our communities (Anderson, 2014). Therefore, adoption of Erin's Law across the U.S. may signal real progress.

## Summary of Registration/Notification Laws

The sex-offender registration/notification laws in the U.S. were enacted in the 1990s and 2000s, and they led to strict requirements for sex offenders to register with law enforcement officials. Registration (the Wetterling Act) then led to public notification (Megan's Law), and these laws were largely overhauled by the Adam Walsh Act (SORNA), which established minimum guidelines for control of sex offenders. Many states and local governments have established more restrictive guidelines, including posting of yard signs to identify a sex offender lives there and establishing "safe zones" to bar sex offenders from living within so many feet (500, 1,000, or even 2,500 feet) of places where children are known to congregate. SORNA co-occurred with the development of a national sex-offender registry (Dru Sjodin National Sex Offender Public Registry).

You may have noticed that each of the laws occurred in response to an assault, usually of a child or young adult. The loved ones of the victim often led the way to a new law in hopes of preventing more sex crimes. There is an untestable assumption that if Megan's parents knew about a registered sex offender in their neighborhood, she would not have been unsupervised and would not have been abducted. The same is true of the other victims. If a national registry existed, would Dru Sjordin have been abducted? Although these assumptions cannot be tested, we can review research on the observed effects of public registration/notification laws.

### Assumptions of Sex-Offender Registration/Notification Laws

The purpose of the sex-offender registration and notification laws has been to "provide ... the public with information about known sex offenders in an effort to assist parents and potential victims to protect themselves from dangerous predators" (Levenson, D'Amora, & Hern, 2007, p. 587). An obvious assumption is that registration and notification will make community members and the police more aware of the whereabouts of known sex offenders. This, however, may not be the case. A Gallup poll revealed that only 23% of adults have actually checked the registry (Saad, 2005). This was true of only 36% of adults with children.

Also, research has consistently shown that sex-offender registries are often inaccurate. One study found that the location of nearly half (49%) of all registered sex offenders in Massachusetts was unknown (Mullvihill, Wisniewski, Meyers, & Wells, 2003). Similarly, more than half of registered sex offenders who were assessed in Florida were either deceased, incarcerated, or not living at the address in the registry (Payne, 2005). As many as 25% of the addresses of registered sex offenders in Kentucky were wrong (Tewksbury, 2002). Although sex offenders are required to register their addresses, it cannot be assumed that this is always done.

It was assumed that registration laws would prevent child molesting and rapes. This, however, begs the question: have registration laws actually led to decreases in such crimes? Several studies have examined this question. One study of rape concluded "that the sex offender legislation seems to have no uniform and observable influence on the number of rapes reported in the [10] states analyzed" (Vásquez, Maddan, & Walker, 2008, p. 188). But does registration decrease the likelihood of recidivism by sex offenders? Maddan (2005) found that registered sex offenders recidivated at approximately the same rate (about 10%) as offenders who were not required to register. Later research also found no differences in sex-offender recidivism among those required to register and those not required to register (Zgoba, Veysey, & Dalessandro, 2010). Still another study, using different samples and study designs, also found that registration had no effect on recidivism rates of sex offenders (Letourneau, Levenson, Bandyopadhyay, Sinha, & Armstrong, 2010).

It is also assumed that convicted sex offenders have a high recidivism rate. As noted in Chapter 1, recidivism rates of convicted sex offenders are relatively low. The overwhelming majority of convicted sex offenders are not re-arrested for another sex offense. Thus, many of the underlying assumptions of sex-offender registration laws have not been supported by existing evidence.

### Effects of Sex-Offender Registration/Notification Laws

Many sex offenders have reported that registration decreases the chances they will re-enter their communities successfully (Levenson et al., 2007), which gives them a greater risk of recidivating. For example, one study reported that a majority of sex offenders suffer negative consequences from registration, such as depression, shame, and hopelessness (Levenson et al., 2007). Additionally, a majority of sex offenders reported job loss as a result of registration (Levenson et al., 2007). Thus, sex-offender registration laws can lead to limited access to education, housing, and employment (Bonnar-Kidd, 2010).

Many registered sex offenders also report being harassed. This includes threats of harassment and property damage (Levenson et al., 2007). As noted in Focus Box 11.1, many of these incidents involve serious physical harm, even sometimes death. Some people who commit vigilante acts against sex offenders view themselves as heroes.

---

*Focus Box 11.1   Cases of Vigilantism*

A gunman was given a life sentence, without the chance of parole, in Washington for gunning down two registered sex offenders. The gunman left behind a note taking credit for the murders and for "taking care of some problems." He was described as unremorseful and apologized only for the collateral damage he caused, not for gunning down the registered sex offenders. When he was captured, he admitted of a plan to continue killing registered sex offenders until he was captured by the police.

Source: (Bartkewicz, 2012)

A 20-year-old gunman turned a gun on himself in Boston, committing suicide as he was about to be captured by police. The gunman-turned-suicide victim had previously killed two registered sex offenders. The sex offenders were identified by going online to a public registry.

Source: (Adams, 2006)

Jack King from the National Association of Criminal Defense Lawyers in Washington described a case of vigilantism that occurred shortly after the sex-offender registry became public in the early 1990s. He described an incident where the brother of a registered sex offender was mistaken for a registered sex offender and was beaten nearly to death using a baseball bat.

Source: (Adams, 2006)

In addition to the sex offender being harassed, family members of sex offenders have also reported harassment (Farkas & Miller, 2007; Levenson & Tewskbury, 2009). Research has shown that relatives of sex offenders also experience depression, frustration, and targeted hostility from other family members who chose not to stay in contact with the registered sex offender (Farkas & Miller, 2007). This often leads to relatives distancing themselves from registered sex offenders, creating further isolation (Levenson & Tewskbury, 2009). Thus, it is clear that sex-offender registration laws can result in negative, collateral consequences that affect relatives of registered sex offenders.

There is a clearly documented perception that many community members believe sex-offender registration laws are useful in that they (1) create a better public awareness, (2) increase community surveillance, (3) deter recidivism by known sex offenders, and (4) promote child safety (Matson & Lieb, 1996). Thus, sex-offender registration laws, which were developed in response to several high-profile cases, have assuaged the public's fear through providing public information about known sex offenders.

The Center for Sex Offender Management, a reputable resource of sex-offender information, summarizes laws regarding sex offenders:

> [M]yths about sex offenders and victims, inflated recidivism rates, claims that sex-offender treatment is ineffective, and highly publicized cases involving predatory offenders fuel negative public sentiment and exacerbate concerns by policymakers and the public alike about the return of sex offenders to local communities. Furthermore, the proliferation of legislation that specifically targets the sex offender population—including longer minimum mandatory sentences for certain sex crimes, expanded registration and community notification policies, and the creation of "sex offender free" zones that restrict residency, employment, or travel within prescribed areas in many communities—can inadvertently but significantly hamper reintegration efforts.
>
> (Center for Sex Offender Management, 2007, p. 1)

## Additional Requirements for Sex Offenders

As noted earlier, SORNA established minimum guidelines (McPherson, 2007). State and local governments could pass additional requirements and limitations on registered sex offenders. These vary a great deal. Below are just a few of the requirements in different jurisdictions:

- Several counties in Southern California passed ordinances forbidding sex offenders to decorate their houses or keep any lights on. They are required to post a sign, "No candy or treats at this residence."

- Those in Louisiana are required to include their status as a sex offender in large red type on their driver's licenses (Silver, 2012).

- Some states require GPS devices, so the police know the whereabouts of known sex offenders (Silver, 2012).

- A law in Gonzales, Texas requires sex offenders to post a sign in their yard, indicating a sex offender lives there (KMOV, 2015).

- Manitowoc, Wisconsin forbids sex offenders from living anywhere in the city. Exceptions exist (e.g., offenders who lived in the city for at least five years prior to the law's passage) (Nesemann, 2015).

These are just a few of the current restrictions placed on sex offenders. One of the most common restrictions, however, is a residence restriction, which is discussed next in greater detail.

### Residence Restrictions

Residence restrictions typically forbid registered sex offenders to live and sometimes just be within so many feet (500–2,500 feet) of areas where children congregate, such as schools, daycare centers, and parks (Mustaine, 2014). Such restrictions are based on unsupported assumptions. For example, it is assumed that these restrictions effectively prevent sex offenders from living near areas where children congregate. Support for this has not been found (Birchfield, 2011). These restrictions also are based on the assumption that sex offenders encounter their victims by going to places where children congregate (Mustaine, 2014). Instead, sex offenders typically choose victims who are acquaintances or relatives (Colombino, Mercado, & Jeglic, 2009).

Although there are many negative consequences of sex-offender laws, one positive consequence is that such laws make the public feel good (Mustaine, 2014). Beyond this, documented benefits are difficult to find. In contrast, there are many negative consequences reported in existing literature. Registered sex offenders subjected to residence restrictions report a high degree of frustration and stress (Tewksbury & Mustaine, 2009). One of the most serious negative consequences involves housing. Nearly one-third of surveyed registered sex offenders in one study reported having to move because of residence restrictions (Tewksbury & Mustaine, 2009). Another one-fifth were forced to move because of either social pressure from the community or financial problems. Many sex offenders have no choice but to live in high-crime neighborhoods (Mustaine & Tewksbury, 2011).

Another serious consequence of residence restrictions is homelessness. Reporters in Miami, Florida highlighted the problem of homelessness among registered sex offenders. Pictured in many newspapers was a series of tents underneath the Julia Tuttle Causeway occupied by sex offenders who believed they had no choice but to live there. This was described as a consequence of a "patchwork of laws" that prohibited sex offenders from living anywhere else. This included a 2,500-foot residence restriction, preventing sex offenders from living near schools. Many organizations legally had their status changed to "school," which eliminated much of the city as a possible place to live. In 2014, the Florida American Civil Liberties Union filed a lawsuit, challenging these laws. The lawsuit alleged that criminal justice officials were aware of the problem and actually directed sex offenders to the tent cities (Flatow, 2014).

Some state and local officials have recognized the negative consequences of these laws. For example, in December, 2015, California reversed previous laws forbidding sex offenders from living near parks, schools, or other places where children congregate. The current law only forbids those who had molested children from living near such areas. Thus, more than 4,200 of the nearly 6,000 sex offenders will not be subjected to the residence restrictions (Associated Press, 2015). Perhaps this is a sign of what is to come: serious reconsideration of laws that were developed on a weak empirical foundation.

## CIVIL COMMITMENT LAWS FOR SEX OFFENDERS

Civil commitment laws have been used in the U.S. for approximately two decades. They allow for persons who meet certain criteria to be involuntarily institutionalized—typically in psychiatric institutions. Civil commitment laws vary from state to state. These laws typically have been used for people with mental illnesses who were in need of treatment. Beginning in the 1960s, emphasis was placed on community-based treatment as opposed to institutionalization (Brooks, 2007). Therefore, many civil commitments resulted in a mandate to community-based treatment, as opposed to in-patient psychiatric care. Most states require that there is an imminent danger that a mentally ill person will kill him/herself or someone else to be civilly committed (Szabo, 2013).

Only recently were civil commitments used for sex offenders. This allows for sex offenders who have already served a prison sentence to be civilly committed and their institutionalization to be continued. The offender can be continuously committed and, therefore, indefinitely institutionalized. We will discuss the background of civil commitment laws for sex offenders, along with their current implementation.

### Leroy Hendricks

Leroy Hendricks had a lengthy history of sex offending, and it was his case that led to civil commitments for sex offenders. Hendricks began his career of sex offending in 1955 when he exposed himself to two young girls. He was caught and pled guilty to two charges of indecent exposure. Later, in 1957, he was convicted of lewdness. This case involved a young girl. He received a short jail sentence for that offense.

Three years later, in 1960, he was working at a carnival when he molested two young boys. He served two years of the sentence when he was paroled. He was again arrested for molesting a young girl who was only seven. He received treatment in a state psychiatric institution and was released. Not too long after that, in 1967, however, he performed oral sex on an eight-year-old girl and fondled an 11-year-old boy.

He was imprisoned and refused to participate in sex-offender treatment. Despite this, he was paroled in 1972. He was diagnosed as a pedophile and entered a treatment program, which he did not complete. Soon after his parole in 1972, he abused two more victims—his stepdaughter and stepson. He continued to abuse them for four years. He also attempted to fondle two teenage boys. He was arrested and convicted and remained in prison until 1994.

## The Kansas Sexually Violent Predator Act

In 1994, the Kansas legislature approved the Sexually Violent Predator Act, allowing "sexually violent predators" to be civilly committed after they completed their criminal sentences. A sexually violent predator included:

> [A]ny person who has been convicted of or charged with a sexually violent offense and who suffers from a mental abnormality or personality disorder which makes the person likely to engage in the predatory acts of sexual violence, if not confined in a secure facility.

Sexually violent offenses included rape, indecent liberties with a child, sodomy, aggravated sodomy, indecent solicitation of a child, sexual exploitation of a child, aggravated sexual battery, and aggravated incest. It also included all of the offenses listed previously that were attempted or committed prior to the enactment of the law (1994). It even included a broad range of offenses that are considered "sexually motivated" (Kan. Stat. Ann. § 59–29a02(a)(Supp. 1996)).

The civil commitment process in Kansas requires the agency in charge of the inmate's release (i.e., the State Department of Corrections) to notify the Attorney General, along with a multidisciplinary team, of the inmate's imminent release. This affects inmates who may meet the sexually violent predator criteria. The multidisciplinary team, providing guidance to the prosecutor, decides whether to file a petition to commit the inmate civilly. The judge decides whether probable cause exists. The inmate is given the right to legal counsel, to present evidence, and to cross-examine witnesses. If probable cause exists, the inmate is transferred to a secure facility for a professional mental evaluation.

The last stage involves a trial that determines whether the inmate is a sexually violent predator. In addition to the rights given at the probable cause hearing, the inmate is also provided the right to elect for a jury trial (which requires a unanimous jury decision), a mental evaluation by a professional, and a standard of proof that involves "beyond a reasonable doubt." Probable cause refers to a standard that involves an adequate amount of evidence, whereas "beyond a reasonable doubt" refers to a stricter standard, requiring more evidence. If it is found that the inmate is a sexually violent predator, he or she is transferred to a secure facility, "until such time as the person's mental abnormality or personality has so changed that the person is safe to be at large" (Kan. Stat. Ann. § 59–29a02(a)(Supp. 1996)).

## The U.S. Supreme Court and the Sexually Violent Predator Act

The jury unanimously decided that Leroy Hendricks was a sexually violent predator and civilly committed him (*Kansas v. Hendricks (1997)*). The case was appealed to the U.S. Supreme Court.

The following excerpt is from the U.S. Supreme Court decision:

> Hendricks admitted that he had repeatedly abused children whenever he was not confined. He explained that when he "get[s] stressed out," he "can't control the urge" to molest children … Although Hendricks recognized that his behavior harms children, and he hoped he would not sexually molest children again, he stated that the only sure way he could keep from sexually abusing children in the future was "to die."
>
> (*Kansas v. Hendricks (1997)*, p. 355)

The U.S. Supreme Court established that civil commitments could be used for sexually violent predators. The Court specifically examined the constitutionality of civilly committing a sexually violent offender on the basis of (1) due process, and (2) double jeopardy. With regard to due process, it was specifically questioned whether a law could be created *ex-post facto* (after the fact). Second, with regard to double jeopardy, the U.S. Constitution prohibits more than one prosecution of the same defendant for the same crime in the same jurisdiction. Hendricks argued that this applied to him; he had completed his sentence for the crime he committed and could not be punished again. The U.S. Supreme Court, however, found that the Sexually Violent Predator Act is constitutional on the grounds that it is a civil proceeding, not criminal. This was a five-to-four decision among the Justices, indicating considerable disagreement.

Civil commitments are generally thought of as rehabilitative and protecting people from harm to themselves and/or others. This is as opposed to criminal proceedings, which are deemed punitive in nature. In 2010, the U.S. Supreme Court expanded the civil commitment of sexually violent predators to those with federal charges (not just state charges) in *U.S. v. Comstock (2009)*.

## Civil Commitment Laws in the U.S.

---

*Focus Box 11.2   An overview of Minnesota*

Minnesota has the highest rate, per capita, of civilly committed sex offenders. One source indicates that over 700 sex offenders are civilly committed (Bakst, 2015). Not a single sex offender who has been civilly committed in Minnesota has been released (Bakst, 2015). It costs approximately $120,000 each year to detain a sex offender in Minnesota. The facility resembles something akin to a prison: razor wire, locked metal doors, and regular headcounts conducted by the staff (Davey, 2015). The controversy is deeply

---

political. For example, the democrat governor, Mark Dayton, proposed a plan—later abandoned—to release a rapist who admitted to sexually assaulting over 60 women. He faced intense criticism. Attempts to provide psychiatric services, such as risk evaluations for sex offenders, have also met criticism (Davey, 2015). Recently, a federal judge, noting that none of the offenders were being "treated," ordered risk assessment of all of the sex offenders who were civilly committed (Bakst, 2015). The focus of conducting risk assessments is to develop a plan to rehabilitate the offenders so they can be released. The judge noted that indefinite commitments were unconstitutional. Sweeping reform measures were laid out, but a legal battle ensued and is still being dealt with in the courts.

Source: (Bakst, 2015; Davey, 2015)

Given that the U.S. Supreme Court has found that the Kansas and federal-level Sexually Violent Predator Acts do not violate any constitutional rights, states are allowed to develop similar laws. Twenty states have enacted such laws: Arizona, California, Florida, Illinois, Iowa, Kansas, Massachusetts, Minnesota, Missouri, Nebraska, New Hampshire, New Jersey, New York, North Dakota, Pennsylvania, South Carolina, Texas, Virginia, Washington, and Wisconsin (Association for the Treatment of Sexual Abusers, 2010). Although the states vary in how civil commitments are carried out, many have been condemned for the few who are rehabilitated through treatment and subsequently released from detention. As noted in Focus Box 11.2, Minnesota fights this battle, as they have the largest number of civilly committed sex offenders.

## CONCLUSION

As noted throughout this textbook and this chapter, there are many myths about sex offenders. More specifically, in this chapter, there are many myths in the form of assumptions about sex offenders and sex crimes that have culminated in what others have deemed as "feel-good" laws (Freeman-Longo, 1996). Thus far, there is little empirical evidence that such restrictive laws lead to fewer sex crimes.

Nevertheless, a series of U.S. laws have paved the way for other countries to implement laws to require sex offenders to register with law enforcement officials. In the U.S., this information is made public, and several states have enacted additional laws, including restrictions on where sex offenders can live. Only recently have there been hints of reconsidering such laws. For the time being, however, it appears these laws will probably stay in place for a considerable time.

## REVIEW POINTS

- Many countries have enacted sex-offender registration laws; however, the U.S. was the first to have these laws and currently has the strictest laws.

- The Wetterling Act, passed in 1994, was the first U.S. law to require sex offenders to register with law enforcement officials.

- The federal Megan's Law, passed in 1996, required that the public have access to information about registered sex offenders.

- The Pam Lynchner Sex Offender Tracking and Identification Act of 1996 led to a national sex-offender registry.

- The Adam Walsh Act, also known as the Sex Offender Registration and Notification Act (SORNA), became law in 2006. It amended previous laws, establishing national guidelines, including a three-tier system of registration requirements.

- The Office of Sex Offending Sentencing, Monitoring, Apprehending, Registering, and Tracking (SMART) is responsible for assisting with the implementation of SORNA laws.

- State and local governments are allowed to implement more restrictive laws than the minimum guidelines established by SORNA. This includes, but is not limited to, posting yard signs to notify others that a sex offender lives there, requiring sex-offender notification on drivers' licenses, and restricting where a sex offender can live.

- Twenty states allow sex offenders to be civilly committed to an institution after they have completed their criminal sentences.

# REFERENCES

18 U.S.C. 16911 (5)

IL PA 096–1524

Adams, G. (2006, April 18, 2006). Maine killings raise vigilantism fears (two sex offenders killed). Retrieved January 15, 2016 from http://www.freerepublic.com/focus/news/1617207/posts

Albro, W. (1997). She refused to give up. Retrieved December 15, 2015, from http://realtor-mag.realtor.org/news-and-commentary/feature/article/1997/04/she-refused-give-up

Anderson, G. (2014). Child sexual-abuse prevention policy: An analysis of Erin's Law. *Social Work in Public Health, 29*(3), 196–206.

Associated Press. (2015, December 14, 2015). California's sex offenders free to live near parks and schools. Retrieved January 2, 2016, from http://nypost.com/2015/12/14/californias-sex-offenders-free-to-live-near-parks-and-schools/

Association for the Treatment of Sexual Abusers. (2000, March 11, 2000). The effective legal management of juvenile sex offenders. Retrieved December 1, 2007, from http://www.atsa.com/ppjuvenile.html

Association for the Treatment of Sexual Abusers. (2010, August 17, 2010). Civil commitment of sexually violent predators. Retrieved January 3, 2016, from http://www.atsa.com/civil-commitment-sexually-violent-predators

Association for the Treatment of Sexual Abusers. (n.d.). Sexual violence prevention fact sheet. Retrieved January 11, 2016, from http://www.atsa.com/sexual-violence-prevention-fact-sheet

Bakst, B. (2015, October 29, 2015). Judge orders review of all Minnesota sex offenders in civil commitment. Retrieved January 2, 2016, from http://www.fox9.com/news/40851395-story

Bartkewicz, A. (2012, September 19, 2012). Unrepentant Washington vigilante who killed two registered sex offenders gets life in prison. Retrieved December 24, 2015, from http://www.nydailynews.com/news/national/unrepentant-washington-vigilante-killed-registered-sex-offenders-life-prison-article-1.1162753

Birchfield, K. B. (2011). Residence restrictions. *Criminology and Public Policy, 10*(2), 411–419.

Bonnar-Kidd, K. K. (2010). Sexual offender laws and prevention of sexual violence. *American Journal of Public Health, 100*(3), 412–419.

Bowater, B. M. (2007). Adam Walsh Child Protection and Safety Act of 2006: Is there a better way to tailor the sentences for juvenile sex offenders? *Catholic University Law Review, 57*(3), 817–851.

Brooks, R. (2007). Psychiatrists' opinions about involuntary civil commitments: Results of a national survey. *Journal of American Academy of Psychiatry and the Law, 35*(2), 219–228.

Center for Sex Offender Management. (2007). Managing the challenges of sex offender reentry. Retrieved January 2, 2016, from http://www.csom.org/pubs/reentry_brief.pdf

CNN. (2008, December 16, 2008). Police: Drifter killed Adam Walsh in 1981. Retrieved January 3, 2016, from http://www.cnn.com/2008/CRIME/12/16/walsh.case.closed/index.html

Colombino, N., Mercado, C. C., & Jeglic, E. L. (2009). Situational aspects of sexual offending: Implications for residence restriction laws. *Justice Research and Policy, 11*(1), 27–44.

Davey, M. (2015). States struggle with what to do with sex offenders after prison. Retrieved January 2, 2016 from http://www.nytimes.com/2015/10/30/us/states-struggle-with-what-to-do-with-sex-offenders-after-prison.html

Enniss, B. (2008). Quickly assuaging public fear: How the well-intended Adam Walsh Act led to unintended consequences. *Utah Law Review, 697*, 697–717.

Erin's Law (IL Pub. Act 096–1524).

Farkas, M. A., & Miller, G. (2007). Reentry and reintegration: Challenges faced by the families of convicted sex offense recidivism. *Criminal Justice and Behavior, 35*(4), 484–504.

Farley, L. G. (2008). The Adam Walsh Act: The scarlet letter of the twenty-first century. *Washburn Law Journal, 47*(1), 471–503.

Flatow, N. (2014, October 23, 2014). Inside Miami's hidden tent city for 'sex offenders'. Retrieved January 3, 2016, from http://thinkprogress.org/justice/2014/10/23/3583307/in-miami-dade-sex-offenders-are-relegated-to-outdoor-encampments/

Freeman-Longo, R. E. (1996). Feel good legislation: Prevention or calamity. *Child Abuse & Neglect, 20*(2), 95–101.

Kan. Stat. Ann. § 59–29a02(a)(Supp. 1996)

KMOV. (2015). Sex offenders required to put identifying signs in yard. Retrieved January 2, 2016, from http://www.kmov.com/story/30706993/sex-offenders-required-to-put-identifying-signs-in-yard

Lave, T. R. (2011). Throwing away the key: Has the Adam Walsh Act lowered the threshold for sexually violent predator commitment too far? *Citation, 14*, 391–429.

Letourneau, E. J., Levenson, J. S., Bandyopadhyay, D., Sinha, D., & Armstrong, K. (2010). Effects of South Carolina's sex offender registration and notification policy on adult recidivism. *Criminal Justice Policy Review, 21*(4), 435–458.

Levenson, J., D'Amora, D. A., & Hern, A. L. (2007). Megan's Law and its impact on community re-entry for sex offenders. *Behavioral Sciences and the Law, 25*(4), 587–602.

Levenson, J., & Tewskbury, R. (2009). Collateral damage: Family members of registered sex offenders. *American Journal of Criminal Justice, 34*(1), 54–68.

Logan, W. A. (2009). Adam Walsh Act and the failed promise of administrative federalism. *George Washington Law Review, 78*(5), 993–1013.

Maddan, S. (2005). Sex offenders as outsiders: A reexamination of the labeling perspective utilizing current sex offender registration and notification policies. Unpublished Ph.D. dissertation, University of Nebraska at Omaha.

Matson, S., & Lieb, R. (1996). Community notification in Washington State: 1996 survey of law enforcement. Retrieved January 15, 2016 from http://wsipp.wa.gov/ReportFile/1242

McPherson, L. (2007). Practitioner's guide to the Adam Walsh Act. *National Center for Prosecution of Child Abuse, 20*(9 & 10), 1–7.

Mullvihill, M., Wisniewski, K., Meyers, J., & Wells, J. (2003, November, 2003). Monster next door: State losing track of sex offenders. *Boston Herald*, p. 1.

Mustaine, E. E. (2014). Sex offender residency restrictions: Successful integration or exclusion? *Criminology and Public Policy, 13*(1), 169–177.

Mustaine, E. E., & Tewksbury, R. (2011). Assessing the informal social control against the highly stigmatized: An exploratory study of differential experiences and resulting stress of registered sex offenders. *Deviant Behavior, 32*(10), 944–960.

Nesemann, M. (2015, December 22, 2015). Manitowoc sex offender ordinance approved. Retrieved January 2, 2016, from http://www.htrnews.com/story/news/2015/12/22/manitowoc-sex-offender-ordinance-approved/77755062/

Payne, M. (2005). Sex offender site criticized. *Southwest Florida News-Press*.

Pennsylvania State Police. (n.d.). Megan's Law Website. Retrieved December 24, 2015, from http://www.pameganslaw.state.pa.us

Prison Legal News. (2015, September 19, 2014). Some states refuse to implement SORNA, lose federal grants. *Prison Legal News*. Retrieved January 3, 2016, from https://www.prisonlegalnews.org/news/2014/sep/19/some-states-refuse-implement-sorna-lose-federal-grants/

Saad, L. (2005, June 9, 2005). Sex offender registries are underutilized by the public. Retrieved January 2, 2016, from http://www.gallup.com/poll/16705/sex-offender-registries-underutilized-public.aspx

Silver, C. (2012). Pariahs among us: Sex offender laws in the 21st century. Retrieved January 2, 2016, from http://www.aljazeera.com/indepth/opinion/2012/10/2012101474052331874.html

SMART. (n.d.). Learn more about the functionality and capabilities of NSOPW: About NSOPW. Retrieved December 24, 2015, from http://www.nsopw.gov

Szabo, L. (2013, January 7, 2013). Committing a mentally ill adult is complex. Retrieved January 2, 2016, from http://www.usatoday.com/story/news/nation/2013/01/07/mental-illness-civil-commitment/1814301/

Tewksbury, R. (2002). Validity and utility of the Kentucky sex offender registry. *Federal Probation, 66*(1), 21–26.

Tewksbury, R., & Mustaine, E. E. (2009). Stress and collateral consequences for registered sex offenders. *Journal of Public Management and Social Policy, 15*(2), 215–239.

Townsend, S. M. (2008). *Primary prevention of sexual violence: A technical assistance guide for planning and evaluation*. Enola, PA: Pennsylvania Coalition Against Rape.

U.S. Department of Education. (2002, October 24, 2002). Disclosure of education records concerning registered sex offenders. Retrieved January 4, 2016, from http://www2.ed.gov/policy/gen/guid/fpco/hottopics/ht10-24-02.html

U.S. Department of Justice. (2008). Frequently asked questions: The Sex Offender Registration and Notification Act (SORNA) final guidelines. Retrieved December 30, 2015, from http://ojp.gov/smart/pdfs/faq_sorna_guidelines.pdf

Vásquez, B. E., Maddan, S., & Walker, J. T. (2008). The influence of sex offender registration and notification laws in the United States. *Crime and Delinquency, 54*(2), 175–192.

Young, C. (2008). Children sex offenders: How the Adam Walsh Child Protection and Safety Act hurts the same children it is trying to protect. *New England Journal on Criminal and Civil Confinement, 34*(Summer), 49–73.

Zgoba, K., Veysey, B. M., & Dalessandro, M. (2010). An analysis of the effectiveness of community notification and registration: Do the best intentions predict the best practices? *Justice Quarterly, 27*(5), 667–691.

## Court Cases

*Kansas v. Hendricks*, 521 U.S. 346 (1997).

*U.S. v. Comstock*, 551 F.3d 274 (4th Cir. 2009).

## DEFINITIONS

**Adam Walsh Act (SORNA):** A federal law enacted in 2006, replacing the requirements of the Jacob Wetterling Act and its amendments. It established a three-tier system of registration, requiring that sex offenders register for 10 years, 15 years, or life, depending on the type of offense committed.

**Campus Sex Crimes Prevention Act (CSPCA):** A federal level law passed in 2000. The Act required that institutions of higher education maintain and disseminate information about known registered sex offenders.

**Dru Sjodin National Sex Offender Public Registry (NSOPR):** Formerly named the National Sex Offender Registry and renamed after Dru Sjodin. The registry includes sex offenders' registration information, regardless of where they live.

**Erin's Law:** A state law adopted in Illinois and several other states. It creates a task force for sex-abuse prevention programs and implements a sex-abuse prevention program in public schools. It is a primary prevention strategy.

**Jacob Wetterling Crimes against Children and Sexually Violent Offender Registration Act (the Wetterling Act):** A federal level law passed in 1994. It requires sex offenders to register with law enforcement officials, usually local police.

**Megan's Law:** A federal law that passed in 1996. It requires that information regarding sex offenders' registration be made public. The law is an amendment to the Violent Crime Control Act of 1994.

**National Sex Offender Registry (NSOR):** Established by the Pam Lynchner Sex Offender Tracking and Identification Act of 1996, it requires a national registry be established for the purpose of maintaining all sex offenders' information, regardless of the state where they live. It was subsequently named the Dru Sjodin National Sex Offender Public Registry.

**Office of Sex Offending Sentencing, Monitoring, Apprehending, Registering, and Tracking (SMART):** This office was established to assist states with the implementation of SORNA's requirements. It also provides information about the implementation of SORNA.

**Pam Lynchner Sex Offender Tracking and Identification Act of 1996:** Established a national registry for sex offenders (National Sex Offender Registry).

**Primary Prevention Strategies:** Action taken before a sex crime has occurred for the purpose of preventing victimization and re-victimization.

**"Romeo and Juliet" Clause:** A clause in the SORNA guidelines that allows for exemption of registration for those who have engaged in consensual sex with a victim who is at least 13 years old and involves an offender who is no more than four years older.

**Secondary Prevention Strategies:** Action taken after a sex crime has occurred and involves an immediate reaction.

**Tertiary Prevention Strategies:** Action taken after a sex crime has occurred for the purpose of managing its impact.

# CHAPTER 12

# *Conclusion*

## CHAPTER OBJECTIVES

- Discuss the myth, "All sex offenders are the same."
- Assess unanswered questions and potential future directions of sex-offender research.
- Identify the effects of myths regarding sex crimes and sex offenders.

As noted in the beginning of this textbook, a great deal of sex-offender research has been conducted over the past several decades. While we know much more about sex offenders today than we knew in the past, there are still many unanswered questions. Researchers have just begun to scratch the surface. Furthermore, throughout history, there has been a pendulum swing from indifference towards sex crimes and sex offenders to a moral panic about them. This has shaped many of the myths that surround sex crimes and sex offenders, which has affected sex-offender identification, treatment and punishment, research, and policy development. In this chapter, we provide a summary of many of the myths that surround sex crimes and sex offenders with attention to potential future directions for research.

## BRINGING IT ALL TOGETHER: ALL SEX OFFENDERS ARE (NOT) THE SAME

One particular myth, *all sex offenders are the same*, is embedded in many of the other myths that have been highlighted throughout this textbook. It has been said that although many sex offenders have common characteristics (intimacy deficits, poor self-control, antisocial tendencies, etc.), their criminal behaviors vary (they commit rape, child molestation, and/or child pornography,).

Sex offenders also have diverse backgrounds. For example, some sex offenders are female (Chapter 7), and some are very young (Chapter 6). Also, some sex offenders are in a position of authority. For example, some clergy, teachers, and law enforcement officials have committed sex crimes (Chapter 8). Most sex offenders know their victim and, therefore, are not strangers, dispelling the myth that a sex offender is someone who attacks a victim on the street, late at night, while the victim is alone. Victims of sex crimes also vary from very young to very old. They include both males and females, although young women are at a particular risk for rape (Chapter 3).

## MYTHS, UNANSWERED QUESTIONS, AND FUTURE DIRECTIONS

### Myths Regarding the Number of Sex Crimes and Sex Offenders and Associated Trends

It has been emphasized in this textbook that it is (wrongly) believed by many that the number of sex crimes and sex offenders has recently increased. This is mired in an emerging culture of "panic," resulting in policies that may or may not decrease sex crimes. Evidence from several sources indicates that the number of sex crimes has actually decreased over the past several years.

There are many unanswered questions surrounding this myth, however. For example, much of the research covered in Chapter 1 is limited to just a few data sources. Most of those data sources require that a crime be reported to law enforcement officials. What we do not know is the true number of sex crimes that occur. We know, for example, that:

- Many victims do not report sex crimes for a variety of reasons.
- Sex crimes have additional investigational obstacles to successful prosecution.
- Victims of sex crimes are often "groomed."
- Most sex offenders know their victims.
- Some sex offenders are in a position of authority to the victim (e.g., teacher or relative).

All of these lead to low reporting of sex crimes. More accurate measures of sex crimes and sex offenders are needed. Research that involves more than one measure of sex crimes, for example, can yield more accurate results. As noted in Chapter 10, the use of polygraph examinations for convicted sex offenders has resulted in increased knowledge about the range of sex crimes they commit. There are opportunities to capture more accurate information about sex crimes and sex offenders.

Another unanswered question is why sex offenders have low recidivism rates. More research is needed to address this question through carefully designed studies that accurately measure recidivism. For example, are sex offenders more likely to recidivate than other types of offenders, such as burglars? As noted by Bader, Welsh, & Scalora (2010), using multiple indicators of recidivism (such as arrest records and reports to child protective service agencies) has revealed higher rates of recidivism than relying only on one measure, such as arrest records. Currently, our knowledge is based on those we know have committed sex crimes because they have been caught, but we do not know about those who have not been caught.

## Myths Regarding Why Sex Offenders Commit Sex Crimes

Although many may (wrongly) believe that one must be "sick" or "mentally ill" to commit a sex crime, researchers have examined a much broader range of theoretical explanations. There is still too little research, however, about why people commit sex crimes. Much of the research regarding sex-offender specific theories (Chapter 2) has simply identified correlates rather than providing a coherent theoretical explanation. Despite a large number of studies showing that sex offenders commit other types of non-sex crimes too—that is, they are generalists—relatively little research has been conducted applying general crime theories to sex crimes and sex offenders.

## Myths Regarding Rapists, Rape, and Rape Victims

There is also a great deal of misunderstanding regarding the context in which rape occurs. A widespread belief is that rapes are spontaneous, violent attacks involving strangers. Research has consistently shown that scenarios like this are the exception, rather than the norm. By and large, rapes are committed against a victim by someone who is known to her or him. A very small percentage of rapes involve strangers. Rapists are usually not impulsive; most rapes are acts of premeditated violence. The idea that once a rapist begins to engage in sex, he (or she) can be provoked to "a point of no return" reinforces the stereotype that rape is an act of uncontrollable passion and symptomatic of high sexual energy. Focus Box 12.1 presents a recent criminal case involving a police officer who committed numerous rapes against victims whose reputations were questionable (reflecting the myth that certain women are "unrapeable").

---

*Focus Box 12.1    Former Oklahoma City Police Officer Targets "Bad Women" for Rape and Sexual Assault*

In December 2015, former Oklahoma City police officer Daniel Holtzclaw was found guilty of 18 counts of rape and sexual assault against over a dozen women between December 2013 and June 2014. By design, Holtzclaw methodically targeted Black/African American teenagers and elderly women with criminal records and histories of drug abuse and sex work. Holtzclaw used his authority to run background checks and outstanding arrest warrants on the women as a means to coerce sex, offering reprieve from warrants and jail time in exchange for sex. Holtzclaw's defense attorney, Scott Adams, acknowledged that the accusers in the case waited months to report his crimes to authorities because they were not "perfect victims" or "perfect accusers." In fact, Adams went so far as to claim that while Holtzclaw was "naïve and very gullible," his victims possessed "street smarts like you can't imagine," effectively portraying Holtzclaw's targets as the predators and responsible for the trauma that they endured. Holtzclaw was sentenced to 263 years in prison for his crimes in January 2016. Critics and commentators have observed that this verdict illustrates the budding momentum of the "Black Lives Matter" campaign, an activist social movement that protests violence against those who are Black/African American and broader issues of police brutality, racial profiling, and abuse of authority. As discussed throughout this textbook, legal decisions regarding sex crimes and sex offenders are often the result of shifting social and political climates, and scientific research plays a major role in shaping some of these shifts.

## Myths Regarding Child Sexual Abuse, Child Molestation, and Child Victims

It is estimated that approximately 1 in 5 girls and 1 in 20 boys is a victim of child sexual abuse. The actual prevalence of this crime is difficult to determine, as child sexual abuse is not uniformly defined and, similar to crimes of rape, suffers from under-reporting. As such, the general consensus among experts is that the prevalence rate is higher than official statistics suggest.

There is a great deal of mythology and public denial surrounding child sexual abuse with regards to offenders and victims. For example, it is widely assumed that people who look and act "normal" cannot sexually abuse children. Closely related is the belief that all offenders who sexually abuse children are pedophiles. Both myths distort the true image of child sexual abusers. On the whole, offenders who commit sex crimes against children are very similar to their non-offending counterparts. Many maintain employment, are active in their communities, are well-educated, and engage in age-appropriate sexual relationships. They are knowledgeable about the importance of securing a "good-guy" image and appear charming, socially responsible, and sincere. Maintaining this image is a component of the grooming process, where offenders establish trust with potential victims and their caregivers.

Many laws and prevention strategies that have been developed in response to child sexual abuse are predicated on the notion of "stranger danger" (i.e., children are taught early on to avoid contact with strangers, presumably to eliminate the risk of victimization). However, very few crimes of child sexual abuse involve offenders that are unknown to the child. As part of the grooming process, child molesters and other child sexual abusers engage in long-term relationships with potential targets and their families. It may be weeks, months, or even years until abusive acts against the child begin.

Further, the majority of child sexual abusers *do not* fit the diagnostic criteria for pedophilia, yet many confuse child molestation and pedophilia. Someone can molest a child and have no sexual attraction to children. This person would be considered a child molester and not a pedophile. Alternatively, someone can have a strong sexual attraction to children, yet not behave sexually toward a child. This person would be considered a pedophile who does not violate any laws. As noted in Focus Box 12.2, two self-proclaimed pedophiles (who also claim not to molest children) founded an organization, *Virtuous Pedophiles*, allowing people similarly inclined toward pedophilia, but wishing to abstain from pedophilic behaviors and actions, to connect with others in a supportive environment. This website, and in particular the statement from one of the founders set out in Focus Box 12.2, provides an example of someone who is a pedophile, yet is not, reportedly, a child molester.

---

*Focus Box 12.2    Mythbuster: Pedophiles Are Not Necessarily Child Molesters*

Nick Devin and Ethan Edwards founded a website, *Virtuous Pedophiles*, that provides a forum for those who have a sexual attraction to children (i.e., pedophilia), yet have not molested any child. Below Nick Devin provides his background:

> *I'm in my mid-60s and married, with four adult children. I have advanced degrees from prestigious universities, a very good job, a lot of friends and am well respected in my community.*
>
> *I am also a pedophile. I am sexually attracted to boys in the early stages of puberty (typically ages 12–14).*
>
> *I've never touched a child in any way that could be considered remotely sexual, and am confident I never will. I've resisted my sex drive for more than fifty years, and I'm long past the age where acting on it is even a remote possibility. I know that many children have been harmed by pedophiles, and I refuse to do anything that could harm a child.*
>
> *On various occasions, I've suffered from low self-esteem and even self-hatred as a result of my pedophilia, feeling that I was somehow immoral as a result of being attracted to kids, even though I never acted on that attraction. With the help of a supportive psychologist, I came to understand that there's nothing morally wrong with being attracted to children as long as I don't have sexual contact with them. I did not choose my sexual orientation, and there is nothing I can do to change it. I cannot be evil simply because I have sexual feelings that I didn't choose and can't change, so long as I don't act on those feelings. In hindsight this strikes me as obvious, but it wasn't at all obvious at the time, and the realization that I am not evil was enormously helpful... To those of you who are reading this, I realize that the concept of someone being sexually attracted to children is extremely distasteful to you, but I'll leave you with this. If you had a child who was unfortunate enough to be sexually attracted to children, would you want him to be alone, to feel dirty and evil, to suffer from depression and self-hatred, to possibly even become suicidal? Or would you instead want him to have access to a place like Virtuous Pedophiles, a place where he could receive support in his efforts to resist his pedophilia, where he could have the example of decent, well-adjusted men who have successfully done so?*

Source: http://www.virped.org/index.php/who-we-are

---

Similar to rape, claims of child sexual abuse are sometimes met with skepticism, and many victims are accused of making false accusations. It is important to note that although many claims of child sexual abuse are unsubstantiated (meaning there is insufficient legal evidence to determine whether a crime has occurred), very few claims are intentionally fabricated.

## Myths Regarding Child Pornographers, Child Pornography, and Victims of Child Pornography

In general, the rate of sex crimes has been decreasing over the past 20 years. For example, as learned in Chapter 1, official statistics show that there was a 35% reduction in the number of arrests for rape between 2005 and 2014. Likewise, victimization surveys (which are able to capture incidents not reported to law enforcement officials) estimate that rape rates have decreased 58% from 1995 to 2010. The trend for child sexual abuse is similar, with studies showing that rates are about half of what they were 20–30 years ago (Finkelhor & Jones, 2006).

Sex crimes involving child pornography, however, have *increased* over the past 20 years. Though child pornography was approaching near-eradication in the 1980s, the Internet dramatically changed the scale and nature of the child-pornography problem. From 2000 to 2009, the total number of arrests for child-pornography production more than doubled (Wolak, Finkelhor & Mitchell, 2012). From an entrepreneurial perspective, child pornography is one of the fastest growing online businesses, generating billions of dollars in annual revenue.

It is widely believed that all individuals who view child pornography will inevitably go on to commit contact offenses against children. However, this is only one of several hypothesized relationships between consumption of child pornography and hands-on offending. For example, some research has indicated that instead of propelling an individual to commit contact offenses against children, viewing child pornography may provide a substitute for actual contact offending (Taylor & Quayle, 2003). Other research has shown that offenders who sexually abuse children may seek out child pornography as an additional form of sexual gratification (Marshall, 2000). In this light, the offender's sexual interest in children drives child pornography consumption, and not the other way around.

It is also assumed that any adult who views child pornography is a pedophile. Although child pornography is a diagnostic indicator of pedophilia (perhaps even more than contact offenses against children), many child pornography offenders do not fit the diagnostic criteria for pedophilia. For example, some may be recreational users (i.e., those who seek out material out of impulse or curiosity). Others may maintain collections or libraries of images, yet do not maintain exclusive sexual interest in children (i.e., they may maintain age-appropriate relationships in addition to viewing child pornography).

Though adult males are the most likely to commit crimes involving child pornography, there has been an increase in the number of youth participating in these crimes. In fact, between 2000 and 2009, the number of arrests for illegal images produced, distributed, and downloaded for youth increased from 22 to 1,198 (an approximate 5,500% increase) (Wolak, Finkelhor, & Mitchell, 2012).

Some of these crimes involve "sexting" incidents, which have been sensationalized in the media as being widespread among youth, but the majority involve youth-produced images that were created as a result of adult solicitation (i.e., cases involving adult offenders who entice adolescent or child victims to produce images).

## Myths Regarding Juvenile Sex Offenders, Crimes, and Victims

Although many assume that sex offenders are usually adults, a substantial proportion of sex crimes are committed by juveniles. A prevalent myth regarding juvenile sex offenders is that they continue to offend as adults. The research shows that very few juveniles who sexually offend go on to commit sex crimes as adults. Many of the questions surrounding juvenile sex offenders concern how to respond to them. Should they be treated, given their low recidivism rates? There is no consensus regarding whether juveniles should be required to register, and if so for how long and for what offenses?

## Myths Regarding Female Sex Offenders, Crimes, and Victims

Over the past decade, many female sex offenders have been portrayed in the media. It has become common to hear about a teacher who has molested a pre-teen or teenage boy. This leaves the impression that female sex offenders are young women, usually pretty, who "fall in love" with a young, male student. It is often couched in terms of a consenting victim. By law, children cannot consent to sexual relationships with adults. Such relationships are abusive. Also, the existing research on female sex offenders has identified many who are not teacher-lovers. Thus, there is a broad range of sex crimes committed by female sex offenders. It has also been documented that female sex offenders do in fact inflict harm on their victims. Many questions still exist regarding female sex offenders. It is not known, for example, whether they exhibit pedophilia. No assessment tool has been designed specifically for women. Does the same type of treatment relied upon for male sex offenders work for female sex offenders? It is not clear whether female sex offenders recidivate at the same rate as male sex offenders.

## Myths Regarding Institutional Abuse

Although there has been considerable effort to eradicate the myth of "stranger danger" (i.e., sex offenders choosing stranger victims), it is still difficult for many people to accept that a sex offender could be someone who is in a trusted position, such as a teacher, daycare provider, or clergy member. Many organizations are ill-equipped to respond to sexual-assault allegations. Future research should identify obstacles in responding appropriately to sexual-assault allegations.

## Myths Regarding Investigating Abuse

A critical component of controlling sex crimes is the arrest of known sex offenders. Law enforcement officials, however, are subject to the same biases everyone else has. That means they are subject to the same moral panic that persists in the U.S. To guard against biases, whether they are in response to the moral panic regarding sex offenders or the many myths regarding the number, characteristics, and recidivism rates of sex crimes and sex offenders, law enforcement officials must conduct investigations in a thorough manner. Although much has been learned about improved strategies for investigating sex crimes, there is considerable room for improvement. Techniques have been developed, such as distinguishing between an organized offender and a disorganized offender (based on crime-scene characteristics), which allow for narrowing potential suspects. This process can also exclude potential suspects, but does not decisively indicate who the offender is. Similarly, geographical mapping and geographical profiling can narrow the scope of an investigation, but it will not indicate that "John Smith" committed the sex crime.

Much of what we know about investigating sex crimes is based on known errors that have occurred during past investigations. For example, it was found that strict guidelines must be in place when interviewing vulnerable victims, as they are highly suggestible (Bull, 2010). Children, for example, must be allowed to provide as much information about the sex crime as possible prior to asking forced-choice questions (e.g., Was the rapist Black or White?). Research is needed that clearly assesses best practices for interviewing victims, witnesses, and suspects.

## Myths Regarding Assessment and Treatment of Sex Offenders

There are two myths that relate to assessment and treatment. First, it is (wrongly) believed that sex offenders have a high rate of recidivism—once a sex offender, always a sex offender. Research has consistently shown that sexual recidivism rates of sex offenders are relatively low. Second, it is often believed that sex offenders cannot be treated. Although research in the 1990s reported virtually no positive effects of treatment (Hall, 1995), subsequent research has revealed that successful completion of treatment leads to lower sexual recidivism rates among convicted sex offenders.

With regard to treatment, cognitive-behavioral treatment programs have yielded positive results (Lösel & Schmucker, 2005). Cognitive-behavioral treatment programs encompass a wide variety of components (such as addressing cognitive distortions, learning to manage emotions, increasing interpersonal skills, addressing empathy deficits, reducing deviant sexual behavior, ensuring relapse prevention, and learning self-management skills), but it has not been determined which factors are the most beneficial and for whom. There are unanswered questions regarding the length of treatment. When should treatment of a sex offender be ended, if ever?

There are still sizeable gaps in assessment tools. For example, although it has been shown that using more than one actuarial assessment increases predictive accuracy, no one has assessed which combination of available assessment tools yields the most valid and reliable risk predictions.

## Myths Regarding Which Community Sanctions Should Exist for Sex Offenders

Given the heinous nature of sex offenses, many may believe that all offenders are given lengthy prison sentences. While some sex offenders do receive lengthy prison sentences, most (60%) live in the community under some form of supervision (Greenfeld, 1997). Due to several high-profile cases of children (and young adults) who were abducted, sexually assaulted, and murdered, registration and community notification laws have been enacted. These laws, however, are based on assumptions that are difficult, if not impossible, to support with existing evidence. It is assumed that if the public is more aware of known sex offenders, preventive action will be taken and, therefore, lead to fewer sex crimes. Although some research shows no reduction in sex crimes as a result of strict laws (Letourneau, Levenson, Bandyopadhyay, Sinha, & Armstrong, 2010), no large-scale, multi-state comparison of the effects of various laws has been published.

Beyond sex-offender registration requirements, it is not known what other types of restrictions should exist for sex offenders. Should there be restrictions on where sex offenders can live, work, or engage in recreation? It is not known whether publicly identifying sex offenders (e.g., sex-offender notification on drivers' licenses, signs in yards, flyers distributed to neighbors, etc.) leads to a reduction in recidivism.

While it is clear that sex crimes are not unique to the U.S., the strictest registration and community-notification laws exist in the U.S. Due to substantial differences in reporting standards across countries, comparisons among different countries are difficult, if not impossible. What is different about the U.S. that has led to a moral panic about sex offenders?

## THE EFFECTS OF SEX-CRIME AND SEX-OFFENDER MYTHS

As noted throughout this textbook, there are many myths regarding sex crimes and sex offenders. The effects of these cannot be overstimated, as they affect every effort to minimize the number of sexual-abuse victims. For example, as noted in Chapter 1, a taboo has always existed regarding any research that involves "sex," including sex crimes and sex-offender research. It is a relatively small group of people who conduct sex-offender research, especially when compared to those in the broader fields of psychology, sociology, social work, and criminology who study other types of crime. We have learned a great deal about sex crimes and sex offenders over the past few decades; however, much of what we know can still be refined and expanded upon.

The myths regarding sex crimes and sex offenders have negatively affected victims. Victims of sexual abuse are reluctant to report for a variety of reasons, including the shame associated with being a victim. Victims receive blame not only from others, but also from themselves. This blame negatively impacts research. For example, research has revealed that positive reactions from others in response to sexual-assault disclosure can lessen the severity of posttraumatic stress disorder (PTSD) symptoms (Ullman & Peter-Hagene, 2014). Critical to understanding sex crimes and sex offenders is to gain information from victims. Without reports of sexual victimization, new knowledge cannot be garnered.

For those who do report, a culmination of myths comes into play. Investigations are hampered by false assumptions about sex offenders, sex crimes, victims, and how to best find out what happened. As noted in Focus Box 12.3, a police officer told a sexual-assault victim that she was "lucky." Needless to say, she did not feel lucky. For other crimes, a car theft for example, it is likely no one questions the car owner like this: "Are you sure your car was stolen? Did you leave it unlocked? Why did you park your car there?," etc. In other words, it would be unusual if a police officer asked the victim what he or she did that led to car theft. For a rape victim, an altogether different story occurs, unfortunately.

---

*Focus Box 12.3   Case in Point: How Can a Rape Victim be "Lucky?"*

In 1999, Alice Sebold, acclaimed author of the novel *Lovely Bones*, published a memoir document-ing her own rape. The title of the book, *Lucky*, reveals a common reaction that many had to her report of rape. The rape took place on a college campus when she was a freshman. She was walk-ing back to her dormitory one night when a stranger appeared and raped her. Alice was not doing anything she should not have been doing. She was not drunk or under the influence of drugs. She was not promiscuous. In fact, she was a virgin. She was not wearing a short skirt or provocative clothing. When attacked, she fought back. She was beaten during the rape, leaving many injuries. The rapist threatened her life. She believed she was going to die. He had a knife. The author notes:

> In the tunnel where I was raped, a tunnel that was once an underground entry to an amphitheater, a place where actors burst forth from underneath the seats of a crowd, a girl had been murdered and dismembered. I was told this story by the police. In comparison, they said, I was lucky.
>
> (Sebold, 1999, n.p.)

Alice eventually identified her rapist to the police, and he was sentenced to prison. She reveals many difficulties associated with rape: the fear of dying during the rape, having to tell her story repeatedly afterwards, not wanting others—including her family—to know about the rape, the uncomfortableness associated with a rape examination, and running into her rapist months after the incident occurred. She also reveals the difficulty of coping afterwards, including depression symp-toms. The book reveals that a rape does not end when the rape incident is over, or even when the offender is apprehended and sentenced. The effects, therefore, can last a lifetime.

---

The myths regarding sex crimes and sex offenders have fueled a moral panic. This, in turn, has led to laws that have lacked empirical support for reducing sex crimes. We have yet to identify effective ways of treating and managing sex offend-ers. As additional research is conducted, more of these myths can be dispelled, and more effective strategies for managing sex offenders can be developed.

## REFERENCES

Bader, S. M., Welsh, R., & Scalora, M. J. (2010). Recidivism among female child molesters. *Violence and Victims, 25*(3), 349–362.

Bull, R. (2010). The investigative interviewing of children and other vulnerable witnesses, Psychological research and working/professional practice. *Legal and Criminological Psy-chology, 15*(1), 5–23.

Finkelhor, D., & Jones, L. (2006). Why have child maltreatment and child victimization declined? *Journal of Social Issues, 62*(4), 685–716.

Greenfeld, L. (1997). *Sex offenses and offenders: An analysis of data on rape and sexual assault.* U.S. Department of Justice, Office of Justice Programs, Bureau of Justice Statistics.

Hall, G. C. N. (1995). Sexual offender recidivism revisited: A meta-analysis of recent treatment studies. *Journal of Consulting and Clinical Psychology, 63*(5), 802–809.

Letourneau, E. J., Levenson, J., Bandyopadhyay, D., Sinha, D., & Armstrong, K. (2010). Effects of South Carolina's sex offender registration and notification policy on adult recidivism. *Criminal Justice Policy Review, 21*(4), 435–458.

Lösel, F., & Schmucker, M. (2005). The effectiveness of treatment for sexual offenders: A comprehensive meta-analysis. *Journal of Experimental Criminology, 1*(1), 117–146.

Marshall, W. L. (2000). Revisiting the use of pornography by sexual offenders: Implications for theory and practice. *Journal of Sexual Aggression, 6*(1–2), 67–77.

Sebold, A. (1999). *Lucky.* New York: Scribner.

Taylor, M., & Quayle, E. (2003). *Child pornography: An internet crime.* Psychology Press.

Ullman, S. E., & Peter-Hagene, L. (2014). Social reactions to sexual assault disclosure, coping, perceived control, and PTSD symptoms in sexual assault victims. *Journal of Community Psychology, 42*(4), 495–508.

Wolak, J., Finkelhor, D., & Mitchell, K. (2012). Trends in arrests for child pornography production: The Third National Juvenile Online Victimization Study (NJOV-3). Durham, NH: Crimes Against Children Research Center.

# NOTES

## CHAPTER 1 INTRODUCTION

1 For additional details, refer to the United Nations Office on Drugs and Crime (www. unodc.org).

## CHAPTER 3 RAPE

1 Colorado, Connecticut, Florida, Georgia, Hawaii, Kansas, Kentucky, Louisiana, Maine, Maryland, Minnesota, Missouri, Montana, Nebraska, Nevada, New Hampshire, New Mexico, New York, Oklahoma, Oregon, Pennsylvania, South Dakota, Tennessee, Utah, Vermont, Washington, West Virginia, Wisconsin.
2 Arkansas, California, Idaho, Illinois, Indiana, Massachusetts, Michigan, Mississippi, New Jersey, North Carolina, North Dakota, Ohio, Rhode Island, South Carolina, Virginia, Wyoming.
3 Alabama, Delaware, Idaho, Louisiana, Missouri, Nebraska, Washington, West Virginia.
4 Alaska, Florida, Illinois, Iowa, Kentucky, Maine, Michigan, Minnesota, Montana, New Mexico, Ohio, Oregon, Pennsylvania, Virginia.

## CHAPTER 6 JUVENILE SEX OFFENDERS

1 See Chapter 2 for a discussion of cycle of abuse.

## CHAPTER 7 FEMALE SEX OFFENDERS

1 The description of the categories, heterosexual and homosexual, simply refers to having male or female victims and does not make assumptions about the offender's sexual orientation.

# INDEX

Note: Information in figures and tables is indicated by page numbers in italics.